Marxism in Latin America from 1909 to the Present

REVOLUTIONARY STUDIES
Series Editor: Paul Le Blanc

Marxism in Latin America from 1909 to the Present
An Anthology

Edited and with an Introduction by
MICHAEL LÖWY

Translated from Spanish, Portuguese,
and French by
MICHAEL PEARLMAN

Humanity
Books

an imprint of Prometheus Books
59 John Glenn Drive, Amherst, New York 14228

Published 1999 by Humanity Books, an imprint of Prometheus Books

First published in French in 1980 as *Le marxisme en Amérique Latine* by Éditions
La Découverte, 1 Place Paul-Painlevé, 75005 Paris

03 02 01 00 99   6 5 4 3 2

Library of Congress Cataloging-in-Publication Data

Marxisme en Amérique latine de 1909 à nos jours. English.
    Marxism in Latin America from 1909 to the present : an anthology / edited and
introduced by Michael Löwy ; translated from Spanish, Portuguese, and French by
Michael Pearlman.
    p.   cm. — (Revolutionary studies)
    Translation of: Le Marxisme en Amérique latine de 1090 à nos jours.
    Originally published in English: Atlantic Highlands, NJ : Humanities Press
International, Inc., 1992
    Includes bibliographical references and index.
    ISBN 1–57392–474–1
    1. Communism—Latin America—History. 2. Socialism—Latin America—
History. I. Löwy, Michael, 1938–   . II. Pearlman, Michael. III. Title.
IV. Series.
HX110.5.A6M3213   1992
324.1'7'0980904—dc20   92–3708
                                                        CIP

Printed in the United States of America on acid-free paper

Contents

vii

PART III. STALINIST HEGEMONY

Introduction

Points of Reference for a History of Marxism in Latin America

While, of course, the history of over sixty years of the workers' movement on a continent cannot be summarized in as many pages, the following observations attempt to establish some points of reference for the study of the evolution of Marxist thought in Latin America, with an emphasis on the question of the *nature of the revolution*.[1]

One of the principal problems that Latin American Marxism has had to confront, in fact, has been defining the character of the revolution in the continent. Such a definition is both the result of a particular analysis of Latin American social formations and the starting point for the formulation of political strategy and tactics; in other words, it is the essential moment of scientific thought and a decisive mediation between theory and practice. A whole series of key political questions—class alliances, a peaceful road to socialism or armed struggle, the stages of the revolution, and so forth—are intimately connected to this central problematic: the nature of the revolution.

Very schematically, we can distinguish three periods in the history of Latin American Marxism: 1) a revolutionary period in the twenties, through 1935, whose most profound theoretical expression is the work of Mariátegui and whose most important practical manifestation was the Salvadoran insurrection of 1932. In this period, Marxists tended to categorize the Latin American revolution as simultaneously socialist and anti-imperialist; 2) the Stalinist period, from the middle of the thirties to 1959, during which the Soviet interpretation of Marxism was hegemonic, as was Stalin's theory of revolution by stages, defining the current stage in Latin America as national-democratic; 3) the new revolutionary period after the Cuban Revolution, which sees the rise (or consolidation) of radical currents whose common points of reference are the socialist nature of the revolution and the necessity of armed struggle, and whose inspiration and symbol, to a great degree, has been Che Guevara.

The problem of the nature of the revolution is ultimately related to certain fundamental theoretical and methodological issues that revolve around the question of how to apply Marxism to Latin American reality.

Marxism in Latin America has always been threatened by two opposing temptations: Indo-American exceptionalism and Eurocentrism.

Indo-American exceptionalism tends to absolutize the specificity of Latin America and its culture, history, or social structure. Pushed to its ultimate conclusion, this American particularism finally judges Marxism itself to be too exclusively a European theory. The most significant example of this approach has been, of course, the APRA (American Popular Revolutionary Alliance),[2] which, under the leadership of Haya de la Torre, at first attempted to "adapt" Marxism to the continental reality, only to later "supersede" it in the service of a *sui generis* and eclectic populism. For Haya de la Torre, "Indo-American historical space-time" is ruled by its own laws, profoundly different from the "European space-time" analyzed by Marx, and thereby demands a new theory which negates and transcends Marxism.[3]

It is Eurocentrism, above all else, that has wreaked havoc on Latin American Marxism. By this term, we mean a theory that limits itself to mechanically transplanting to Latin America those models of European economic and social development that explain Europe's historical evolution through the nineteenth century. For each aspect of European reality studied by Marx and Engels—the contradiction between capitalist productive forces and feudal relations of production, the historically progressive role of the bourgeoisie, the bourgeois-democratic revolution against the absolutist feudal state, and the like—one must laboriously seek the Latin American equivalent, thereby transforming Marxism into a Procrustean bed upon which reality must be pitilessly cut or stretched according to the needs of the particular case. Using this method, the agrarian structure of the continent is classified as feudal, the local bourgeoisie is deemed progressive if not revolutionary, the peasantry is considered indifferent to collectivist socialism, and so on. In this problematic, all specificity of Latin America is implicitly or explicitly denied and the continent seems conceived as some kind of tropical Europe, with its development delayed by a century and under the domination of the North American empire.

These two temptations are strictly opposed and contradictory, but paradoxically lead to a common conclusion: that socialism is not on the order of the day in Latin America. According to Haya de la Torre,

Before the socialist revolution that will bring the working class to power, our people must pass through previous periods of economic and political transformation and perhaps through a social revolution that will achieve national emancipation from the imperialist yoke and Indo-American economic and political unification. The proletarian revolution will come later.[4]

Starting from the specificity of Latin America, the Apristas (for example, Carlos Manuel Cox) criticize Mariátegui for not having understood the difference between industrial European societies and essentially agrarian Indo-American societies, and of having thereby invented the myth of a Latin American working class with a revolutionary calling.[5]

Indeed, the Eurocentric current (which found inspiration in Stalin's writings) comes to a precisely analogous conclusion: the economic and social conditions in Latin America are not ripe for a socialist revolution; for the moment, the goal is to realize a democratic and anti-feudal historical stage (as in Europe in the eighteenth and nineteenth centuries!). For example, Alejandro Martínez Cambero, a theoretician of the Mexican Communist Party, wrote in 1945:

> The objective and subjective conditions in which we find ourselves do not permit the immediate inauguration of socialism in Mexico. Have the productive forces in our country developed to the point that a break with those capitalist relations of production that currently exist is both necessary and possible? We think not! Objectively, economic conditions and the mode of production (in its fundamental bases, and not only in isolated industrial centers) are not yet essentially capitalist.[6]

The creative application of Marxism to Latin American reality means precisely the overcoming of these two tendencies, the *aufhebung* (transcendence) of the dilemma between a hypostatized particularism and a universalist dogmatism—the dialectical unity between the specific and the universal in a concrete and rigorous model. In our opinion, it is not accidental that the majority of those thinkers who share this methodological position, from Mariátegui to Gunder Frank, to cite two well-known examples, arrive at precisely the opposite conclusion: the revolution in Latin America will be socialist, or it will not be.

One of the problems that has served as a point of departure for questioning the Eurocentric model has been the issue of the historical stages of social development in Latin America. In their analysis of the structure of productive relations, a number of Marxist investigators of the forties and fifties, such as Sergio Bagú, Marcelo Segall, and Caio Prado Jr., denied that Latin American social formations had originally been local versions of European feudalism. Starting from these investigations, Andre Gunder Frank, Luis Vitale, and others developed an analysis of the specifically capitalist dimension of the Latin American productive structure and of its combination with precapitalist forms, emphasizing that the evolution of its socioeconomic stages has not been identical to that experienced in Europe from the Middle Ages through the era of industrial capitalism. By showing that the cause of underdevelopment, regional inequality, and the profound misery of the peasantry is not feudalism, but the particular character that capitalism has taken in Latin America (colonial and, later, semi-colonial or dependent forms), these authors criticize the Eurocentric thesis on the "anti-feudal" dimension of the development of capitalism in Latin America. In their view, one can logically conclude from a Marxist understanding of the specificity of Latin America that only anti-capitalist measures in the context of a revolutionary socialist process can resolve the agrarian problem on the continent and open the way to harmonious economic and social development. Note how such an interpretation articulates certain fully "classic" Marxist concepts, while fully acknowledging the unique character of Latin American economies and societies.

In addition, this problematic is related to the indigenous question; it involves discovering the particularity of the Latin American peasantry in relation to the European model. Here lies the interest of a Mariátegui or a Diego Rivera in the study of pre-Columbian modes of production, trying to reencounter certain collectivist traditions that could lead the Indo-American peasantry to behave differently than the smallholding European peasants described by Marx in the *Eighteenth Brumaire*. Here also lies the preoccupation of a Hugo Blanco or a Ricardo Ramírez with analyzing the dual nature of the oppression to which the indigenous peasantry is subjected and the simultaneously socioeconomic and ethno-cultural (or national) character of its rebellion. While the "dogmatic" current only recognizes the peasant struggle as a bourgeois-democratic one,[7] similar to that of the peasantry in the French Revolution, the concrete-dialectical point of view captures the specificity of the Latin American peasantry that flows from its cultural traditions and the capitalist character of its exploitation, and reveals the explosive, revolutionary socialist potential of the masses of rural workers (El Salvador in 1932, Cuba in 1957–61, to cite only two).

Another significant debate in this context is that over the question of dependency. Can Latin America liberate itself from imperialist domination and experience an independent, autonomous capitalist development, like those European nations (Italy, Germany) that unified and emancipated themselves from foreign domination in the nineteenth century? The trend represented by Mariátegui, which is still developing within a new Marxist social science, rejects the European model here, too. The Latin American bourgeoisie arrived too late on the historical scene. Within the context of the capitalist mode of production, they are inevitably condemned to dependence and submission to the economic and political-military power of imperialism. The only road to ending their semi-colonial domination by the North American metropolis and the hegemony of multinational monopolies, the only way to escape exogenous underdevelopment, is to break with the capitalist system itself—to take the socialist path.

Obviously, the development and hegemony of one or the other of these two foci of Latin American Marxism, whether the Eurocentric or concrete-dialectical one (leaving aside eclectic and exotic Indo-Americanism, which tends to fall outside the bounds of Marxism), depends not only on the individual talent of a particular thinker, but also and above all on the historical situation of the workers' movement around the world and in Latin America. In this regard, the period of the twenties, the era of "original Communism" before the dogmatization and impoverishment brought on by the triumph of Stalinism, was particularly favorable to an "open" focus, as is the new era that opened with the Cuban Revolution. Nevertheless, this did not prevent the appearance of creative and rich Marxist investigators even during the most difficult period (1935–59), whether at the margins of the Communist movement or at its center.

Marxism was first introduced and disseminated through Latin America by German, Italian, and Spanish immigrants toward the end of the nineteenth century. The first workers' parties arose, the first thinkers availed themselves of Marxist ideas, and a socialist current appeared, inspired by the Second International; its moderate wing was represented by Juan B. Justo (1865–1928) and his Argentine Socialist Party (founded in 1895), and the revolutionary wing by Luis Emilio Recabarren (1876–1924) and his Socialist Workers Party of Chile (founded in 1912).

Juan B. Justo was the first translator of *Capital* into Spanish, but it is difficult to consider him the first Latin American Marxist because of his eclectic and semi-liberal ideas. His party was connected to the Second International, but Germán Ave-Lallemant (1835–1910), a German immigrant Marxist and Argentine correspondent for the *Neue Zeit*, considered the leading circles of the Argentine SP to be "bourgeois ideologues" or, at best, "followers of Turati."[8]

The first significant attempts to analyze Latin American reality in Marxist terms and to establish a revolutionary political orientation came with the appearance of a Communist current. The Communist parties arose in the twenties from two distinct sources: the left, internationalist wing of certain Socialist parties (Argentina, 1918) and the majority of those parties that rallied to the October Revolution (Uruguay, 1920, and Chile, 1922); and the evolution toward Bolshevism of certain anarchist or anarcho-syndicalist groups (Mexico, 1919, and Brazil, 1922). The strength of these parties remained quite limited for some time: the Chilean CP, already the strongest, had no more than 5,000 members in 1929.

During the early years, their orientation was inspired in large measure by the resolutions of the Third International, particularly the January 1921 document "On the Revolution in America: A Call to the Working Class of the Two Americas," and the January 1923 proclamation "To the Workers and Peasants of South America."[9]

Clearly, these texts simultaneously attribute agrarian, anti-imperialist, *and* anti-capitalist tasks to the revolutionary struggle in America. Unity between the proletariat and the peasantry is conceived in the context of a strategy of "uninterrupted" revolution capable of leading Latin America directly from an underdeveloped and dependent capitalism ("backward and semi-colonial" in the terminology of the Third International) to the dictatorship of the proletariat. They explicitly deny the idea of a historical stage of independent "national and democratic" capitalism and emphasize the complicity of the local bourgeoisies with imperialism. In passing, let us note that these documents never refer to "feudalism" in the countryside and describe the peasant struggle as being directed against agrarian capitalism.

To support their position, these documents analyze the stagnation of the Mexican Revolution and compare it with the October Revolution as an example of the growing over of the democratic revolution toward socialism.

Of course, the Russian Revolution exercised a profound influence on the workers' movement and among the intelligentsia of Latin America.[10] Luis Emilio Recabarren was perhaps the most typical example of a historic workers' leader who turned to Bolshevism under the influence of October. A typographer and founder of the Socialist Workers Party of Chile, Recabarren led its transformation into the Communist Party, the Chilean section of the Third International, in 1922. The writings and speeches of Recabarren, a real mass leader and popular tribune, center on the irreconcilable class struggle between capitalists and workers in the mines and factories, a struggle whose historic outcome can only be the socialist revolution and proletarian power. Nevertheless, his thought retains a certain "workerist" shading, underestimating the national and agrarian questions. His profound and sincere adherence to the Russian Revolution does not signify a real appropriation of the Leninist problematic.

Julio Antonio Mella (1903–29) was the first and most brilliant example of a political "archetype" frequently encountered in the social history of Latin America: the student or young revolutionary intellectual, the romantic anti-capitalist spirit who finds in Marxism an answer to the passion for social justice.[11]

A founder of the Anticlerical League of Cuba (1922), the Federation of University Students (1923), and the Cuban section of the Anti-Imperialist League of the Americas (1925), Julio Antonio Mella participated in the creation of the Cuban Communist Party (1925) and was elected a member of its Central Committee. Because of his activities against the dictator Machado ("the ass with claws," in the famous phrase of the Communist poet Rubén Martínez Villena), he was arrested and forced into exile in Mexico. He joined the Mexican CP, but in 1928 developed differences with its leadership, which accused him of "Trotskyist" tendencies.[12] Mella organized Cuban emigres in Mexico and prepared an armed landing on the island, but was assassinated by agents of Machado on January 10, 1929, at the age of twenty-six.[13]

How did Mella envision the revolutionary struggle in Cuba? With the war cry "Wall Street must be destroyed," he calls for the formation of an anti-imperialist united front, composed of "workers of all tendencies, peasants, students, and independent intellectuals"; he refuses to include the national bourgeoisie, which he considers an accomplice of imperialist domination.[14] He exhorts Cuban soldiers to no longer defend "the exploiters, the native and foreign bourgeoisie," and to join their class brothers, the workers and peasants.

Mella saw the struggle against the Machado dictatorship as a war to the death between the proletariat and the dominant classes: "We have no homeland. We have only class enemies. Class war has broken out—brutal, violent, and bloody."[15]

The question of nationalism and national liberation occupied a central place in Mella's work. He enthusiastically supported the movement of Sandino, who was struggling against the North American invasion of Nicaragua at the head of his peasant guerrilla army. On the other hand, he harshly criticized the "populist" nationalism of Haya de la Torre's APRA, which claimed to be the "Kuomintang of Latin America." In an anti-APRA pamphlet published in 1928, Mella rejects "a united front on behalf of the bourgeoisie, the classic betrayer of all truly emancipatory national movements," and emphasizes that "the definitive struggle for the destruction of imperialism . . . is not only a petty-bourgeois national struggle, but a proletarian international one, since it is only by abolishing the cause of imperialism, which is capitalism, that truly free nations can exist."[16] These concepts are situated on the same political terrain as the Comintern texts of 1921–23 (one can verify the fact simply by comparing them) and advance the same strategy: the fusion, "telescoping," or combination of the anti-imperialist and anti-capitalist dimensions of the Latin American revolution.

A convinced and militant internationalist, Mella was at the same time profoundly integrated into the culture and revolutionary traditions of Cuba. Like the Castroists later, he considered himself a disciple of José Martí and heir to his democratic, revolutionary, and anti-imperialist message.[17]

This dialectical synthesis between the universal and the particular, the international and the Latin American, is reencountered even more clearly in the work of José Carlos Mariátegui (1894–1930), undoubtedly the most vigorous and original thinker that Latin America has yet known. A writer and journalist, Mariátegui became a socialist in 1919 and discovered Marxism and Communism during a long stay in Europe (1920–23), particularly in Italy. Upon returning to Peru, he integrated himself into the workers' movement and actively participated in the establishment of unions of industrial and agricultural workers. In 1926, he founded the review *Amauta*, which gathered around it the cultural and political vanguard of Peru and Latin America; it also published numerous European literary and political texts (Breton, Gorky, Lenin, Marx, Rosa Luxemburg, Romain Rolland, Ernst Toller, Leon Trotsky). In 1927, Mariátegui participated in the congress of the Workers' Federation of Lima, all of whose delegates were arrested by the government and accused of mounting a "Communist plot." Ill and disabled, Mariátegui was interned in a hospital under police surveillance.

After having participated for a time in the activities of the APRA (1927), Mariátegui broke with Haya de la Torre and founded the Socialist Party; he wrote its program, which declared the party in accord with the Third International. Rejecting fusion proposals from the APRA, he drily responded:

> The vanguard of the proletariat and class-conscious workers, faithful to action on the terrain of the class struggle, repudiate any tendency that would mean a fusion with the forces or political bodies of other classes. We condemn as opportunist all politics that put forward even the momentary renunciation by the proletariat of its independence of program and action, which must be fully maintained at all times. We therefore repudiate the APRA tendency.[18]

Mariátegui was also the founder of the workers' journal *Labor* in 1928, and of the CGTP (General Confederation of Peruvian Workers) in 1929. While carrying out his political activity, Mariátegui continued his theoretical work. In 1928, he published his most important book, *Seven Interpretive Essays on Peruvian Reality*, the first attempt at a Marxist analysis of a concrete Latin American social formation.

Unable because of illness to participate in the first Latin American Communist Conference (Buenos Aires, 1929), Mariátegui sent two theses, on the indigenous question and the anti-imperialist struggle, with the Peruvian delegation; they provoked intense debate and polemic. Finally, in 1928–29, he wrote *Defense of Marxism*, developing his own philosophical and ethical-social concepts against those of Henri de Man and Max Eastman. Mariátegui did not take sides in the conflict between Stalin and the Left Opposition, but his articles on the issue barely hide his regret over the defeat of Trotsky:

> He has an internationalist, ecumenical sense of the socialist revolution. His notable writings on the transitory stabilization of capitalism (*Where Is England Going?*) are among the most well-informed and keen criticisms of the epoch. But this very internationalist sense, which gives him such prestige on the world scene, is at the moment robbing him of his power in the practice of Russian politics.[19]

Mariátegui has been accused of Eurocentrism by his Aprista adversaries and, on the other hand, of Indo-American "national populism" by certain

Soviet authors.[20] In reality, his thought is characterized precisely by a fusion between the most advanced aspects of European culture and the millenarian traditions of the indigenous community, and by an attempt to assimilate the social experience of the peasant masses into a Marxist theoretical framework.

Mariátegui has often been considered heterodox, idealist, or romantic. It is true that his works, especially *Defense of Marxism*, show the profound influence of Italian idealism (Croce, Gentile), Bergson, and above all, Sorel. Nevertheless, this ethical-social voluntarism must be understood as a reaction against an economistic and vulgar materialist version of Marxism. In this sense, the Marxist thought of Mariátegui presents notable similarities to the "Fichteanism" of the young Lukács and the "Bergsonianism" of the young Gramsci, both of them also forms of antipositivist revolt (against the "orthodox" Marxism of the Second International).[21] This attempt at a revolutionary renovation of Marxism, despite its idealist excesses, permits Mariátegui to free himself from the neo-Kautskyian evolutionism, with its rigid and determinist version of the succession of historical stages, that the Comintern was beginning to disseminate throughout Latin America. It is interesting to note that at the very moment Stalin and Martynov were developing the concept of a bourgeois-democratic revolution as an autonomous stage in China, Mariátegui was explicitly stressing the historical fusion between socialist and democratic tasks in Peru:

> Insufficiently profound and critical minds might suppose that the liquidation of feudalism is a typically and specifically liberal and bourgeois measure, and that to attempt to convert it into a socialist task is to romantically bend the laws of history. These shallow theoreticians oppose socialism with one simplistic criterion as their sole argument—that capitalism has not exhausted its possibilities in Peru. The partisans of this idea will be astonished to discover that the task of socialism, when it comes to power in the country, depending on the hour and the historical compass to which it must adjust, will to a great degree be the realization of capitalism, or better, the realization of the historical possibilities that capitalism still contains. . . .[22]

Mariátegui's method, his interpretation of dialectical materialism, plays a fundamental role, therefore, in his rejection of "stagism" (Menchevik and/or Stalinist), which sees historical development ruled by "natural laws" in which the sequence—feudalism, backward capitalism, advanced capitalism, socialism—is as immutable as the sequence of seasons of the year.

The decisive sociopolitical hypothesis of Mariátegui is that "in Peru, there is not, and there never has been, a progressive bourgeoisie with a national sensibility that declares itself liberal and democratic and bases its politics upon the postulates of its theory."[23] Of course, the leading Peruvian

Communist could not ignore the contradiction between this claim and the orientation sponsored by the Comintern in China during this period. He tried to escape this predicament by invoking hypothetical ideas about "national civilization" to explain why the Chinese bourgeoisie, as opposed to the Peruvian, was participating in the anti-imperialist struggle.[24]

It is from his analysis of the native bourgeoisie that Mariátegui developed his conception of revolutionary strategy in the preamble to the program of the Socialist Party (1928):

> The emancipation of the economy of the country is only possible through the action of the proletarian masses in solidarity with the worldwide anti-imperialist struggle. Only proletarian action can first push forward, and later realize, the tasks of the bourgeois-democratic revolution, which the bourgeois regime is incompetent to develop and fulfill.[25]

Beyond the borders of Peru, Mariátegui includes all Latin America in his analysis. The Latin American revolution can only be a socialist revolution that includes agrarian and anti-imperialist objectives. In a continent dominated by empires, there is no place for an independent capitalism; the local bourgeoisie has arrived too late on the historical scene.[26]

In certain writings on Peru, Mariátegui seems to suggest that the socialist road is possible, particularly in the countryside, because of the survival of remnants of an "Incan communism." This idea in particular is one of the axes of his communication on the indigenous question to the first Latin American Communist Conference. We should draw analogies here not with populist ideas, but with the writings of Marx and Engels on the Russian *mir* and its role in the transition to socialism of Czarist Russia. Perhaps we could also speak of an anti-capitalist romanticism in Mariátegui, of a critique of bourgeois civilization that is really a nostalgia for older precapitalist communities, as in Bergson and Sorel (and also in Lukács and Gramsci before their adherence to Marxism)? We should refrain from simplifying his complex and subtly shaded thought; his idyllic vision of the past is limited by the rigorous context of his historical materialist problematic. In the program of the Socialist Party, Mariátegui clearly attempts to emphasize this:

> Socialism finds the elements of a socialist solution to the agrarian question both in the continued existence of rural communities and in the large agricultural enterprises. . . . But this . . . absolutely does not signify a romantic and ahistorical tendency to the reconstruction or resurrection of Incan socialism, which corresponded to historical conditions which have been completely superseded and whose only remnant is the habit of cooperation and socialism among the indigenous peasants, which can be useful within the context of a clearly scientific productive technique.[27]

Along with cadres and thinkers who were authentically revolutionary and internationalist and, like Mella and Mariátegui, simultaneously capable of independent thought, Latin American Communism began to see another type of leader developing by the end of the twenties. These leaders were much more directly connected from an intellectual and political point of view to the Comintern apparatus of Stalin, whose various turns they followed with an exemplary faithfulness. The first, and one of the most talented, of this group was Vittorio Codovilla (1894–1970), General Secretary of the Argentine CP. Born in Italy, Codovilla arrived in Argentina in 1912 and shortly afterward joined the Socialist Party. In 1918, he was one of the founders of the International Socialist Party, which soon became the Argentine Communist Party, a section of the Third International. Toward the end of 1924, Codovilla participated in a meeting of the Enlarged Executive Committee of the Communist International as a representative of the Argentine CP. He was rapidly integrated into the Comintern apparatus and, in 1926, helped adopt a resolution in the Central Committee of the Argentine CP that condemned Trotskyism and solidarized with the leadership of the Communist Party of the Soviet Union.

In 1929, Codovilla participated in the first Latin American Communist Conference in Buenos Aires. This was at the beginning of the so-called Third Period of the Comintern (1929–33), which was characterized by an "offensive" political strategy and the rejection of any agreements with Social Democracy (baptized "social-fascism" by Stalin). Codovilla presented a report, "The International Situation, Latin America, and the Danger of War," on behalf of the South American Secretariat of the Communist International. This report is very significant. On the one hand faithfully echoing the Stalinist doctrine of "social fascism," Codovilla elaborates the concept of "national fascism," which he applies to various Latin American governments, including Mexico (the Mexican CP readopted this term in the early thirties to criticize Lázaro Cárdenas). On the other hand, while in the midst of a turn toward a revolutionary offensive, he emphasizes that "the character of the revolution in Latin America is that of a bourgeois-democratic revolution." In other words, Codovilla understands perfectly well that revolution by stages is to be the unshakable foundation of Comintern strategy for Latin America, independent of tactical turns to the right or left.[28]

While certain parties, like the Argentine CP, followed the Third Period orientation of the Comintern in all its rigid and sterile orthodoxy (the struggle against "national fascism," etc.), others saw this left course as a stimulus to their own autonomous revolutionary inclinations. This was the case for the Communist Party of El Salvador—founded in 1930 by union cadres and an ex-student, Agustín Farabundo Martí (1893–1932)—which in

1932 organized the only mass insurrection in the history of Latin America to be led by a Communist party.

The social situation in El Salvador, then under the military dictatorship of General Martínez, is summarized perfectly in these sentences from a report by U.S. Major A.R. Harris, military attache for Central America, during a tour in El Salvador:

> Thirty or forty families own nearly everything in the country. They live in almost regal splendor with many attendants. . . . The rest of the population has practically nothing. . . . I imagine the situation in El Salvador today is very much like France was before its revolution, Russia before its revolution and Mexico before its revolution. The situation is ripe for communism and the communists seem to have found that out.[29]

Facing government repression against party propaganda and the Communist press, Farabundo Martí (who had fought in 1929 with Sandino's guerrillas) declared: "When one cannot write with the pen, one has to write with the sword." The Communist Party, which led the first workers' and peasants' unions, chose to prepare an insurrection, basing themselves primarily on revolutionary work in the ranks of the army, where the conflict between (indigenous) peasant soldiers and (European-American) officers, the sons of the oligarchy, had sharpened.

But the government, informed of Communist preparations, unleashed a wave of preventive repression, arresting some of the principal leaders of the Salvadoran CP (Farabundo Martí, Alfonso Luna, Mario Zapata, and Miguel Mármol) and shooting soldiers suspected of Communist sympathies. In response, a peasant insurrection inspired and led by the Communists broke out in January 1932, especially in the regions of the large coffee plantations. Red detachments of indigenous peasants, armed mostly with machetes and a few rifles, occupied some villages for a few days and established ephemeral "local soviets." It seems that more than 40,000 combatants participated in the rising.[30]

What was the political program of the movement? A series of documents and calls to action by the Communist Party of El Salvador clearly show that the objective was nothing less than a socialist revolution—power for workers', soldiers', and peasants' councils seeking "the implacable destruction of the national bourgeoisie and imperialism."

In fact, there was no real central political and military coordination of the insurrection. Since the red networks in the army had already been destroyed, the local insurrections could be put down one by one (with the aid of the oligarchy's "civic guard"). What then occurred has passed into Salvadoran history as El Matanza, "The Slaughter." For weeks, the army shot, murdered, and burned its way through peasant villages, executing some 20,000 men, women, and children in the red regions. After a mockery of a trial, Farabundo Martí, Luna, and Zapata were themselves executed. The only survivor among the party leadership was Miguel Mármol, a workers' leader who was left for dead by a firing squad.

What was the Comintern's relation to this unprecedented (and unrepeated!) episode in the history of the Latin American Communist parties? According to Mármol (in his 1970 recollections), the International played no role; the leadership of the Salvadoran CP took this decision with complete independence.[31] The reaction of official representatives of the Communist movement after the events tends to confirm this. While saluting "the heroic struggle of the workers and peasants of El Salvador," the organ of the Communist Party of the United States criticized "the putschist and left sectarian tendencies" of the Salvadoran CP,[32] and David Alfaro Siqueiros, leader of the Mexican party, pointed out that the uprising had been a mistake, since under any circumstances the North American imperialists would have intervened directly to stop a red victory.[33] Marmol's self-criticism, forty years later, is situated in a quite different problematic:

> Our errors were rightist, not leftist, ones. Our mistakes included, on one hand, vacillation in the application of a fundamentally correct line, which kept us from taking advantage of an adequate opportunity, surprise, the maintenance of the initiative, etc. In addition, our errors included a great disregard for the material means of insurrection: arms, transport, economic measures, communications, etc.[34]

Therefore, we can conclude that the 1932 rebellion constituted a quite singular event in the history of Latin American Communism because of the mass character of the armed struggle, its openly socialist program, and its autonomy in relation to the Comintern. The fact that this episode has been more or less "forgotten" or disregarded by the official Communist movement is evidently the consequence of these peculiarities, which increasingly stood in contradiction to the new orientation of the Communist parties. It was only rediscovered and "rehabilitated" by Castroism in the seventies.[35] The current attitude of official Communism toward the 1932 revolt can be seen in a book by Graciela A. García (of the Guatemalan CP). While devoted to "revolutionary struggles in Central America," this historical work only mentions the Salvadoran rising in passing—in one sentence—as "the tragic events of 1932, planned by the dictator Martínez to destroy the union movement once and for all."[36]

The other (and final) attempt in Latin America at armed insurrection under Communist leadership was the red rebellion of 1935 in Brazil. Nevertheless, this rising was radically different from the one in El Salvador both in style and substance. First, it was not really a popular insurrection by an armed people, but in essence a failed military rebellion. Second, the program of the movement was not socialist, but merely national-democratic. Third, this 1935 action, unlike that in El Salvador, was scrupulously discussed, planned, and decided upon by the Comintern.

It seems that in December 1934, at a meeting of Latin American Communist parties in Moscow, a decision was taken to launch an insurrectionary movement led by a popular anti-imperialist front. A certain number of Comintern representatives were sent to Brazil to advise the Communist Party, among them "Harry Berger" (the pseudonym of the German Communist leader and former deputy Artur Ewert) and Rodolfo Ghioldi of the Argentine CP.[37] At the Seventh Comintern Congress (July 1935), a number of speakers touched on the Brazilian question. Dimitrov himself spoke openly of the struggle for power, and the Brazilian delegate made it understood that an insurrection was being prepared.[38]

The man selected to lead the movement was Luis Carlos Prestes (1898–1990), a legendary personality in Brazil. In 1924, as an army captain, he had participated in a military uprising of young officers against the oligarchy of coffee planters that had dominated Brazil since the end of the nineteenth century. After the failure of the movement in the large cities, he formed a column of several thousand soldiers and officers that withdrew to the interior of the country. For three years, they recrossed Brazil from north to south, from east to west, successfully escaping all attempts by government troops to surround them. The group adopted the name the "Prestes Column," and its chief became a popular hero, nicknamed the Knight of Hope. In 1926, the last survivors of the column were forced to take refuge in Bolivia, and Prestes went into exile in Argentina. The rising of 1924 was one episode in a broader movement of struggle by young officers, mostly lieutenants (tenentes in Portuguese, hence the name of the movement, tenentismo), which had begun in 1922 with a revolt in Fort Copacabana in Rio and continued until 1930. The program and ideology of tenentismo were quite vague and confused: against the rural oligarchy, for democracy, for progress, for national independence, and so on. Around 1930, the movement split. While the right wing joined the bourgeois politician Getulio Vargas to launch the so-called Revolution of 1930, Prestes radicalized and, after a brief pro-Trotskyist interlude, moved closer to the Brazilian CP.[39] In 1931, he accepted an invitation from the Comintern to come to the U.S.S.R. He soon became a Communist and worked with the Latin American Secretariat of the Comintern. In 1935, he returned to Brazil, took over the leadership of the Communist Party, and organized the insurrectionary movement.

Before the return of Prestes, the Communists and the tenentista left wing had created the ANL (the National Liberation Alliance) and elected the Knight of Hope as honorary president. The ANL grew quite rapidly and obtained considerable success. The official leaders were left *tenentista* officers (former members of the Prestes Column), but the real organizers were Communist cadres. By May 1935, there were 1,600 branches of the ANL. Its direct opponent was the Integralist Party, a Brazilian variant of fascism; these groups confronted each other in street fighting, especially in São Paulo. The program of the ANL was moderate enough: national and democratic reforms compatible with a popular front strategy. It was its chosen method of struggle, armed insurrection, that distinguished the ANL from a popular front.

On July 5, 1935, Prestes, having returned to Brazil, made a memorable speech in which he accused Vargas and the government of having betrayed both the ideals of the *tenentista* movement and their commitments from the 1930 revolution, raising the slogan "All power to the ANL." Vargas immediately outlawed the National Liberation Alliance, and preparations for the rising intensified. In November 1935, a military rebellion finally broke out, starting in the north; various battalions led by noncommissioned officers revolted in the cities of Natal and Recife. They succeeded in taking power in Natal and installing a Popular Revolutionary Government in the province. Some days later, government troops reinforced from the south put down the rebellion. It was a few weeks before other troops from the Third Infantry Regiment (under Captain Agildo Barata) and the Military Aviation School revolted in Rio, the country's capital. Other regiments that were supposed to rise did not do so, and the movement was crushed in its shell after hours of fierce combat.

Apparently, the leaders of the Brazilian CP were counting on the support of the "progressive bourgeoisie" (in particular, the governor of Rio de Janeiro State). Indeed, as Abguar Bastos, a historian sympathetic to the Communists, recognized: "The progressive bourgeoisie—industrial, commercial, and intellectual—that had committed themselves to the movement did not take a single step to join the revolution. . . . After the risings . . . the whole bourgeoisie joined with Vargas to finish with 'communism.'"[40]

Actually, the rising had been conceived as an entirely *military* movement. There was no true mobilization and arming of the worker and peasant masses (except for a few places in the north). Its failure was followed by an immense wave of repression, with thousands of executions, mass torture, and the jailing of tens of thousands of political prisoners. Prestes himself was arrested and jailed for ten years. His wife, the German-born Communist Olga Benario, was turned over to the Gestapo. Artur Ewert was driven insane under Brazilian police torture.

The 1935 action was the product of a transitional period. Its program was popular-frontist, but its insurrectionary method corresponded more closely to tendencies of the Third Period. The almost totally military (and non-popular) character of the rebellion derived from two factors: the *tenentista* origin of Prestes and the leaders of the ANL, accustomed to conspiracies and military risings, and especially the nature of the ANL program itself, which did not call for the masses to arm themselves. Since the revolution was defined as national-democratic, it was natural to count on the so-called progressive bourgeoisie and the nationalist (bourgeois) wing of the army.

In this sense, the Brazilian rebellion of 1935 was both the last revolutionary uprising inspired by a Latin American Communist party and the first step toward the politics of class collaboration that would orient the Communist movement for most of its history from the thirties onward.

After the death of Mella and Mariátegui, a process of impoverishment of Marxist thought began in Latin America that would last for decades. One exception during the thirties was the Argentine sociologist Aníbal Ponce (1898–1938). Ponce, a disciple, friend, and collaborator of the celebrated thinker José Ingenieros (who was ideologically close to positivism), only became a Marxist after 1928, when he declared at a memorable conference that the ideals of the Russian Revolution were the very ideals of the May Revolution (the "Jacobin" revolution of May 1810 that proclaimed the independence of Argentina from Spanish colonial power), "in their full significance." A sympathizer of the Communist Party, he chaired the 1933 Latin American Conference against Imperialist War in Montevideo, but he played no significant role in the Argentine workers' movement.

Ponce was the author of various works of history and sociology, of which the most widely known are *Education and Class Struggle* (1937) and *Bourgeois Humanism and Proletarian Humanism* (1935). These writings, particularly the latter, reveal not only a knowledge of universal culture, but also a real command of historical materialism. On the other hand, the few works by Ponce on Latin America seem distant from any Marxist problematic. His biography of Sarmiento, the great nineteenth-century Argentine writer and *caudillo*, is quite apologetic and does not analyze this figure and his political role in class terms.[41] If we compare Ponce with Mariátegui, we have to recognize that his general sociological writings are on a level with the notable works of the Peruvian Marxist, while his works on Latin America are much less interesting than those of the author of the *Seven Interpretive Essays on Peruvian Reality* and are of an essentially pre-Marxist character. Was this difference, as well as Ponce's marginal political role, due solely to psychological and individual causes? It seems to us that an explanation should also be sought in the differences between these two periods in the Latin American workers' movement, the thirties being less favorable to unity between the universal and the particular, or between theory and practice.

By 1936, the process of the Stalinization of the Communist parties, which had developed in an unequal and contradictory way since the late twenties, was crystallized and completed. By Stalinism, we mean the creation in each party of a leading apparatus—hierarchical, bureaucratic, and authoritarian— that was intimately connected from an organic, political, and ideological point of view to the Soviet leadership, and that faithfully followed all the turns of its international orientation. The result of this process was the adoption of the doctrine of revolution by stages and the bloc of four classes (the proletariat, peasantry, petty bourgeoisie, and national bourgeoisie) as the foundation of their political practice; their goal was the realization of the national-democratic (or anti-imperialist or anti-feudal) stage. This was a doctrine elaborated by Stalin and applied in China, and later generalized for all the so-called colonial or semi-colonial countries (including, of course, Latin America). Its methodological starting point is an economistic interpretation of Marxism already found in Plekhanov and the Mensheviks: in a semifeudal and economically backward country, the conditions are not "ripe" for a socialist revolution.[42]

To avoid any misunderstanding, let us reemphasize that from a subjective point of view, for a majority of Communist militants and leaders, these two phenomena were accompanied by a sincere conviction that, first, the U.S.S.R. was the homeland of socialism, whose defense was a primordial imperative, and second, that the democratic-national revolution would open the road toward the final objective of the workers' movement—socialism.

Regis Debray has written, concerning the relation between Latin American Communism and the Comintern:

> Latin America always followed either too soon or too late. Every turn in the world situation is out of phase with turns in the continental or regional situation. The Communist parties, following the directives of the Comintern, find themselves in the counter-current of regional events, confronting their specific tasks from precisely the opposite direction.[43]

To us, this problematic is not situated solely at the Latin American level. The orientation of the Stalinized Comintern was also "against the current" in Asia and Europe (Germany 1929–33). Nevertheless, while in Asia (China, Vietnam) some Communist parties followed their own autonomous orientation in practice, without breaking with the Comintern, in Latin America (as in the majority of European countries), the Communist parties unconditionally followed the "general line" as defined by the Soviet leadership, limiting themselves to adapting it, poorly more often than not, to the specific conditions of their countries (adaptations that permit them a certain room for maneuver and explain the sometimes important differences in the parties' tactics).

The first manifestation of this new period, characterized by the hegemony of the "Stalin phenomenon" over Latin American Marxism, is the popular front.

The worldwide turn toward the popular front, that is, toward an antifascist alliance of Communist, Socialist, and bourgeois-democratic parties, as outlined in 1934, was officially sanctioned by the Seventh Comintern Congress in 1935. After this, each Latin American Communist Party attempted to apply the new orientation, seeking allies for a local popular front. In the majority of countries on the continent, in the absence of social-democratic parties, alliances were made directly with bourgeois forces considered liberal or nationalist, or simply non-fascist. In Peru, the CP, rejected by the APRA, joined the Democratic Front, which supported the candidacy of Manuel Prado, a representative of the traditional liberal oligarchy.[44] In Colombia, the CP supported the Liberal Party—a support that would take an increasingly unconditional character (according to the official history of the party published in 1960). In 1938, the Colombian CP even broke with the left of the Liberal Party to support Eduardo Santos, the head of the Liberal right.[45] In a similar way, the Mexican CP broke with General Mújica, leader of the left of the Party of the Mexican Revolution (the ruling party), in 1939 to support the moderate wing represented by Ávila Camacho.[46] In Cuba, the CP, unable to unite with social democrats, liberals, or democrats, finally supported Fulgencio Batista in January 1939, for the simple reason that he had a line of "effective collaboration between Cuba and the United States against the fascist threat."[47]

The only country in which it was possible to constitute a popular front with certain similarities to the European model was Chile. Here the CP and the SP united under the hegemony of the Radical Party, represented by Aguirre Cerda, who was elected president in 1938.[48] For the Chilean CP, the objective of the Popular Front was the realization of the national-democratic stage through an independent and progressive development of Chilean capitalism.[49] The Socialist Party's position was more complex. Founded in 1933 by a fusion of various small socialist parties and groups, and strengthened in 1937 by the adherence of the Communist Left (the Trotskyist faction expelled from the CP), the Chilean SP was not a social-democratic party, but rather a unique political formation that paid allegiance to Marxism in its program and called for a "workers' dictatorship" and a "Socialist Republic of Latin America." Nevertheless, its principal leader in the thirties, Air Commodore Marmaduque Grove, one of the leaders of an ephemeral, twelve-day Socialist Republic established by a military rising in 1932, was politically eclectic, closer to socialistic nationalism than to Marxism. The SP resisted the call for a popular front for some time, pointing out that it would transform the workers' parties into instruments of bourgeois-democratic radicalism, since they could not adopt a socialist program that would frighten their capitalist allies. Nevertheless, at its Fourth Congress in 1937, the SP decided to join the Popular Front that was already being created by the CP and the Radical Party. Having rapidly become a mass party, the SP was and would continue to be extremely heterogeneous, both politically and ideologically, and unite the most diverse currents, from Trotskyism to "classic" social democracy, in a flexible and unintegrated federation.[50]

The Chilean Popular Front lasted in a variety of forms until 1947, and until 1952 was an alliance between the CP and a wing of the SP. During these fourteen years, the Radical Party allied at times with the Communists against the Socialists, and at times with the Socialists (or one of its currents) against the Communists. For example, in 1946, the Radical president, Duhalde, attacked the CP with the support of the Socialist right wing. In 1947, the new Radical president, González Videla, attacked the SP with the support of the CP (which was participating in the government), but reversed alliances with the start of the Cold War in 1948, and outlawed the CP (with the support of the Socialist right). In 1952, when the CP and a wing of the SP finally joined to create a united front, the workers' movement was so demoralized that its common candidate, Salvador Allende, obtained only 6 percent of the vote.

We can summarize the historic role of the Popular Front by comparing the following analyses. According to a North American academic historian, "The victory of the Popular Front prevented a revolution and taught the masses to use the ballot box instead of the sword."[51] A Chilean Communist has stated: "The triumph of the Popular Front in 1938 and of the Democratic Alliance in 1946 showed precisely that the working class and the Chilean people could conquer the government otherwise than by insurrection."[52] Lastly, Oscar Waiss, a Chilean left socialist (with a Trotskyist background), claimed: "The Popular Front was a gigantic political error that rehabilitated a decomposing Radical Party and stole the revolutionary initiative from the masses. The Popular Front was an act of social mystification . . . that never attempted to modify the structure of landed property or regain the ownership of our fundamental wealth."[53]

If the popular front in Latin America at first had an anti-imperialist program (1935–36), this aspect tended to disappear as an accommodation developed between the U.S. and the U.S.S.R. against Nazi Germany. In general, the politics of the Communist parties toward the United States during the thirties and forties closely followed the turns of Soviet foreign policy. The most striking example is the Argentine CP, which had always been the most faithful to the U.S.S.R. Some statements by P. González Alberdi, a well-known leader of the Argentine CP, regarding Franklin

Delano Roosevelt's United States demonstrate a change in positions to keep in step with Soviet views. In 1933, during the Third Period, he wrote, "In Cuba, the formidable revolutionary movement of the Antillean masses has shown that Roosevelt is as imperialist as Hoover" (*Informaciones*, October 1933). In 1938, when the U.S.S.R. was allied with the Western powers, Gonzalez Alberdi wrote that "the Italo-Nazi attempts to promote anti-imperialism against the Yankees have failed. The nations of the continent have understood that close collaboration with Roosevelt, who cannot be considered a representative of the imperialist forces to the north, does not at all diminish each country's autonomy nor affect its individual dignity" (*Orientación*, December 15, 1938). Finally, in 1940, after the Molotov-Ribbentrop pact: "In the name of the struggle against Nazism, Yankee imperialism conspires against the public liberties of the American nations" (*La Hora*, July 14, 1940).[54]

While the German-Soviet pact was in force, Ernesto Giudici, a leader of the Argentine CP, published an interesting book which included, on the one hand, a radical (and justified) attack against Anglo-American imperialism and its domination of Argentina and, on the other hand, a quite astonishing analysis of the fascist phenomenon:

> We should appreciate that the aspirations of the masses often lay behind this fascist ideology. And because they come from the people, it matters little whether their ideological form is fascist or not. The necessary political rectification can occur in the mass movement itself—which has developed with little regard for the reactionary ideology that some attribute to it.[55]

After June 1941 (and Hitler's invasion of the U.S.S.R.), the opposite analysis was developed in Argentina and elsewhere on the continent. In the context of the antifascist alliance between the United States and the U.S.S.R., any propaganda against North American imperialism was harshly criticized and branded by the Communist parties as a maneuver in the service of fascism.[56]

During 1944 and 1945, a phenomenon known as Browderism developed in Latin America. In the euphoria brought on by the Teheran accords, Earl Browder, the leader of the Communist Party of the United States, declared the start of an era of friendship and close collaboration between the socialist camp and the United States that was destined to continue even after the war. Browder drew "excessive" conclusions from this historical perspective and converted the CPUSA into a vague "political association." This practice was condemned as liquidationist by the international Communist movement in a speech by Jacques Duclos (leader of the French CP) in April 1945. But the Latin American Communist parties had also been swept away by Browderism. For example, in a book *Marching Toward a Better World*, published in 1944, Vittorio Codovilla had written the following:

International cooperation between the most important capitalist countries, and between these countries and the U.S.S.R., with the purpose of creating a better world, shows that the United States and England have agreed upon an economic policy to be followed in Latin America that aims to contribute to economic, political, and social development in a progressive manner. . . . This agreement should be based upon the cooperation of these two great powers with democratic and progressive governments in Latin America, to carry out a common program that, while creating a market for their capital that is ten or twenty times greater than at present, will contribute to the independent development of these countries and permit them within a few years to eliminate the backwardness in which they have wallowed for many decades.[57]

Browderism also had consequences for the Communist parties on the national political level. In Cuba, for example, after having participated in General Batista's government from 1943 to 1944,[58] the Popular Socialist Party (the new name of the Cuban CP) published a pamphlet in 1945 entitled *Collaboration between Bosses and Workers*, to commemorate an important breakfast meeting in Havana between the association of industrial employers, the government, and the (Communist) leaders of the Confederation of Cuban Workers.[59] In Mexico, the major union confederation (the CTM) and the main employers' association signed a national unity agreement in 1945, and *The Voice of Mexico*, the organ of the Mexican CP, celebrated the event with a banner headline, "Historic Worker-Boss Pact: Solid Base for the Growth and Progress of the Country." It is interesting to note that one of the points of this agreement solemnly declared as its goal "to reject the theory of economic self-sufficiency and act on the theory of economic interdependence and financial and technical cooperation with the other countries of the continent for our common benefit, as part of an international program that considers the needs of the world's other peoples." According to *The Voice of Mexico*, the agreement was "proper," "impeccably formulated," and "patriotic," and reflected the new conditions in Mexico and the world that "require an alliance of the workers and the capitalists."[60]

The Duclos article of 1945 and the removal of Earl Browder from the leadership of the CPUSA inaugurated a period of self-criticism and rectification, which led to the abandonment both of the perspective of "harmonious" agreement with the United States and of those organizational measures that were considered liquidationist. Nevertheless, this new period, which could be called Post-Browderism, was characterized by the continuation of a "national unity" orientation. In Mexico, for example, in

November 1945 (well after the Duclos letter), the journal of the Mexican CP developed the following thesis: "The objective of the development of capitalism in Mexico is a revolutionary objective, since it signifies the growth of a national economy, the removal of the eagle's claws that keep the country a semi-colony, the elimination of semi-colonial vestiges, the realization of agrarian reform, and the democratic and general development of the country thanks to an anti-imperialist agrarian revolution."

Also, according to this article, the measures proposed by the Mexican CP "are, like the agrarian reform, bourgeois measures that will permit the development of capitalism in Mexico, the industrialization of the country, and its liberation from any imperialist intervention."[61] The Soviet historian Anatol Shulgovsky, author of a work on the history of modern Mexico, writes about this period that the "Marxist" ideology of the Mexican workers' movement could be compared to the "legal Marxism" of Czarist Russia (P. Struve and others), whose central theme was that the working class should support industrial development as a precondition to future social struggle. Nevertheless, Shulgovsky only refers explicitly to the orientation of the "Marxists" around the leadership of the CTM (Lombardo Toledano) and does not mention that the Communist Party put forward a similar orientation.[62]

One of the most famous episodes of post-Browderism was the attitude toward Peronism adopted by the Argentine CP. Deeply convinced that Perón and his supporters were fascists, the Argentine Communists participated in the formation of the Democratic Union, a broad anti-Perón coalition whose forces, according to Vittorio Codovilla (in his report to the National Conference of the CP in December 1945), included the following:

1. All the traditional parties.
2. The most conscious and combative part of the workers' and peasants' movement.
3. Most of the worker and peasant youth and the immense majority of university youth, professors, professionals, and the middle classes.
4. The majority of industrialists, commercial entrepreneurs, farmers, cattlemen, and financiers.
5. The majority of the army and navy and a section of the uniformed police.
   Despite this, the Democratic Union still has an overly limited character, since some progressive sectors of the Conservative Party are not participating.[63]

Their participation in this alliance, which was also supported by Spruille Braden, the U.S. ambassador to Argentina (who mistrusted Perón's demagogic nationalism), had long-term consequences for the CP. A sharp divide opened between the majority of the Argentine working class, who supported Peronism, and the Communists, who were accused by Perón of collaborating with the military and the most conservative section of landed proprietors ("the oligarchy").

A similar situation developed in other countries of the continent, especially in Bolivia, where the PIR (Revolutionary Left Party, pro-Soviet) joined with the tradition parties of the oligarchy in 1946 to overthrow the government of the MNR (National Revolutionary Movement), which they considered pro-fascist. The most notable exception was Brazil, where the Brazilian CP supported the populist caudillo Getulio Vargas in 1945— among other reasons because he had participated on the side of the allies in World War II (unlike Perón and Villaroel, the Bolivian president supported by the MNR).[64]

It is interesting to note that it was in this period, when the politics of the Communist Party were extremely moderate, that the first signs were seen of a mass left opposition to the Communists in the very heart of the workers' movement.

The Communist Left Opposition and Trotskyism appeared in Latin America in the early thirties, first in Brazil and then in Chile. In 1933, the Chilean Left Opposition, an affiliate of the International Left Opposition, was established by an important section of the Chilean CP (led by Manuel Hidalgo, Humberto Mendoza, Oscar Waiss, and others) that had split from the party in 1931. Nevertheless, the majority of the members of this group joined the Socialist Party in 1937, and Trotskyism then became one of the diffuse ideological tendencies of Chilean socialism. It was above all in Bolivia that the Trotskyist opposition really succeeded in implanting itself. Founded by J. Aguirre Gainsborg and Tristán Marof, the POR (Revolutionary Workers Party), the Bolivian section of the Fourth International, developed a significant influence in the workers' movement after World War II. In 1946, a congress of the FSTMB (Federation of Mineworkers of Bolivia), meeting in the city of Pulcayo, approved a set of theses of clearly Trotskyist inspiration, whose central axis was the strategy of transforming the bourgeois-democratic revolution into a socialist revolution in an uninterrupted process, under the leadership of the proletariat allied with the peasantry.

This conception, the perspective of a revolution that combines democratic, agrarian, national, and anti-capitalist tasks and the rejection of a strategic alliance with the native bourgeoisie (considered incapable of playing a meaningful revolutionary role) which is logically derived from it, radically differentiates Trotskyism from the "orthodox" Communist current (as does, of course, its independence from the U.S.S.R.).

Because of its vision of revolutionary strategy, the Latin American current inspired by the ideas of Trotsky can be considered as the continuator of the ideas of Latin American Communism of the twenties, especially those of

Mariátegui, to whose political inheritance the Trotskyists constantly appeal.[65] Denounced as "provocateurs" and "agents of fascism" by the Communist parties, forced by them to the margins of the workers' movement, and internally divided by fratricidal quarrels, the Trotskyists in many countries were reduced to sects composed essentially of intellectuals. Before the Cuban revolution, Trotskyism did succeed in implanting itself in the working class and the unions in Bolivia and, to a lesser degree, in Argentina and Chile, where they played a real political role. This was the case, in particular, for the militants of the POR, who played a decisive role in the creation of the COB (Bolivian Workers Confederation) during the Bolivian revolution of 1952–53. The first program of the COB, published at the end of 1952 and of clearly Trotskyist inspiration (and probably written by González Moscoso, a leader of the POR), points out: "The proletariat will realize the tasks which are historically those of the bourgeoisie."[66] The POR also inspired peasant land occupations in 1952–53 that forced the MNR government to decree a land reform.[67]

During 1948–54, the so-called Cold War broke out on an international scale, starting with a generalized imperialist offensive against the U.S.S.R., followed by a hardening of the latter and of the international Communist movement. After 1948, Communist parties were outlawed in Latin America (for example, in Brazil and Chile) and police harassed Communist unionists (for example, the assassination of Jesús Menéndez, a leader of the Cuban sugar workers). Governments elected with Communist votes (or supported by them) in 1945–46, such as Grau San Martín in Cuba, González Videla in Chile, and Miguel Alemán in Mexico, drew inspiration from the U.S. political scene and unleashed witch hunts and anticommunist repression.

In response (and following the new orientation of the U.S.S.R.), the Latin American CPs refurbished their anti-imperialist credentials and, to a certain extent, relaunched the class struggle against their bourgeoisies. The Cold War period saw a new left turn by pro-Soviet Communism in Latin America. But, unlike 1929–35, no revolutionary mass action was led by the Communist parties, and, most importantly, this new turn by no means threatened the essential foundation of these parties' strategy for the continent: the "Stalinist" interpretation of Marxism, the theory of revolution by stages, and the bloc of four classes for the realization of the national-democratic revolution.

The most characteristic events of this period undoubtedly occurred in Guatemala from 1951 through 1954, when the PGT (Guatemalan Labor Party—Communist) became one of the principal political forces in the country during the presidency of Jacobo Arbenz. Hegemonic in the workers' and peasants' unions, the PGT saw its tasks in the context of a national-democratic revolution, in alliance with those sectors of the bourgeoisie and the armed forces it considered progressive. The party statutes, approved at its second congress, clearly stated: "The PGT does not propose to struggle immediately for the establishment of socialism in Guatemala. It orients its immediate struggle against feudal backwardness and the imperialist oppression under which our country suffers."[68]

The events that followed are now well known. After the Arbenz government expropriated a certain number of properties of the United Fruit Company, an army of mercenaries trained by the U.S. invaded Guatemala in June 1954. The government's armed forces defended themselves with little conviction, and their general staff finally abandoned Jacobo Arbenz and rallied to Colonel Castillo Armas, leader of the invading forces, thanks to the mediation of John Peurifoy, the U.S. ambassador to Guatemala. But for some exceptional local actions, the workers' and peasants' movement (and the PGT), unarmed, was unable to resist.[69] The victory of Castillo Armas cleared the way for massive and bloody anticommunist repression, a true white terror, while the United Fruit Company retook its expropriated land.

How was such a defeat possible? In 1955, the leadership of the PGT published a self-critical balance sheet that recognized the party "did not follow a sufficiently independent line in relation to the democratic national bourgeoisie." In particular, "the PGT contributed to sowing illusions in the army and did not unmask the true positions and counter-revolutionary activity of the army High Command."[70] Yet this self-criticism did not question the strategic foundation of the PGT's orientation (its conception of the stages of historical development, etc.), but only the tactical errors committed in the concrete application of this stagist strategy. Thus the PGT in 1955 reaffirmed the necessity of forming a bloc with the national bourgeoisie for a democratic and patriotic revolution.[71]

In most countries of the continent, the years 1948–53 saw the Communists facing murderous repression by the police and military and responding with courage and tenacity. It is also undeniable that a real radicalization took place in certain countries during the Cold War. The Communists found themselves at the head of large strike movements (Brazil, 1953–54), or participated in peasant guerrilla actions (Colombia, 1949–55). But for the continent's other Communist parties, the political hardening did not necessarily signify any concrete revolutionary activity. The Cuban example is quite significant in this regard.

After Batista's military coup (1952), the PSP energetically denounced the reactionary and pro-U.S. character of the putsch, but the party was not outlawed and its daily paper, *Hoy*, continued to appear, a fact which possibly influenced its politics.[72] The PSP did not lead violent actions against the Batista regime, and it denounced the July 26, 1953, attack on Moncada as "a putschist attempt, a desperate form of adventurism, typical of petty bourgeois circles lacking in principles and implicated in gangsterism."[73] This did not stop Batista from unleashing a brutal wave of anticommunist repression and outlawing the PSP.

The PSP's preoccupation with being mistaken for "adventurists" could be seen again in the party journal, *Fundamentos*, in June 1957 (six months after the landing in Cuba of the fighters of the July 26 Movement under the leadership of Fidel Castro): "It is important to reaffirm . . . that today, like yesterday, we reject and condemn, and we will continue to reject and condemn, terrorist and putschist methods as ineffective, harmful, and contrary to the interests of the people."[74] The orientation put forward by the party at this time was "change" by the peaceful road, "without violence or suffering," a purpose for which the PSP was "ready, today like yesterday and forever, to make any sacrifice and any honorable concession, upon the basis, of course, of the supreme interests of the working class, the people, and the homeland."[75] The goal of these changes was Batista's overthrow and the accomplishment of the democratic revolution and national liberation through an alliance between the PSP and the progressive bourgeoisie.[76]

During 1958, the PSP finally integrated itself into the July 26 Movement's struggle against the dictatorship. Several militants and some leaders of the party (notably Carlos Rafael Rodríguez) headed for the mountains to participate in the armed struggle, honorably contributing to the guerrilla triumph in January 1959. The PSP, however, remained a moderating influence inside the Cuban revolutionary movement, which in its opinion should have remained within the limits of the national-democratic stage. Thus Blas Roca (General Secretary of the PSP), in his report to the Eighth National Assembly of the party (August 1960), emphasized:

> The Cuban revolution . . . is a revolution which, by the historical tasks that it faces and accomplishes, can be correctly qualified as an agrarian revolution, a revolution of national liberation, a patriotic and democratic revolution. . . . The national bourgeoisie, which benefits from the revolution and has recently obtained great profits because of the growing purchasing power of the people and the larger number of consumers, supports the revolution but is frequently frightened by its radical measures and by the threats, bluster, and attacks of North American imperialism. . . . Within limits to be established, it is necessary to guarantee the profits of private enterprise, its normal functioning and development. It is necessary to stimulate zeal and increase productivity among the workers of these enterprises.[77]

We can therefore conclude that the PSP did not play an important role in the preparation and unleashing of the armed struggle against Batista (1953–57) or in the transition of the Cuban Revolution toward socialism (August–October 1960). This was not the result of specific limitations of the PSP, but the consequence of the fundamental political orientation of the continent's official Communist movement: revolution by stages and a bloc with the national bourgeoisie. In this sense, the politics of the PSP from 1953 to 1960 were an example of how difficult it was for the traditional Communist parties to play a real revolutionary role, despite the self-denial, courage, and devotion of their members.

The death of Stalin (1953) and the Twentieth Congress of the CPSU (1956) inaugurated a new epoch in "pro-Soviet" Latin American Communism that continues until today. The dissolution of the Cominform (1956) did not signify the abolition of the political and ideological links between the Communist parties and the Soviet leadership. The orientation of the U.S.S.R. toward institutionalized peaceful coexistence and its turn toward moderation after the end of the Cold War was translated by the Latin American Communist parties into a political line supporting bourgeois governments considered progressive and/or democratic, such as Juscelino Kubitschek in Brazil and Frondizi in Argentina. The theoretical foundation for this line was summarized in a May 1958 declaration of the Brazilian CP, according to which the contradiction between the proletariat and the bourgeoisie

does not demand a radical solution in the current stage. In the present conditions of the country, capitalist development corresponds with the interests of the proletariat and the whole people. . . . The proletariat and the bourgeoisie are allied around the common objective of struggle for independent and progressive development in opposition to North American imperialism.[78]

The hegemony of Stalinism over Latin American Marxist thought from the thirties until the Cuban Revolution did not mean that no scientific contributions to Marxist thought were made in this period. In a number of countries, the postwar period saw an increase in research, especially in Marxist economic history, both inside and outside the Communist parties, questioning the prevalent schematic interpretations of the continent's socioeconomic formations, particularly the tendency to impose the European feudal model onto Latin American agrarian structures. The pioneering work of Sergio Bagú, *The Economy of Colonial Society*, which appeared in 1949, advanced the following thesis, probably for the first time:

The economic structure which is born in America in the period under our study was of a colonial capitalist rather than a feudal type. . . . The metropolis creates Iberian America in order to integrate it into the cycle of nascent capitalism, not to prolong the languishing feudal cycle.[79]

Soon after, Caio Prado Jr., a well-known historian connected to the Brazilian Communist Party, published his *Economic History of Brazil*, which proceeds from the following analysis:

As a whole, seen from a worldwide and international perspective, the colonization [of the tropics] seems a vast commercial enterprise . . . [whose] purpose is to exploit the natural resources of a virgin territory in the interest of European commerce. . . . The Brazilian colony is constituted with these characteristics, articulated in a purely productive and mercantile organizational form.[80]

Similarly in Chile, Marcelo Segall's research criticized the partisans of the theory of Latin American feudalism and insisted on the importance of mining, a typically capitalist industry, in the colonial economy.[81] We should mention the important work of certain Argentine Trotskyist authors during this period, especially Nahuel Moreno and Milcíades Peña (although Peña's work was only published later), on the capitalist aspect of Spanish and Portuguese colonization and its combination with precapitalist social relations.[82] Nahuel Moreno insists on the combination of different productive structures:

If it is true that the purposes of the European colonization were capitalist and not feudal, the colonists did not establish a capitalist system of production because there was no army of free labor on the market in America. Thus the colonists, to exploit America in a capitalist manner, were obliged to call upon non-capitalist productive relations: slavery or the semi-slavery of the indigenous people.

Meanwhile, the "official" historians of the Communist movement continued to defend the traditional theory against time and tide. For example, Hernán Ramírez Necochea, historian of the Chilean CP, insisted on the thesis that the Chilean colonial economy "mainly possessed diverse elements of a strictly feudal type. . . . It had characteristics *acquired by European feudalism at the end of the Middle Ages*. . . . Manufacturing and even mining were not independent activities, and feudal relations of production predominated there also."[83]

For Trotskyist historians, this debate was directly connected to their critique of the doctrine of the bourgeois-democratic (anti-feudal) stage of the Latin American revolution. For other authors, some of them militants or sympathizers of the Communist parties, their historical discoveries did not transcend the context of their scientific specialty; they did not develop their political consequences, nor were they taken into consideration by the leadership of their parties. In a work published in 1966, Caio Prado Jr., a well-known Brazilian CP intellectual, complained of the impossibility of having the results of his "heretical" research acknowledged inside the party:

It was impossible to oppose the witness of the facts, as convincing as they were, to conceptions that were so deeply rooted . . . because the facts themselves were considered only through the deforming lenses of these false conceptions. . . . We continued and still speak to Brazil, in deference to the old schema originally based on the European experience, of this bourgeois-democratic revolution destined to eliminate the supposed "feudal remnants" in our country.[84]

Incidentally, this testimony shows it was not scientific ignorance that was at the source of these theoretical errors, but the reverse.

Unlike developments in economic history, there were very few scientific works of Marxist sociology in this period that were oriented toward current questions. One of the rare exceptions was the work of Silvio Frondizi (1907–74), a revolutionary militant and professor of sociology, history, and law at the University of La Plata, whose philosophic, socioeconomic, and political writings reveal a profound knowledge of European culture and the Marxist classics as well as a concrete understanding of Latin American reality. The more directly engaged and political character of his writings on Latin America distinguishes his work from that of the economic historians. In *Argentine Reality: An Essay in Sociological Interpretation*, Silvio Frondizi, aided by a team of young collaborators including Milcíades Peña, Marcos Kaplan, Ricardo Napuri, and Marcelo Torrens, developed an economic, social, and political analysis of the Argentine social formation as it existed after 1943; its central axis is an attempt at understanding the Peronist phenomenon. Criticizing the Communist Party's identification of Peronism as Nazism (in 1945), Frondizi analyzes the Bonapartist nature of Perón's regime, his role as a pseudo-arbiter above social classes, and his capacity to neutralize the workers' movement through "state control." He also points out that the defeat of the Peronist experiment was not accidental, but the result of the organic incapacity of the Argentine bourgeoisie (like that of "semi-colonial" countries in general) to accomplish a real democratic revolution. This historical task can only be accomplished under the leadership of the proletariat, but in this case, "it is not a question of realizing the bourgeois-democratic revolution as a self-enclosed stage, but of realizing bourgeois-democratic tasks in the forward march of the socialist revolution."[85]

The audacity of his theoretical and political ideas kept Silvio Frondizi relatively isolated during the fifties, with little influence on the organized workers' movement. His role became more important in the sixties and seventies, when he established relations with the armed revolutionary organizations. He was assassinated by the Argentine Anti-Communist Alliance in 1974.

The Cuban Revolution obviously constituted a capital turn in the history of Latin American Marxism and in the history of Latin America itself.[86]

After the destruction of Batista's dictatorial state and its repressive apparatus by the guerrillas, led by the young lawyer Fidel Castro (b. 1927), the Cuban democratic revolution experienced a process of "growing over" toward socialism, which ended with the installation of a proletarian-type state in 1960–61. The democratic and nationalist measures of 1959–60—radical land reform, expropriation of the imperialist oil refineries, etc.—rapidly ran up against the opposition and growing hostility not only of foreign capital and the financial oligarchy, but the totality of the dominant classes of the island. In August 1960, the Castro regime expropriated the principal sectors of North American capital in Cuba (telephone, electricity, sugar mills). Next, facing economic sabotage and the suspension of production by the Cuban bourgeoisie, the revolutionaries of the July 26 Movement took over abandoned factories. Finally, the expropriation of all the national big bourgeoisie and the de facto abolition of capitalism in Cuba followed in October 1960, as did the creation of workers' and peasants' militias, the foundation of a new state. The proclamation of the socialist nature of the revolution by Fidel in May 1961 (following the defeat of the counterrevolutionary invasion at the Bay of Pigs) was only the explicit and official sanction of an existing reality.

The conclusion to which the leaders and leftist militants of the July 26 Movement had come is summarized in a remark by Fidel in December 1961:

We had to make an anti-imperialist and socialist revolution. Well, the anti-imperialist and socialist revolution could only be one revolution, because there is only one revolution. This is the great dialectical truth of humanity: imperialism, and socialism against imperialism.[87]

Some of the Cuban revolutionaries held this perspective from the beginning of 1959, notably Guevara, who since April 1959 had proclaimed himself a partisan of the "uninterrupted development of the revolution" as far as the destruction of the existing social system and its economic foundations.[88] For most others, practice preceded theory, and their discovery of Marxism and the socialist path took place in the course of the revolutionary process itself: "It is thanks to the revolution that we will acquire a great fund of experience. The revolution is revolutionizing us internally."[89]

The exceptional fact of the Cuban Revolution is that a whole political team of petty-bourgeois origin, emboldened by a Jacobin ideology (inspired by José Martí), passed into the camp of the proletariat and became Marxist in a truly unprecedented collective "ideological metamorphosis." It was their determination to fully and unconditionally carry out radical democratic transformations that led Fidel and the left of the July 26 Movement to discover in the socialist revolution the only path capable of realizing these historic tasks. Free of the paralyzing stagist schemas of the PSP, the Castroist leadership did not fear transcending the bourgeois-democratic framework and taking anti-capitalist measures. It was therefore not by chance that the first socialist revolution in America was made under the leadership of revolutionaries outside the ideological mold of traditional Communism, with its evolutionist conception of the historical process and its economistic interpretation of Marxism.[90]

The Cuban Revolution clearly overturned the traditional problematic of the hegemonic Marxist current in Latin America. On the one hand, it showed that armed struggle is an effective way to destroy a reactionary and pro-imperialist power, and an indispensable preliminary condition for the passage to socialism. On the other hand, it demonstrated the objective possibility of a revolution combining democratic and socialist tasks in an *uninterrupted* revolutionary process. These lessons, in eminent contradiction to the orientation of the Communist parties toward peaceful change and an alliance with the industrial bourgeoisie for the democratic, progressive, and national development of capitalism, obviously stimulated the appearance of Marxist currents inspired by the Cuban example.

A new revolutionary period for Latin American Marxism therefore began after 1959—a period that has recovered some of the vigorous ideas of the "original Communism" of the twenties. There was no direct political and ideological continuity between the two periods, but the Castroists have reclaimed Mariátegui and rescued Mella and the 1932 revolution in El Salvador from historical oblivion.[91]

The leader and revolutionary thinker who best symbolizes and epitomizes this new period for Marxism in Latin America is Ernesto "Che" Guevara (1928–67), not only because of his historic role in the Cuban Revolution, but especially for the profound influence of his writings and practical activity on the new revolutionary currents of the continent.

This influence is exercised through a series of closely connected themes that constitute the central axis of Che's Marxism:[92] The first theme is the creation of a new man as the ultimate purpose of the revolution, and the rejection of economic measures of socialist construction that are based on "the worn-out arms left to us by capitalism (the commodity as economic unit, profitability, individual economic interest as motivating whip, etc.)."[93] The second theme is the socialist character of the Latin American revolution, a revolution that must overthrow "the imperialists and the local exploiters at the same time."[94] According to the famous formula of his *Message to the Tricontinental Congress* (which has served as an ideological and programmatic banner for the whole revolutionary left of the continent), "The national bourgeoisies have totally lost their ability to resist imperialism— if they ever had any—and now form its rear guard. There are no other alternatives: either socialist revolution or a caricature of revolution."[95]

Regarding Cuba, Guevara examines the methodological premises for a Marxist analysis of the transformation of the democratic revolution into a socialist one in an important 1964 essay. He poses the question of how the transition to socialism is possible in a semi-colonial, under-industrialized country. He ironically rejects the stagist position that answers, "like the theoreticians of the Second International," that Cuba "has broken all the laws of the dialectic, of historical materialism, of Marxism." Starting from a completely different understanding of Marxism and the dialectic between subject and object and between economics and politics, he emphasizes that in Cuba, the revolutionary forces "are leaping over stages" to "force the march of events, but within the context of what is objectively possible."[96] Guevara's critique is valid not only against Menshevism and the Marxism of the Second International, but also against all those in Latin America who avail themselves of the rigid, determinist, and natural-scientific evolutionism of the stagist theory elaborated by Stalin.

Guevara's third theme is that armed struggle is a necessary condition for this socialist revolution, since the victory of the proletariat implies the destruction of the bourgeois military apparatus. For Guevara, rural guerrilla warfare, seen as a continuation of workers' political struggle by other means, is the surest and most realistic form of armed struggle. But he insists:

> To attempt to wage this type of warfare without the support of the population is the prelude to inevitable disaster. The guerrillas are the fighting vanguard of the people. . . . They are supported by the peasant and worker masses of the region and the whole territory in which they act.[97]

Under the influence of the work and the example of Che, the speeches and writings of Fidel Castro, the programmatic documents of the Cuban leadership—the First and Second Declarations of Havana (1960 and 1962)— and above all, the living and concrete example of the Cuban Revolution itself, a new revolution current, Castroism, was born in Latin America. One of the most fundamental characteristics of this current's interpretation of Marxism is a certain "revolutionary voluntarism," both political and ethical, in opposition to all passive and fatalistic determinism:

> The duty of every revolutionary is to make the revolution. We know that the revolution will be victorious in America and the world, but it is unworthy of a revolutionary to sit on the doorstep of his house and wait for the corpse of imperialism to pass by.[98]

From this comes the idea that it is not necessary to wait for all conditions to be met to initiate the armed struggle, since the guerrilla *foco* itself can contribute to the creation of these conditions.

The first Castroist organizations appeared at the beginning of the sixties, following splits in the youth movement of certain populist parties (APRA in Peru, Democratic Action in Venezuela) or the traditional Communist parties. During an early period (1960–68), most of these movements started on the path of rural guerrilla warfare, trying to recreate the achievement of the Cuban July 26 Movement. These were the guerrillas of the FALN (Armed Forces of National Liberation, led by Douglas Bravo) and the MIR (Revolutionary Left Movement, led by Américo Martín) in Venezuela, the FAR (Revolutionary Armed Forces, led by Turcios Lima) and the MR-13 (November 13 Revolutionary Movement, led by Yon Sosa) in Guatemala, the MIR (led by Luis de la Puente Uceda) and the ELN (National Liberation Army, led by Héctor Béjar) in Peru, the FSLN (led by Carlos Fonseca Amador) in Nicaragua, the June 14 Movement in the Dominican Republic, and finally Guevara's ELN in Bolivia.

In 1967, the congress of the Organization of Latin American Solidarity (OLAS) met in Havana, constituting the highest political expression of this first period of Castroism on the continent. The historic significance of this congress lies, first, in its glorious perspective of the continental coordination, for the first time since Bolivar, of the Latin American revolutionary process, and second, in its unequivocal and unambiguous proclamation of the unity of the democratic and socialist content of the Latin American revolution: "The nature of the revolution is the struggle for national independence, emancipation from the oligarchies, and the socialist road to full economic and social development."[99] The OLAS also took a position in favor of guerrilla warfare as the most effective method of struggle in most countries of the continent.

Around this time, the work of the young French philosopher Regis Debray appeared, coherently and radically developing some of the ideas implicit in the Castroist current at the time. His book *Revolution in the Revolution?* had a big impact, and his main propositions, the priority of the military over the political and the guerrilla *foco* as the core of or substitute for the political party, were adopted by an important number of Castroist organizations.

Because of their "militarist" and voluntarist orientation, most of these guerrilla movements were either fully or partially defeated, both in a military and political sense. After some conjunctural successes, the fighters and their leaders were decimated, and the guerrilla centers either disappeared (as in Bolivia and Peru) or were isolated and marginalized (in Venezuela and, to a certain degree, Colombia). In general, the guerrillas succeeded in establishing local links with sectors of the poor peasantry, but the absence of a mass movement and political organization on the national scale limited the extension of the armed struggle.

A new stage in the development of Castroism, characterized particularly by the growth of *urban* guerrilla movements with considerable political impact, began after 1968. These included the Tupamaros National Liberation Movement (led by Raúl Sendic) in Uruguay, the PRT-ERP (Revolutionary Workers Party—People's Revolutionary Army, led by Roberto

Santucho) in Argentina, the ALN (Action for National Liberation, led by Carlos Marighella) and the MR-8 (October 8 Revolutionary Movement, led by Captain Carlos Lamarca) in Brazil, and the MIR (led by Miguel Enríquez) in Chile. While having bases in the countryside, these movements were fundamentally urban. They found significant support in student and intellectual milieus, and to a lesser degree in the shantytowns and among certain radicalized sectors of the working class. Most were destroyed or extremely weakened by the brutal repression unleashed by military regimes during the decade. Some drew a self-critical balance sheet of their "militarism" and their inability to root themselves organically in the worker and peasant masses, and tried to reorient their political practice.

After 1974, the Castroist current organized itself into a Junta of Revolutionary Coordination, whose members were the PRT-ERP, the Chilean MIR, the Tupamaros, and the Bolivian ELN. The junta went into a profound crisis after 1977–78 because of internal differences and the weakening of its member groups.

Paralleling the growth of the Castroist current, the Cuban revolution stimulated an intensive development of Marxist social science. For the first time, Marxism developed on a massive scale in Latin American universities and enriched the study of sociology, political economy, history, and political science. The ideas of North American social science and its imitators in Latin America, the developmentalist theories of CEPAL (U.N. Economic Commission for Latin America) with their dualistic problematic (modern vs. archaic society), and the congealed theories of the traditional left (generally Stalinist in origin) were questioned and criticized in a series of works of theoretical and empirical research. A critique of some of the common dominant themes of these theories was formulated in a concise and polemical manner in a celebrated essay by the Mexican sociologist Rodolfo Stavenhagen, *Seven Erroneous Theses on Latin America* (1965), in an article by Luis Vitale, *Latin America: Feudal or Capitalist?* (1966), and in a more developed manner by Andre Gunder Frank in *Capitalism and Underdevelopment in Latin America* (1967). A large quantity of important and novel Marxist research on the key subjects of Latin American reality has appeared since the beginning of the sixties: dependence and underdevelopment, populism, unions and their connection to the state, the workers' and peasants' movement, the agrarian question, marginality, and others. While at times defending contradictory theses, there is no doubt that these works—for example, those of Alonso Aguilar, Arturo Anguiano, Octavio Rodriguez Araujo, José Aricó, Mario Arrubla, Vania Bambirra, Roger Bartra, Carlos Blanco, Julio Cotler, Arnaldo Córdova, Fernando Henrique Cardoso, Francisco Delich, Enzo Faletto, Roberto Fernández Retamar, Adolfo Gilly, Octavio Ianni, Marcos Kaplan, Ernesto Laclau, Rigoberto

Lanz, Héctor Malave Mata, Héctor Silva Michelena, José Álvaro Moisés, Gilberto Mathias, José Nun, Francisco de Oliveira, Juan Carlos Portantiero, Aníbal Quijano, Eder Sader, Germán Sánchez, Sergio de la Peña, Theotonio Dos Santos, Enrique Semo, Azis Simao, Paul Singer, Edelberto Torres Rivas, Tomas Vasconi, Francisco Weffort—all have made a rich and stimulating contribution to the Marxist interpretation of Latin America.

It is important to emphasize that the new Marxist social science is not limited to the academic milieu and frequently plays a role in ideological debates and struggles in the workers' movement. For example, among those authors closest to the revolutionary left, such as Gunder Frank, Rui Mauro Marini, Aníbal Quijano, and Luis Vitale, economic and social research has been explicitly connected to a certain conception of political strategy. Their common problematic is situated on the following axes:

1. The rejection of the theory of Latin American feudalism and the characterization of the historical colonial structure and the present agrarian structure as essentially capitalist.
2. The critique of the concept of a "progressive national bourgeoisie" and the perspective of a possible independent capitalist development in Latin American countries.
3. An analysis of the defeat of populist experiments as being the result of the very nature of the Latin American social formations, their structural dependence, the political and social nature of the local bourgeoisies, etc.
4. The discovery of the source of economic backwardness not in feudalism or in precapitalist obstacles to economic development, but in the character of dependent capitalist development itself.
5. Finally, the impossibility of a "national-democratic" road to economic and social development in Latin America and the necessity of a socialist revolution as the only realistic and coherent response to underdevelopment and dependency.

There is no doubt that the Cuban Revolution has been a powerful stimulant to such questioning of established social science. In a more general way, the Cuban Revolution has created an ideological climate favorable to a rebirth and renewal of Latin American Marxism and to its emancipation from the model of Marxism-Leninism put forward by the Soviet Union. Above all, the triumph of the Cuban Revolution has struck a mortal blow against the classic ideological argument of bourgeois thought on the continent: that Marxism is a European doctrine, viscerally alien to the idiosyncrasies of Latin American peoples.

During the sixties, Cuba itself saw a flourishing of sociological, historical, and philosophical research, a witness to the existence of a creative and open Marxism whose most notable expression was the journal *Pensamiento Crítico* (Critical Thought), which was published from 1967 to 1970.

Still, Castroism has not been the only revolutionary current developing in Latin America since 1959. To a lesser degree, Trotskyism and Maoism have also seen significant growth.

The consolidation of Trotskyism during this period has occurred, among other reasons, because the Cuban Revolution has been seen by sectors of radicalized youth as a confirmation of certain theses of those currents influenced by the ideas of Trotsky and/or the Fourth International, especially the theory of permanent revolution as a process leading to the growing over of the democratic revolution into a socialist one. Also, Trotskyism has been able to grow as a result of the crisis of the traditional Communist movement after the Cuban Revolution, and because of the Castroist polemic against the moderate politics of the Latin American Communist parties.

From 1961 to 1963 in Peru, a Trotskyist militant, Hugo Blanco, led one of the largest mass peasant movements in the recent history of the continent—a series of land occupations by peasant unions in the Convención Valley. Hugo Blanco also tried to organize a peasant militia to defend the movement against the landowners and the police, but repression by the armed forces destroyed the peasant unions, and their leaders were arrested.[100]

The Trotskyists' sympathy for the Cuban Revolution and the absence of anti-Trotskyist prejudices among the Castroists permitted the establishment of collaborative relations between the two currents in a series of countries, which for a time went as far as a certain political and/or organizational symbiosis.

Thus in Chile, Trotskyists (Luis Vitale and others) participated in the foundation of the MIR in 1965. The organization was influenced by their ideas even after their departure some years later, and Trotskyists have considered the MIR to be the closest to their ideas of all the Castroist groups.

In Bolivia, the POR of González Moscoso and the ELN of Inti Peredo collaborated closely from 1969 to 1971, even partially fusing their military wings.

Finally, in 1965 in Argentina, a fusion between a Castroist group and a Trotskyist organization gave birth to the PRT (Revolutionary Workers Party), which was the Argentine section of the Fourth International from 1969 to 1973.[101]

This Trotskyist-Castroist alliance crystalized at the Ninth Congress of the Fourth International (1969), which proclaimed an orientation toward armed struggle and the integration of the Trotskyist organizations into the OLAS current. During the seventies, however, strategic and tactical divergences led to an estrangement between the two tendencies, which nevertheless maintain fraternal relations in most countries. Trotskyism developed during this new period, especially in Mexico, where the PRT (the Mexican section of the Fourth International) grew rapidly (with important influence in independent peasant unions); also in Colombia, Brazil, and Peru, where the FOCEP (Workers', Peasants', and Students' Front), a predominantly Trotskyist coalition, received 12 percent of the vote in the June 1978 elections to the Constituent Assembly.

The relationship between Maoism and Castroism, on the contrary, has been mostly conflictive. Maoism appeared in the continent as a consequence of the Sino-Soviet polemic and as a result of splits in the traditional Communist parties. The first Latin American Maoist group was the Communist Party of Brazil (PCdB), the product of a dissident current that left the Brazilian Communist Party (PCB) in 1962. The Communist Party of Brazil was founded by a section of the old leadership of the party that supported Stalin and was discontented with the Twentieth Congress and de-Stalinization; they found their major preoccupations echoed in the Chinese critique of Khrushchev. The orientation of the PCdB combined a return to the politics of the offensive of the Cold War period (1949–53) and an attempt to apply the revolutionary strategy of the Chinese CP. The Brazilian Maoist party thus extolled the "bloc of four classes" and the establishment of a popular revolutionary government by peoples' war (conceived as "the encircling of the cities by the countryside"), whose task would be to accomplish an anti-imperialist and anti-landlord revolution. The Maoists found themselves in agreement with the pro-Soviets in denying the socialist character of the revolution in its present stage and in insisting upon the necessity of a front with the national bourgeoisie; they nevertheless insisted upon the hegemony of the proletariat in this class alliance, and on the necessity of armed struggle. During the sixties, the PCdB refused to engage in armed actions and severely criticized the activities of the Castroist guerrillas (ALN, MR-8, etc.) as not being real peoples' warfare. Nevertheless, in 1971–73, the party participated in a peasant guerrilla action in Amazonia that was decimated by the Brazilian army. Around this time, the PCdB was reinforced by the adherence of an important section of Popular Action, an organization that originated in the Christian left and had been hegemonic in the Brazilian student movement in the sixties.

Organizations similar to the PCdB appeared in other countries: the PCML (Marxist-Leninist Communist Party) of Peru, the PCML of Bolivia, the PCML of Colombia, and so on. The latter distinguished itself from the other groups by creating an important rural guerrilla organization, the EPL (Army of Popular Liberation), in 1967. On the other hand, the refusal of the PCML of Bolivia (led by Oscar Zamora) to support Che's guerrillas in 1967 was one of the themes of the political confrontation between Maoism and Castroism on the continent. During the seventies, the new Chinese foreign policy (rapprochement with the U.S., an ambiguous attitude toward

Pinochet) provoked a profound crisis inside the Maoist current, most of whose organizations (notably the Communist Party of Brazil) drew closer to Albania. Today, Maoism hardly exists as a current in Latin America.

The development of Castroism, Trotskyism, and Maoism in Latin America after 1959 has represented a challenge to the hegemony of the traditional Communist parties over the workers' movement.

These latter parties reacted in a variety of ways to the Castroist organizations. Certain ones (Argentina, Brazil, Colombia, Chile) from the beginning refused to cooperate at all with the new currents, classifying them as petty-bourgeois adventurists. Others periodically attempted to collaborate with the armed Castroist groups (Bolivia, Venezuela, Guatemala); very rapidly, profound divergences on the role of armed struggle itself (as a strategy or a tactic) provoked a split in which members of the Communist military cadre (Douglas Bravo in Venezuela) or sectors of the Communist youth (Inti Peredo in Bolivia) joined the ranks of the Castroist guerrillas. Finally, some parties, notably the Uruguayan (under the leadership of Rodney Arismendi), participated in the OLAS and succeeded in establishing a *modus vivendi*, even collaborating with the Castroist current (the Tupamaros).

The party that experienced the deepest crisis after the Cuban Revolution was probably the Brazilian CP.[102] Deeply involved with the populist regime of President João Goulart and confident in the "national-democratic" sector of the Brazilian armed forces, the PCB was surprised by the military putsch of April 1964 that established the dictatorship that remained in power until the eighties. However, unlike the Guatemalan PGT, which issued a self-criticism of its insufficient independence from the bourgeoisie after the fall of Arbenz in 1954, the PCB, in a Central Committee resolution, in May 1965, emphasized the "sectarian and leftist" tendency of the party during 1962–64, a tendency which "isolated [it] from the united front of important sectors of the national bourgeoisie."[103] The 1964 defeat and this self-critical line (considered a rightist one by the opposition) provoked an internal crisis in the party, which was sharpened by the impact of the OLAS conference. After 1967, many militants and some of the principal leaders of the PCB (including Carlos Marighella, Joaquim Câmara Ferreira, Mario Alves, Apolônio de Carvalho) left the party to found revolutionary left organizations and engage in armed struggle.

Some parties, like the Chilean CP, on the other hand, had no important splits (except for some youth sectors that rallied to the MIR) and remained impermeable to the influence of the Cuban Revolution. Thanks to its organizational strength and ideological coherence, the Chilean CP became the hegemonic force in what can be considered the most important attempt to establish a peaceful road to socialism, the Popular Unity government in Chile.

We must emphasize that, in the face of hesitations by the Socialist Party, which was profoundly influenced, on the rank-and-file level, by Castroist and Trotskyist tendencies, the Communist Party was *the most moderate* working-class tendency in the Allende government. Convinced for years that Chile could not become socialist without passing through an "anti-oligarchic and anti-imperialist" stage,[104] the Communist Party tried with all its means to assure a *modus vivendi* between the Popular Unity government and those bourgeois forces it considered progressive, by limiting nationalizations,[105] through dialogue with the Christian Democracy, and especially through collaboration with the armed forces, within which, according to the Communist leaders, "a professional consciousness and respect for the constitutionally established government reigns."[106]

In conclusion, we can say that the tragic events of September 1973 were not foreseen by the Chilean CP, and would have been difficult for it to foresee, considering the party's conception of the nature of the state apparatus and its relation to social classes.

Finally, a few words on socialist currents in Latin America. Social democracy has not effectively implanted itself in the continent. The principal exceptions until the seventies were the Socialist parties of Argentina and Uruguay, which played a significant role in the workers' movement for many years under the leadership of E. Frugoni in Uruguay and of Juan B. Justo, Alfredo Palacios, Américo Ghioldi, Alicia Moreau de Justo, and others in Argentina. But the Cuban Revolution also had an impact here, provoking the radicalization of sectors of these parties. In the sixties, various splits occurred in the Argentine SP, both to the right (the Democratic Socialist Party of Ghioldi and Nicolás Repetto) and the left (the Vanguard Socialist Party of David Tieffenberg and others; one of the socialist tendencies, led by Juan Coral, united in 1972 with the "La Verdad" group of Nahuel Moreno to form the Trotskyist-oriented Socialist Workers Party). Consequently, the Argentine social-democratic current has been weakened and marginalized, nearly disappearing as an important political or trade union force. A similar process took place in Uruguay, where the most combative sections of the Socialist Party created the Tupamaro movement (under Raúl Sendic).

The Chilean Socialist Party, unlike the parties of Argentina and Uruguay, has never joined the Socialist International. Actually, this party is not at all a typically social-democratic party, even if there have always been social-democratic currents within it. Its sympathy for the Yugoslav and, later, the Cuban revolutions and its political alliance with the Communists placed it in contradiction to traditional social-democratic doctrine (although this began to change at the end of the seventies, when a section of Chilean socialists drew closer to the Socialist International). This is also true of the

Revolutionary Socialist Party of Ecuador and the Venezuelan MAS (Movement toward Socialism) of Teodoro Petkoff. Today, most of the parties and movements that call themselves social-democratic and are members of the Socialist International are populist-style parties that have little to do with Marxism or the workers' movement: the APRA of Peru, the Brazilian PDT of Leonel Brizola, Democratic Action (AD) in Venezuela, the PLN of Costa Rica, the Jamaican PNP, the PRD of the Dominican Republic, and others.

The major Latin American parties that consider themselves socialist, such as the Chilean SP, the Revolutionary Socialist Party of Uruguay, and the MAS (Movement toward Socialism) in Venezuela, cannot be considered social democratic parties, if one takes into account their stated adherence to Marxism, their program and strategy, their international relations, and other factors. In fact, positive attitudes toward the October Revolution have been predominant within the various currents of Latin American Marxism from the twenties until today.

Despite the defeat of the majority of the guerrilla movements of the sixties and seventies, the new revolutionary period of Latin American Marxism initiated by the Cuban Revolution has not been exhausted. The victory of the Nicaraguan Revolution and the development of revolutionary fronts in Central America are witness to the continuation of this dynamic, which is also manifested under new forms throughout the continent.

The Sandinista National Liberation Front was founded in 1961, under the influence of Cuba and Guevarism. However, *Sandinismo* is not a simple copy or imitation of the Cuban model. Carlos Fonseca and his friends formulated their own theory and orientation, corresponding to Nicaragua's revolutionary traditions. The Sandino legend—his epic struggle against the U.S. Marines, his cowardly assassination by Somoza's men in 1934—was a heritage transmitted from generation to generation. It represented a hidden, repressed, underground, but incredibly tenacious tradition of the oppressed that included the ideas of Sandino, the General of Free Men: an explosive mixture of intransigent anti-imperialism and social rebellion. Outlawed by the state and ignored by the Stalinist PSN, this popular revolutionary culture fused with Marxism to become the new *Sandinismo*. Interpreting Sandino in a Marxist context and translating Marxism into the language of Sandinista culture, Carlos Fonseca and his comrades forged the revolutionary ideology of the FSLN.

It is not by chance that the old Communist Party of Nicaragua (the PSN) remained marginal to the revolutionary process, as in Cuba, criticizing the Sandinista Front as "ultra-leftist," "adventurist," and "influenced by Maoism and Trotskyism."

In certain respects, the Sandinista revolution resembles the Cuban one: the armed overthrow of a disgraced dictatorship, the creation of a revolutionary power based on the arming of the people, agrarian reform, confrontation with imperialism, the deepening of the revolution, and so forth. However, certain original characteristics were specific to Nicaragua: a much more important role played by the poor and young population of the cities, the lesser significance of the rural guerrilla war in comparison with urban insurrections, and the mass participation of Christians.

However, unlike Cuba, where the growing over of the democratic into the socialist revolution occurred quite rapidly (in about two years), in Nicaragua, ten years after the victory of the insurrection in July 1979, a mixed economy still existed and many capitalists retained their property. The violation of bourgeois order was at first *political*: the destruction of the state apparatus of the dominant classes and the establishment of a revolutionary state based on the Sandinista Army, the popular militias, the unions, the Sandinista Defense Committees, and other bodies. The economic changes took place more slowly and incompletely: the expropriation of the property of Somoza and his clique and, later, a sufficiently radical agrarian reform. While the majority of property remained in private hands (which created many difficulties for the revolution, besides), the control of owners over their enterprises was quite limited.[107] Another particular feature of the Nicaraguan Revolution was the establishment by the Sandinista government of a political regime based on democratic rights, political and trade union pluralism, freedom of the press, and the right to organize. Elections that were recognized by international observers as truly free and democratic (the first in Nicaragua's history!) were held in 1984 and resulted in a 67 percent majority for the FSLN in the Constituent Assembly. Authoritarian mistakes (notably in regard to the Miskito Indians) were progressively corrected. The Sandinista revolutionary-democratic experiment, with all its contradictions and limitations, has been an important contribution to Marxist thought on the transition to socialism in Latin America.

The defeat of the Sandinistas in the 1990 elections was above all the result of the terrible consequences of the North American economic blockade and the counterrevolutionary war organized by the United States against the Nicaraguan people. But Sandinista errors also contributed to this setback: insufficient internal democracy in the Sandinista party, compulsory military service, excessive economic concessions to the private sector, etc. Nevertheless, the FSLN remains a powerful social force, supported by more than 40 percent of the population.

The Nicaraguan Revolution has had a profound impact on the whole continent, but especially in Central America. In El Salvador, it has helped to inspire the development of popular organizations and guerrilla fronts. Coming from diverse origins—Castroist, Maoist, left Christian, dissident Communist—these fronts transcended focoism and combined military activity with extensive efforts at popular organization (among workers, peasants, students, and others). The popular movement provoked the overthrow of the military dictatorship of General Romero in 1979; but, disunited, the revolutionary fronts and their mass organizations could not take power. Unity was established soon after, with the founding of the Farabundo Martí National Liberation Front (FMLN) in 1980, which adopted the heritage of early Salvadoran Communism and the insurrection of 1932. The FMLN and its political expression, the Revolutionary Democratic Front (FDR), today control a third of the country's territory and enjoy wide popular support in the cities and the countryside. Without massive military and economic aid from the United States, the power of the Salvadoran army and oligarchy would have been overthrown long ago. As in Nicaragua, many revolutionary militants in El Salvador are Christians; for a long time, the main base of the rural guerrillas has been the FECCAS, the Christian Federation of Salvadoran Peasants, created by progressive Jesuits. At the beginning of the eighties, internal confrontations (the murder of Comandante Ana María, the suicide of Cayetano Carpio) greatly weakened the FMLN, but in recent years, the front has succeeded in overcoming these divisions and moved toward greater unity. Along with the development of rural guerrilla struggle, the social movement in the cities has grown stronger and more unified, in particular with the founding in 1986 of the UNTS (National Union of Salvadoran Workers), which unites the major unions of the country.

The Sandinista victory also encouraged the revolutionaries of Guatemala, even if their movement is not as large as that in El Salvador. The different Guatemalan guerrilla fronts, united since 1985 in the URNG (National Revolutionary Union of Guatemala), have succeeded in implanting themselves in the indigenous Mayan peasant communities, unlike their predecessors in the sixties. Radicalized Christians and their base communities have also played an essential role here. However, systematic massacres by the army and the forced military organization of the rural population have for the moment succeeded in weakening the Guatemalan revolutionary organizations.

In these three Central American nations, the revolutionary vanguard was created through the fusion of Marxism with popular traditions of social struggle and anti-imperialism that have remained in the collective memory of the oppressed: the struggle of Sandino against American intervention in Nicaragua (1927–34), the 1932 insurrection in El Salvador, and the centuries-old struggle of Native Americans against colonization in Guatemala. Currents with a variety of origins are found in the three liberation fronts—even the "historic" Communist parties participate in El Salvador and Guatemala—but it is the new Marxist forces, sometimes inspired by

Guevarism, that are hegemonic. The attractiveness of socialist and Marxist ideas to a significant section of the "Christian masses" and the most radicalized sectors of the clergy is one of the characteristic aspects of the Central American revolution and is unprecedented on such a scale.

The role of Christians is also important for understanding certain new political and social movements in the Southern Cone of Latin America, especially the formation of the Workers Party (PT) and the United Workers' Center (CUT) in Brazil. The industrialization process, directed by the military regime in association with multinational capital, led to the emergence of a new working class that mobilized in large strikes in 1978–79, especially in the ABC region (the industrial suburbs of São Paulo). Facing state repression, militant unionists like Lula (the leader of the metal workers' union) became politicized and took the initiative in the struggle against the military, creating a Workers Party independent of the liberal bourgeois opposition forces of the Brazilian Democratic Movement Party (PMDB). The new Workers Party rapidly received the support and adherence of many trade unionists and organizers of ecclesiastical base communities, as well as leftist intellectuals, former militants of the guerrilla fronts of the sixties, and Marxist groups (notably the Trotskyists). The CUT was created in 1982 under the impetus of PT trade unionists, uniting the class-struggle currents of the workers' movement that today, with ten million members, have become the hegemonic force in Brazilian unionism. With around 400,000 members and millions of voters, the PT is currently the main working-class and popular opposition to the "New Republic" created as a compromise between the military and the liberal bourgeoisie. The Workers' Party as such does not claim to be Marxist, but most of its leaders are, and its revolutionary, democratic, and socialist program is undoubtedly of Marxist inspiration. Actually, the development of the PT has for the first time accomplished a fusion between Marxism and the workers' movement, which until that point had been dominated by Vargista populism (with the support of the Stalinist CP).

Neither the revolutionary upsurge in Central America nor the formation of the new workers' and peoples' movement in Brazil can be understood without a consideration of a new and unexpected phenomenon—the radicalization of large Christian sectors and their attraction to Marxism.

The Second Vatican Council undoubtedly contributed to this evolution, although not in a direct way, since its resolutions did not transcend the limits of a modernization, an *aggiornamento*, a liberal opening. But this opening, by disturbing the old dogmatic certainties, made Catholic culture permeable to new ideas and "external" influences. Opening itself to the modern world, the Church could not avoid the social conflicts that shake this world, especially in Latin America. It is in this context that many

Christians—at first, mostly intellectuals: theologians, Jesuits, lay experts, students—were finally attracted to Marxist analyses and proposals (as occurred with the majority of the continent's intellectuals during the sixties).

Liberation theology did not create this change; it is a product of it. More precisely, it is the particular expression of a social movement created by the involvement of Christians in neighborhood associations, trade unions, student movements, peasant leagues, centers of popular education, leftist political parties, and revolutionary organizations. This movement, which we could call liberation Christianity, appeared in the sixties (remember Camilo Torres!), well before liberation theology. But the latter, by giving a legitimacy and a theory to the movement, had contributed to its diffusion and development.

The theme of liberation had begun to concern the most advanced theologians (who were unsatisfied with the dominant "theology of development") by the end of the sixties. But it was in 1971, with a book by Gustavo Gutiérrez, a Peruvian Jesuit and ex-student of the Catholic universities of Louvain and Lyon, that liberation theology was truly born. In this work, *A Theology of Liberation*, Gutiérrez put forward a certain number of controversial ideas that were destined to profoundly subvert Church doctrine. Influenced by Marxism—he refers particularly to the writings of Mariátegui, Ernst Bloch, and dependency theorists—Gutiérrez does not see the poor as an object of pity or charity, but as *the subject of their own liberation*. Rejecting "developmentalism . . . which has become merely synonymous with reformism and modernization," that is, limited, timid, and ineffective measures that only aggravate dependence, the Peruvian theologian unhesitatingly proclaims:

> Only a radical destruction of the present state of affairs, a profound transformation of property relations, the coming to power of the exploited class, a social revolution, will end this dependence. Only they will allow the transition to a different society, a socialist society.[108]

Note that this position is much more radical than those put forward by the Latin American Communist parties in this period.

Shortly after, in April 1972, the first continent-wide meeting of the movement "Christians for Socialism" took place in Santiago, organized by two Chilean Jesuits, the theologian Pablo Richards and the economist Gonzalo Arroyo, with the support of the Mexican bishop Sergio Mendez Arceo. This ecumenical movement, joining Catholics and Protestants, pushed the logic of liberation theology to its ultimate conclusion—that is, an attempt at a synthesis between Marxism and Christianity—which soon led to its interdiction by the Chilean church hierarchy. The final resolution of the 1972 meeting proclaimed their adherence as Christians to the struggle for socialism in Latin America:

> The real context for a living faith today is the history of oppression and the liberation struggle against oppression. To situate oneself in this context, however, one must truly participate in the process of liberation, joining parties and organizations that are authentic instruments for the working class struggle.

Thanks to the work of Gutiérrez, the Brazilian brothers Leonardo and Clodovis Boff, Frei Betto (jailed for several years by the military dictatorship for his support to Marighella's movement and now the main animator of Brazil's base communities and an advisor to the Workers Party), Jon Sobrino and Pablo Richards in Central America, and the active participation of clergy (the Cardenal brothers and Miguel D'Escoto) in the Sandinista government, the growth of liberation theology has provoked a reaction from the Vatican: the famous "Instruction on Some Aspects of Liberation Theology," by Cardinal Ratzinger's Congregation for the Doctrine of the Faith, which denounces liberation theology as a new heresy based on its "indiscriminate" use of Marxist concepts.

Whatever the result of the current Vatican offensive (and we cannot assume that it will not score some points), the position of Christians on the field of the class struggle will never be what it was before the appearance and growth of liberation Christianity.

For many years, the question of an alliance with so-called "left Christian" sectors has been a tactical preoccupation of the workers' movement and Marxists in Latin America. During his trip to Chile in 1971, Fidel Castro spoke of the possibility of Christians and Marxists moving from a tactical to a strategic alliance. Yet today, after the Central American as well as the Brazilian experience, we should no longer speak in terms of alliances, but of organic unity. This is because Christians are already an essential component of the revolutionary movement and, in certain cases, even of its revolutionary vanguard. They often bring a moral sensibility, experience in popular work "at the base," and a utopian urgency that can only serve to enrich the movement. What attracts certain radicalized Christians to Marxism is not only its scientific value as an analysis of society; it is also, or even especially, its ethical opposition to capitalist injustice, its identification with the cause of the oppressed, and its active participation in their struggle for revolutionary emancipation.

Even today, a large part of the population of Latin America is under the domination of conservative or repressive military regimes whose armed forces specialize in the arrest, torture, and assassination of Marxist militants of various tendencies: pro-Soviet Communists and Maoists, Castroists and Trotskyists, revolutionaries and reformists. Beyond the necessary political debates and the inevitable ideological confrontations, an increasing number of militants consider that the unity in action of all the currents in the workers' movement who consider themselves socialist and Marxist is, more than ever, an urgent imperative. As Mariátegui wrote on May Day, 1924:

> To form a united front is to carry out an act of solidarity in regard to a concrete problem and an urgent necessity. This does not mean renouncing the theories that each party holds or the position that each occupies in the vanguard. A variety of tendencies and a diversity of ideological currents are inevitable in this immense human legion that is called the proletariat. The existence of tendencies and well-defined and distinct groups is not an evil; it is on the contrary a sign of an advanced period in the revolutionary process. What matters is that these groups and these tendencies know how to act in concert while confronting the concrete reality of the day. . . . Let them not employ their weapons . . . to injure each other, but to combat the social order, its institutions, its injustices, and its crimes.[109]

PARIS, OCTOBER 1990

Notes

1. For a relatively well-documented history of Latin American communism, see the work of Boris Goldenberg, *Kommunismus in Lateinamerika* (Stuttgart: Verlag Kohlhammer, 1971), which, despite its faults and a tendency toward anticommunism, is certainly superior to similar works published in the United States, all of which are profoundly marked by the Cold War.
2. The APRA (American Popular Revolutionary Alliance) was founded by the Peruvian Víctor Raúl Haya de la Torre while in Mexican exile. Ideologically eclectic, it was inspired mainly by the Mexican Revolution, elaborating a unique "Indo-Americanist" doctrine. During the twenties, the APRA was a movement with a continent-wide character, with sections in several Latin American countries, but little by little it became restricted to Peru, where it remains a mass party. Originally, the APRA declared itself anti-imperialist, but its anti-imperialist character progressively faded and ultimately disappeared.
3. According to Haya de la Torre, "*Aprismo* formulates a new interpretation of Marxism for Latin America, transferring the Einsteinian concept of space-time into the socio-historical domain for this complex agglomeration of regions and races, of forms of production and culture. *Aprismo* negates and transcends Marxism" (in Victor Alba, *Politics and the Labor Movement in Latin America* [Stanford: Stanford University Press, 1968], p. 169). But Aprista theory essentially is situated outside the bounds of Marxism, and its Indo-American exoticism has never been a hegemonic current in Latin American Marxist thought, even if it has had an influence on certain authors or political groups (for example, the "national left" in Argentina).
4. Ibid., p. 147.

5. Cf. Carlos M. Cox, "Reflexiones sobre José Carlos Mariátegui," in *El marxismo latinoamericano de Mariátegui* (Buenos Aires: Ed. Crisis, 1973), pp. 185–186: "Mariátegui claimed that the proletariat, an incipient one in Peru as in all of Latin America, will accomplish those tasks that historically must be realized by the bourgeoisie. . . . Mariátegui has thus made a myth of the proletariat."
6. A.M. Cambero, "Perspectivas del socialismo en México," *La Voz de México*, November 25, 1945, p. 7.
7. See, for example, a Brazilian Maoist text that declares in trenchant terms: "To claim that socialism is the task of the current stage of the revolution . . . is to deny the role of the peasantry. In the current circumstances in Latin America, the peasant movement, the principal base of the revolution, is essentially democratic" (*A linha revolucionaria do Partido Comunista do Brasil* [Rio de Janeiro: Ed. Caramuru, 1971], p. 282).
8. Cf. Germán Ave-Lallemant, "Kapitalismus und Sozialismus in Argentinien," *Die Neue Zeit*, Year 23, v. 2 (Stuttgart, 1905), p. 454.
9. See the selections from these documents in this book. Significantly, these documents fell into obscurity after the thirties and were ignored even by well-informed observers like Regis Debray, who wrote that the first official document of the Communist International on Latin America was a protest against the U.S. invasion of Nicaragua during the time of Sandino. Cf. Debray, *La critique des armes* (Paris: Seuil, 1975), v. 1, p. 42.
10. On the influence of 1917 on intellectuals, see the selection from Aníbal Ponce, the Argentine Marxist sociologist.
11. The archetype here is the legendary character "The Student," in *El recurso del método* (translated as *Reasons of State* [New York: Knopf, 1976]) by the great Cuban writer Alejo Carpentier.
12. Cf. *Claridad*, Bulletin of the Left Opposition (Mexico City) n. 5, March 1931.
13. The thesis of Julián Gorkín, Victor Alba, and others that Mella was executed under the orders of a G.P.U. agent (Vittorio Vidali) seems to us an anticommunist myth.
14. Cf. Julio Antonio Mella, "Los estudiantes y la lucha social," in *Hombres de la revolución: Julio Antonio Mella* (Havana: Imprenta Universitaria, 1971), p. 37, and Mella, "Cuba, un pueblo que jamás ha sido libre," in *J. A. Mella, documentos y artículos* (Havana: Ed. de Ciencias Sociales, Instituto Cubano del Libro, 1975).
15. Mella, "El grito de los martires," 1926, *Hombres*, pp. 17, 19. This article refers to the assassination of workers by Machado; see a longer selection in this book.
16. Mella, "Que es el APRA?," ibid., pp. 77, 97.
17. Mella, "Glosas al pensamiento de José Martí," ibid., pp. 41–47. José Martí, a poet and revolutionary, was the principal leader of Cuba's liberation struggle against the Spanish metropolis (and the whims of the North Americans) in the nineteenth century. His "Jacobin" ideology was close to being socialist.
18. José Carlos Mariátegui, "Sobre un tópico superado," *Amauta*, n. 28, January 1930, in *Ideología y política* (Lima: Ed. Amauta, 1971), p. 211. Shortly after his break with Haya, Mariátegui wrote to Eudocio Ravines: "Whatever the course of national politics, and particularly of those elements with which we had collaborated and apparently identified (we have now discovered that this was only in appearance), those of us who have dedicated ourselves to socialism have the obligation to demand the right of the working class to organize itself into an independent party." See this letter in R. Martínez de la Torre, *Apuntes*

para una interpretación marxista de la historia social de Perú (Lima: Ed. Peruana, 1948), v. 2, p. 335. We thank the Peruvian historian Héctor Milla for calling our attention to this document.

19. Mariátegui, "Trotsky y la oposición comunista," February 1928, in *Obra política* (Mexico City: Ed. Era, 1979), pp. 218–219. According to Pierre Naville (in a 1971 conversation), there was correspondence between Mariátegui and the European Left Opposition.

20. See, for example, V.M. Miroshevski, "El 'populismo' en el Perú," in José Aricó, ed., *Mariátegui y los orígenes del marxismo latinoamericano* (Mexico City: Ed. Pasado y Presente, 1978), pp. 55–70.

21. On the affinity between Mariátegui and Gramsci or Lukács, see the excellent article of Robert Paris, "El marxismo de Mariátegui," ibid., pp. 119–144. Paris, for example, compares the formula "so much the worse for reality," that Mariátegui attributes to Lenin, with Fichte's remark, "so much the worse for the facts," that Lukács, in 1919, saw as the essence of the Bolsheviks' revolutionary politics.

22. Mariátegui, preface to L.E. Valcárcel, *Tempestad en los Andes*, 1927 (Lima: Ed. Universo, 1975).

23. Mariátegui, *Seven Interpretive Essays on Peruvian Reality* (Austin: University of Texas Press, 1988).

24. Mariátegui, "Carta colectiva del grupo de Lima," in *El proletariado y su organización*, (Mexico City: Ed. Grijalbo, 1970), p. 11.

25. Mariátegui, "Principios programáticos del Partido Socialista," in *Obra política*, p. 270.

26. See the selection in this book.

27. Mariátegui, *Obra política*, p. 270.

28. Cf. *El movimiento revolucionario latinoamericano, versiones de la Primera Conferencia Comunista Latinoamericana, June 1929* (Buenos Aires: Correspondencia Sudamericana), pp. 19–27.

29. Cited in Thomas P. Anderson, *Matanza: El Salvador's Communist Revolt of 1932* (Lincoln: University of Nebraska Press, 1971), p. 83.

30. See the documents of the 1932 insurrection in this book.

31. Roque Dalton, *Miguel Mármol* (Willimantic, CT: Curbstone Press, 1987), ch. 6, pp. 211–271. According to an academic historian of the 1932 rebellion, Farabundo Martí had Trotskyist tendencies and was on bad terms with Moscow. Cf. Anderson, *Matanza*, p. 68.

32. Quoted by Anderson, ibid., p. 83.

33. Roque Dalton, "Miguel Mármol: El Salvador 1930–32," *Pensamiento Crítico*, n. 48, January 1971, p. 72.

34. Ibid., p. 69.

35. Roque Dalton, a Salvadoran Communist in exile in Cuba, published his interview with Mármol in the Cuban journal *Pensamiento Crítico* in 1971. (Mármol's autobiography, edited by Dalton, has been published in English by Curbstone Press, Willimantic, CT—translator.)

36. Graciela A. García, *Páginas de lucha revolucionaria en Centroamérica* (Mexico City: Ed. Linterna, 1971), p. 101.

37. Heinz Neumann, another leader of the German Communist Party who was more or less "in disgrace" in 1935, had also been proposed for this dangerous job because of his experience as an organizer of the Canton insurrection of 1927. In the end, he was not sent; he later disappeared in the Soviet Union, a

victim of the Moscow Trials. Cf. Margarete Buber-Neumann, *La Révolution mondiale* (Paris: Casterman, 1971), ch. 20.

38. See Helio Silva, *1935, A revolta vermelha* (Rio de Janeiro: Ed. Civilizaçao Brasileira, 1970), pp. 117, 286–287.

39. In a 1973 autobiographical article, Prestes recognized the influence that the Trotskyists had on his evolution and pointed out that his July 1930 manifesto contained "typically Trotskyist" opinions. Cf. Prestes, "Comment je suis venu au parti," *Nouvelle Revue Internationale*, n. 174, 2/1973, p. 223.

40. Abguar Bastos, *Prestes et a revolução social* (Rio de Janeiro: Ed. Calvino, 1946), p. 323.

41. Domingo Faustino Sarmiento, author of the famous novel *Facundo*, was president of the Argentine Republic, 1868–74. According to Aníbal Ponce, "rarely has a man of state better known the needs of his people." See *Sarmiento, constructor de la Nueva Argentina* (Madrid: Ed. Espasa-Calpe, 1932), p. 199. On the other hand, according to the Cuban Marxist writer Roberto Fernández Retamar, Sarmiento was "the implacable ideologue of the Argentinian bourgeoisie who was attempting to transport the schemas of the metropolitan bourgeoisies, concretely the North American, to his country. . . . He was perhaps the most important and most active of the bourgeois ideologues in our continent in the nineteenth century." See Roberto Fernández Retamar, *Calibán, apuntes sobre la cultura de nuestra América* (Buenos Aires: Ed. La Pléyade, 1973), p. 98.

42. The term "ripe" itself typifies a "naturalist" and non-dialectical conception of the laws of economic and social development. On this subject, see Michael Löwy, *Dialectique et Révolution* (Paris: Ed. Anthropos, 1973).

43. Regis Debray, *La critique des armes* (Paris: Seuil, 1974), v. 1, pp. 42–43.

44. Cf. Goldenberg, *Kommunismus in Lateinamerika*, p. 94.

45. Cf. *Treinta años de la lucha del Partido Comunista de Colombia*, 1960 (Medellín: Ed. La Pulga, 1973), pp. 40, 47, 48.

46. See Mújica's open letter of July 14, 1939, in Adolfo Gilly, *La revolución interrumpida*, (Mexico City: Ed. El Caballito, 1972), p. 389.

47. Blas Roca, *La unidad vencerá el fascismo* (Havana: Ed. Sociales, 1939), p. 12.

48. At the convention of the Popular Front in 1938, the Communist Party played a decisive role in the selection of Aguirre Cerda, the leader of the right wing of the Radical Party, over the Socialist Marmaduque Grove as presidential candidate. Cf.

49. Cf. "A Program of Action for the Victory of the Chilean People's Front," *The Communist*, v. 20, n. 5, May 1941.

50. The Chilean Socialist Party was strongly influenced by Titoism after 1948 and, to a certain degree, by Castroism after 1960. For the thirties, see Julio César Jobet, *El Partido Socialista de Chile*, 3rd ed. (Santiago: Prensa Latino-americana, 1971), v. 1.

51. John Reese Stevenson, *The Chilean Popular Front* (New York: Greenwood Press, 1942), p. 136.

52. Galo González, "Xᵉ Congres du P.C. du Chili, avril 1956," in Luis Corvalán, *Chili, les Communistes dans le marche au socialisme* (Paris: Ed. Sociales, 1972) p. 36.

53. Oscar Waiss, *Nacionalismo y socialismo en América Latina*, 1954 (Buenos Aires: Ed. Iguazú, 1961), p. 139.

54. Paulino González Alberdi was one of the main leaders of the Argentine CP

from the twenties onward. The quotations are taken from J. Abelardo Ramos, *Historia del stalinismo en la Argentina* (Buenos Aires: Ed. del Mar Dulce, 1969) p. 176.

55. Ernesto Giudici, *Imperialismo y liberación nacional*, 1940 (Buenos Aires: Ed. Crónica, 1974), pp. 3–4. See the longer selections in this book.

56. For example, see the Mexican CP's criticism of the "anti-imperialist demagogy of the Trotskyists" in Blas Manrique, "El aplastamiento de los reptiles trotskistas: ésa debe ser una tarea de los antifascistas," *La Voz de México*, May 13, 1945.

57. Quoted by Ramos, *Historia*, pp. 190–191. In the same vein, see a letter from Blas Roca to Earl Browder, published by the Cuban CP in 1945: "Dear friend, your book is a document of inestimable value for the Latin American people. . . . Until now, we have maintained that it is only by the nationalization of all foreign investment and property, in violent opposition to English and North American interests, that we could attain the highest degree of economic development. . . . The collaboration that the United States, England, and the U.S.S.R. have established at Teheran has opened another perspective. For us, it opens the perspective of obtaining these progressive results through collaborating in a common program that you suggest to us . . . the collaboration with England and the United States in a total plan to harmoniously resolve our sharpest and most urgent economic problems" (Blas Roca, *Estados Unidos, Teherán y la América Latina, una carta a Earl Browder* (Havana: Ed. Sociales, 1945).

58. When Batista resigned in 1944, the Cuban CP sent him a letter declaring: "Since 1940, our party has been the most loyal and consistent supporter of your governmental measures and the most energetic promoter of your platform, inspired by democracy, social justice, and the defense of national prosperity." Blas Roca, *Los socialistas y la realidad popular* (Havana: Ed. del PSP, 1944).

59. Blas Roca and Lázaro Peña, *La colaboración entre obreros y patrones* (Havana: Ed. Sociales, 1945). See p. 21, where Blas Roca explains that "we are in the process of proclaiming a form of class collaboration."

60. *La Voz de México*, April 12, 1945, pp. 1, 7.

61. Carlos Sánchez Cárdenas, "La revolución mexicana y el desarrollo capitalista de México," *La Voz de México*, November 20, 1945, p. 1.

62. Anatol Shulgovsky, *México en la encrucijada de su historia* (Mexico City: Ed. Fondo de Cultura Popular, 1969), p. 494.

63. Cited by the newspaper of the Mexican CP, *La Voz de México*, January 13, 1946.

64. Nevertheless, the PCB also had a post-Browderist "national unity" orientation. For example, in a book published in 1945, Luis Carlos Prestes wrote: "It is through its union organizations that the proletarian class can aid the government and the employers find practical, rapid, and effective solutions to the grave economic problems of the day" (Prestes, *União Nacional para a Democracia e o Progresso* [Rio de Janeiro: Ed. Horizonte, 1945], p. 25.) On this subject, see the notable work of F. Weffort, "Origens do sindicato populista no Brasil," *Estudos CEBRAP*, n. 4, April–June 1973.

65. See, for example, E. Espinoza, "Aniversario de la muerte de Mariátegui," *Clave: tribuna marxista* (Mexico City), n. 8–9, April–May 1940.

66. Liborio Justo, *Bolivia, la revolución derrotada* (Bolivia: Ed. Cochabamba, 1967), p. 156.

67. On the role of the POR in the countryside, cf. R.W. Patch, "Bolivia," in *Social Change in Latin America Today* (New York: Council on Foreign Relations, 1960), p. 121.

68. In Jaime Díaz Rizzotto, *La Révolution au Guatemala, 1944–54* (Paris: Ed. Sociales, 1971), p. 261. The report of General Secretary José Manuel Fortuny to the Second Congress is even more explicit: "We communists recognize that because of these special conditions, the development of Guatemala must take the capitalist road for some time" (J.M. Fortuny, *Relatorio sobre la actividad del Comité Central al Segundo Congreso del Partido*, Guatemala City, December 11, 1952).

69. It is known that Che Guevara was in Guatemala at this time and that he vainly attempted to struggle against the pro-American invasion. According to his first wife, Hilda Gadea: "Ernesto told me that he insistently proposed to the Youth Alliance [Communist] to go to the front and fight, and that many youths, inspired by him, were prepared to go. Once or twice he presented the same proposal to the PGT, but his requests went unheeded, with the response that the army had taken the necessary measures and the people ought not be concerned" (Hilda Gadea, *Che Guevara, años decisivos* [Mexico City: Ed. Aguilar, 1972], p. 65. On the polemic between Che and Fortuny, both in exile in Mexico in 1955, see p. 117 of the same book).

70. *La intervención norteamericana en Guatemala y el derrocamiento del régimen democrático* (Ed. Comisión Política del PGT, 1955), pp. 31–32.

71. Ibid., p. 42.

72. Cf. J. Arnault, *Cuba et le Marxisme* (Paris: Ed. Sociales, 1963), p. 48.

73. "Carta a los militantes," Executive Committee of the PSP, August 30, 1953. Cited by K.S. Karol, *Guerrillas in Power* (New York: Hill and Wang, 1970), p. 139.

74. *Fundamentos*, n. 149, December 1956–June 1957, p. 9.

75. Ibid., p. 8.

76. Ibid., pp. 3–6.

77. Blas Roca, *Balance de la labor del partido desde la última asamblea nacional y el desarrollo de la revolución* (Havana: n.p., 1960), pp. 42, 80, 87.

78. *Declaraçao sobre a politica do Partido Comunista do Brasil* (Rio de Janeiro: Ed. Comité Central do PCB, March 1958), pp. 15, 18.

79. Sergio Bagú, *Economía de la sociedad colonial: ensayo de la historia comparada de América Latina* (Buenos Aires: Ed. El Ateneo, 1949), pp. 39, 68. We should also mention the earlier works of Silvio Zavala, *La Encomienda indigena* (Madrid, 1935), and José Miranda, *La función economica de la encomienda en las origenes del régimen colonial* (Mexico City, 1947), on the Spanish *encomienda* regime, but they remained halfway between the traditional conception of feudalism and the new thesis introduced by Bagú.

80. Caio Prado Jr., *Historia economica do Brasil*, (São Paulo: Ed. Brasiliense, 1957), p. 23.

81. Marcelo Segall, *Desarrollo del capitalismo en Chile* (Santiago: n.p., 1953).

82. Cf. Nahuel Moreno, "Cuatro tesis sobre la colonización española y portuguesa," *Estrategia* (Buenos Aires), n. 1, September 1957, and Milcíades Peña, "Claves para entender la colonización española en la Argentina," *Fichas*, n. 10, 1966. Also see George Novack, *Understanding History* (New York: Pathfinder Press, 1980), ch. 6, "Hybrid Formations."

83. Hernán Ramírez Necochea, *Antecedentes económicos de la Independencia de Chile*

(Santiago: Ed. Universitaria, 1967), p. 50. (The italics are the editor's—M.L.).
84. Caio Prado Jr., *A revolução brasileira*, 1966 (São Paulo: Ed. Brasiliense, 4th ed., 1972), p. 288.
85. Silvio Frondizi, *La realidad argentina, ensayo de interpretación sociológica*, v. 2, *La revolución socialista* (Buenos Aires: Ed. Praxis, 1956), p. 234.
86. Since the Cuban Revolution and events in Latin America after 1959 are much better known than those of the previous periods, we limit ourselves here to situating this period in the wider context of the evolution of Marxism in the continent.
87. See the selection in this book.
88. Ernesto Guevara, "A New Old Che Guevara Interview," 1959, in R. Bonachea and N. Valdes, eds., *Che: Selected Works of Ernesto Guevara* (Cambridge: M.I.T. Press, 1969), p. 372.
89. Fidel Castro, "Discours de la séance inaugurale du 9ᵉ cycle de l'Université populaire," December 2, 1961, in *Trois discours sur la formation du Parti uni de la révolution socialiste cubaine* (Paris: Embassy of Cuba in France, 1962), p. 55.
90. It is nevertheless true that the Cuban Revolution would have had difficulty surviving the U.S. economic blockade and intervention without the economic and military support of the U.S.S.R.
91. The writings of Mella, the founder of the Cuban CP, were published in Cuba only after the Castroist revolution. The PSP had not published these writings since the thirties.
92. Cf. Michael Löwy, *The Marxism of Che Guevara: Philosophy, Economics, and Guerrilla Warfare* (New York: Monthly Review Press, 1973).
93. Ernesto Guevara, "Socialism and Man in Cuba," 1965, in Bertram Silverman, ed., *Man and Socialism in Cuba: The Great Debate* (New York: Atheneum, 1973), p. 342.
94. Ernesto Guevara, "Guerilla War: A Method," 1963, in Bonachea and Valdes, *Che*, pp. 89–103.
95. See the selection in this book.
96. Ernesto Guevara, "The Meaning of Socialist Planning," in Silverman, *Man and Socialism*, p. 102.
97. See the selection in this book.
98. *Second Declaration of Havana*, 1962. See the selection in this book.
99. See the selection in this book.
100. Militants of the FIR (Revolutionary Left Front), a Peruvian Trotskyist organization of which Hugo Blanco was a member, carried out the first "bank expropriations" in Latin America under the leadership of Daniel Pereyra in 1961–62.
101. In 1968, a group led by Nahuel Moreno left the PRT, opposing the perspective of engaging in armed struggle against the Argentine military regime, and later formed the PST (Socialist Workers Party). As for the PRT, it split from the Trotskyist Fourth International in 1973, taking a political and ideological orientation close to the political line of the Vietnamese Communist Party.
102. The Venezuelan CP also underwent a serious crisis in 1969–70, which led to the departure of a large part of its leadership and important sectors of its base, who went on to form the MAS (Movement toward Socialism), led by Teodoro Petkoff. The major cause of the split was not armed struggle, but rather the issue of the party's relations with the U.S.S.R., which had been put into question by the invasion of Czechoslovakia in 1968. The split was there-

fore similar to that which occurred in the Greek Communist Party in the same period.

103. Cf. Carlos Rossi, "Le P.C. brésilien," *Révolution permanente en Amérique latine* (Paris: Maspero, 1972), p. 15.
104. See, for example, the report of the General Secretary to the XIV Party Congress in November, 1969. Luis Corvalán, *Camino de victoria* (Santiago), September 1971, p. 323.
105. The famous "Millas Plan," put forward by the Communist Finance Minister, even foresaw the return of certain properties expropriated during the "employers' strike" of October 1972 to their former owners.
106. Cf. Corvalán, *Camino de victoria*, pp. 425–426. In an interview with *L'Humanité* (the newspaper of the French CP), Corvalan, the General Secretary of the Chilean CP, emphasized: "In ultra-revolutionary circles, it is being claimed that a confrontation with the army is inevitable and irrevocable. . . . In the final analysis, to consider an armed confrontation to be inevitable implies, and some are suggesting this, the immediate formation of workers' militias. In the current situation, this would be a signal of a lack of confidence in the army. But the army is not impervious to the new winds that are blowing and penetrating all corners of Latin America" (*L'Humanité*, January 7, 1971).
107. For a detailed study of these questions, see the excellent study of Paul Le Blanc, *Permanent Revolution in Nicaragua* (New York: Fourth Internationalist Tendency, 1984).
108. See Gustavo Gutiérrez, *A Theology of Liberation* (Maryknoll, NY: Orbis Books, 1973), pp. 26–27.
109. Mariátegui, "El primero de mayo y el frente único," 1924, in *Obra política*, pp. 253–254.

About This Anthology

The purpose of this anthology is to fill a vacuum and provide a useful tool for researchers and activists. In fact, there are practically no other real anthologies of politically significant Marxist texts from Latin America. One of the rare works of this type, the small volume by Luis Aguilar (*Marxism in Latin America* [New York: Knopf, 1968]), a Cuban who emigrated to the U.S. after the Cuban Revolution, suffers from the drastic limitations of a pocket-book of North American "Kremlinology."

It is obvious that any selection of texts contains a certain degree of arbitrariness, and this anthology does not escape the rule. Nevertheless, our purpose has been to assemble documents from the different currents of Latin American Marxism, including those minority and oppositional currents that have been neglected by official academic histories (and by the Communist parties). While of course including theoretical, sociological, economic, and historical developments, the central focus of most of these documents is the *political struggle*.

The method of this anthology is decidedly *historicist*, considering the evolution of Marxist thought in the context of the social and political struggles of each historical period in Latin America. Moreover, it bases itself on the supposition that the history of Marxism in Latin America cannot be considered a world apart, separate from the international context. We thus emphasize the connections with the developments in the international workers' movement at each stage.

We have only chosen texts that deal with Latin America itself; we have therefore been obliged to sacrifice a number of quite interesting writings on Marxist method, socialist theory, and Leninism that at times have constituted important contributions to international Marxist thought. These works could perhaps be the subject of another anthology.

We have also been forced to neglect (with a few exceptions) some specifically economic or sociological writings that have flourished in Latin America, especially since 1960, with the appearance of a new Marxist social science of great richness and quality. Again, another volume would be necessary.

Finally, we have not been able to include selections from some significant currents of Latin American Marxism because of a lack of space: for example, the so-called national left, which has emphasized the national dimension of the struggle on the continent (such as Jorge Abelardo Ramos in

Argentina and Carlos Malpica and the journal *Marka* in Peru), and an "African-American Marxist" current that includes Franz Fanon himself—who was born in Martinique and wrote *Black Skin, White Masks* (1952) on the condition of African Americans in the French colonies of the Antilles—Jacques Stéphen Alexis, the writer, poet, and leader of the Communist Party of Haiti who was assassinated by the Duvalier dictatorship, the Brazilian historian Clovis Moura, the currents influenced by the Black Power movement in the English-speaking Caribbean, and others.

Our anthology begins in the twentieth century. While there certainly were theoreticians and organizations that proclaimed themselves to be Marxists by the end of the nineteenth century, their influence was quite limited and their political role was marginal.

Abbreviations

AD	Democratic Action
ALN	Action for National Liberation
ANL	National Liberation Alliance
APRA	American Popular Revolutionary Alliance
CENUS	National Council of Trade Union Unity
CEPAL	U.N. Economic Commission for Latin America
CGTP	General Confederation of Peruvian Workers
COB	Bolivian Workers' Central
CSTB	Bolivian Workers' Confederation
CTM	Mexican Workers' Confederation
CUT	United Workers' Center
EGP	Guerrilla Army of the Poor
ELN	National Liberation Army
EPL	Popular Liberation Army
ERP	Revolutionary Army of the People
FALN	Armed Forces of National Liberation
FAPU	United Popular Action Front
FAR	Revolutionary Armed Forces
FDR	Revolutionary Democratic Front
FECCAS	Christian Federation of Salvadoran Peasants
FIR	Revolutionary Left Front
FLN	National Liberation Front
FMLN	Farabundo Martí National Liberation Front
FOCEP	Workers', Peasants', and Students' Front
FSLN	Sandinista National Liberation Front
FSTMB	Bolivian Mineworkers' Federation
FUN	National United Front Party
FUP	Proletarian United Front
JCR	Council of Revolutionary Coordination
LP-28	February 28 Popular Leagues
MAS	Movement toward Socialism

MIR	Revolutionary Left Movement
MNR	National Revolutionary Movement
MR-8	October 8 Revolutionary Movement
MR-13	November 13 Revolutionary Movement
OLAS	Organization of Latin American Solidarity
ORDEN	Democratic Nationalist Organization
OSPAAL	Organization of Solidarity with the Peoples of Asia, Africa, and Latin America
PCB	Brazilian Communist Party
PCdB	Communist Party of Brazil
PCM	Communist Party of Mexico
PCML	Marxist-Leninist Communist Party
PCV	Communist Party of Venezuela
PDT	Democratic Labor Party
PGT	Guatemalan Labor Party
PIR	Revolutionary Left Party
PLN	National Liberation Party
PMDB	Brazilian Democratic Movement Party
PNP	People's National Party
POR	Revolutionary Workers Party
PP	Popular Party
PPS	Popular Socialist Party
PRD	Dominican Revolutionary Party
PRI	Institutional Revolutionary Party
PRM	Party of the Mexican Revolution
PRT-ERP	Revolutionary Workers Party-People's Revolutionary Army
PRV	Party of the Venezuelan Revolution
PSN	Nicaraguan Socialist Party
PSP	Popular Socialist Party
PT	Workers Party
PUM	United Mariateguista Party
UDN	National Democratic Union
UNTS	National Union of Salvadoran Workers
URNG	National Revolutionary Union of Guatemala

PART I
The Introduction of Marxism in Latin America

1

Socialism before 1914

FREE TRADE*

Juan B. Justo

Juan B. Justo (1865–1928), a doctor and journalist, was the founder of the Argentine Socialist Party (1896) and author of the first Spanish translation of Volume 1 of *Capital* (1895). While he can be considered one of the first authors to disseminate Marxism in Latin America, his writings in fact owe more to positivist sociology (Comte, Durkheim, and Spencer) than to Marx. Associated with the moderate wing of the Second International (he attended the Copenhagen Congress in 1910) and the Socialist International after World War I, Justo was the principal leader and theoretician of a Latin American social-democratic current that, outside of Argentina and, to a lesser degree, Uruguay, has never become an important political force on the continent.

His major scientific work is *The Theory and Practice of History*, an eclectic combination of Marxist, liberal, and positivist ideas. We reproduce here a short passage from this work that advocates free trade for Argentina. Justo was an impassioned free-trader; in his intervention at the Berne Socialist Conference of 1919, he advocated international free trade as the only guarantee against future wars and proselytized for "world economic unification" through the abolition of tariffs.[1] Justo's ideas have been severely criticized by most Argentine Marxists as a semi-apologia for imperialism and as a radical misunderstanding of the national question in Latin America.

Freeing working people from taxation is another of the great tasks of workers' democracy.

Instead of demanding that the well-to-do pay the taxes necessary to maintain a political machine that operates on their own behalf, governments throw the burden of public spending onto the shoulders of the people in the form of taxes on their lives and labor. In Spain, taxes on consumption took 400 million pesetas from the population in 1907. Only 160 million made

---

*Juan B. Justo, *Teoría y práctica de la historia*, 1909 (Buenos Aires: Ed. Libera, 1969), pp. 485–486. (Most of the titles for the selections were chosen by the editor.)
[1]See Juan B. Justo, *Internacionalismo y patria* (Buenos Aires: Ed. La Vanguardia, 1933), pp. 26–27.

their way to the public treasury; the rest disappeared in the workings of the complex fiscal apparatus needed to take this amount from consumers. In the Argentine Republic, tariffs greatly increase the price of everything that is imported for working-class consumption: from rice, salt, sugar, and coffee to fabrics and everyday clothes; from the oil that working people use to light their homes to the galvanized sheets that serve as their roofs. Every one of these taxes means a decrease in real income. To these, add the duties on the implements that the people need to work, from the artisan's tools to the tailor's needle and thread, and the fees that are demanded of all those who work for themselves, from bakers to midwives. In the province of Buenos Aires, isn't there a tax on vegetable gardens that produce for the market, but not on the country mansions and parks of the rich? The new democracy must abolish these hated burdens that the bourgeois state uses to oppress working people.

The workers' party that celebrates the worldwide festival of May Day from its headquarters in Brussels is internationalist by nature and design and should not be fooled by the fraud of industrial nationalism or protectionism. For us, the remaining barriers to commerce between peoples are as barbaric as those that hindered trade between provinces 150 years ago; we should support them only to the extent necessary for the continued existence of already established companies, whose failure would hurt the workers they employ.

The workers' party uses this same criterion to judge the contributions of time and blood that the state demands of the proletariat for military purposes.

The association of workers' parties strengthens world peace. This is true internationally, just as in the Austrian Empire—a heterogeneous conglomeration of perpetually feuding races, languages, and religions that has found unity and stability with the growth of Social Democracy. Neither imperialism nor fanatic nationalism will find the workers' party its tool. It distrusts both the militarist actions of capitalism and the patriotic spirit into which degenerate and incompetent oligarchies tend to fall as the end of their rule approaches. The workers' democracy supports only defensive wars against barbaric foreign enemies and wars that open new areas of the physical and biological environment to the rational action of man. Among civilized people, all issues should be resolved by negotiation. The new politics insists upon reducing war spending (which still consumes an enormous portion of the public treasury), democratizing military institutions, and limiting the personal obligations imposed by them. In France, the barracks are beginning to be used for the professional, cooperative, and civic education of its citizens.

THE RICH AND THE POOR*

Luis Emilio Recabarren

Unlike Juan B. Justo, Luis Emilio Recabarren (1876–1924), who was also one of the first Marxist thinkers of Latin America, exemplifies the revolutionary current of the continent's newborn socialist movement. More an influential educator and propagandist than a theoretician, Recabarren was a founder of the Socialist Workers Party of Chile in 1912 (which later became the Communist Party, the Chilean Section of the Third International, in 1922). During 1916–18, he was active in the Argentine Socialist Party, opposing the reformist tendency led by Justo, and participated in the founding of the International Socialist Party (the future Argentine Communist Party).

The following selection comes from a lecture given by Recabarren in September 1910 on the occasion of the centennial of Chile's independence. It is one of the first attempts at a Marxist analysis of the process of emancipation of the Spanish colonies in America and of its results from the point of view of working people. The text is notable for its class combativity and its rejection of patriotic bourgeois mythology, but it lacks an anti-imperialist dimension.

This lecture, written on the occasion of the first centennial of what is called the *political emancipation of the people*, will precisely analyze the country's political situation.

The bourgeoisie, through its writers, always speaks to us of "the great men who gave us our homeland and our freedom," and has tried to etch this phrase into the minds of the people, having them believe it relevant for everyone.

I myself, in turn—thinking about the members of my class—contemplating the thirty-four years of my life, do not find one circumstance that convinces me that I have had a homeland and that I have had freedom. . . .

Where is my homeland and where is my freedom? Did I have it during my childhood, when, instead of going to school, I had to go to the workshop to sell my meager labor power to an insatiable capitalist? Do I have it today, when capital takes the full product of my work, without my enjoying a single atom of my own production?

I believe that a homeland means a satisfying and full home life, and that freedom only exists when this exists. The enormous multitude that populates the cities and the countryside—do they have such a life? They don't even have a home! They don't have a home! And anyone without a home has no freedom! All the great founders of political economy have affirmed this principle: "Anyone who has no home has no freedom!"

Who can contradict me?

---

*Luis Emilio Recabarren, "Ricos y pobres," September 3, 1910, in *Obras* (Havana: Ed. Casa de las Américas, 1976), pp. 74–76, 79–80.

Did those who defeated the Spanish on the battlefield think at any point about the people's freedom? Those individuals, seeking their own nationhood, wishing to be independent of the monarchy, sought this independence for themselves, not for the people.

Celebrate the people's political emancipation! I consider this a sarcastic phrase or perhaps an ironic joke. It's just like our bourgeoisie proclaiming "O, Sovereign People!" when they see ragged, idle, and wasted men. Let them celebrate the political emancipation of the capitalist class, the ones who enjoy the nation's wealth; that seems more reasonable.

Those of us who have understood for years that we have nothing to do with this so-called anniversary of national independence feel we must explain to the people the real significance of this day. In our view, it should only be commemorated by the bourgeoisie, since it is they who rose against the Spanish crown in 1810 and conquered this land to enjoy all the advantages that independence would provide. But the people, the working class, which had always lived in misery, gained nothing, absolutely nothing, with the liberation of this land from Spanish domination. Once the war had ended and independence was consolidated, the so-called fathers of our country, whose names the bourgeoisie wishes to immortalize, who led the common soldier in the countryside in the fight to dislodge the Spaniard from this land, did not even consider giving the proletariat the same freedom the proletariat had conquered for the bourgeoisie, reserving for them the same slavery under which they had always lived. . . .

This meanness of spirit and lack of morality kept the bourgeoisie from giving the republic, which had been born through the efforts of its slaves, the radiance of a true greatness that would have shown the founders of the homeland to be great men. How small they seem to us today!

Until 1823, the year of Chile's first constitution, there was not a single law displaying any generosity toward the people, recognizing any of their rights, or even considering them as worthy members of society.

Here we see what lot fell to the people during these revolutionary days, which gave the bourgeoisie the power to administer the natural and social wealth of this part of the planet, while leaving the people sunk in their long-suffering misery.

And if all this is true, what do the people have to celebrate on this anniversary? What the people really do on this day, urged on by the bourgeoisie, is spend their money on torrents of liquor that this same bourgeois class sells them to keep the money in their insatiable coffers.

If the people were not appreciated in our early years as an independent nation, much less were they afterwards. The people were excluded from the first elections, and we might even say that fraud and government intervention in elections were born along with the republic. Let us see what the conservative caudillo M.J. Irarrázaval said in the Senate during the session of November 11, 1889, when the Law of Communal Autonomy was being discussed:

> I have here the first Act of Government Intervention. I can't help but deplore the fact that O'Higgins began this series of disgraceful acts. That intervention had a certain polite air of shamefacedness; he concealed the matter, so as not to be compromised in any way—since he would have lost influence.

Irarrázaval made these comments in relation to a letter of O'Higgins in which he recommended the election of some of his friends as deputies. But this same Irarrázaval, who is credited with magnificent intentions on behalf of the people and their rights, made the following claim in the Senate on August 5, 1874, during the debate on the Law of Cumulative Voting: "I point out to this chamber *that I am not saying or claiming that any minority whatever has a right to representation.*"

With this, Irarrázaval showed he was not considering the people's interests. Nor did he want it thought that by defending the cumulative vote he was claiming to defend the interests of the popular classes. Irarrázaval supported the cumulative vote so that all the social interests of the bourgeoisie might be represented in Congress. The people's interests were not taken into account.

If this has been the case, as seen on various occasions from 1810 until today, there is no reason for the working class to rejoice at the periodic arrival of this date.

The glorious day of the people's emancipation has not yet arrived. The popular classes still live as slaves: tied to the economic order with the chain of wages, which is the cause of their misery; tied to the political order with the chains of bribery, fraud, and intervention, which negate all their activity and forms of popular expression; tied to the social order with the chains of their own ignorance and vice, which keep them from being considered useful members of our society.

A people who live subjected to the whims of an unjust, immoral, and criminally organized society—what concern is it of theirs to celebrate the 18th of September? None! The people should absent themselves and should not participate in the festivals with which their executioners and tyrants celebrate the independence of the bourgeois class, which in no way represents the independence of the people, either individually or collectively.

PART II
The Revolutionary Period

2

Documents of the Leninist
Comintern (1921–23)

The two documents of the Third International that we reproduce here are of the greatest interest. We do not know who drafted them or which Latin Americans participated in their editing. Comparing them with Latin American Communist texts written during the thirties and after allows us to measure a profound change of orientation, language, and problematic in the international and Latin American Communist movements.

ON THE REVOLUTION IN AMERICA*

The central idea of the first text is the revolutionary alliance of workers and peasants against U.S. imperialism and the local bourgeoisie. The hypothesis of a continental extension of the revolution, so dear to the Castroist current in the sixties, appears here for the first time. On the other hand, the question of immediate unity between the workers of South and North America seems more dated, corresponding to a period when revolutionary currents played an important role in the U.S. workers' movement.

SOUTH AMERICA: COLONIAL BASE FOR
NORTH AMERICAN IMPERIALISM

Placing the whole world under its control: this is the goal of North American imperialism. But just as the key to British imperialism is its colonial system, North American imperialism rests upon its exploitation and domination of South America.

The peoples of South America foolishly delude themselves when speaking of their own independence. In the imperialist epoch, there is no independence for small peoples; they are reduced to the status of vassals of the Great Powers. North American imperialism has subjugated the peoples of South America in the economic realm through commerce and the penetra-

---

*"Sur la révolution en Amérique. Appel à la classe ouvrière de deux Amériques," *L'Internationale communiste*, n. 15, January 1921, pp. 3311–3314, 3321–3324.

tion of capital and in the political realm through the Monroe Doctrine. Where is the independence of these peoples? Forced under the tutelage of the North American government, at times by force of arms like the peoples of Central America, at times by unspeakable diplomatic pressure and bloody intrigue (as in Mexico), their industrial development is at the mercy of North American finance.

Actually, South America is a colony of the United States, a source of raw materials, cheap labor, and, of course, fabulous profits. Its immense and still unexploited territories serve as an outlet for North American machinery and capital and as an open field for exploitation by North American industry.

The necessity of adapting to the consequences of the world war definitively transformed South America into a colony of the United States. But this is merely the consummation of prior developments.

While England, Germany, and France were formidable competitors of the United States in South America before the war, the Monroe Doctrine had already succeeded in assuring the political hegemony of North American imperialism (and therefore its economic hegemony).

The history of the Monroe Doctrine gives an idea of the nature of capitalist thievery and Machiavellianism.

Formulated nearly a hundred years ago with the stated purpose of defending the two Americas against monarchist and colonial intrigues from Europe, the Monroe Doctrine actually reflected the rivalry between the United States and England. Later, it was interpreted in conformance with the needs of North American capitalist development, becoming what it is today—a means for North American imperialism to dominate South America and defend its hegemony against any imperialist rival.

Fifty years ago, President Grant gave the Monroe Doctrine an imperialist cast, which was formulated even more clearly by President Cleveland during the Anglo-American dispute over Venezuela. During the presidency of the impetuous Roosevelt, the Monroe Doctrine became the manifest expression of North American imperialism. But completing the work of President Roosevelt was a task that fell to President Wilson. So it would be more correct today to refer to the Monroe Doctrine as the Roosevelt-Wilson Doctrine. President Wilson, interpreting the Monroe Doctrine in 1913, proclaimed the right of the United States to oppose the domination of Mexico's petroleum deposits by British capital. Pan-Americanism, while considered a method for the democratic unification of the peoples of the two Americas, is actually a way of assuring U.S. hegemony. At the exact moment President Wilson was defending the principle of Pan-American unity, Undersecretary of State Lansing declared the Monroe Doctrine to be the *national* property of the United States, conceived and upheld in its interest. Isn't imperialism the purest negation of democratic unity?

It is precisely in the name of the Monroe Doctrine that the United States has abolished the independence of the Central American republics. It is in the name of this very doctrine that they maintain an occupation army in Nicaragua, Honduras, Haiti, and the Dominican Republic, ruining the smaller peoples whose independence they have abolished (these actions were particularly prominent during Wilson's presidency). It is still in the name of the Monroe Doctrine that the United States bases and maintains its economic and financial hegemony over South America.

The war has allowed the expropriation of German property in South America. From an economic and financial point of view, Germany no longer plays any role in the Central and South American market. The decline of France has been extreme, while England has fallen to the second rank, without hope of retaking a primary position. The markets of South America are falling increasingly into the hands of the United States.

The peoples of South America constitute the foundation of North American imperialism. South America absorbs an enormous quantity of capital and machinery (and, generally, all the products of the metallurgical industry). On the other hand, the United States suffers from a lack of raw materials that South America has in abundance.

The full importance for the United States of its hegemony in South America was expressed by its opposition to the League of Nations (for the good reason that the latter annulled the Monroe Doctrine) and in President Wilson's urgent demand that this Pan-American doctrine never be modified and be fixed inviolably by treaty. Its hegemony in South America also has found expression in the politics of the Panama Canal (as well as its struggle to be master of the Pacific). The recent U.S. project to purchase and fortify some Caribbean islands located near the canal reveals the aggressive designs of the United States; its proposal to England to liquidate that nation's debt in return for the cession of its interests in South America is also proof of the political orientation of the United States. Economically, American imperialism has not yet definitely established its hegemony in South America, but this is its conscious goal. Just as German imperialism cherishes the goal of economically, financially, and politically linking Central Europe with Germany, American imperialism pursues the linkage of South America and the United States, uniting the two Americas in a single imperialist bloc. Hegemony in Central Europe would serve as a foundation and motor force for German domination over the world. The same aggressive designs serve as a foundation for U.S. hegemony in the two Americas.

An American empire, with its unfathomable wealth and innumerable sources of raw materials, would have infinitely greater power than any previous empire; it would be a formidable force for conquest and destruction. The development of American power constitutes the greatest danger for world security, the freedom of peoples, and the liberation of the proletariat.

Workers of the two Americas, this is the danger you must avert.

THE URGENT REVOLUTIONARY TASKS IN SOUTH AMERICA

The revolutions that periodically shake Mexico, Venezuela, and other countries do not directly interest the masses. But they must be taken advantage of if we are to effectively develop the movement of the revolutionary masses and express the interests of the proletariat and the poor peasantry. Only a revolutionary movement of this kind can liberate the peoples of South America from the grip of their national exploiters and North American imperialism.

Socialism has done nothing to develop this revolutionary mass movement. In South America, socialism has scandalously betrayed the interests of the masses. It is now only a miserable reformist combination, a plaything of the democratic petty bourgeoisie or, as in Mexico, the semi-military, semi-revolutionary sport of a few adventurers (aren't Obregón and his allies "socialists too"?). It is an urgent and essential revolutionary task to discredit this socialism, destroy its influence, and recruit revolutionary socialist elements to communism.

This task consists, above all, of organizing a resolute and conscious Communist Party, with a clear idea of its goals, in every country of South America. This party will not necessarily be powerful at birth; it need only have a clear and precise program, agitate resolutely on behalf of its principles and revolutionary tactics, and be implacable in its struggle against those who mislead and betray the masses. A party of this type must be composed of the best and most honest representatives of the masses. It must lay out a program for a truly revolutionary movement and dedicate itself fully to mass action, setting out patiently but firmly on the broadest revolutionary path toward the highest ends.

It is only with the cooperation of the Communist Party that revolutionary clarity and honesty can be introduced into the South American movement; it is only in this way that the movement can ally itself with the revolutionary movement in the United States and the Communist International, and give the South American masses their legitimate place in the army of the world revolution.

The agrarian question is a problem of the highest order. Agriculture occupies first place in South America (even Argentina, the most developed country in South America from a capitalist point of view, has fewer than 400,000 industrial workers among a total population of more than eight million).

Horribly exploited, the peasantry lives in the darkest misery, under a crushing yoke, and serves as canon fodder for military adventures. The Mexican experience is both characteristic and tragic. The agricultural workers have revolted and made revolutions, only to see the fruits of their victory stolen by capitalists, exploiters, political adventurers, and socialist charlatans. The peasants, oppressed and duped, should arise to revolutionary action and organization. They should be educated in the idea that neither they nor the workers can be emancipated unless they ally with the revolutionary proletariat against capitalism.

The Communist Party must penetrate among the peasantry, not with formulas and abstract theories, but with a practical program able to move them to struggle against the large landowners and capitalists. The revolutionary unity of the poor peasantry and the working class is indispensable; only the proletarian revolution can liberate the peasantry by breaking the power of capital, and only the agrarian revolution can save the proletarian revolution from the danger of being crushed by the counterrevolution.

In South America, the army is composed mainly of poor peasants, which better serves our revolutionary agitation. This agitation must be systematically organized to unite soldiers, workers, and peasants in joint action against the landowners, the capitalists, and the government.

The unions, which do not organize the large bulk of industry (as in the United States), tend to be revolutionary. But the leaders of the unions are often traitors. This is the case in Mexico, where Morones and his ilk exploit the workers and use these organizations for their personal profit. We must throw out these leaders and liberate the unions from these blackmailers and their reactionary influence. We must destroy the American Federation of Labor (AFL), whose leaders are counterrevolutionaries; we must boycott the AFL and organize class-struggle unions in South America and the United States. It is also imperative to join the Red International of Trade Unions, the international that mobilizes unions throughout the world to struggle against imperialism and for world revolution.

A Communist nucleus must be created in every union. While seeking to organize all the workers, it should march hand in hand with the conscious political movement. Together with the local Communist Party and the Communist International, the unionized workers will become a powerful force for the American revolution.

While carrying out all the measures indicated above, and as their direct consequence, we must purge the South American movement of its syndicalist aspects. Syndicalism (especially its proletarian version) reflects revolutionary aspirations, but lacks any knowledge of the measures necessary to realize them. Revolutionaries should use the good side of syndicalism, while rejecting the bad side. The theory and program of world revolution are drawn from Marxism, not syndicalism. Syndicalists are opponents of political parties. The Communist Party is the practical realization of the syndicalist idea of "conscious minorities," cleansed of petty-bourgeois anarchism and definitively linked to the real struggle of the working masses for the proletarian revolution. Syndicalists are opponents of parliamentarism. The Socialist Party's parliamentarism is a betrayal of the working class and the revolution. By contrast, the parliamentarism of the Communist Party is the revolutionary recognition of the fact that we must utilize all means, even the parliamentary tribune, as long as we have not yet organized the mass movement that will sweep away the parliament. Syndicalists are opponents of the dictatorship of the proletariat. Life itself proves the necessity of this dictatorship; rejecting the dictatorship of the proletariat means rejecting the revolution. This summarizes the questions that life and revolutionary experience authoritatively demand that the masses resolve on the basis of communist theory and action.

The unity of the revolutionary movement of South America will be completed by its union with the revolutionary movement of the United States. This unity is a life-and-death matter. The revolution of the proletariat and the poor peasantry in any country of South America will immediately provoke armed intervention by the United States. This will require the revolutionary intervention of the U.S. proletariat as a consequence. The movement will spread to the other countries of South America, and this will be a stage on the road to the *American revolution.*

Revolution in our country and proletarian revolution in the United States: this is the slogan of the revolutionary proletariat and the poor peasantry of South America.

The political experience of the proletarian revolution in Russia has an international importance. It has put into relief the forms of the proletarian struggle for power: mass action, workers' councils, and proletarian dictatorship. The Communist International is the result and the expression of this experience.

The workers of the two Americas will learn how to adapt this experience to their own struggle. Their revolutionary integrity and experience will teach them instinctively to adapt theory to practice and practice to theory.

The collapse of capitalism and the coming of the world revolution are the decisive events of our epoch, and they must determine the forms and goals of the international struggle of the proletariat.

Workers of the two Americas, unite! The Communist International calls you to action!

Long live the world revolution!

The Executive Committee of the Communist International

TO THE WORKERS AND PEASANTS OF SOUTH AMERICA*

This document, published in early 1923, is a resolution adopted at the Fourth Congress of the Communist International in November 1922. It is probably the first Comintern document addressed specifically to the workers of Latin America.

The declaration insists, above all, on the close association between U.S. imperialism and the ruling classes of Latin America. From this, it derives the strategic unity between the anti-imperialist struggle and the struggle against the Latin American bourgeoisie. As in the 1921 text, only the working class and the peasantry are considered revolutionary classes.

Comrades:

The Fourth Congress of the Communist International, meeting in Moscow on the fifth anniversary of the Russian Revolution, calls on all the workers and peasants of South America to prepare for the class struggle and support the revolutionary action of the world proletariat.

THE ROLE OF THE UNITED STATES OF AMERICA

The European war represented the beginning of the final crisis of capitalism. The conflicts among the international bourgeoisie resulted in the most terrible slaughter in history for the purpose of deciding which of the two imperialist groups would impose its hegemony. The proletarians were sacrificed by the millions on the battlefields for the benefit of capitalist imperialism, which seeks a solution to the acute crisis that is inevitably leading it to bankruptcy.

War could not resolve this crisis. The internal crises of European capitalism have increased and, at the same time, the class struggle has intensified. The Treaty of Versailles is a source of new conflicts. The proletarian masses increasingly recognize that only the Revolution can abolish capitalist antagonisms. The incredible repression to which we are witness today and the implacable bourgeois offensive point to the critical situation of the capitalist states.

Only North American imperialism increased its power during the war. The United States is currently the strongest imperialist power. But new causes for inter-imperialist struggles have appeared since the war. The antagonisms between North America, England, and Japan once again threaten world peace. Yankee imperialism is growing and laying the bases for future conflicts that will demand bloody new sacrifices from the work-

---

*"Aux ouvriers et paysans de l'Amérique du Sud," *La Correspondance internationale*, n. 2, January 20, 1923, pp. 26–27. Cf. "To the Workers and Peasants of South America," *Inprekorr* (Berlin), v. 3, n. 9, January 23, 1923, p. 74.

ing masses. The United States has become the center of international bourgeois reaction against the proletariat.

THE SPREAD OF YANKEE IMPERIALISM

Yankee imperialism is trying to extend its influence to all the regions of the world. In Asia, in Africa, on the shores of the Pacific, it is seeking new spheres of exploitation. It is above all in Latin America where United States imperialism is asserting its domination, whether under a supposedly economic form or through open political domination. In South America, it seeks a secure market for its exports, which European capitalism can no longer assure due to the rotting of its social base.

The Monroe Doctrine allows the North American imperialists to assure their economic conquest of Latin America. Loans, new investment by North American capital in industrial, commercial, and financial enterprises, railroad and shipping concessions, the acquisition of oil fields—these multiple forms of the expansion of Yankee economic penetration—show how North American capitalism wishes to convert South America into the base of its industrial power.

Economic precautions also lead the different national bourgeoisies to intervene in imperialist struggles in Central America, Panama, Colombia, Venezuela, and Peru. The bourgeoisies of all the Americas are laying the basis for reaction against the proletariat by calling international police congresses. When the workers of South America oppose the criminal actions of Yankee capitalism, such as during the trial of Sacco and Vanzetti, the ruling classes repress these proletarian demonstrations to prove their self-interested and deliberate submission to the imperialism of the North. The Pan-American unity of the bourgeoisie is an evident fact, as is its objective, the maintenance of class privilege and a regime of oppression.

THE DUTY OF THE PROLETARIAT OF SOUTH AMERICA

Workers and peasants of South America! Capitalist imperialism is introducing the same international antagonisms into your countries that led to the bloodiest war and tremendous reaction among the peoples of Europe. It is time to unite the revolutionary forces of the proletariat, since the capitalists of all the Americas are uniting against the working class.

Comrades, the workers and peasants of South America still lack disciplined organizations of class struggle and the requisite unity of action. Your ruling class is supported by the formidable power of the United States in crushing your efforts, repressing your liberating actions, and preventing any revolutionary movement of your oppressed masses.

Workers and peasants! The Communist International calls upon you. Do not forget there are Communists in the United States ready to aid your revolutionary struggle. The common struggle of the working class of all the states of the Americas against all the allied American capitalists is a vital necessity for the exploited class. It is the only road to your salvation. The heroic example of the Russian Revolution, which is carrying on a fierce struggle against international capitalism, will help you understand the destiny that awaits if you remain indifferent while the possessing class intensifies its capitalist exploitation. Antagonisms within the world of high finance and industry are intensifying in your countries, and world imperialist conflicts threaten to drag them, and yourselves, into the slaughter.

Comrades, oppose the bourgeois offensive with proletarian unity. Organize yourselves and join your revolutionary activity to the actions of the working class and peasantry of all the Americas and all the countries of the world. Struggle against your own bourgeoisie and you will be struggling against Yankee imperialism, which embodies the highest degree of capitalist reaction. Rally around the banner of the Russian Revolution, which has laid the foundation of the world proletarian revolution.

Like the Russian Revolution, you should prepare to transform any attempt at war into an open struggle of the working class against the bourgeoisie. Likewise, carry your actions against imperialism through to the end, preparing for the proletarian dictatorship that will destroy bourgeois dictatorship throughout the Americas. If you remain divided and disorganized, the American bourgeoisie will devour you, crush your activities, and intensify capitalist exploitation by robbing you of your previous achievements. The struggle against your own bourgeoisie will increasingly become the struggle against world imperialism and a battle of all the exploited against all the exploiters.

Comrades! Organize! Strengthen your Communist parties and create them where they do not already exist. Join your actions to those of the Communists of all the Americas. Organize the struggling proletariat into the Red International of Labor Unions and create sections of the Communist International and the Red International of Trade Unions throughout the Americas.

Long live the Red International of Trade Unions! Long live the Communist International! Long live Soviet Russia! Long live the revolutionary proletariat of America and the World Revolution!

3

The Impact of
the October Revolution

THE RUSSIAN REVOLUTION AND
CHILEAN WORKERS*

Luis Emilio Recabarren

Toward the end of 1922, Recabarren left for Moscow to take part in the Fourth Congress of the Communist International and the Second Congress of the Profintern (the Red Trade Union International). On his return to Chile in 1923, he published a book, *Worker and Peasant Russia*, containing an essay on his trip to the U.S.S.R., as well as texts by Lenin and Trotsky. In the selection below, he criticizes capitalist democracy in Chile in the light of the experience of workers' power in the Soviet Union. This text illustrates the manner in which the October Revolution was received by the most radicalized sectors of the Latin American workers' movement and represents an early attempt at a Marxist analysis of bourgeois parliamentarism in Latin America.

The objections that Russia has not yet created a Communist regime are totally devoid of reason and seriousness. Whoever reads Trotsky's report carefully would understand what it means to build a workers' state on the ruins of a capitalist regime that vanished in the whirlwind of the greatest war that has ever beset humanity—the European war that spread across the world from 1914 to 1918. The capitalist regime created a mountain of devastation during the war, and the capitalist counterrevolution fought to reconquer power until 1922; yet, despite all the difficulties caused by war, counterrevolution, hunger, a dearth of culture among the people, and the want of working-class cooperation from other countries—despite all of this, worker and peasant Russia is victoriously growing and prevailing.

These problems, and others found in the pages of this book, show the

---

*Luis Emilio Recabarren, "La Rusia obrera y campesina," 1923, in *Obras escogidas* (Santiago: Ed. Recabarren, 1965), v. 1, pp. 182–185.

reader how unreasonable it is to demand that the Communists rapidly construct a new regime, considering the destruction and chaos left by the departing regime and the problems later created by foreign capitalism. To refuse to believe or appreciate these matters is to deny reality.

We have shown that the whole working population is the source of state power once they are able to choose the components of this power and are able to revoke it. If elections are carried out in the workplace, if the members of the Soviets are elected in real assemblies, then these elections differ completely from those in other countries. In Russia, it is true—*it is an actual reality*—that the people elect their administrators. In Russia, the people *truly* have electoral rights.

In Chile, we have no electoral rights. When voter registration opens, citizens who are not recommended by influential politicians are harassed. Registration is done at the whim of the biggest taxpayers during hours when most citizens work.

Some oppose the mass registration of the tenants on large estates as being, in effect, a counterweight to the supposed intelligence of the city electorate. But voting rights are still bought and sold in the city, the signatures of absent or dead electors are forged, and ballots are falsified as needed by the political leaders of the capitalist class.

This is a *timeworn, undeniable reality in Chile*. These actions negate all our legal prerogatives and make a lie of any talk about rights and freedom. When it is said that Chile is a country where *democracy* is an established tradition, this is precisely a lie. There is no democracy in Chile. The government is organized to serve the interests of the big capitalists, without in any way taking into account the interests of the other inhabitants of the nation. Whoever honestly examines the government's behavior would have to recognize this truth.

To deceive the people, they say: "Isn't it true that worker-democrats are members of the government?" And we ask: "With whom do the worker-democrats govern?" Everyone recognizes that the democrats are governing alongside and with the consent of the country's biggest capitalists, or with the representatives of these big capitalists. Legislating in the company of these big capitalists, they must serve their particular interests. They thereby forsake the interests of the working class, since the government of a country can *never* serve both interests at the same time. This is the *truth*.

The capitalists, who are quite clever, have allowed some democrats into the Congress, even into the government, but on the condition that they serve only capitalist interests. But bringing democrats into the government feeds the people's illusion that they might someday expect reform to come in this way. And while the workers keep hoping, they *do not struggle, fold their arms, and wait for these promises to be fulfilled,* while the capitalist class tranquilly continues exploiting and oppressing the population.

This is what democracy has accomplished: it has lulled the working classes to sleep with this pretty story.

Democracy is something like a toy with which the capitalist exploiter deludes and entertains the people to appease their anger and misdirect their attention. What abuse has been eliminated in the country since the democrats have been in the government? . . . Have the tyranny and abuses of the national police been stopped? Has the system of paying workers in scrip and the suppression of free trade in minerals been terminated? Have the slanderous trials of organized workers been stopped? Has the persecution of the workers' press and the workers' federations ended? Have the violations of the laws against work on Sunday, the law on work accidents, and the law for the suppression of alcoholism been eliminated?

What have the democrats accomplished in exchange for cooperating with the capitalists? *We would like to know!* They have gotten a few jobs for a few friends, and acquired the *conceit* of considering themselves in power—when, in reality, they are there merely to serve the interests of the capitalists, not those of the people.

In Russia, the workers *never* believed the lies of democracy and took straight to the road of *revolution,* which is shorter and more secure. This has allowed them the victory that we Communists now celebrate.

THE OCTOBER REVOLUTION AND ARGENTINE INTELLECTUALS*
Aníbal Ponce

Aníbal Ponce (1898–1938), an Argentine Marxist thinker and disciple of the famous sociologist José Ingenieros, was the author of several original and profound works of social science, the most well-known being *Bourgeois Humanism and Proletarian Humanism* (1935). A professor of psychology at the University of Buenos Aires, he was dismissed from his chair by the Argentine government in 1936, accused of "communist propaganda contrary to the social order and the institutional regime." The passage below is a selection from his biography of José Ingenieros and describes the atmosphere in the non-conformist intellectual milieu after the World War I. It shows the prevailing sympathy toward the October Revolution, even if the distinction between Bolshevik "maximalism" and anarcho-syndicalism was far from clear.

---

*Aníbal Ponce, *José Ingenieros, su vida y su obra,* 1926, in *Obras Completas* (Buenos Aires: Ed. Héctor Matera, 1957), pp. 88–90.

The university reform movement, which began as a protest against out-dated schools, quickly became a true student revolution (May 1918). A new generation came to life, loudly proclaiming its restlessness for renovation. The whole country, preoccupied with other matters, responded fearfully to their energy and enthusiasm. With passions stirred up by the press and taken advantage of by politicians, the student youth of Córdoba took by storm the strongest bastions of the conservative reaction.

Meanwhile, the nation's apparent neutrality could not keep the taint of faraway tragedy from reaching us. Rival factions poisoned the spirit with their mutual hatreds, and the war touched home, school, and party. The lies of the capitalist press, the propaganda of the English press agencies, our long-time love of France, the apparent idealism of President Wilson—all these seemed to confer the task of defending revolutionary ideals upon the Allied armies.

Isolated voices came later: Romain Rolland, Barbusse, Frank, Latsko. Their eyes reddened by the fire, their words nearly overcome by emotion, these *prophets* shouted to us of the horror of these deceitful lies. It was not a war for right or justice: industrialists on one side, industrialists on the other; coke and steel vs. coal and oil. Poor human beasts perished by the millions, while others gained glory, received honors, and multiplied their riches a hundredfold.

No one realized, though, how our twenty-year-old hearts beat at this decisive moment of history. We lived these exciting years in uncertainty and confusion, our ears alert to distant rumors. Yes, we knew with absolute certainty that feudal society was in agony, and that among the debris of a ruined world, the city of the future was being designed. From faraway Russia, a bonfire's glow arrived with its swelling mute clamor, as monumental and ambiguous as the ideas of the multitude. These events were so shocking, followed so dizzily upon one another, and so shook the world's mental cast that, for us, they pushed back the limits of the possible. As in Milton's verse, we saw the dawn break at noon.

But how, among this tumult of voices, are we to hear the words to point our way? Who will take the tremendous responsibility of being our guide and guardian? In their turn, we see the unworthy spectacles of these serious times: the professional politicians moving in the shadows, the country's intellectuals moved to silence. Fear is everywhere—the hypocritical fear that always betrays a humiliated home and homeland, the fear that would soon find its comic note in the "Great Collection," and its tragic face in the "January Week."

Only one man would speak, and our eyes turned toward him. Thousands of students and workers warmed the auditorium of the New Theater on the night of that memorable meeting (November 22, 1918), as if the intense expectations were sending a tremor of emotion through every member of the audience. Ingenieros finally arrived and, with a simple sincerity that was all his own, stepped forward to the stage as if it were his lecture hall. With broad strokes, he outlined the revolutionary panorama of the prewar years as they had occurred, with their unequivocal signs: the transformations of politics, labor legislation, the rebirth of ethical ideals. A thousand signs in the workshops, the schools, the parliaments, and on the barricades presaged the imminence of a decisive crisis. No one was unaware that a war between the biggest European capitalist states would bring forth, as its logical consequence, the definitive triumph of the most radical aspirations of the left. But the "Great War" came, and few, very few, around the world could escape the collective insanity. The smoke clouds of the war seemed blinding. Most took sides with one or the other fighting bands, as if the real end of war lay in armed victory. It was at the beginning of 1918 that a decisive turn took place in Russia. The Fifth All-Russian Congress of Soviets proclaimed a new Constitution for its liberated people and inaugurated a new chapter in the philosophy of political rights—imparting a new character to the republican system of government, nationalizing the means of production, and suppressing the parasitism of the leisure classes. Despite the lies telegraphed around the world by self-serving governments, Ingenieros maintained that the Maximalists represented the true meaning of Social Revolution as it was imagined before the war, and as such represented a ray of hope in the dying eyes of Reclus.

The inevitable mistakes, the apparent contradictions among its earliest measures, or the excesses of sectarianism and terror might disturb the judgment of the tired or the terrified. But for those who view the course of history with a panoramic vision that ignores the trivial, the Russian Revolution marks the arrival of social justice in the world. Let us prepare to welcome it; let us struggle to form the clear consciousness of its new aspirations in our collective soul. "And this new consciousness," Ingenieros finished, "can only be formed in one section of society—among the youth, among the innovators, among the oppressed, the thinking and active minority in every society, and the only ones able to understand and nurture the future."

Ingenieros was never dearer to us than that night.

4

The First Great Latin American Marxists

THE CLASS WAR IN CUBA*
Julio Antonio Mella

Julio Antonio Mella (1903–29), founder of the Cuban Communist Party, was one of the first Latin American Marxists to analyze the phenomenon of imperialist domination over the countries of the continent, its relation to local dictatorships, and the strategy for the workers' movement that flows from this reality. His writings, "rediscovered" after the Cuban Revolution, have an extraordinary intensity of expression and an intransigent revolutionary orientation. The 1925 text below refers to the assassination of several workers' leaders and militants by agents of the dictator Machado; it is characteristic of a period when the class struggle and the anti-imperialist struggle were intimately linked in the eyes of Latin American Communists.

This pamphlet is a response to the bloody offensive by our tyrant and his master—Yankee capitalist imperialism. It is also a homage to the only revolutionary cadre in Cuba willing to defend freedom at the cost of their own lives. This is a homage to these workers and peasants and to the few students and intellectuals who have dared to face the attacks of the tyrant. This is a memorial to the fallen. Your memory will never be betrayed by us, the living. This is an inspiration to those who struggle, and the revenge of us who are yet to die.

One—another—yet another. There are too many to count. There is nothing left to feel when we hear of more deaths. We are soldiers in battle and know that the list of martyrs will grow daily. We have lost our humanity. Hatred fires our hands—hands longing to be claws; vengeance fills our stares with a mad glow—stares that yearn to be rays of death. All this has killed what humanity might yet live in the oppressed.

---

*Julio Antonio Mella, "El grito de los mártires," 1926, in *Hombres de la revolución: Julio Antonio Mella*, (Havana: Ed. Imprenta Universitaria, 1971), pp. 17–24.

We have no homeland. We have only class enemies.

Class war has broken out—brutal, violent, and bloody. Quiet the frightened, screaming mouths! Shame on the weeping cowards! Punish the wretched who refuse to struggle! Praise to the brave standing in the vanguard! No more theoretical discussions and foolish Byzantinism. Let action speak with its unambiguous eloquence!

The heroic past of our class guides and encourages us. The cries of the victims sacrificed in the ditches of the Commune of 1871; the screams of the martyrs of 1905, sacrificed in the snows of Czarist Russia; the worldwide clamor of the rebellion of 1917: this is the music of our proud struggle. Those who left their workshops only to fall in the jungles during the struggle for independence; those murdered in the first general strike in the republic's early days; those who valiantly succumbed during the proletarian epic of imperialism's rapid and violent industrialization of Cuba: it is they who blazed the trail! Forward!

Díaz Blanco, you irrigated the improvised barricades of Havana with your blood. You fell, shot by our exploited brothers who murder unwittingly in the service of our common masters—the imperialists, the capitalists, and their tyrant. You, proletarian revolutionary, are our herald.

Your blood, flowing through the streets of Havana, has written a message that workers read with emotion as they go to their prisons and when they return home. Its words are: "Justice! Justice! Justice!"

Varona, fellow fighter, who could have prophesied your tragic end? Magnificent leader, a giant in body and mind, you were made for the vanguard of the Proletarian Army. As large as a gladiator, death itself seemed to fear you. Your disturbing words, like the struggle in Cuba's countryside, were prophecy heralding a new era. Your leadership of powerful strikes in the sugar mills gave hope to a proletariat avid for new conquests. Greetings, general of the young, red proletarian armies of Cuba! As the years pass and the proletariat destroys all social tyranny, you will also have been a herald.

You fell victim to a treacherous murder, killed by a servant of the tyrant sent from the Presidential Palace expressly to find you. The ruling of the official tribunals, with a last vestige of integrity, exonerated you of the fantastic accusation of being a terrorist. But who can pardon you after the tyrant's personal "justice"? To him, you merited death; you were an oppressed worker, you struggled against foreign imperialism on behalf of your comrades, and the tyrant could never pardon this crime.

The last cry that escaped your lips when you fell still resounds in the ears of the proletarians of Cuba: "Vengeance! Vengeance! Vengeance!"

Cuxart, unfortunate and obscure worker, you knew nothing of class war. You knew nothing of the hatred the rich and their lackeys of the tyrannical

regime have for us. You were happy "because you fulfilled your duty."
You did your work punctually, and nothing more. . . . Who would have
guessed you would be the object of these criminal sycophants?

Our leader is all-powerful. Our leader is theatrical, like an actor or a
tyrant. Our leader safely enjoys his passions. A "conspiracy," a "crime,"
was invented. You, unfortunate worker, became the plaything of this farce.
But for the monsters that hatched this nonsense about a supposed assault,
there were congratulations in the press, promotions, and other rewards.

While you were prisoner, another of our brothers, a soldier in the
service of the tyrant, meted out punishment under the Law on Fugitives.
What irony!

Comrade Cuxart! You fell, but the soldier who assassinated you has
terrible nightmares. Each night he sees your body appear like a ghost above
the memorial wall of La Cabaña. He sees your face rise next to the martyrs
who fell in the Ditch of the Laurels, defending the independence of Cuba
against the tyranny of Old Spain. This ignorant soldier has serious worries.
He doesn't understand why your face is there with the martyrs of the
Revolution. He doesn't know that it is a crime to kill a "worker dog." But
he calls his buddies and tells them his dreams.

(O Cuban soldiers, workers, and peasants, oppressed by the Machado
tyranny, when will you learn, like Russians oppressed by Czarist tyranny,
that you are a single class, that you are brothers, that you have common
bosses, and that the factories, the fields, and the power are yours and yours
alone? The workers and peasants create the wealth and you, soldiers, defend
the exploiters, the foreign and native bourgeoisies. When will you understand that your parasite officer is a servile tool of the Yankee plantation and
railroad bosses, and that together they oppress you, soldiers, and your
brothers, the workers and peasants?)

Late at night by the sea, near where the *Maine* was sunk so that a few
brigands could commit the crime of seizing Cuba, soldiers come to listen.
They cannot explain the ghosts' appearance. But from their breasts comes a
unanimous shout, and this cry can be heard by the masses of soldiers:
"Revolt! Revolt! Revolt!"

Grant, you came from the homeland of the omnipotent Yankee. But
nothing could save you. In that country, as in Cuba and many others, you
are not a citizen simply because you were born inside its borders. The only
citizens of the United States of America are the rich, who come to Cuba as
conquerors, giving orders through the ambassador to protect their interests.
You were a worker and fighter, so you did not have your government's
protection. Not at all! It happened after the epic, month-long railroad
strike, with its dead, injured, and disappeared. One night, an "unknown
person," as the bourgeois papers say, put the cold barrel of a revolver to

your chest. Its bullet ended your life and made you one more martyr to our cause.

North American worker, may your treacherous death at the hands of agents of the imperialist companies—agents who might as easily be soldiers as the companies' paid guards—awaken the nation of Lincoln. May they learn that the financial oligarchy that rules the world from Wall Street is the worst enemy of the people of the United States.

In any case, the thousands of comrades who filed by your corpse in Camaguey heard a cry of redemption screaming from your bloody wound: "Down with imperialism!"

Lopez, O warrior, I have no words for you. The author of these lines now feels like an orphan. A novice in the struggle, he gained his experience through your example and through your actions.

Oh, your proletarian word, your union work, your organizing skill! The Workers' Federation of Havana, the National Workers' Confederation, the Congresses of Camagüey and Cienfuegos are powerful organs of class struggle. But you, fighter, were their soul. Despite your disappearance, you are still the teacher of the Cuban proletariat.

(Teacher, it is not a tear I offer you as homage, nor is it these lines, which are not literature, but an act of revolution. What I offer you is the solemn promise to follow your path, to continue your work, and to cooperate so that the new proletarian generation to which I belong might move beyond the last in our struggle.)

No one knows your whereabouts. Can we revolutionaries choose how we die? We die as soldiers, wherever our enemy's bullets find us. Were you kidnapped? Are you alive? Then you will return to the struggle with even more enthusiasm. Were you murdered? "The revolutionary has no resting place other than the grave," said Saint-Just more than a century ago.

Teacher, brother, and comrade, the deeds you performed are silent monuments to your memory. When the hour of our triumph arrives, we, the oppressed class, will have been victorious in large part because of what you began. You will have no avenues named after you in bourgeois cities, nor statues in public parks. But every proletarian will know that the organizations you founded are the best monuments to your memory.

We salute you, fighter! The organizations you left us are our red battalions. Soon they will cry out against the day's tyrants, against imperialism, against native capital and its allies: "To the attack! Attack! Attack!"

You, comrades who are still alive (forgive me if I do not name you, in case you have not been struck by the tyrant's glare), persecuted comrades, candidates for sacrifice, as we all are in this struggle, let us say together, in a single shout:

"Forward!"

THE PROLETARIAT AND NATIONAL LIBERATION*

Julio Antonio Mella

Mella was also one of the first Latin American Marxists to analyze and criticize populist nationalism. This passage is a selection from a polemic against Haya de la Torre's APRA (American Popular Revolutionary Alliance) that was published as a pamphlet by Mella in Mexico in 1928.

Without excluding tactical support to bourgeois nationalist movements, Mella insists upon the complicity between the continent's national bourgeoisies and imperialism, and upon the primacy of class contradictions.

His thesis attributing to the proletariat the historical task of liberating Latin America from imperialist domination is characteristic of this early period of Latin American Communism.

The Communists will aid national liberation movements, as they already have done in Mexico, Nicaragua, etc., despite their having a bourgeois-democratic basis. No one denies this necessity, as long as they are truly emancipatory and revolutionary. But here is what Lenin's theses at the Second Comintern Congress still advise: "The Communist International should support national liberation movements in the colonial and under-developed countries (despite their having a bourgeois-democratic basis, as they all do [J.A.M.]), only on the condition that the elements of the future proletarian parties who are Communists in more than name unite and educate themselves in the consciousness of their own special tasks, i.e., the struggle against the bourgeois-democratic movements in their own nations. The Communist International must enter into a temporary alliance with bourgeois democracy in the colonial and underdeveloped countries, but should not merge with it, and under all circumstances should maintain the independence of the proletarian movement, even in its most rudimentary form."[1]

Here we have the Marxist view of the united front, clearly presented by that most faithful and practical interpreter of Karl Marx, Nikolai Lenin. The Apristas have not yet shown that they can better interpret him, despite their desire to make us think so.

This is not merely "theory"; we have lived this reality in America.

The Communist Party of Mexico has been supporting the struggle of the liberal, democratic, and revolutionary bourgeoisie against imperialism and

---

*Julio Antonio Mella, "La lucha revolucionaria contra el imperialismo," 1928, in *Hombres de la revolución: Julio Antonio Mella* (Havana: Ed. Imprenta Universitaria, 1971), pp. 76–78.

[1] V.I. Lenin, "Preliminary Draft Theses on the National and Colonial Questions," in *Theses, Resolutions, and Manifestos of the First Four Congresses of the Third International*" (London: Ink Links, 1980), p. 80.

its local allies, the Catholic clergy and the reactionary, professionally seditious officers. The Communists have been doing the same in the case of Nicaragua. The Cuban Communists, while not fusing with the Nationalist Party and maintaining the independence of the proletarian movement, would support this party in a revolutionary struggle for real national emancipation, if such a struggle were carried through to the end. In the struggle against the "prorogation of powers," the immediate political issue for Yankee imperialism, they supported all those against "prorogation," whether or not they were workers or Communists. In Chile, it was the strong Communist Party that fought for a united front against the imperialist dictatorship of Ibáñez. But they have never considered leaving the working class isolated or abandoning them to other classes—because when conditions change, as they are at the moment in Mexico, the workers might be orphaned and leaderless. APRA's "united front" really does just this, by not speaking concretely of the role of the proletariat and presenting us with an abstract united front, which is nothing more than a united front on behalf of the bourgeoisie, the classic betrayer of all truly emancipatory national movements. According to Lenin, "the national liberation movements of the colonies and the oppressed nationalities have learned through bitter experience that there is no salvation outside the victory of soviet power": in other words, the victory of the workers' revolution over imperialism in each country.

Betrayals by the national bourgeoisies and petty bourgeoisies have a rationale that is already understood by the whole proletariat. They struggle against foreign imperialism not to abolish private property, but to defend their own property against attempted theft by the imperialists.

In their struggle against imperialism (the foreign thief), the bourgeoisies (the local thieves) unite with the proletariat, who serve as excellent cannon fodder. But they understand in the end that it is better to ally with imperialism, as they ultimately pursue similar interests. The progressives become reactionaries. When the working class in its forward march becomes a danger to both the foreign and the local thieves, they betray the promises made to the proletariat to get them on their side. This is the reason for the hue and cry against Communism.

On the other hand, the United States (this is one characteristic of modern financial imperialism) does not want to seize Latin America and destroy all the property of their ruling classes, but rather wants to rent their services and even improve their situation, provided that it can exploit them for its own purposes. What the United States wants for every nation in Latin America is a good bourgeois country with a stable government—a regime in which the national bourgeoisies are minor partners in big business. In exchange, they concede them the privileges of "governing" and having national anthems, flags, and even armies. This form of domination is more economical.

Moncada in Nicaragua; the Kuomintang in China (an organization the Apristas claim to copy); the new politics of the Mexican petty bourgeoisie; and all the rose-colored diplomacy carried out at the Havana Conference by the many nations that call themselves free, but who allied themselves with imperialism: all these finally demonstrate that our analysis is indeed correct.

To speak concretely, only the proletariat can obtain absolute national liberation, and this will be by means of a workers' revolution.

PROLOGUE TO *TEMPEST IN THE ANDES**
José Carlos Mariátegui

José Carlos Mariátegui (1894–1930), the founder of Peruvian Communism, is probably the most important Marxist thinker that Latin America has yet produced. Besides his philosophical and sociological writings (*Defense of Marxism*, 1928–29; *Seven Interpretive Essays on Peruvian Reality*, 1928), Mariátegui drafted numerous political texts of great interest beyond their conjunctural aspects, since they touch upon fundamental issues for the Latin American workers' movement.

This document is among the most characteristic of Mariátegui's thought, as much for its references to Sorel (in opposition to "mediocre positivism"), whom he tries to integrate into his Marxist vision, as for its socialist position on the indigenous question. His admiration for the Incan past is not carried as far as a "restorationist" position, since he recognizes the irreversible character of certain "conquests of Western civilization." One of the important passages in the text might lend itself to misinterpretation. When he claims that one of the functions of socialism is to "realize capitalism," what he means by this paradoxical formulation is made clear by the immediate context of the paragraph: only a socialist revolution can carry through the agrarian task of bourgeois democracy (liquidating feudalism).

After having given us a schematic outline of the history of the Tawantin-suyu in his works *De la vida inkaika* (On Incan Life) and *Del Ayllu al Imperio* (From the *Ayllu* to the Empire), Luis E. Valcárcel with this book offers us a dynamic vision of the indigenous present. This book announces "the coming of a world," the appearance of the new Indian. It therefore cannot be an objective critique or neutral analysis; it must be a passionate affirmation, an exalted protest.

Valcárcel sees the indigenous renaissance clearly because he believes in it. A germinating historical movement cannot be understood in its full transcendence except by those who are struggling for its fulfillment. The

---

*José Carlos Mariátegui, "Prólogo a *Tempestad en los Andes*," in *La polémica del indigenismo* (Lima: Ed. Mosca Azul, 1976).

socialist movement, for example, is only fully understood by its militants. The same is not true for an already realized movement. The phenomenon of capitalism has not been understood and explained as fully and precisely by anyone as by socialists.

The role of Valcárcel in this work, if we judge it as Unamuno might, is not that of professor, but of prophet. He does not propose merely to register those facts that announce or signal the formation of a new indigenous consciousness, but to translate their intimate historical meaning, thereby helping this indigenous consciousness to encounter and be revealed to itself. In this case, as in perhaps no other, interpretation becomes creation.

Tempest in the Andes is not presented as a work of doctrine or theory. Valcárcel feels the revival of the Quechua race. This resurrection is the theme of his work. One does not prove that a people is alive by reasoning or theorizing, but by showing it to be alive. This is the procedure followed by Valcárcel, who, rather than documenting the extent and the route of the indigenous renaissance, is preoccupied with showing us evidence of its reality.

The first part of *Tempest in the Andes* has a political intonation. Valcárcel puts the emotions and the ideals of the Incan resurgence into his vehement prose. It is not the Incan Empire that is reviving; it is the Incan people, who, after four centuries of slumber, have once again started on the march toward their destiny. Commenting on Valcárcel's first book, I wrote that neither the conquests of Western civilization nor the vital consequences of the colonial and republican periods could be renounced.[1] Valcárcel recognizes these limits to his longing.

The second part of the book, a collection of pictures, full of color and movement, presents us with indigenous rural life. Valcárcel's prose assumes a fondly bucolic accent when he evokes, with simple images, the rustic enchantment of farming in the *sierra*. The vehement pamphleteer reappears in his description of the "*mestizo* villagers," outlining the sordid portrait of a parasitic, obsolete, diseased, alcoholic, and worm-eaten people in whom the qualities of both the Spaniard and the Indian have degenerated in an unfavorable mixture.

---

[1] Here is exactly what I wrote (*Mundial*, September 1925): "Valcárcel goes too far, which almost always happens when one gives free reign to the imagination. Western civilization is neither as exhausted or rotten as Valcárcel supposes. Nor once it has acquired its experience, technique, and ideas can Peru mystically renounce such valid and precious instruments and return with bitter intransigence to its old agrarian myths. The Conquest, with all its evil, was an historical deed. The Republic, as it exists, is an historical reality. Abstract mental speculations and pure spiritual concepts have little or no power against historical facts. The history of Peru is but a piece of human history. A new reality has been created in these four centuries. Torrents from the West have created it. It is a weak reality; but it is, in any case, a reality. It would be overly romantic to choose to ignore it."

In the third part, we assist at the characteristic episodes of the Indian drama. The landscape is the same, but its colors and voices are different. The georgic *sierra* of the planting, the harvest, and the *Kaswa* becomes the tragic *sierra* of the *gamonal* and the *mita*. The brutal despotism of the *latifundista*, the *kelkere*, and the policeman weigh down on the peasant *ayllu*.

In the fourth section, the *sierra* rises, pregnant with hope. It is no longer a race united in resignation and renunciation that lives here. A strange wind sweeps the villages and fields of the *sierra*. The "new Indians" appear: here, the teacher and agitator; there, the laborer, the shepherd—different than before. The Adventist missionary is not extraneous to their arrival, but Valcárcel accompanies an appreciation of his work with a prudent reserve, for one reason: as Alfredo Palacios warns, these missions can assume the role of outpost for Anglo-Saxon imperialism. The "new Indian" is not a mythic, abstract being, only given life by the prophet's faith. We feel him alive, real, and active by the end of this "movie of the *sierra*," which is how the author himself defines his book. What distinguishes the "new Indian" is not education, but spirit (literacy does not redeem the Indian). The "new Indian" waits. He has a goal. This is his secret and his power. The rest is peripheral. I, too, have recognized him in more than one messenger of the race that has come to Lima. I recall the unexpected and impressive type of agitator that I met four years ago in the person of the Indian Ezequiel Urviola, from Puno. This encounter was the strongest surprise that Peru had reserved for me on my return from Europe. Urviola represented the first spark of a fire to come. Tubercular and hunchbacked, he succumbed after two years of indefatigable work. It does not matter today that Urviola no longer lives. It is enough that he did. As Varcarcel says, the *sierra* today is pregnant with Spartacuses.

The "new Indian" explains and indicates the true nature of *indigenismo*, which in Valcárcel has one of its most passionate evangelists. Faith in the indigenous resurgence does not proceed from a process of the material "Westernization" of the land of the Quechua. It is not the civilization or the alphabet of the white man that is lifting the soul of the Indian. It is the myth, the idea of the socialist revolution. The hope of the indigenous people is absolutely revolutionary. This very myth, this very idea, is the decisive agent in the awakening of other failing ancient peoples and races: Hindus, Chinese, etc. Today, as never before, world history tends to be guided by the same compass.

Why should the Incan people, who constructed the most developed and harmonious communist system, be the only group insensitive to the world's emotions? The close relationship between the indigenous movement and the world's revolutionary movements is too obvious to document. I have already said that I came to an understanding and realization of the importance of the indigenous people through socialism. The case of Valcárcel precisely confirms my personal experience. A man with a broad intellectual background, influenced by his traditionalist tastes, guided by different sorts of influences and studies, Valcárcel resolves his *indigenismo* politically, through socialism. In this book he tells us, among other things, that "the indigenous proletariat awaits its Lenin." A Marxist's language would be no different.

The indigenous program lacks historical concreteness as long as it remains on a philosophical or cultural plane. To gain this concreteness—that is, to acquire reality, corporeity—it must become a political and economic program. Socialism has taught us to pose the indigenous question in new terms. We have stopped considering it abstractly as an ethnic or moral problem, and now recognize it concretely as a social, economic, and political problem. And we therefore feel that, for the first time, we have clarified and demarcated the issue.

Those who have not yet broken out of the context of their liberal bourgeois education and, basing themselves on an abstract and literary position, continue to confuse themselves with the racial aspects of the problem, forget that it is fundamentally dominated by politics, and therefore by economics. They employ a pseudo-idealist language to obfuscate reality, which lies hidden behind its attributes and consequences. To the revolutionary dialectic they oppose an absurd and confused criticism, according to which the solution to the indigenous question does not lie in reform or political action, since their immediate effects would not influence a complex multitude of customs and vices that can only be transformed through a slow and regular evolution.

History, fortunately, resolves all doubts and dispels all ambiguities. The Conquest was a political act. It brusquely interrupted the autonomous development of the Quechua nation, but did not imply a sudden substitution of native laws and customs by those of the conquerors. Nevertheless, this political act opened a new period in all arenas of life, both spiritual and material. This change of regime was enough to untie the life of the Quechua people from its moorings. Independence was another political act. It did not result in a radical transformation of the economic and social structure of Peru, but it nevertheless inaugurated another period in our history. If it did not better the condition of the indigenous peoples in practice, because it barely touched the colonial economic infrastructure, it changed their legal position and cleared the way for their political and social emancipation. If the republic did not continue down this path, the responsibility for this omission lies exclusively with the class that took advantage of the work of the liberators, which was so potentially rich in creative principles and values.

The indigenous question no longer allows for the mystification to which it has been subjected by a mob of lawyers and literati who are consciously or unconsciously tied to the interests of the *latifundistas*. The moral and material misery of the indigenous race too clearly appears as a simple consequence of the economic and social regime that has weighed upon it for centuries. This regime, the successor to colonial feudalism, is called *gamonalismo*. Under its rule, one cannot seriously speak of the redemption of the Indian.

The term *gamonalismo* does not only designate a social and economic category that includes the *latifundistas* and large landowners. It signifies a phenomenon. *Gamonalismo* is not represented only by the *gamonales* themselves. It includes an extensive hierarchy of functionaries, intermediaries, agents, parasites, etc. The literate Indian himself becomes an exploiter when he puts himself at the service of *gamonalismo*. The key factor in this phenomenon is the hegemony of the giant semi-feudal landowners in the politics and machinery of the state. Consequently, it is this factor that must be acted upon if we wish to radically attack this evil, which some insist upon contemplating only in its episodic or subsidiary manifestations.

The liquidation of *gamonalismo*, or of feudalism, could have been carried out by the republic in the context of its liberal and capitalist principles. But for reasons I have already discussed in other studies, these principles have not effectively and fully directed our historical process. Sabotaged by the very class that was charged with applying them, they have been powerless for more than a century to redeem the Indian from a servitude that is absolutely at one with its feudal counterpart. Now that these principles are in crisis around the world, it would be useless to wait for them to suddenly acquire an unexpected creative vitality in Peru.

Revolutionary or even reformist thought can no longer be liberal, but must be socialist. Socialism appears in our history not by chance, imitation, or fashion, as superficial minds suppose, but as a historical necessity. On the one hand, we who profess socialism logically and coherently propose the reorganization of the country on a socialist basis. And, maintaining that the economic and political regime we are combating has gradually become a force for the colonization of the country by foreign capitalist imperialists, we proclaim that, at this moment in our history, it is impossible to be truly nationalistic or revolutionary without being a socialist. On the other hand, in Peru, there is not, and there has never been, a progressive bourgeoisie with a national sensibility that declares itself liberal and democratic and bases its politics on the postulates of its theory. With the sole exception of the traditionally conservative elements, there is no one in Peru who, with greater or lesser sincerity, does not claim for himself a certain dose of socialism.

Insufficiently profound and critical minds might suppose that the liquidation of feudalism is a typically and specifically liberal and bourgeois measure, and that to attempt to convert it into a socialist task is to romantically bend the laws of history. These shallow theoreticians oppose socialism with one simplistic criterion as their sole argument—that capitalism has not exhausted its possibilities in Peru. The partisans of this idea will be astonished to discover that the task of socialism, when it comes to power in the country, depending on the hour and the historical compass to which it must adjust, will to a great degree be the realization of capitalism, or better, the realization of the historical possibilities that capitalism still contains, in the sense that this serves the interests of social progress.

Valcárcel, who does not start from any ideological a priori (as might be said of myself or those elements of the younger generation known to be closest to me), discovers this same path through the natural and spontaneous work of probing and studying the indigenous question. The work he has written is not one of theory and criticism. It is somewhat evangelical, even apocalyptic. One will not find here the exact principles of the revolution that will restore the indigenous race to its place in the history of the nation. But here are its myths. And since the elevated spirit of George Sorel, reacting against the mediocre positivism that had infected the socialists of his era, discovered the perennial value of the Myth in the creation of great popular movements, we have known well that this is an aspect of the struggle we must not neglect or underestimate, while being fully realistic.

Tempest in the Andes has arrived at the right moment. Its voice will move all sensitive consciences. It is a passionate prophecy announcing a new Peru. And it matters not that for some it is facts that create prophecy, and for others, prophecy that creates facts.

THE INDIGENOUS QUESTION IN LATIN AMERICA*

José Carlos Mariátegui

Mariátegui sent a communication to the 1929 Latin American Communist Conference on the problems of the indigenous peasants and their involvement in the class struggle. The following are some sections of this report. Mariátegui attributed much importance to Incan collectivist traditions as a factor favoring the development of Communism among the peasant masses of the Andean region.

---

*José Carlos Mariátegui, "El problema de la razas en América Latina," in *El movimiento revolucionario latinoamericano, versiones de la Primera Conferencia Comunista Latinoamericana*, June 1929 (Buenos Aires: La correspondencia sudamericana, 1929), pp. 277–279, 290–291.

Nevertheless, it would be unfair to characterize his position as "populist"; for Mariátegui, the political hegemony of the proletariat is still the condition for the transition to socialism.

Mariátegui was the first Latin American Communist to discuss the agrarian question and its relation to the indigenous question, trying to apply the Marxist method in a creative way to a specifically Latin American phenomenon. It is noteworthy that this problematic would be raised after Mariátegui, especially by the "heretics" and dissidents of the Latin American Marxist movement and, later, by the Castroist current.

The coming of the republic does not substantially transform the country's economy. A simple change of classes occurs: a government of landowners, *encomenderos*, and native professionals succeeds the courtly government of the Spanish nobility. The *mestizo* aristocracy seizes power, lacking either economic ideas or political vision. The movement for emancipation from the metropolis passes unnoticed by the country's four million Indians. Their state of servitude has continued from the Conquest to our day, despite laws intended to "protect" them that cannot be applied while an economic structure based on the vestiges of feudal landowning persists in our social system.

The new ruling class, passionately greedy for wealth, dedicates itself to enlarging its *latifundios* with land belonging to the indigenous communities—some of which even disappear in various regions. With the theft of the land that had been held in common by the member families of the *ayllu*, they are forced to look for work, and become *yanacones* or peons of the *latifundistas* who had violently dispossessed them.

Nothing remains of the ancient *ayllu* other than one or another physical or ethnic trait, custom, religious or social practice that can be found in the innumerable communities that had previously made up the "little kingdom," or *curacazgo*. But if all the elements of compulsion and solidarity have been eliminated from this latter institution, which had been the political intermediary between the *ayllu* and the empire, it has, on the other hand, kept its particular identity and its informal character in some underdeveloped areas, where important elements of social integration have been maintained since the Conquest.

These communities are built on the common ownership of lands that they cultivate and maintain through agreements and ties of consanguinity that unite the various families that form the *ayllu*. The fields and pastures belong to the community and form the patrimony of the collectivity. The members of the community live on the land and maintain themselves with its crops. The constant efforts made to keep their land from being seized by their powerful neighbors or by other communities serve as sufficient incentive to stay organized as a single group. Even today, the communal lands belong to the whole *ayllu*, or rather to the group of families that make up the community. Some lands are distributed, while others remain as commons whose administration is carried out by agents of the community. Each family has a piece of land to cultivate, but they cannot sell it, because it does not belong to them; it belongs to the community.

In general, there are two types of land: those which are cultivated in common for some "saint" or community and those cultivated separately by each family.

But the collectivist spirit of the indigenous peoples is not only revealed by the existence of these communities. The secular custom known as the *minka* still persists in Peru, Bolivia, Ecuador, and Chile: work which a *parcelero*, even if he is not a member of a community, cannot perform without help, or because of sickness or similar reasons, is carried out with the cooperation and aid of the neighboring *parceleros*, who in turn receive part of the harvest if it is large enough, or additional help for themselves at a later time.

This cooperative spirit, which exists even outside the communities, is manifested in special ways in Bolivia, where mutual agreements are made between poor, indigenous, small landholders to work their land in common and divide the product. Another form of cooperation seen in Bolivia is that between an Indian who owns nothing more than a small piece of land near a city and an Indian who lives in the city as a relatively well-paid worker or artisan. The latter has no spare time, but he can obtain seed and work implements that the other needs; the former supplies the land and his individual labor, and at harvest time, they divide the harvest in pre-established proportions.

These and other forms of extracommunitarian cooperation, along with the existence of numerous communities (approximately 1,500 communities with 30 million hectares of land cultivated by 1,500,000 members in Peru and approximately an equal number of communities in Bolivia with fewer members, since many of them have been uprooted from the land to work the mines) that produce higher yields than the *latifundios* in some regions, attest to the vitality of primitive Incan collectivism, which, given the necessary means for cultivating and mechanizing the *latifundios*, is capable of quickly multiplying its productivity.

The Sixth Congress of the Comintern has again pointed out the possibility that peoples with a rudimentary economic system can move directly to a collective method of economic organization without suffering the long evolution through which other peoples have passed. We believe that among "backward" peoples, no group compares to the indigenous Incan people in combining such favorable conditions for transforming (under the hegemony of the proletariat) their primitive agrarian communism, which persists both in concrete structures and a deep collectivist spirit, into one of the most solid bases of the collectivist society foreseen by Marxist Communism.

Only a class-based revolutionary movement of the exploited indigenous masses will allow for a real liberation of the race from exploitation, and thereby favor the possibility of its political self-determination.

The indigenous question, in the majority of cases, is identified with the land question. The ignorance, backwardness, and misery of the indigenous people are merely results of their subservience. The feudal *latifundio* maintains the exploitation and absolute domination of the indigenous masses by the landowning class. The Indians' struggle has invariably centered on the defense of their lands against dispossession and absorption by the *gamonales*. Thus, there is an instinctive and profound indigenous demand: the demand for land. Giving an organized, systematic, and definite character to this demand is a task on which the union movement and our political propaganda must actively collaborate.

The "communities," which have demonstrated a quite astounding level of resistance and persistence under conditions of extreme repression, represent a natural factor for the socialization of the land. The Indian has an established habit of cooperation. Even when communal property becomes individual property (and not only in the *sierra*, but also on the coast, where a greater degree of cultural amalgamation weighs against indigenous customs), cooperation is still maintained and heavy labor in carried out in common. The "community" can become a cooperative with minimal effort. Awarding the land of the *latifundios* to the "communities" is the necessary solution to the agrarian question in the *sierra*. On the coast, where large landholders are also all-powerful but communal property no longer exists, the solution inevitably tends toward the privatization of the land. The *yanacona*, a type of harshly exploited sharecropper, should be supported in his struggle against the landowner. The natural demand of these *yanaconas* is for the land that they work. On the haciendas that are directly exploited by their owners with the labor of *peones*, who are recruited in part from the *sierra* and therefore lack a local connection to the land, the terms of the struggle are different. The demands for which they must struggle are the freedom to organize, suppression of the *enganche* (forced recruitment), wage increases, the eight-hour day, and the enforcement of labor laws. Only when the *peon* has won these demands will he be on the road to his definitive emancipation.

It is very difficult for trade union or political propaganda to penetrate into the hacienda. Each hacienda on the coast is a fiefdom. No organization that does not accept the patronage and tutelage of owners and management is allowed, and only sports or recreational associations are found there. But the increase of automobile traffic, little by little, is opening a breach in the barriers that keep the haciendas closed to propaganda. This is the reason for the importance of the organization and active mobilization of transport workers in the development of working-class mobilization. When the *peones* on the haciendas know that they can count on the fraternal solidarity of the unions and understand its value, the will to struggle that is missing today will easily be awakened. The nuclei of adherents of trade unionism that are gradually formed on the haciendas will have the task of explaining themselves in whatever protests that develop, and of taking advantage of the first opportunity to form their own organizations, to the degree that circumstances permit.

For the progressive ideological education of the indigenous masses, the workers' vanguard has at its disposal those militant elements of the Indian race that enter into contact with the union movement in the mines or urban centers, assimilate its principles, and qualify themselves to play a role in the emancipation of their race. Workers coming from the indigenous milieu often return there temporarily or permanently. The idiom allows them to effectively fulfill a mission as instructors of their racial and class brothers. The Indian peasants will only truly understand people from their midst, who speak their own language. They will always distrust the white, the *mestizo*; in turn, the white and *mestizo* can only with the greatest difficulty take on this hard work of coming to the indigenous milieu and bringing class propaganda.

THE LATIN AMERICAN SOCIALIST REVOLUTION*

José Carlos Mariátegui

The following text, taken from a document edited by Mariátegui on behalf of a group of Lima militants (the nucleus of the future Communist Party), is part of a debate with the APRA. It describes, in incisive and thorough terms, the socialist character of the continental revolution as the only realistic alternative to domination by North American imperialism.

The very word revolution, in this America of so many small revolutions, quite lends itself to ambiguity. We must rigorously and intransigently rehabilitate it. We must restore its strict and exact meaning. The Latin American revolution will be nothing more or nothing less than a stage, a phase of the world revolution. It will simply and purely be a socialist

---

*José Carlos Mariátegui, "Carta colectiva del grupo de Lima," June 1929, in *El proletariado y su organización* (Mexico City: Ed. Grijalbo, 1970), pp. 119–121.

revolution. To this word you many add, according to the particular case, whatever adjective you like: "anti-imperialist," "agrarian," or "national revolutionary." Socialism supposes, precedes, encompasses all of these.

To a plutocratic, imperialist North America, we can effectively counterpose only a socialist Latin or Ibero-America. The era of free competition in the capitalist economy has finished in all areas and in all of its aspects. We live in the era of monopolies, or better yet, of empires. The Latin American countries came late to capitalist competition. The inside lanes had already been assigned. The destiny of these countries in the capitalist order is that of being simple colonies. Differences of language, race, and spirit have absolutely no decisive weight. It is ridiculous to still speak of the contrast between a materialist, Anglo-Saxon America and an idealist Latin America, between a blonde Rome and a pallid Greece. All these are unpardonably discredited topics. Rodó's myth no longer touches the soul in a useful or fundamental manner, nor has it ever. Let us inexorably put aside all these caricatures and semblances of ideologies and geographies, and let us seriously and honestly take account of reality.

Socialism is certainly not an Indo-American theory. But no theory, no contemporary system, is or could be. And socialism, although born in Europe as was capitalism, is neither specifically nor particularly European. It is a worldwide movement from which none of the countries that move in the orbit of Western civilization can escape. This civilization moves toward universality with a force and with means that no other civilization has ever possessed. Indo-America, in this world order, can and must have its own individuality and style, but not its own culture or particular destiny. A hundred years ago, we owed our independence as nations to the rhythm of Western history, which has inevitably imposed itself upon us since the era of colonization. Freedom, Democracy, Parliament, the Sovereignty of the People: all the great words pronounced by men of that era came from the European repertoire. History, nevertheless, does not measure the greatness of these men by the originality of their ideas, but by the effectiveness and genius with which they served them. And the peoples that have advanced furthest on our continent are those where they took root the soonest and best. Interdependence and solidarity between peoples and between continents were nevertheless much less then than now. Socialism, ultimately, is in the American tradition. Incan civilization was the most advanced primitive communist organization that history has known.

We certainly do not want socialism to be absolute, abstract, indifferent to the facts and to changing, mobile reality; it should be germinating, concrete, dialectical, operative, powerful, and capable of movement. *Amauta* is not a diversion, nor the game of pure intellectuals. It professes a historical ideal, affirms an active and popular idea, and is obedient to a contemporary popular movement. In the struggle between two systems, between two ideas, it would not occur to us to be spectators, nor to invent a third way. Originality, taken to the extreme, is a literary and anarchic preoccupation. On our banner, we inscribe a single, simple, and great word—socialism (and with this slogan, we affirm our absolute independence from the ideas of a petty-bourgeois and demagogic Nationalist Party).

THE ANTI-IMPERIALIST POINT OF VIEW*
José Carlos Mariátegui

This text is from a document drafted by Mariátegui and presented by the Peruvian delegation to the First Latin American Communist Conference (Buenos Aires, June 1929). It takes up the key question of the dialectical relation between the class struggle and the anti-imperialist struggle, and sketches an unusual and penetrating analysis of the connections and contradictions between the North American metropolis and the local bourgeoisie and landowners. It is one of the most well-known political texts of Mariátegui, reissued by many Latin American revolutionary groups after the Cuban Revolution.

1. To what degree is the situation of the Latin American republics similar to that of the semi-colonial countries? The economic condition of these republics is undoubtedly semi-colonial, and this characteristic of their economies tends to be accentuated as capitalism, and therefore imperialist penetration, develops. But the national bourgeoisies, who see cooperation with imperialism as their best source of profits, feel themselves secure enough as mistresses of power not to be too greatly preoccupied with national sovereignty. The South American bourgeoisies, not yet facing Yankee military occupation (with the exception of Panama), are not disposed to admit the necessity of struggling for their second independence, as Aprista propaganda naively supposes. The state, or better yet the ruling class, doesn't seem to feel the need for a greater or more secure degree of national autonomy. The revolution for independence is relatively too near, its myths and symbols too alive in the consciousness of the bourgeoisie and petty bourgeoisie. The illusion of national sovereignty still lives on. It would be a serious mistake to claim that this social layer still has a sense of revolutionary nationalism, as in those places where it does represent a factor for anti-imperialist struggle in semi-colonial countries enslaved by imperialism, for example, in Asia in recent decades.

---

*José Carlos Mariátegui, "Punto de vista anti-imperialista," 1929, in *Obra política* (Mexico City: Ed. Era, 1979), pp. 273–278.

Over a year ago, in our discussion with Aprista leaders in which we rejected their desire to propose the creation of a Latin American Kuomintang, we put forward the following thesis as a way to avoid Eurocentric plagiarism and to accommodate our revolutionary activity to a precise appreciation of our own reality:

> Collaboration with the bourgeoisie and even many feudal elements in the anti-imperialist struggle in China is explicable in terms of race and national culture that are not relevant for us. A Chinese nobleman or bourgeois feels himself Chinese to the core. He matches the white man's contempt for his stratified and decrepit culture with his own contempt and pride in his millennia-long tradition. Anti-imperialism can therefore find support in such sentiments and in a sense of Chinese nationalism. Circumstances are not the same in Indo-America. The native aristocracy and bourgeoisie feel no solidarity with the people in possessing a common history and culture. In Peru, the white aristocrat and bourgeois scorn the popular and the national. They consider themselves white above all else. The petty-bourgeois *mestizo* imitates their example. The Lima bourgeoisie fraternizes with the Yankee capitalists, even with their mere employees, at the Country Club, the Tennis Club, and in the streets. The Yankee can marry the native *señorita* without the inconvenience of differences in race or religion, and she feels no national or cultural misgivings in preferring marriage with a member of the invading race. The middle-class girl has no qualms in this regard, either. The girl who can trap a Yankee employed by the Grace Company or the Foundation does it with the satisfaction of thereby raising her social position. The nationalist factor, for these inescapable objective reasons, is neither decisive nor basic to the anti-imperialist struggle in our environment. Only in countries such as Argentina, where there is a large and rich bourgeoisie proud of their country's wealth and power and where the national character for this reason has clearer contours than in more backward countries, could anti-imperialism (perhaps) penetrate more easily among bourgeois elements. But this is for reasons related to capitalist expansion and development, rather than for reasons of social justice and socialist theory, as in our case.

The betrayal by the Chinese bourgeoisie and the failure of the Kuomintang have not yet been understood in their full magnitude. Their capitalist style of nationalism (one not related to social justice or theory) demonstrates how little we can trust the revolutionary nationalist sentiments of the bourgeoisie, even in countries like China.

As long as the imperialists are able to "manage" the sentiments and formalities of these states' national sovereignty and are not forced to resort to armed intervention or military occupation, they can definitively count on the collaboration of their bourgeoisies. While they may depend upon the imperialist economy, these countries, or rather their bourgeoisies, consider themselves as much the masters of their own fate as Romania, Bulgaria, Poland, and the other "dependent states" of Europe.

This factor of political psychology should not be discounted in the precise estimation of the possibilities of anti-imperialist action in Latin America. Neglect of this matter has been one of the characteristics of Aprista theory.

2. The fundamental difference between us in Peru who originally accepted the APRA (as a project for a united front, never as a party or even as an effective organizer of struggle) and those outside Peru who later defined it as a Latin American Kuomintang is that the former remain faithful to the revolutionary, socioeconomic conception of anti-imperialism; the latter, meanwhile, explain their position by saying: "We are leftists (or socialists) because we are anti-imperialists." Anti-imperialism thereby is raised to the level of a program, a political attitude, a movement that is valid in and of itself and which leads spontaneously to socialism, to the social revolution (how, we have no idea). This idea inordinately overestimates the anti-imperialist movement, exaggerates the myth of the struggle for a "second independence," and romanticizes that we are already living in the era of a new emancipation. This leads to the idea of replacing the anti-imperialist leagues with political parties. From an APRA initially conceived as a united front, a popular alliance, a bloc of oppressed classes, we pass to an APRA defined as the Latin American Kuomintang.

For us, anti-imperialism does not and cannot constitute, by itself, a political program for a mass movement capable of conquering state power. Anti-imperialism, even if it could mobilize the nationalist bourgeoisie and petty bourgeoisie on the side of the worker and peasant masses (and we have already definitively denied this possibility), does not annul class antagonisms nor suppress different class interests.

Neither the bourgeoisie nor the petty bourgeoisie in power can carry out anti-imperialist politics. To demonstrate this we have the experience of Mexico, where the petty bourgeoisie has just allied with Yankee imperialism. In its relations with the United States, a "nationalist" government might use different language than the Leguía government of Peru. This government is clearly, unabashedly pan-Americanist and Monroeist. But any other bourgeois government would carry out the same practical policies on loans and concessions. Foreign capital investment in Peru grows in direct and close relation to the country's economic development, the exploitation of its natural riches, its population, and the improvement of its routes of communication. How can the most demagogic petty bourgeois oppose this capitalist penetration? With nothing but words; with nothing but a quick, nationalist fix. The taking of power by anti-imperialism, if it were possible, would not represent the taking of power by the proletarian masses, by socialism. The socialist revolution will find its most bloody and dangerous enemy (dangerous because of their confusionism and demagogy) in those petty bourgeois placed in power by the voices of order.

Without ruling out the use of any type of anti-imperialist agitation or any action to mobilize those social sectors that might eventually join the struggle, our mission is to explain to and show the masses that only the socialist revolution can stand as a definitive and real barrier to the advance of imperialism.

3. These factors differentiate the situation of the South American countries from that of the Central American nations. There, Yankee imperialism, by resorting to armed intervention without the slightest hesitation, does provoke a patriotic reaction that could easily win a part of the bourgeoisie and petty bourgeoisie to an anti-imperialist perspective. Aprista propaganda, conducted personally by Haya de la Torre, has obtained better results here than in any other part of America. His confusionist and messianic perorations, which claim to be related to the economic struggle, actually appeal to racial and emotional factors, thereby meeting the necessary conditions for impressing the petty-bourgeois intellectual. Class parties and powerful, clearly class-conscious union organizations are not destined for the same quick growth here as in South America. In our countries, the class factor is more decisive and more developed. There is no reason to resort to vague populist formulas behind which reactionary tendencies can only prosper. At the moment, *Aprismo*, as propaganda, is limited to Central America; in South America, it is being totally liquidated, a consequence of the populist, "bossist," and petty-bourgeois deviation that sees it as a Latin American Kuomintang. The next Anti-Imperialist Congress in Paris, which will have to unify the anti-imperialist organizations and distinguish between anti-imperialist programs and agitation and the tasks of class parties and trade unions, will put an absolute end to this question.

4. Do the interests of imperialist capitalism necessarily and inevitably coincide with the feudal and semi-feudal interests of our countries' landowning classes? Is the struggle against feudalism unavoidably and completely identical with the anti-imperialist struggle? Certainly, imperialist capitalism uses the power of the feudal class to the degree that it considers it the politically dominant class. But their economic interests are not the same. The petty bourgeoisie, even the most demagogic, can end up in the same intimate alliance with imperialist capitalism if it, in practice, dilutes its most conspicuous nationalist impulses. Finance capital would feel more secure if power were in the hands of a larger social class that is in a better position than the old, hated feudal class to defend the interests of capitalism and serve as its guard and water boy by satisfying certain overdue demands and distorting the masses' class orientation. The creation of a class of small-

holders, the expropriation of the *latifundios*, and the liquidation of feudal privileges are not in opposition to the interests of imperialism in an immediate sense. On the contrary, to the degree that feudal vestiges still remain despite the growth of the capitalist economy, the movement for the liquidation of feudal privileges coincides with the interests of capitalist development as promoted by imperialist experts and investments. The disappearance of the large *latifundios*, the creation of an agrarian economy through what bourgeois demagoguery calls the "democratization" of the land, the displacement of the old aristocracies by a more powerful bourgeoisie and petty bourgeoisie better able to guarantee social peace: none of this is contrary to imperialist interests. The Leguía regime in Peru, as timid as it has been in regard to the interests of the *latifundistas* and *gamonales* (who support it to a great degree), has no problem resorting to demagogy, declaiming against feudalism and feudal privilege, thundering against the old oligarchies, and promoting a program of land distribution to make every field worker a small landowner. *Leguiísmo* draws its greatest strength from precisely this type of demagogy. *Leguiísmo* does not dare lay a hand on the large landowners. But the natural direction of capitalist development— irrigation works, the exploitation of new mines, etc.—is in contradiction to the interests and privileges of feudalism. To the degree that the amount of cultivated land increases and new centers of employment appear, the *latifundistas* lose their principal power: the absolute and unconditional control of labor. In Lambayeque, where a water diversion project has been started by the American engineer Sutton, the technical commission has already run up against the interests of the large feudal landowners. These landowners grow mainly sugar. The threat that they will lose their monopoly of land and water, and thereby their means of controlling the work force, infuriates these people and pushes them toward attitudes that the government considers subversive, no matter how closely it is connected to these elements. Sutton has all the characteristics of the North American capitalist businessman. His outlook and his work clash with the feudal spirit of the *latifundistas*. For example, Sutton has established a system of water distribution that is based on the principle that these resources belong to the state; the *latifundistas* believe that water rights are part of their right to the land. By this theory, the water was theirs; it was and is the absolute property of their estates.

5. And is the petty bourgeoisie, whose role in the struggle against imperialism is so often overestimated, necessarily opposed to imperialist penetration because of economic exploitation? The petty bourgeoisie is undoubtedly the social class most sensitive to the fascination of nationalist mythology. But the economic factor which predominates is the following: in countries afflicted with Spanish-style poverty, where the petty

bourgeoisie, locked in decades-old prejudice, resist proletarianization; where, because of their miserable wages, they do not have the economic power to partially transform themselves into a working class; where the desperate search for office employment, a petty government job, and the hunt for a "decent" salary and a "decent" job dominate, the creation of large enterprises that represent better paid jobs, even if they enormously exploit their local employees, is favorably received by the middle classes. A Yankee business represents a better salary, possibilities for advancement, and liberation from dependence on the state, which can only offer a future to speculators. This reality weighs decisively on the consciousness of the petty bourgeois looking for or in possession of a position. In these countries with Spanish-style poverty, we repeat, the situation of the middle classes is not the same as in those countries where these classes have gone through a period of free competition and of capitalist development favorable to individual initiative and success and to oppression by the giant monopolies.

In conclusion, we are anti-imperialists because we are Marxists, because we are revolutionaries, because we oppose capitalism with socialism, an antagonistic system called upon to transcend it, and because in our struggle against foreign imperialism we are fulfilling our duty of solidarity with the revolutionary masses of Europe.

5

The Red Revolt in El Salvador (1932)

DOCUMENTS OF THE COMMUNIST PARTY OF EL SALVADOR*

The following texts are calls, proclamations, and documents issued by the Communist Party of El Salvador during the peasant insurrection of 1932, the only mass armed rising ever led by a Latin American Communist Party.

This event must be situated in the context of the left turn of the Comintern (the Third Period), but was essentially an expression of an authentic and autonomous revolutionary movement "from below." The appeals to soldiers in the Communist Party proclamations were not merely rhetorical, but corresponded to real Communist influence in the army.

These documents were published in the Cuban journal *Pensamiento Crítico* by the Salvadoran Communist poet Roque Dalton as an appendix to the memoirs of Miguel Mármol, the only survivor among the leaders of the Communist Party of El Salvador in 1932.

COMMUNIST MANIFESTO FOR THE SOLDIERS OF AHUACHAPÁN

Comrade Soldiers:

We workers and peasants, under the leadership of the Central Committee of the Communist Party of El Salvador, have nothing to hope for from the current government, which is in the hands of the rich. You know that the comrades of the canton of Santa Rita are on strike, demanding a wage increase and a decrease in rents that leave almost nothing for the agricultural workers. The capitalist Rogelio Arriaza and Rafael Herrera Morán, another capitalist, got the National Guard drunk so they would murder our striking comrades. The government, being a rich man's government, has sent

---

*Roque Dalton, "Miguel Mármol: El Salvador, 1930–32," in *Pensamiento Crítico*, n. 48 (Havana), January, 1971, pp. 98–106. For Mármol's complete memoirs, see Roque Dalton, *Miguel Mármol* (Willimantic, CT: Curbstone Press, 1987).

45

troops to crush the workers. You, comrade soldiers, are members of our exploited class and should not shoot a single bullet at the workers. The workers, peasants, and soldiers should unite to establish a workers' and peasants' government. You should repudiate your officers and commanders because they are all against the workers. Name your own delegates and reach an agreement with us. Finish off your commanders and officers and form a Red Army of soldiers and commanders named by yourselves, the soldiers. Not one bullet against us! The delegates of the soldier comrades should take orders from the Communist Party. The Central Committee of the Communist Party will lead us to victory over the rich thieves.

Ahuachapán
January 7, 1932

International Red Aid, El Salvador Communist [Party], National Executive Committee

(Confidential and Urgent)
Comrade:

We expect that the masses will not become disheartened or discouraged at the appointed hour. Be certain that the United States will look favorably on the insurrection and consider it a reaction by the Araujoists. They will immediately recognize the existence of a state of war, which is indispensable to us at the moment. We will meanwhile take the reins of power, which is our objective. Afterwards, with arms already in hand and with the aid of comrades of all the Americas, especially the United States, we can confront any unexpected situation. This is a life or death struggle.

For the victims of reaction and imperialism,
For the National Executive Committee,
Ismael Hernández, General Secretary

Plan to be Carried Out by the Revolutionary Military Committee on the . . . of This Month [January] in the Struggle for the Taking of Power by the Workers, Peasants, and Soldiers, by Resolution of the Central Committee of the Communist Party of El Salvador

1. This CC of the PCS [Communist Party of El Salvador] names a Revolutionary Military Committee under the leadership of this CC that will consist of the comrades: [names].
2. The Revolutionary Military Committee is authorized by this CC to organize the immediate insurrection mandated by this broadened CC in its meeting of the 8th of this month.

3. All members of the party will be under the orders of the Revolutionary Military Committee, to whom they owe the strictest obedience.

Workers of the world, unite.

For the CC,
Octavio Figueira, Interim General Secretary
January 9, 1932

WHY SOLDIERS SHOULD TAKE PART IN THE PROLETARIAN REVOLUTION

First, the soldier is a worker or peasant exploited by the rich in factories, workshops, and fields. While still young, he is called to the barracks, where he is forced to carry a weapon to defend the riches that he as a worker or peasant has produced for the wealthy. The soldier, living under the oppression of the barracks, feels discontented despite the lies of his commanders and officers, because he feels that they are his enemy, because these very commanders and officers belong to the class that exploits him in the workshops, factories, and fields.

An example of this is the coup of December 2 of last year. During this coup, our soldier discovered that fighting for his commanders did nothing but improve their lot, while he himself remained a slave. So while everything went well for the commanders, who enjoyed the whole thing, the soldier was not even paid; while the cadets got promotions, the slave was dying of hunger.

All of this is to make you understand, comrade soldier, that your interests are the same as those of the working classes that your commanders and officers are forcing you to kill when they are struggling in defense of their rights, like better wages, shorter hours, and lower rents. We must fight for the same reason the rich refuse to pay you: because of the crisis that the rich are throwing on our backs and yours, while they live like princes with their grand banquets and parties.

Now more than ever, your duty as a proletarian, your duty as someone exploited like a worker, peasant, or soldier, is to organize yourself. You have a weapon in your hand that will let you effectively help your class, which, led by the Communist Party, will take power to end the exploitation of man by man.

Don't shoot a single bullet at your own comrades from the fields and workshops. Do not obey your commanders and officers when they order you to stain your hands with the blood of the oppressed, since you, like them, are a victim of native capital and of imperialism. Salute the flag of the revolution and love it, because it will bring you the freedom that your commanders and officers and the government of the rich have denied you for so long.

Long live the Communist Party, which will bring the workers, peasants, and soldiers to power! Long live the Red Army, in which the soldier will have human rights and will not be a slave like in the army of the rich!

COMMUNICATION FROM MILITANTS TO THE PARTY CENTRAL COMMITTEE IN THE DAYS BEFORE THE INSURRECTION, AND A REPORT TO THE REVOLUTIONARY MILITARY COMMITTEE OF SAN SALVADOR

Comrade Commander:

I would like to discuss the following points in a broad and comprehensive manner so we can create an effective movement and real results: 1) What points must be secured to advance the struggle? This is of vital importance, because we must have a definite strategy. 2) What material means can we count on and where will our provisioning sites be, or don't we have any? 3) How are the different sectors organized and who is commanding them, so we can be sure to coordinate our activities? 4) Where will the different sectors concentrate at the start of the action? 5) The most rapid means of communication must be used at the necessary moment. 6) What political measures should be taken with the inhabitants of the places that we take? This is also of vital importance. 7) Who will lead the purely military activity? 8) The exact hour when we all must be at our posts.

Greetings,

(signed) Magón

RED COMMANDER'S CREDENTIALS

Communist Party of El Salvador

Section of the Communist International

Central Committee

This Central Committee hereby names COMRADE *Inocente Rivas Hidalgo* as RED COMMANDER OF THE RED ARMY FORCES, which will operate in the . . . zone and in taking the city of San Salvador. The forward march of the revolutionary struggle is his absolute responsibility until the final victory over the exploiting class.

Given at the General Quarters of the Red Army of El Salvador, the 16th day of January 1932.

For the merciless destruction of the native bourgeoisie and imperialism.

For the Central Committee,

Octavio Rodríguez

Interim General Secretary

[In the lower left-hand corner is a seal with a hammer and sickle and a five-pointed star, surrounded by the words (with two spelling errors): COMMUNIST PARTY/C.C. SEC. SALVADOR III. According to the army and the police, more than 1,500 of these documents were confiscated.]

Manifesto of the Communist Party of El Salvador to the Soldiers of the Army

San Salvador, January 20, 1932
Comrades:

The Central Committee of the Communist Party addresses you at this moment, when the working classes of the republic are beginning the armed struggle for the conquest of power. They will use this power to liberate themselves and you from the yoke of capital and the large landowners, who have condemned to hunger so many families of workers in the factories, workshops, railroads, plantations, ranches, and other capitalist enterprises, with salaries so low they do not remedy the misery of all of us who produce their wealth.

You know of the massacres committed by the governments of Romero Bosque, Araujo, and Martínez (on the orders of the rich and the imperialists) against the workers of Santa Tecla, Sansonate, and Zaragoza, and most recently, on the fifth of this month, in the canton of Santa Rita in Atiquizaya. You also know of the strikes that we workers have declared to force the rich to increase our pay, since we cannot live with the same miserly wages we have always earned. The rich and their government do not want us, the organized workers, to demand our rights. This is why they have killed and are still killing us, and have imprisoned and are still imprisoning hundreds of workers, whom they have sentenced to build the Cojutepeque highway, even though these strikes have been carried out in a highly organized manner.

This Central Committee has led the workers in the municipal and parliamentary elections. Everyone has seen that the Communist Party is the largest party in all the cities and towns, having obtained the majority of the votes, as even the newspapers of the rich have noted. But despite this majority, the Martínez government, which is the creature of the rich, has not allowed us, the workers, to take our posts in the city halls or our seats in the National Assembly.

The rich and the government understand that workers in these posts would have favored our class, the poor, which has lived under the yoke of slavery its whole life.

For these reasons, the Central Committee of the Communist Party has armed itself to unite all working men and women and all peasant men and women to conquer power and establish a workers', peasants', and soldiers' government. Councils in which the workers, peasants, and soldiers will be represented will have the power to pitilessly crush the rich and the bourgeoisie in general by giving land to the peasants and soldiers and protecting the poor peasants with their small piece of land (since our struggle is against the really rich with their giant plantations and ranches, and not against those who barely have a tiny plot of land on which to be buried).

The armed rising of the worker and peasant masses, led by this Central Committee, must receive all the help, all the support that you, comrade soldiers, are able to give as our brothers in the struggle to the death against the rich exploiters. They are the ones who have condemned you to the strict discipline of the barracks, who don't pay you, and use you only to oppress the very class of the poor to which you also belong.

As the armed struggle begins, as the great masses of workers arise to the cry of the revolution, you should select delegates to receive general instructions from the Central Committee.

You should elect Soldiers' Committees among yourselves and name a soldier as Red Commander to lead you in this rising along with the Central Committee. You should not take a single shot at us. Long live the Red Army! Long live the Central Committee of the party at the head of the proletarian revolution! Down with the commanders and the officers!

Manifesto of the Central Committee of the Communist Party to the Working Classes of the Republic: Workers, Peasants, and Soldiers

Comrades:

The Communist Party is leading the proletariat toward the final victory, which will only be won when hunger, unemployment, and all other forms of slavery to which we, the workers, are condemned by the rich and the imperialists have been ended. We have carried out a fierce struggle on behalf of the workers against our rulers and the big landowners. At first, the rich and their government tried to discredit us by saying that the Communist Party was a bunch of thieves. We workers are thieves—according to those who steal our labor and pay us a miserable wage, according to those who kill us slowly, who condemn us to live in filthy quarters, without water, without electricity, or in stinking barracks, or to work day and night in the fields in the sun and rain. We are called thieves for demanding the wages due us, shorter hours, and lower rents, which are now so high that the rich keep nearly the whole harvest and steal our labor.

To these lies they add murder, beatings, jail, and exile for the fighting comrades of our class. We have witnessed the massacres of working men and women, and even children and older workers, in Santa Tecla, Sansonate, and Zaragoza, and most recently in Ahuachapán. According to the rich, we workers have no rights at all—not even to speak. Our newspapers have been outlawed, our letters opened and stolen. Although the Communist Party is the largest and most disciplined party, during our struggle to elect mayors and deputies of our class, the government and the rich shamelessly demonstrated that as long as their class is not removed from power by our own action, we will remain its slaves. In Ahuachapán, after not allowing our comrades to vote, the National Guard brutalized us by order of the rich. Our comrades in Ahuachapán are now valiantly defending themselves from these assassins with arms in hand.

Under these circumstances, the Central Committee of the Communist Party, which represents the opinions of all the working men and women of the republic and which can count on the moral and material support of all the workers of the world, under the direction of the Communist International,

ORDERS:

The arming of all the workers and peasants and the establishment of the General Headquarters of the Red Army of El Salvador.

The general insurrection of working men and women until the establishment of a workers', peasants', and soldiers' government.

Comrade workers: Arm yourselves and defend the Proletarian Revolution! Comrade railworkers: Take the railroads and put them at the service of the revolution!

Comrade peasants: Take land from the large plantations and farms, protect those who do have a small plot of land, and defend your revolutionary conquests with your weapons, with no mercy for the rich!

Comrade soldiers: Don't take a single shot at the revolutionary workers and peasants! Kill your commanders and officers! Place yourselves under the orders of the soldier comrades who have been named Red Commanders by this Central Committee!

Comrades: Form workers', peasants', and soldiers' councils!

All power to the workers', peasants', and soldiers' councils!

San Salvador, January 21, 1932,
at the General Headquarters of the
Red Army of El Salvador,
Central Committee

__6__

The 1935 Insurrection
in Brazil

PROGRAM OF THE POPULAR NATIONAL REVOLUTIONARY GOVERNMENT*

This text is from the period preceding the Communist Party-inspired Brazilian military insurrection of 1935, an event that constituted a transition between the tactics of the Third Period and the era of the popular front.

The Program of the Popular Revolutionary Government is a document of the National Liberation Alliance (ANL), a political-military coalition between the Brazilian Communist Party and the left wing of the *tenentista* movement, which led the uprising of November 1935. Its programmatic orientation was relatively moderate and did not challenge the existence of capitalist rule in Brazil.

With the main objective of eliminating misunderstandings, as well as responding to the questions of many comrades in the alliance, we will move on to give some concrete information on the character of the Popular Revolutionary Government, for whose establishment we are struggling as liberators of Brazil and as true democrats—that is, as active members of the National Liberation Alliance.

1. All those who claim our organization is a simple front for the Communist Party are slandering the ANL and obviously carrying out the work of police provocateurs. The ANL is a broad, national, united front of all those Brazilians who wish to struggle for national independence against foreign imperialism that enslaves us, and against fascism, which in a country like ours is the instrument of the most heinous terror in the service of imperialism, which is incapable of maintaining its domination by the old methods employed until the present.

Likewise, they understand nothing of our intentions as liberators of

*"Programa do Governo Popular Nacional Revolucionario," in Helio Silva, *1935: A revolta vermelha* (Rio de Janeiro: Ed. Civilização Brasileira, 1969), pp. 443–447.

52

Brazil, or are simply provocateurs in the service of our adversaries, who pretend to confuse the National Popular Revolutionary Government, for which the ANL is fighting, with a soviet government—the democratic dictatorship of the workers, peasants, soldiers, and sailors.

Under current conditions in Brazil, which faces the threat of the most terrible fascism and the complete imperialist colonization of our nation (which continues to be cynically sold out by the government of national betrayal of Getulio and his most faithful lackeys in the states), we members of the ANL proclaim the necessity of a government that truly grows out of the people in arms (a people, meaning the totality of the population of a country, excluding only imperialist agents and the insignificant minority that follow them). This government will not only be a government of workers and peasants, but a government in which all social layers and all important, weighty currents of public opinion are represented. It will be a Popular Government in the strict meaning of the word, since it will be supported by the large popular organizations, such as the unions, peasant organizations, cultural organizations, the armed forces, the democratic political parties, etc. It will have men of real political prestige at its head, men in each locale who truly represent the people or a local population. At the head of such a government, as the uncontested leader with the greatest popular prestige in the whole nation, no one could be found to substitute for Luis Carlos Prestes. For the great majority of the nation, the name Prestes represents a guarantee that such a government would truly and effectively struggle to carry out the program of the ANL. It is the guarantee that such a government will not follow the path of previous governments, the path beaten by Vargas, the path of the complete abandonment of the promises of 1930 and of open and cynical national treason.

Here we should make an opportune clarification. With the impressive growth in the popular prestige of the ANL, many elements now claim to agree with its program, and even with the establishment of a popular government in Brazil, but without Prestes, or at least without Prestes being a central and decisive figure in such a government. It might appear at first glance that this is an exclusively personal matter and nothing more. But this is not true. All supporters of the alliance should understand the obviously counterrevolutionary basis of such a tendency. To remove the popular, national, and revolutionary figure of Prestes from the leadership of the government represents a conspiracy by those who fear the application of the program of the ANL, the struggle against imperialism, and the satisfaction of popular interests. It is a desire to retrace the path of 1930: the path of betrayal, the path of the progressive liquidation of the real revolutionaries. This is why we need to show the people that the defenders of this point of view are already organizing the counterrevolution inside our ranks.

2. The Popular Government, as the representative of the interests of the great mass of the population, will only be able to exercise power under the direct control of the people, practicing democracy in its highest sense through the complete freedom of thought, freedom of speech, freedom of the press, and freedom of organization by religion, race, color, etc. The Popular Government will only be able to exist by practically fulfilling all measures demanded by the people through their diverse organizations. The Popular Government will be our country's first practical democracy and will really be the government of the people, since the people will intervene directly in such a government with their suggestions and demands, while participating practically in carrying out measures that concern them. At the head of such a government will have to be men of real popular prestige, men who truly interpret the will of the great popular majority. In these conditions, all social layers will have to be represented in the Popular Government, including the national bourgeoisie, through its truly anti-imperialist and antifascist elements. The Popular Government, a government arising from the people in arms, will not only be a government of workers and peasants, but will be the government of a broad united front of all Brazilian anti-imperialists.

3. But at the same time, this government will be a National Revolutionary Government, because this government will be profoundly revolutionary, confronting imperialism and its agents, and not recognizing the sanctity of either profits or treaties or anything that really signifies the selling of Brazil to foreign capitalists. In confronting imperialism, the National Revolutionary Government will be truly national and revolutionary—profoundly, radically, and energetically revolutionary. In this sense, it is necessary to emphasize that only this government is capable of energetically confronting foreign domination. With the support of the whole people, with power wielded by leaders of great popular prestige, under the direct influence of the large mass organizations and supported by the armed forces of the whole country, it will be the first government in our nation capable of exercising the harshest dictatorship against the imperialists and their agents within the context of popular democracy. Democracy, yes, but for the people, for the Brazilians, and for all those who work honestly without exploiting Brazil; but the harshest, most energetic, and most terrible dictatorship against foreign feudalism and its agents in Brazil, the Brazilians who sell their country to imperialism. Granting freedom to the agents of imperialism would mean denying the national revolutionary content of such a government, and would mean suicide for this liberating revolution.

4. The Popular Revolutionary Government will not liquidate the private ownership of the means of production, nor take the factories and national

enterprises under its control. This government, initiating the free development of the forces of production, does not intend the socialization of
industrial and agricultural production. In Brazil's current situation, it will
only be possible to liquidate feudalism and slavery and give guarantees for
the free development of the country's forces of production by establishing a
real democracy. But since the strategic heights of the economy are now in
the hands of imperialism, the National Revolutionary Government, by
appropriating and nationalizing such enterprises in a revolutionary manner,
will from the start hold large sectors of production in its hands. This will
incontestably constitute a strong factor on the side of the free development
of the nation's productive forces, which will guarantee the further progressive development of Brazil.

5. The Popular Government will immediately take all the necessary
measures to guarantee the execution of a minimum of social legislation,
which will include essential measures, such as, among others: a) an eight-
hour day, with fewer hours for minors; b) equal pay for equal work; c) a
minimum wage in accordance with the cost of living in each locality, as
determined by the workers' organizations; d) mandatory, paid time off
every week; e) yearly paid vacations; f) hygienic conditions in the workplace; g) two months of paid leave before and after childbirth; h) workers'
committees to oversee this legislation in each workplace; i) social security
for the unemployed; j) pension and retirement accounts, etc.

The Popular National Revolutionary Government will immediately take
all measures necessary to lower the cost of living by decreasing and even
ending taxes on petty trade, such as the production tax, consumption taxes
on primary necessities, lowering railway and maritime tariffs on widely
used articles, etc. The Popular Government will take all necessary measures
to guarantee popular education, wipe out illiteracy, and raise the intellectual
level of the masses, etc., by making education mandatory. The Popular
Government will take all measures necessary to guarantee the people's
health, increasing the number of hospitals and clinics, distributing medica-
tion to the people without charge, and bettering the living conditions of the
great urban masses by appropriating buildings which today belong to
imperialism and its national lackeys.

The Popular Government, by nationalizing the banks, will guarantee
existing deposits that belong to all those who are not national traitors as
direct and indirect agents of imperialism.

The Popular Government will use a tax on the profits of the large foreign
and national companies and the large national capitalists as its fundamental
source of revenue to pay public expenses, eliminating all taxes today paid by
the people.

6. In the countryside, the Popular Government will be led by men with

the confidence of the great working masses, and will naturally defend the interests of these masses against the large feudal landholders, the landed gentry who exploit nearly the whole of our peasant population under the harshest conditions of feudalism and slavery, and who are directly linked to the imperialist exploiters. The Popular Government will obviously end the medieval submission of the peasants to the landowner, as well as abolish all their feudal dues. Guaranteeing the possession of the land to those who work it and guaranteeing land to all those who wish to work, the Popular Government will demand that capitalist proprietors in the countryside fulfill the social legislation established by the revolution. The Popular Government, though, will not expropriate those who do not use feudal means of exploitation. By guaranteeing the freedom of commerce, lowering tariffs, ending all taxes on production, etc., it will allow an enormous and unheard of expansion of the national internal market.

7. The Popular National Revolutionary Government, respecting the rights of the officers of the army and the armed forces of the whole country (including the generals), will only take rigorous measures against traitors to Brazil, against officers who send their troops against the people or try to organize the counterrevolution on behalf of imperialism. The Popular Government will have no mercy for these elements. But it will unify the rest of the armed forces, including its experienced cadre, with the workers and peasants in arms, and will create a great national revolutionary army, an army capable of victoriously struggling against an imperialist invasion and the counterrevolution, an army based on voluntary discipline whose leaders will be men with the confidence of their soldiers.

8. One more word on the form to be taken by the Popular Government. Nothing will give form to the fruits of the revolution other than its very existence, its very revolutionary reality. But if we must deal with such a question, we can say that nothing indicates it is impossible for the Popular Government to take the same outward form as governments that have ruled until now: a central government led by a president, with a cabinet of ministers (so that the most characteristic popular anti-imperialist currents may be represented), and similar governments in the states and municipalities, led by individuals with popular prestige in these states or municipalities.

ALL POWER TO THE NATIONAL LIBERATION ALLIANCE!*

Luis Carlos Prestes

This speech by Luis Carlos Prestes—the legendary leader of the revolutionary Prestes Column of 1924–27 and General Secretary of the Brazilian Communist Party—given shortly after his return to Brazil (after several years in the Soviet Union), was the Communist Party's "declaration of war" against the government of Getulio Vargas, which had been installed by the "Revolution of 1930." Prestes presents himself as the continuator of the revolutionary-democratic traditions of *tenentismo* (the lieutenants' movement of the twenties) that had been abandoned and betrayed by Vargas and the former *tenentes* who had rallied to his support. The speech had a tremendous impact, and the Vargas government took it as a pretext to outlaw the ALN.

The cannons of Copacabana thunder! The heroic comrades of Siqueira Campos fall! The soldiers of São Paulo rise with Joaquim Tavora, and for twenty days the workers' quarter is barbarically bombarded by generals in the service of Bernardes! Then, the retreat. The heroic struggle in the bushes of the Paraná! The risings in Rio Grande do Sul! The column marches through the country's whole interior, awakening the population of the most remote backlands to the struggle against the tyrants who sell Brazil to foreign capital. What energy, what bravery! Thirteen years of bloody struggles, of unending combat, of successive victories, the darkest treachery, of illusions burst like soap bubbles in a blast of reality! But the struggles continue, because victory has not yet been achieved and the heroic fighter cannot stop halfway; because the goal is the national liberation of Brazil, its national unification, its progress, and the well-being and freedom of its people. The persistent and heroic fighter is this very people, who from the Amazonas to Rio Grande do Sul, from the coast to the Bolivian frontier, are united—but united by suffering, by misery, by the humiliation in which they vegetate, and the impossibility of national unity under the semicolonial and semi-feudal conditions of present-day Brazil. We, supporters of the alliance from all of Brazil, once again raise high the banner of the "Eighteen of the Fort," the banner of Catanduvas, the banner that waved in the gates of Teresina in 1925, after crossing all of Brazil from south to north! Today, the National Liberation Alliance is made up of millions who are continuing these struggles. The National Liberation Alliance is today the continuator of the battles for Brazil's liberation from the imperialist yoke begun by Siqueira Campos, Joaquim Tavora, Portela, Benevolo, Cleto

---

*Abguar Bastos, *Prestes e a revolução social* (Rio de Janeiro: Ed. Caláino, 1946), pp. 304–305, 309–311, 313–315.

Campelo, Jansen de Melo, Djalma Dutra, and thousands of soldiers, workers, and peasants throughout Brazil. We are the heirs of our people's best revolutionary traditions, and we march forward into struggle and toward victory with the memory of our heroes!

The contest has begun. The two camps are more clearly defined before the masses. On one side stand those who wish to consolidate the most brutal fascist dictatorship in Brazil, liquidate the people's remaining democratic rights, and complete the sale of our nation into the servitude of foreign capital. On this side is Integralism, the terrorist shock troops of reaction. On the other side stand all those in the ranks of the National Liberation Alliance, those who wish to defend all the national liberties of Brazil and want land, bread, and freedom for its people. This is not a struggle between two "extremisms," as the hypocritical defenders of a "liberal democracy" that has never existed (and which people know only through the bloody dictatorships of Epitacio, Bernardes, Washington Luís, and Getulio Vargas) would like us to believe. The struggle has begun between the liberators of Brazil, on one side, and traitors in the service of imperialism, on the other.

This moment demands of all honest men a clear and definite position: for or against fascism, for or against imperialism. There is no possible or justifiable middle way. This is why the National Liberation Alliance is a vast and broadly organized national united front. The danger that threatens us, the danger growing daily, now obliges us to give the greatest importance to creating the broadest bloc of all classes oppressed by imperialism and feudalism, and therefore by the threat of fascism. This is our decisive task at the present stage of the Brazilian Revolution. The united front does not oblige its members to renounce the defense of their own ideas and opinions. No, this would sow confusion among the revolutionary masses and weaken their revolutionary strength. Recognizing all the political, religious, philosophical, and ideological differences we might have, we know as revolutionaries that the present moment demands, above all, the concentration of all our forces for the struggle against imperialism, feudalism, and fascism. All individuals, groups, currents, organizations, and even political parties, whatever their program, ought to join the National Liberation Alliance—the only condition being that they really wish to struggle against the implantation of fascism in Brazil, against imperialism and feudalism, and for democratic rights. And with our iron will to carry out this work, we must confront all those currents or individuals who, for whatever reason, want to obstruct this national, revolutionary united front. All the individuals, groups, associations, and political parties that participate in the alliance ought to obstruct these efforts with all their energy and implacably denounce these culprits as traitors to Brazil and its people.

The forces of the National Liberation Alliance are already large, but they can and ought to be larger, embracing millions, because its program speaks to all those who work, all those who suffer from imperialist and feudal domination, especially the proletariat and the great masses of the country-side. Proletarian unity, which is invincible, which overcomes all difficulties posed by reaction, is one of the great strengths of the revolution. Each recent strike raises the capacity for struggle of Brazil's heroic proletariat and increases the confidence this class inspires, as the leader of the revolution, among all Brazil's revolutionaries. Peasant struggles, while still spontaneous and lacking a clear orientation, are a good indication of the hatred and concentrated energy that have developed, through centuries of suffering and misery, among the millions who hope for better days. But the soldiers and sailors of Brazil will be with the revolution, and therefore with the alliance. The best officers of the country's armed forces, those who are incapable of leading their soldiers against the liberators of Brazil, will be with the alliance, as will many of those who have already shown in previous struggles that they will be with the people against imperialism, feudalism, and fascism.

As in the era before 1888, the military men of Brazil will not agree to play the role of "slave hunters" for imperialism and its local lackeys. All the heroic fighters of the armed movements that have shaken the country since 1922 will be with the alliance. The heroic youth of São Paulo who decided to defend democracy and liberty in the trenches against the Vargas dictatorship in 1932, youth whose leaders now consort with the government, will join the alliance. The working-class youth and students of the whole country, who are struggling for a better future and are prepared to give all their enthusiasm and energy to the struggle for Brazil's national liberty (where they will stand in the vanguard), will be with the alliance. The women of Brazil—workers and intellectuals, housewives, mothers, sisters, girlfriends, and daughters of workers—will be with the alliance. Despite all the lies and slanders of the mercenary press, they will join the alliance because they understand and feel that only the alliance can give bread to their children and end the brutal exploitation under which they live. Religious women, like all religious people, whether Catholic or Protestant, Animists or Positivists, above all want freedom to practice their religion, and the alliance defends this freedom. Even Brazilian priests, the poorest, those who, having joined the Church, will not sell out their homeland to imperialism or neglect their duty to the poor, will be with the alliance. Naturally, the heads of the Church, the rich and well-fed cardinals and archbishops, as members of the ruling class and lackeys of imperialism, are against the alliance. In the past, Frei Caneca, Father Miguelinho, and many others have struggled alongside the people for the independence of Brazil, against the will of the bishops and archbishops, who ordered them to murder. The artisans, small merchants, and businessmen, squeezed by taxes and the imperialist monopolies, on the one hand, and the greater and greater misery of the popular masses, on the other, earn less each day; to the degree they grow impoverished, they become simply poorly paid intermediaries in the exploitation of the people by imperialism and indirect taxation. They will be with the alliance. The people of color of Brazil, the heirs of the glorious traditions of Palmares, will be with the alliance, because only the broad democracy of a truly popular government can forever end privileges of race, color, and nationality and give Black people in Brazil the widest panorama of freedom and equality, free of any reactionary prejudice, for which they have been bravely struggling for more than three centuries.

In the people's eyes, there is no pretext for struggling against the united liberation front. This is why the ranks of the National Liberation Alliance are open to all those who want to fight for an anti-imperialist, anti-feudal, and antifascist program that can only be carried out by a popular revolutionary government. . . .

The National Liberation Alliance already reflects the tremendous revolutionary strength of our people and their immeasurable willingness to sacrifice in the struggle for the national liberation of Brazil. The recent events in Petropolis and the vigor with which the people of São Paulo forced the Integralista leaders into a cowardly retreat speak well of the potential for a national united front.

We are therefore marching quickly toward the establishment of a popular revolutionary government throughout Brazil, a government of the people against imperialism and feudalism, which will practically demonstrate to the broad working masses of the country what democracy and freedom really are. The popular government, carrying out the program of the alliance, will unify Brazil and save the lives of millions of workers threatened by hunger, tormented by sickness, and exploited by imperialism and the large landowners. The distribution of the lands of the giant plantations will increase internal commercial activity and open the way to a more rapid industrialization of the country, independent of any imperialist domination. The popular government will open the perspective of a new life for Brazil's youth, guaranteeing work, health, and education.

The strength of the masses upon which such a government will depend is the best guarantee for the defense of the country against imperialism and counterrevolution. The people's army, the national revolutionary army, will be able to defend the integrity of the nation against an imperialist invasion and at the same time liquidate all counterrevolutionary forces.

But power can only fall into the hands of the people after the most difficult struggles. The main opponent of the alliance is not only the corrupt

Vargas government, but, most importantly, the imperialists, those who serve them, and those who are trying with all the means at their disposal to stop the establishment of a popular revolutionary government in Brazil. The howls of the mercenary press, sold to the imperialists, are the most obvious signs of the resistance being prepared by reaction. The working masses and all members of the alliance must be attentive and vigilant. This is war, and everyone must occupy their posts. The masses themselves should take the initiative to defend their own meetings, guarantee the safety of their leaders, and prepare actively for the attack. The idea of an offensive is maturing in the consciousness of the masses. Its leaders must organize and guide it.

Working people of all Brazil! On guard in the defense of your own interests. Come take your place with the liberators of Brazil!

Soldiers of Brazil! Attention! The tyrants want to use you against your brothers in the struggle for the liberation of Brazil!

Soldiers of Rio Grande do Sul, heroic heirs of the best revolutionary traditions of the land of the gauchos! Prepare yourselves, organize yourselves. This is the only way you can turn the weapons with which they hope to eternally maintain the shame of the present against the tyrants who oppress you!

Honest democrats of Brazil! Heroic people of Minas Gerais, the traditional home of great struggles for democracy! Only with the National Liberation Alliance can you continue the struggles begun by your ancestors!

Northerners and Northeasterners! Hold fast to your great national energy! Organize yourselves to defend a Brazil that is your own!

Peasants of all Brazil, fighters of the Northeast backlands! The popular revolutionary government will guarantee you the lands you seize! Prepare to defend them!

Brazilians!

All you throughout the country who are united by suffering and humiliation! Express your hatred of your rulers and make this an irresistible and invincible force for the Brazilian Revolution! You have nothing to lose, and the immense riches of all Brazil to gain. Tear the claws of imperialism and its lackeys from Brazil! All to the struggle for the national liberation of Brazil!

Down with fascism!

Down with the abominable Vargas government!

For a popular national revolutionary government!

All power to the National Liberation Alliance!

Luis Carlos Prestes
July 5, 1935

PART III
Stalinist Hegemony

7

The Popular Front in Latin America

THE POPULAR FRONT IN CHILE*
Carlos Contrera Labarca

This article by the General Secretary of the Chilean CP dates from 1938, the early period of the popular front, and furnishes information on the discussions inside the workers' movement during the creation of the front, particularly on the subject of a common presidential candidate. Contrera Labarca harshly polemicizes against the Trotskyists, who were quite influential inside the Socialist Party and opposed opening the popular front to the right. It is also interesting to note the extremely moderate tone in relation to North American capital, which should be understood in the context of the international conjuncture at the moment (attempts at a U.S.–U.S.S.R. accommodation).

STRENGTHENING AND BROADENING THE PEOPLE'S FRONT

But the unity of the working class is not enough, either. Allies must be secured for it.

The People's Front constitutes the structure of a broad alliance of classes which has been proved effective by reality. The Trotskyite slanders that this alliance is a betrayal of the revolution have demonstrated once again Trotskyism's role as servant of fascism.

Who can doubt that the existence and struggle of the People's Front prevent reaction from destroying all the democratic liberties? It is evident that the government has been able to adopt various reactionary measures and that it will be able to do so as long as it remains in power.

Would it have been possible to prevent a great many of these measures? Yes, if the People's Front had been strengthened and widened as the Communist Party has urged insistently.

---

*Carlos Contrera Labarca, "The People of Chile Unite to Save Democracy," *The Communist* (New York) n. 11, November 1938, pp. 1037–1040, 1041–1042.

64

The sectarian conceptions, the maneuvers of the Trotskyites to undermine the People's Front, and their influence on certain sections of the Socialist Party, constitute a serious obstacle to the accomplishment of these tasks.

The extreme and alarming dilatoriness of the work in rural districts, which is one of the most notorious weaknesses of the People's Front, shows a typically Trotskyite influence.

The agrarian program, recently elaborated, contemplates the satisfaction of the demands not only of the poorest, but of the broadest sections of the agricultural population, and aims to rehabilitate agriculture and bring prosperity and well-being to the farms. It tries to combat, above all, the great feudal landlords, to isolate them and prevent them from utilizing the peons, tenants, semi-proprietors, etc., against the popular movement. It seeks at the same time to link up the interests of the farmers with the purchasing power of the working class and of the toiling masses.

The obstinate resistance to carrying on a resolute work of winning over the toiling masses of Catholics is likewise of Trotskyite origin. While the Communist Party works with the slogan, "Catholic workers, we offer the out-stretched hand," the Trotskyites find space in the Socialist press to pile up the counterrevolutionary arguments intended to impede the expansion of the antifascist front.

Because of the semi-colonial character of the country, with its economy crushed and deformed by imperialism, its national industry carried on under very difficult and precarious conditions, there are certain sections of the Chilean bourgeoisie which can and must be won for national liberation by a progressive and democratic policy.

Important sections of the political parties of the right have had moments of vacillation, offering opportunities, which should have been seized, of inviting them to come into the popular movement, with assurances of the satisfaction of their desires for order, progress, and democracy.

The armed forces, by means of an intense mass campaign, must be attracted into the sphere of influence of the antifascist movement, not for the purposes of conspiracy, but so that they may perform their duty of guaranteeing the validity of the constitutional rights.

The possibilities of extending the bounds of the People's Front are still immense. Yet the Trotskyites say, "All who ought to be in the People's Front are already there." This attitude of arrogance and self-sufficiency and overestimation of the capacity of the People's Front must be opposed with a realistic and active policy which will lead to these objectives:

1. Unite 95 percent of the population around the democratic program of the People's Front and the candidacy of Señor Aguirre, utilizing every little

possibility of strengthening and broadening the struggle against Gustavo Ross and fascism and eliminating any motive of discord or division which may separate allies;

2. Divide and disperse the enemy, utilizing without fear the contradictions and difficulties which rage in their midst, until the fifty families of the oligarchy are completely isolated;

3. Discipline the forces of the people, accumulating their energies for joint attacks on the enemy, avoiding premature and divided efforts and acts of impatience and provocation.

To the Communist Party belongs the lofty mission of making the whole country understand the tremendous gravity of the situation, the real magnitude of the dangers lying in wait, and the road which must be followed, warning the people that there is yet time to save democracy and the very life of the republic, but that tomorrow may be too late.

One Candidate of the Antifascist People

To choose the candidate for the presidency of the republic the Communist Party proposed the only democratic procedure: a convention broader than the People's Front, of all the democratic and antifascist forces. The Radicals proposed that they be recognized at once as having the "best right" to provide the candidate from their ranks and that the People's Front should select the candidate from a list of those names; the Socialists proposed a plebiscite. After a long contest the idea of the convention prevailed; but it was not to be so broad as we wished.

In the "Convention of the Left" two candidates were presented: Señor Pedro Aguirre, by the Radical Party, and Señor Marmaduque Grove, by the Socialist Party. They locked horns in a dangerously intransigent battle; but neither of them could be elected, in conformity with the pact, without the agreement of the other. Both solicited the support of the Communist Party. In view of the many ballots that were taken without result, and the danger of breaking up the convention and destroying the People's Front, the Communist Party publicly addressed both parties, urging them, in the name of the people, to lay aside their partisan and selfish interests and seek jointly the one candidate who would unite all the democratic forces of the country.

The situation took on extraordinary complications as the anti-People's Front elements actually made a united front against the convention. The right of the Radical Party speculated with the "danger" of Communist-Socialist alliance in favor of candidate Grove, defrauding the Radical Party of what it expected as the majority party. The Socialist Party thought itself entitled to the candidacy because of the great popularity of its leader, Grove;

but, unfortunately, it launched the slogan "Grove to power," under the influence of the Trotskyites. This false slogan aroused grave misgivings, created dangers by its leftist character, did not unite the People's Front, and tended to the isolation of the proletariat.

It then became necessary for the Communist Party to make them hear the voice of the people demanding antifascist unity and one democratic candidate. The Tenth National Congress of our party meeting at this time pointed out the necessity of taking into consideration:

1. The real level of the Chilean revolutionary movement, that is, making an exact appraisal of the correlation of the class forces in the present stage of the revolution;
2. The degree of political experience and revolutionary education of our working class and of the people;
3. The vital necessity of maintaining and developing the combative unity of all the democratic and antifascist forces around the proletariat, that is, of translating into acts the slogan: "All Chile against Ross and fascism!"

Fortunately, under the tremendous pressure of the people, the convention came to an agreement, on the basis of the withdrawal of the Grove candidacy and the unanimous election of Señor Aguirre.

Señor Aguirre expressed the applause and jubilation of the country when, a few hours after his election, he attended the closing session of the Tenth Congress of the Communist Party and extolled the unshakable and consistent unity policy of our party.

FOREIGN ALLIES

We have spoken of the necessity of winning allies within the country for the victory of the people over fascism. But this is not enough. It is necessary to win allies on the international scale as the patriots of 1810 conceived it. It must be recalled that notable foreigners then contributed their knowledge and gave their blood and their lives for the cause of our emancipation.

The People's Front establishes the necessity that the working class of the world and the other democratic forces lend it due collaboration and aid. The help of the proletariat and the people of North America is particularly valuable.

The Trotskyites are trying to obscure this grave problem. They utilize the legitimate popular feeling of hatred toward imperialism to concentrate the attack on Yankee and English imperialism, which has the greatest volume of investments in Chile. It is a way of helping the penetration and domination of the fascist governments.

It is a political monstrosity to identify the people of the United States with the Yankee imperialist enterprises which oppress our country. Wall Street is the ruthless enemy of democracy, not only in Chile, but in the

United States as well. The enemies of the North American people are the enemies of the Chilean people.

The realignment of the democratic and progressive forces in the United States favors notably the creation of correct relations between our countries.

GOOD NEIGHBOR POLICY

On the basis of the good neighbor policy and its consistent application, relations can and must be established with the Roosevelt administration, which is attacked so violently by Wall Street. The good neighbor policy, according to a strictly realistic criterion, is a useful instrument for the purposes of the struggle for peace and democracy.

As for foreign capital invested in Chile, the people have always respected and always will respect the provisions of the political Constitution of the state which guarantee the property of foreign capital and, in general, of all capital, requiring at the same time that the capitalists, national and foreign, respect them on their side. The people have never ceased to recognize the need for the cooperation of foreign capital and are still disposed to solicit this cooperation in the future, if the national interest requires it. The riches of Chile form an integral and inseparable part of its right of existence as an independent and free nation and must be allocated to the service of maintaining and extending democracy and safeguarding peace among the people, on the basis of concerted action.

Consequently, the People's Front has the mission of defending, above all, the national sovereignty, applying the Chilean law to all equally, and enforcing the strict observance of the social legislation in all its integrity; it will not permit the existence of monopolies, concessions, or privileges, of any kind whatever, which can endanger the well-being and security of the county. It will consider an act of hostility to the national sovereignty any attempt of the foreign enterprises to intervene in domestic policy with the purpose of stimulating, directly or indirectly, the rebellion of the reactionary and fascist forces, whether by lending them economic or financial cooperation, by creating clandestine deposits of arms in its properties, or by utilizing the flags of foreign states to effect or facilitate contraband, espionage, or conspiracies.

Such are, therefore, the conditions for a "new deal," or for a people's treatment of the foreign capitalist enterprises, in accordance with which the government of Chile shall no longer be a vassal but a government of the people, by the people, for the people of Chile. Manifestly, Chile reserves the right to throw full light on the relations which have existed hitherto between the foreign capitalists and the Chilean governments and politicians.

A LEFT CRITIQUE OF THE CHILEAN POPULAR FRONT*

Humberto Mendoza

Humberto Mendoza (also known under the pseudonym Jorge Lavín) was one of the dissident Communist leaders who split from the Chilean CP in 1930 and affiliated with the International Left Opposition in 1933. Mendoza and most of the members of his organization, the Communist Left, decided to join the Socialist Party in 1937, becoming an important left wing of the party. The critique of the Chilean People's Front that Mendoza developed in his 1942 book *And Now?* (from which the following passages come) was inspired by European Trotskyism but attempted to come to grips with the specificity of phenomena in Chile.

The persistence of this problematic in the ideology of the Chilean Socialist Party can be seen in the 1972 republication of large portions of this work in a collection of party documents published by the socialist historian Julio César Jobet.

In Chile, under the current regime, the working classes have not taken power simply because there are Socialist Party ministers. In fact, what has happened is that the working classes are in danger of losing their party. The dialectic of the political process is slowly leading the Socialist Party to represent interests that are ever more foreign to the working class and closer to those of national and international capitalism.

In capitalist society, which is fundamentally based on the class struggle, democracy can only be a function of exploitation. We have seen that freedoms the Constitution claims to be inviolable are eliminated whenever it suits the ruling classes.

Workers, peasants, office employees, professionals, and small business-men all feel the weight of a regime of injustice, hunger, and unemployment. They see, feel, and suffer this reality. But if their consciousness of this exploitation moves them into action to destroy it, the full weight of "capitalist democracy" makes itself felt: clubs, bullets, jails, and mass arrests. Hunger confronts the unemployed and the exploited with the real meaning of capitalist democracy, or rather, the reality of capitalist dictatorship.

Why don't the workers strike and demonstrate to demand this "popular government" carry out its program? Are the working masses eating better than before? Are there more jobs, better salaries, and more rights than under previous governments? The most naive workers see they have won nothing, and in fact have lost a great deal. They have lost their freedom of action. Their heroic, red-letter days of struggle as an organized class are

---

*Humberto Mendoza, "El Frente Popular a la luz del socialismo revolucionario," 1942, in J.C. Jobet and A.C. Rojas, *Pensamiento político del PS* (Santiago: Ed. Quimantú, 1972), pp. 35–39, 42–44.

behind them. Today's ruling classes defeated the autocratic and feudal regime in a revolutionary manner and destroyed established political relations with blood and fire. Now these same classes think like kings and czars, who considered themselves rulers by divine right. They want to maintain power at any cost, and oppose society with the very resources that society has put at their disposal.

> And when the bourgeoisie now make their appeal to force in order to save the collapsing "economic order" from the final crash, by so doing they only show that they are caught in the same illusion as Herr Dühring: the illusion that "political conditions are the decisive cause of the economic order"; they show that they imagine, just as Herr Dühring does, that by making use of the "primitive phenomenon" [of] "direct political force," they can remodel those "facts of the second order," the economic order and its inevitable development; and that therefore the economic consequences of the steam engine and the modern machinery driven by it, of world trade and the banking and credit developments of the present day, can be blown out of existence with Krupp guns and Mauser rifles.

So says Engels in his famous work *Anti-Dühring*, written around 1877, when the working class had not forgotten the lessons of the Commune and the butchery by the Versailles troops in the streets of Paris.

We know that the capacity of resistance and the very breadth of democratic institutions in each country are in direct relation to its economic development. "Wherever the bourgeoisie occupies an important role in economic life, it also occupies it in the political sphere." In Chile, where the predominance of the bourgeoisie in the political arena is unquestionable and the prestige of democratic institutions still sufficient to wager on their solvency, the level of economic development is *not* of such a magnitude to guarantee its absolute predominance.

The petty bourgeoisie plays an important role in agriculture, commerce, the university professions, and the state and financial bureaucracy. It tends to play a role of the first magnitude in politics whenever a decrease in proletarian activity leaves room for the threat of a capitalist offensive to develop.

If the correlation between the economic base and the political superstructure is direct and well known, why does the bourgeoisie play the largest political role here in Chile, where there is no major industrial development? But this is not always the case. Whenever the Chilean bourgeoisie opens an offensive against institutions that it had previously used to exploit society, it does so knowing that these institutions no longer serve to defend this battle front against a working-class offensive. Its political incompetence had not yet allowed it to find the way to win the confidence of the petty bourgeoisie. But it is certain that the relative solidity of democratic institutions merits an ostensible and temporary respect on its part for the formal appearances of democracy.

Furthermore, this is the key to the politics of the Popular Fronts and all combinations that tend to hide or disguise economic contradictions between social classes.

But the process of decomposition of capitalist society continues apace, despite all the political temporizing by the working-class parties. And the danger is ever greater that the bourgeoisie will react against the proletariat, destroy its institutions, and install fascism.

The possessing classes decrease in size to the degree that capital is concentrated and centralized. Parallel to this centralization of wealth comes a centralization of power, decreasing the number of those who enjoy and exercise it. By the very dialectic of this process, the oppression of the working classes increases to unimagined levels. Violence, once a measure applied through the intermediary of forms and institutions created to camouflage its use, becomes the primary, open, and blatant method that the possessing classes brandish as the basis for the maintenance of their rule. The sharpening of the clashes between those who possess everything and those who possess little or nothing continues, gaining intensity and self-consciousness.

The social revolution becomes increasingly visible and essential to broader and broader sectors of the population.

And we cannot escape this conjuncture with good intentions or with bad and false politics. At this moment, we must live or we must die, and we will struggle to live.

The Socialist Party must once and for all make the proletariat and the laboring classes understand that "even the most democratic bourgeois republic is only an instrument for the oppression of the working class by the bourgeois class, the oppression of the proletarian masses by a handful of capitalists." The development of the productive forces shatters relations of production, and this unconscious process must acquire, through the intermediary of our party's activities, the conscious leadership necessary and indispensable for the victory of the socialist revolution. The new imperialist war is only the result of the immense power of the technology perfected by capitalism breaking through national boundaries and attempting to overcome this contradiction by raising them to the level of an international political struggle for the establishment of new relations of production.

The proletariat, supported by the masses of the countryside, in struggling for its rights and demands does nothing more than exercise the historic right that the bourgeoisie applied against the autocracy in 1789.

If the bourgeoisie made use of terror to annihilate the resistance of the defeated regime and to organize in turn the system that we know as capitalist democracy, there is no reason of any kind to forbid the proletariat from organizing its own dictatorship to exterminate the resistance of the bourgeoisie and organize proletarian democracy.

CUBA: THE POPULAR FRONT WITH BATISTA*

R.A. Martínez

There was no real popular front in Cuba, but rather an alliance between the Communist Party and Colonel Fulgencio Batista that lasted from 1939 to 1944, when the latter resigned the presidency. In 1943, the president of the CP, the writer Juan Marinello, was a minister without portfolio in the Batista government. The following article situates the continental political context in which this unique front was created—the pan-American alliance against the fascist threat, under the aegis of Roosevelt, Batista, Lombardo Toledano (General Secretary of the Confederation of Mexican Workers), and the Cuban Communist Party.

The former correspondent of *L'Unita* (the Italian CP daily newspaper) in Havana, Saverio Tutino, wrote the following on Batista's political profile in 1939: "For most Cubans, he personified the anti-nation; it was he who represented fascism, even if the exigencies of North American policy demanded he join the antifascist front on the international level. Batista had massacred workers and been responsible for the assassination of national heroes such as Antonio Guiteras."

THE LATIN AMERICAN SIGNIFICANCE OF THE CUBAN DEMOCRATIC UPSURGE

The growing and ever expanding democratic movement of Cuba is becoming one of the most important influences in the shaping of the democratic antifascist front in our hemisphere. In the measure that the democratic movement grows in Cuba, the foreign policy of its government, inspired by Colonel Fulgencio Batista, constitutional head of the Army, acquires greater antifascist content and Latin American scope. And in Cuba the democratic movement, without doubt, is continuing its impetuous growth.

The perspective foreseen by the Tenth Plenum of the Communist Party (July 1938) and by the Third Congress, held last January, has been further confirmed by recent developments: on the one hand, the people's movement has continued its growth and consolidation; Colonel Batista has become an integral part of the progressive forces. On the other hand, reaction and fascism are gathering their forces and planning desperate measures to overthrow Batista and crush the people's movement.

---

*R.A. Martínez, "The Latin American Significance of the Cuban Democratic Upsurge," *World News and Views* (London), v. 19, n. 18, April 1, 1939, pp. 367–368.

From January 23 to January 28, the congress for trade union unity was held. It was attended by 1,517 delegates representing over 800 unions and fraternal organizations. The Cuban Confederation of Workers that was created includes in its ranks every union in Cuba and has an affiliated membership of over 500,000 workers. Lazaro Peña, a Negro tobacco worker, one of the most beloved leaders of the Cuban working class, was elected General Secretary. The congress was also attended by an imposing delegation from the Mexican Confederation of Workers, headed by its Secretary, Vicente Lombardo Toledano, who made a historical speech exploding the fascist-Trotskyist theory of the non-existence of the fascist threat in Latin America, regarding it as a smoke screen for United States imperialists to carry on their imperialist policies. A fraternal delegate from the Committee for Industrial Organization also attended the congress.

The congress, besides dealing with all basic problems confronting the Cuban working class: the struggle for the application of existing social legislation, organizational problems, the position of the proletariat in relation to the incoming Constituent Assembly, the struggle against war and fascism, etc., paid special attention to the problems of the Cuban peasantry. A large number of fraternal delegates from peasant organizations attended the congress, and after reporting on their problems suggested that a National Peasant Bureau should be created for the purpose of "helping in the preparation of the Provincial Peasant Congress, that will lead to the National Peasant Congress." The Cuban peasantry supported by the powerful C.T.C. and the progressive movement in general will soon overcome its organizational backwardness.

The rulers of Cuba, and especially its outstanding figure, Colonel Batista, understand that the promotion of the well-being of the people and its maintenance, the defense of its democratic institutions, is intimately connected with the struggle against fascism, not in Cuba alone, but in our hemisphere and throughout the world. The courageous attitude of the Cuban delegation in Lima was no circumstantial occurrence, but an expression of the maturing antifascist policy of the Cuban government. This has been proved by Colonel Batista's trip to Mexico, which should be considered as the most serious attempt to give life to and broaden the Lima decisions.

At the great meeting organized by the Mexican Confederation of Workers in Mexico City with the participation of nearly 100,000 workers, Colonel Batista proclaimed the need for "the alliance of the people of our hemisphere, regardless of nationality, race, color, or language" to fight fascism. At the joint reception of the Mexican Chambers, Batista reiterated his pledge of loyalty to the cause of Republican Spain, and to the cause of world democracy. Batista also reassured Mexico of the determination of the

Cuban people to fight side by side with the Mexican people if fascism dare attack the nation.

Upon his return to Cuba, Colonel Batista has further elaborated on his progressive and democratic aims. One example will suffice. At the great meeting called by the C.T.C. to welcome him, Batista stated: "The Communist Party in Mexico, as well as in Cuba, and in France and the U.S.A. where they are recognized as legal forces, instead of elements of disturbance, are acting as promoters of democracy."

In Camaguey, in another speech, Colonel Batista declared that "Communism was an element of progress and democracy."

The growing strength of Cuban democracy and its increasing continental influence has led the forces of fascism and native reaction to intensify [their] attack not only against the workers' organizations and democratic parties and their leaders, but to place Colonel Batista in the center of their attack.

The line of the reactionaries follows the international pattern—throwing out workers from factories (they have even instructed their followers to keep only one servant and to use only one automobile), non-payment of taxes; in many provinces the sugar planters have stopped cutting and refining cane. Politically, they are blocking all progressive legislation and preventing the passage of the Warren Bros. Law (the law that recognized the Cuban gold debt), upon which depends the granting of the $50,000,000 negotiated during Batista's trip to Mexico.

The Communist Party of Cuba, whose profound political understanding of the situation is more responsible than anything else for the changes that have taken place, after considering these recent changes has reached the conclusion that it is necessary to "abandon all the out-of-date formulations that are still heard in the party." The situation has changed so that the slogan of the party must be: "With Batista, against Reaction," meaning that we must work openly for the support of the masses to Batista's policies.

8

The German-Soviet Pact and Its Repercussions in Latin America

IMPERIALISM AND NATIONAL LIBERATION*

Ernesto Giudici

This book, written by Giudici (an important leader of the Argentine CP) in 1940, is an interesting example of the theories developed by the Latin American Communist movement during the years 1939–41 (from the Molotov-Ribbentrop pact until the Nazi invasion of the Soviet Union). He denounces the misdeeds of U.S. imperialism and promotes the necessity of leading an intransigent struggle for the national liberation of Argentina; he also develops an analysis of fascism that is, at the least, ambiguous. This conception only appeared during the brief interlude between the two pro-Roosevelt and antifascist periods (1936–39 and 1941–45).

At one time, all popular movements, including the bourgeois revolution in Europe, expressed their aspirations in terms of religious beliefs or the interests of the Church. But this religious form was transitory. What persisted was the economic and political revolution occurring in the midst of the old society. Something similar has happened with fascism in the post-war political climate. The demagogy of the fascist program seemed to express many popular desires. Many confused national liberation movements were forced to express themselves in a fascist context for the same reason that, in other circumstances, German imperialism was obliged to adopt fascist forms of struggle on the international level while [it] smashed all proletarian and popular activity internally: to make room for themselves in a world dominated by England and the United States, countries that were

*Ernesto Giudici, *El imperialismo y la liberación nacional*, 1940 (Buenos Aires: Ed. Crónica, 1974), pp. 3–8.

75

pacifistic because they were satisfied for the moment. Fascism, in this case, is the transitory form. What is central and decisive is imperialism, which, not having its own political color, adopts the political form (democratic, as in England, or fascist, as in Germany) which best suits its interests in a particular stage or for a particular purpose.

We should appreciate that the aspirations of the masses often lie behind this fascist ideology. And because they come from the people, it matters little whether their ideological form is fascist or not. The necessary political rectification can occur in the mass movement itself—which has developed with little regard for the reactionary ideology that some attribute to it (which is why we must seek contact with this movement). There are popular layers that think they can struggle against the oligarchy within the context of fascism. They struggle in their own way and with their political weaknesses. And we cannot reject them, but must move toward them to convince them of their mistake. These layers suffer as much as, and even more than, other popular layers. The struggle should not be directed against them under the pretext that we are opening a battle against fascism, but rather with them against the oligarchy and fascist leaders or theoreticians, who are connected more closely than is apparent.

Political clarification cannot be postponed in the current circumstances. Our confusion comes from certain types of criticism that we do not always confront because it is easier to include fascist ideology, political mistakes, and clearly reactionary intentions in the same category. One kind of criticism that complicates a clear understanding of the problem is Rosista nationalism. Rosas, in fact, opposed everything foreign. France and England blockaded the Río de la Plata and Buenos Aires, and Rosas confronted the blockade. In hindsight, this seems an authentically nationalist attitude. But was it really? No, that nationalism was fictitious. It stood in opposition to the development of the nation. The cattle-raising oligarchy wished to live peacefully on its ranches while maintaining colonial and semi-feudal forms. Foreign capital and liberals under the patronage of "foreignizing" groups were hostile to them. Thus the country was closed, not to foreigners, but to progress from abroad. The situation was similar to that in Spain during the Napoleonic invasion. Napoleon was a foreigner in Spain, but he also represented the bourgeois revolution as it was projected throughout Europe. As Marx established, this struggle against the foreigner in Spain both united and confused the sincere nationalist desires of some sectors with the reactionary motives of the monarchical and feudal classes, who exploited these nationalist sentiments to their own advantage. What is geographically "national," directed outward, does not by itself define national liberation. What is national (in the sense of sovereignty) must be connected to *internal* progressive action in the economic, social, and political spheres.

National liberation must be a revolutionary step forward, connecting the nation to the progressive rhythm of the most advanced nations. Moving backward, stagnating, is not national liberation. National liberation is not xenophobic isolation, but cooperation with the most progressive elements against the most reactionary, which in each country seek support among the most backward sectors. Sweeping out the Rosista "nationalists" is also national liberation. Certainly, those who claim to struggle against England, but really wish to return to a pre-Anglophilic Argentina, merely serve England by offering up to them (as they have done historically) a backward, agrarian country made to measure for imperialist ambitions.

Despite this, we would like to express a political reservation. In countries more backward than Argentina, the struggle against foreign imperialism can bring non-democratic sectors or parties to a position of leadership, because of the incipient nature of their democracy. This is not the fundamental question. A perfect democracy is not a necessary precondition for the struggle against imperialism, since democracy has been delayed, restricted, and deformed wherever imperialism dominates. We must act with what is, not with what we wish would be. Once the liberation movement has been initiated, the politically reactionary elements will be swept away. Democracy will flourish as the movement grows and new, young, progressive, and revolutionary forces arise. We point this out again because we have often seen essentially progressive popular movements that, because of their environment, appear to be struggles among caudillos that lack democratic, principled integrity when judged disdainfully from Buenos Aires with an arrogant political elitism. Demanding democratic, principled integrity from such movements is like reproaching the masses for their backwardness and lack of culture. It is a vicious circle. Imperialist domination forces the backward nations into even greater backwardness, and one must escape this backwardness in some way. One must break the vicious circle somewhere. And when the popular masses erupt and their actions open new opportunities, their backwardness is thrown in their face! Let's allow them to move forward. Once in motion, all of these aspects will be overcome. We should not allow ourselves to be fooled either by the backwardness of the masses or the anti-democratic appearance of the anti-imperialist movement. Imperialism can rule hidden behind the mantle of democracy, and any struggle against it will oblige measures of force that, seen superficially, seem less democratic. But democracy is not a question of form, but of content. It resides in its aspirations, in its construction, in its movement. If measures of force, even dictatorship, aim to strengthen the power of the masses in struggle against the oligarchy, they are not really anti-democratic, but are acts of a strong democratic government, a democratic dictatorship. We revolutionaries should not allow ourselves to be deceived by appearances: a government is democratic if it finds its support in the great masses and satisfies their necessities, as opposed to those of the reactionary oligarchies. This, we repeat, must be taken into account in many Latin American countries where democracy cannot be established in one blow because they lack the necessary economic and social conditions. There can be no democracy where an oligarchy, dominated by imperialism, rules over the backward masses; the formation of a liberal national bourgeoisie is a precondition of political democracy. This is why we were prudent to wait before categorizing the coup of Colonel Busch in Bolivia as reactionary. Against whom was this coup directed and where did it look for and find support? If it were really directed against Anglo-Yankee imperialism, with the purpose of defending the national economy and the exploited masses, the new government would be progressive, *despite its dictatorial form.* The same could be said about Estigarribia's government in Paraguay, assuming that both movements are directed against oligarchic and imperialist reaction. We say "assuming," because we do not want to make a definitive judgment without deepening the analysis. We are only taking these cases as examples of what could be Latin American dictatorships with a progressive content. Everything depends on the political development of each country.

9

Browderism and the Postwar Period

FOR THE INDUSTRIALIZATION OF MEXICO*
Vicente Lombardo Toledano

Vicente Lombardo Toledano (1894–1958) was one of the most important figures of the Mexican workers' movement and the country's left intelligentsia. A trade-union and political leader during the thirties—as Secretary-General of the CTM (Mexican Workers' Confederation) and a leader of the PRM (Party of the Mexican Revolution, the government party)—Lombardo Toledano was also the author of a large number of works, including books on philosophy, law, education, trade unionism, agriculture, socialism, and Marxism. His theoretical ideas are a unique synthesis of Marxism and the ideology of the Mexican Revolution or, more precisely, of Stalinism and the nationalism of the Mexican state. Various critics have compared Lombardo's thought—which exercised an important influence in Mexico for some time—with Russian "Legal Marxism," as theories whose major function was justifying capitalist economic development in the name of historical materialism. The following selections are taken from a speech given by Lombardo Toledano in September 1944, before an Assembly of the Revolutionary Sector (trade union, peasant, and popular organizations under the leadership of the PRM). The theme, cooperation among different class interests united in support of the country's industrialization, is typical of his political writings.

REVOLUTIONARIES DO NOT PROPOSE THE IMMEDIATE ESTABLISHMENT OF SOCIALISM IN MEXICO

Many people naively believe—as do others, not through ignorance but through perversity, acting as simple provocateurs—that this war is the historic opportunity to actually and immediately establish a socialist regime throughout the world. This is untrue for Mexico. Mexican socialists and

---

*Vicente Lombardo Toledano, *El nuevo programa del Sector Revolucionario de México* (Mexico City, 1944), pp. 14–15, 16–17.

Mexican Marxists that I know; non-socialist revolutionaries who have struggled to destroy the vestiges of feudalism, to overcome our lack of natural resources, and to defend our homeland from imperialism; liberals who do not share some of the concrete ideas of members of today's revolutionary current: all, absolutely all, have agreed for some time that we will not attempt to achieve the abolition of the regime of private property in Mexico during the postwar period. We do not aim to establish socialism in our country, because neither the historical domestic conditions nor international circumstances make propitious such a transcendental task. We have agreed that the postwar period is not the time for socialism and that our goals, objectives, and tasks are those which are logically, naturally, and inevitably connected to the old, historical objectives of the Revolution begun in 1910, the Revolution of Reform and the Revolution of Independence. We wish only the fulfillment, the unfolding, the development, and the advancement of yesterday's ideas, enriched with new methods and forms for their application. We want to be a people with possibilities for culture, possibilities for work, and possibilities to live in a civilized manner; we do not want Mexico to be a semi-colonial country, but a sovereign nation, truly free as much from a political as a material point of view . . . .

WHAT IS ESSENTIAL IN OUR NEW PROGRAM

Transforming poor land into rich land, building factories where there are none, improving and augmenting transportation, increasing the amount of national wealth: these are obviously not the tasks of the workers and peasants alone. They are also the tasks of the other sectors of the country, the work of the whole people, and must be the goals and objectives of all sectors and all people of Mexico, on the condition they accept that the only valid solutions for our country are those which aspire toward progress and not those which look backward.

To transcend the goals of any single sector, of any one social class, is the great, immediate historic task. It is the work of all: peasants, workers, artisans, small businessmen, non-exploiting and non-speculating big merchants, businessmen, and bankers. All who directly or indirectly contribute to production and the economic development of the country, without exception—big businessmen and small businessmen, big bankers and honest merchants, peasants, workers, artisans, professionals, middle-class people, and the national army—think that Mexico's solution lies in its emancipation and in the abolition of the miserable conditions in which the Mexican people live.

The revolutionary sector of Mexico therefore thinks that the new program of the revolutionary sector will be a program in which all the legitimate interests of all the country's social sectors are considered. More prosperity in the future—without this, there will be no collective progress for the nation. There is no industry that can maintain itself, let alone prosper, in a country where the great majority of available consumers are unable to buy. But to do this, a radical, profound reform of Mexican agriculture is necessary. It must move from traditional, archaic agriculture to the category of a modern industry.

The immense majority of the people, made up mainly of the rural masses, would benefit from such a plan. The Mexican proletariat cannot prosper, therefore, without progress for the peasant masses. There can be no numerical increase of the proletariat nor any progress in wages and benefits in a country where the natural development of the factories has been halted because of the absence of an internal market. And unfortunately, we cannot yet aspire to be a country that exports manufactured goods to other nations on a large scale.

And what is true in regard to the proletariat is much more so in regard to the capitalist class. There can be no progress or just profits for the national bourgeoisie, Mexican industrialists, bankers, technicians, or honest merchants unless the Mexican peasant raises his standard of living and our country's incipient proletariat develops as a factor of consumption.

Nevertheless, we are not claiming that the most important step for Mexico to take in the postwar period is improving its agriculture so as to remain an agricultural country, even a modern one. It is obvious that the agricultural future of Mexico is in the cultivation of high-priced, high-income products from the high plains and the development of tropical agriculture. But the economic future of Mexico principally depends on its industrial development.

To industrialize Mexico, to revolutionize our country through industry, to organize production indivisibly, in accordance with a prudent plan full of economic stimulation, is the only solution that can be offered to a country that not only wishes to live better—an old secular aspiration—but that will, or might, be the object of interference from powerful foreign economic forces in the postwar period.

THE POPULAR PARTY*
Vicente Lombardo Toledano

In 1947, Lombardo Toledano founded the Popular Party (PP, later the Popular Socialist Party, PPS). It was not an opposition party, as he himself explained, but a method of cooperating with the government.

---

*Vicente Lombardo Toledano, *Un nuevo partido para la defensa de México y de su pueblo*, mimeographed copy of stenographic version of a speech in May 1947, v. 5 of a collection of Toledano's writings published by the PPS, pp. 25–26, 27–28.

The following paragraphs come from a speech he gave on the occasion of the constitution of the PP. He puts forward the new party's program and its "division of labor" with the official party (the Institutional Revolutionary Party, PRI).

To the degree we are less dependent on foreign countries, the Revolution will have fulfilled its most important historical objective. This is why we say that all the democratic and progressive sectors of Mexico are equally concerned with the objectives of the Revolution. Raising the standard of living of the people is of equal interest to the proletariat as to the peasants, the middle classes, and the progressive bourgeois organizations. Defending the sovereignty and independence of the nation is of equal importance to the proletariat, the peasants, the urban petty bourgeoisie, and the country's progressive big bourgeoisie. It concerns the nation itself. This is why we have proclaimed the unity of all national forces. In short, this means that if the current objectives of the Revolution are of such a magnitude, such significance, and such importance, we must logically conclude that all these sectors ought to participate in every way possible in the coming of the new regime that is replacing the Díaz dictatorship.

One of the fundamental aspects of a modern nation's life is political activity.

When we speak of creating a new political party, we are simply speaking of creating one more instrument to contribute to reaching the objectives of the Revolution. This is why it would be wrong to speak of creating a new party to destroy those few revolutionary forces that do exist. This would be naive, counterproductive, and suicidal for ourselves. Those who think we are attempting to build the Popular Party by trying to destroy the Institutional Revolutionary Party, the PRI, are completely wrong. Those of us who transformed the Party of the Mexican Revolution (PRM), who built it not only materially but ideologically and contributed to the birth of the PRI, declare (or at least I do, and I think many others agree with me) that the Institutional Revolutionary Party should be maintained, for various reasons . . . .

This is why, when we speak of a new party, we are logically speaking in the first place of a party independent of governmental power. The Popular Party, above all, must be a party of the revolutionary sector that has the necessary freedom of action, carrying out in our own way a function that no official party could ever fulfill.

So we must work on this basis, with this principle of independence from the state, the government, and public power. Independence does not mean opposition. It means mutual respect, coordination, alliance, association, and common work. But in relation to the PRI particularly, we must differentiate between the tasks of the Popular Party and the Institutional Revolutionary Party.

Some examples will definitely help explain the differences in function and responsibility of these two organizations. Can the PRI, I ask, carry out the constructive self-criticism that it needs—for example, denouncing the poor work of a member of the cabinet or the mistakes of the government as a whole—without compromising the president of the republic and the government, or without provoking a grave crisis in the government itself? Wouldn't the censure of a minister or a state secretary by the party in government be taken as the opinion of a president of the republic who wanted to get rid of him, but for particular reasons didn't want to abuse him? If the party of government attacks a member of the Cabinet, wouldn't it be said: "Why doesn't the president ask for his resignation or ask him privately to quit his government?" What would be the effect of an official party attack on a member of the Cabinet? A political crisis. Can the government party attack a state governor without this attack being taken as the opinion of the president of the republic?

As for international politics, can the governing party express its opinions on international relations without compromising the government and the president of the republic—unless it reiterates the views of the minister of foreign affairs and is thereby useless?

From this point of view, the official party must echo the government, and its role as critic is nonexistent—which is logical. This is why a party of government like the PRI has the function that it in fact fulfills: coordinating the political activities of functionaries who think in a like manner, while the very historical evolution of Mexico allows no other type of activities or class of civic action.

THE ARGENTINE COMMUNISTS AND PERONISM*
Vittorio Codovilla

In 1945, the Argentine CP participated in the formation of a coalition, the Democratic Union, which included pro-U.S. political organizations opposed to Peronism (which the CP considered a fascist movement).

In a report to the December 1945 party conference, portions of which we republish here, Vittorio Codovilla insistently developed this analysis of "Nazi-Peronism" in relation to the gigantic general strike in support of Perón (October 17–18, 1945), who had been forced from his position as Minister of Labor by

*Vittorio Codovilla, *Batir al nazi-peronismo para abrir una era de libertad y progreso* (Buenos Aires: Ed. Anteo, 1946), pp. 14–15, 18–19, 20.

right-wing officers. In the elections of 1946, Perón was elected president with 1,480,000 votes against 1,210,000 for the Democratic Union.

The Argentine CP later rectified its analysis of Peronism, but its "error" of 1945–46, the inability to distinguish between populist nationalism in a dependent country and the fascism of an imperialist metropolis, weighed heavily on the party's political future.

We should point out that this error was not that of the Argentine CP alone, since other pro-Soviet parties adopted similar positions (for example, the Bolivian PIR in relation to the MNR). Once again, the international context (the politics of the U.S.S.R.) is essential to understanding the question.

What are the essential weaknesses of the Democratic Union?

The first is that it is an *incomplete* union, since the *progressive* wing of the Conservatives and some provincial parties who are disposed to a common struggle for the same objective are not yet participating. These gaps in the democratic unity bloc give a margin of maneuver to the most reactionary elements of the oligarchy and Nazi-Peronism, who are interested in keeping Conservatism from adding its electoral weight to the Democratic Union and thereby assuring the triumph of the Radicals.

Now, with our authority as partisans of a non-exclusive unity and as people who spare no efforts to create a union of all forces opposed to Peronism, we Communists declare that, whatever course this unity movement follows, anyone who claims to be an enemy of Nazi-Peronism but refuses to vote for the Democratic Union is committing *treason against democracy*, wittingly or not, since they would then be favoring the candidates of continuity.

Besides its incompleteness, its main weakness is that it is united around a limited objective, the victory of the Radical presidential candidacy, and that forces allied in the Democratic Union are not united on all terrains of struggle. In fact, there is resistance to the creation of common lists for the election of governors, senators, and national and provincial deputies. This means that the united front is not sufficiently solid and effective. It is not understood that the presentation of joint electoral lists is desirable to assure that representatives of all the politically and socially democratic sectors enter the next parliament, to stop the dispersion of our votes, and to keep the Nazi-Peronists from obtaining representation that does not correspond to their real influence among the people. Our slogan must be: *No seats for the Peronists!* This way we can avoid the introduction of a fascist Trojan horse into the Parliament. This is why I feel that we Communists ought to insist to our allies that we march united, not only in the *presidential* elections, but also the elections for *deputies, senators, and governors* . . . .

Our country is a typical example. Look at Peronism's "anti-imperialist" demagogy and you will see that beneath it all is only blackmail and the selling of our country to the highest bidder. The Peronists talk against imperialism in general, but they specialize in attacking Yankee imperialism.

Why? Because English trusts and monopolies, who support Peronism to a great extent, are dominant in our country. Whenever the need for international economic measures or sanctions is advanced to force the military-fascist dictatorship to abandon power and allow the Argentinian people to freely express their will through the ballot box and have the government that they wish, the reactionary sectors of British politics immediately rise up, maintaining they cannot support such measures or sanctions since they would prejudice the interests of Great Britain and its trade with Argentina. And whenever democratic sectors of the United States government repudiate the Nazi-Peronist dictatorship, a position that has been expressed in the speeches of some North American diplomats, voices of "calm" immediately arise from the higher circles of American industry and finance, fearing that an energetic stance by the United States would favor the large English monopolies and trusts that operate in our country.

And so it goes—these verbal skirmishes between Nazi-Peronists and the American and English governments last for months and years, with no practical result to benefit the Argentine people . . . .

Those of us who have lived as exiles in fraternal countries have seen the intense participation of these peoples in the drama and struggle of the Argentine people expressed by the *warmth and caring spiritual solidarity* with which we were welcomed. I refer particularly to the Chilean, Mexican, and Uruguayan peoples, and in many cases to the government and authorities of these countries also.

And the idea has spread widely in all of these countries that the Argentinian people are struggling to destroy a dangerous Nazi-fascist front in America, and for that reason, our people's struggle is not only a democratic struggle of a national character, but also a struggle for the freedom of all the peoples of Latin America. We can now claim that the Argentinian people's cause, the struggle for the crushing of Nazi-Peronism, *has been transformed into the cause of all those who love democracy and freedom in America.*

Throughout America, a powerful movement of solidarity has been formed with the Argentinian people and with our brothers and neighbors of Paraguay and Bolivia, who also are dominated by regimes of force that are to a great degree supported by Nazi-Peronist influence and by the Munich-like politics of certain foreign oil and mining monopolies.

On behalf of the Communist Party, we would like to express our profound thanks to the American peoples, especially the peoples and governments of Chile, Uruguay, and Mexico, for their many useful displays of solidarity. We should mention among the most important and effective acts of solidarity those of the brave Chilean miners, especially the rugged coal miners of Lota, who *practically* demonstrated, with their repeated refusal to send fuel to the Nazi-Peronist dictatorship, how one *can and ought* to fight fascist, dictatorial regimes: by economically isolating and strangling them . . . .

The October 18 strike was successful in part because of the social demagogy that we saw imposed by violence. It is a fact that this strike took place in accordance with a pre-established plan and was led by a united command with the explicit support of the police. This is why the Peronists were able to cut off electricity, cut the railways, paralyze transport, and keep people from going to work. We shouldn't delude ourselves; Nazi-Peronism knows how to act *boldly and effectively.* This "strike," as well as the excesses committed by the armed Peronist bands for this purpose, should be seen as the *first serious attempt* by the Nazi-Peronists to unleash a *civil war.*

THE WORKER-BOSS PACT*
Mexican Communist Party

In April 1945, the Confederation of Chambers of Industry and the Mexican Workers' Confederation (CTM), under the leadership of Lombardo Toledano, signed a national unity pact. *The Voice of Mexico,* the organ of the Communist Party, saluted this historic event and presented the following political, social, and economic justification. It is characteristic of the "Browderist" period because of its insistence upon collaboration not only with the national bourgeoisie, but with North American imperialism itself (at this time, the last months of World War II, it was still allied with the U.S.S.R.).

Saturday, April 7, 1945, is a historic date for Mexico, with significance beyond its borders. The Alliance Pact was signed that day; the highest representatives of the Mexican workers and capitalists announced their decision to act together on behalf of a program of common goals, a program of goals that involve the whole Nation:

1. To struggle for full economic autonomy and the economic development of the country, and to raise the material and cultural conditions of the people.
2. To renovate, reaffirm, and consolidate—for peace—the alliance that has been formed during the war under the policy of national unity proclaimed by President Ávila Camacho.
3. To work for a modern, prosperous, and cultured Mexico, free of misery, insalubrity, and ignorance, through the maximum utilization of its natural resources, the development of its productive capacity, the growth of its national income, the proliferation of commodities and services, the

---

*"Histórico pacto obrero-patronal," *La Voz de México,* April 12, 1945, pp. 1, 7.

development of transportation, communication, and public works, and the improvement of health and educational institutions.
4. To reject the theory of economic self-sufficiency, and act on the theory of economic interdependence and financial and technical cooperation with the other countries of the continent for our common benefit, as part of an international program that considers the needs of the world's other peoples.
5. The meeting was carried out without disparaging the particular views of the consenting classes and without weakening any rights granted by law.
6. The participants elaborated a joint economic program to present to the government for the solution of the problems caused by the war and those which will be presented by peace.

The pact is so proper, so impeccably formulated, and so patriotic that no one has been able to put forward a serious argument against it—not one!

BUILDING NATIONAL UNITY FOR THE LONG TERM

This pact represents a tremendous achievement for unity—so great that the enemies of unity and the homeland have received a strong, sharp blow.

The movement for national unity has been growing. Once a political idea, national unity is becoming increasingly concretized in deeds. But few events (it would not be exaggerating to say none) have so clearly expressed the development of this movement as the worker-industrialist pact of April 7.

This pact merits the enthusiastic, energetic support of all Mexicans. It has taken much work. It is an aspiration being fulfilled after overcoming many obstacles. The figure of Vicente Lombardo Toledano, the tireless standard-bearer of this aspiration, stands out for his formidable and persistent efforts.

The world was thrust into a brutal war of aggression and conquest by Hitlerism, and it has arisen in a just war against the Nazi bandits and their allies and lackeys. Since then, the patriots of Mexico have raised the banner of national unity, defined as the union of all Mexicans, whatever their ideology, religious beliefs, or social class, for the defense of the homeland and its freedom, well-being, and progress.

At the Ninth National Congress of the Communist Party in May 1944, Dionisio Encina, the General Secretary of the PCM, presented the following clear and precise call on behalf of the Mexican Communists:

We state that the independence and progress of Mexico are the order of the day. We declare that, within this context, it is possible and indispensable that all sectors, classes, groups, and forces of the nation, all men and women of differing ideologies and beliefs, unite around these common goals; we, firm defenders of this national unity, will struggle tirelessly to assure it.

Unity of the Mexican nation to contribute more effectively to winning the war; unity of the Mexican nation in the foreseeable future after the victory, for the independent development of our homeland and its participation in universal, peaceful, just, popular, and solid cooperation for many generations.

With the proper politics upheld by the revolutionary sectors, with the indefatigable and indomitable activity of the leader of unity, Lombardo Toledano, the unity movement continued on course. New difficulties arose. But the national dynamic and the actions of the most conscious and responsible sectors of Mexican life have led to the advancement of the national unity movement.

UNITY ADVANCES. THE ENEMY MANEUVERS.

This situation was analyzed by the recent meeting of the National Committee of the Communist Party, which, referring to industrialization and in regard to the demand that Mexico should acquire machinery from the United States, affirmed: "This demand reflects a sentiment and a postulate of national unity that the National Chamber of Industry defended in the following manner: as equality of access to the equipment we believe the world's most advanced nations should provide to the developing countries to make possible their rapid development, which is in the interests of all."

Since the historic pact was signed, some, in alarm and desperation, have gone through vile contortions to oppose it. Leaving themselves open to exposure if they openly attack the pact, they have for the most part taken the road of intrigue, insult, and repugnant maneuver.

They insist upon raising the "specter" of Communism, but this specter increasingly seems a mere scarecrow. The policy of the PCM—laid out in the preceding paragraphs—is just reaching stride.

They claim to be suspicious about the "real purposes" of Lombardo Toledano, but they cannot change the indisputable fact that Lombardo Toledano has played a decisive role and has been the most active in making the pact possible.

In this whole campaign against Mexico and the formidable advance for national unity signified by the pact, we cannot overlook the perverse labor of the *Excélsior* newspapers, which speak with a defeatist, malevolent voice.

EXCÉLSIOR: THE SCORPION

The *Excélsior* newspapers are biting their own tails and confusedly poisoning themselves with their own venom.

Feigning a benevolent attitude that has fooled no one, the morning

Excélsior made the following statement about the pact: "No citizen who loves his country could refuse to support it."

To whom does this statement refer? Who doesn't love their country? In other words, who is a traitor to our homeland, according to *Excélsior*? Who has stumbled upon the venomous sting of *Excélsior*?

The traitor to the homeland, according to *Excélsior*, is its own stepchild, the afternoon *Últimas Noticias*. "No citizen who loves his country could refuse to support it." And this is what that "citizen," the *Últimas Noticias*, says: "the celebrated pact proposed by those leaders who went to London and which the captains of Mexican industry accepted, moved by their patriotism—though incorrectly, in our judgment."

Could there be more obvious proof of the game and the role played by the *Excélsior* newspapers as organs of fascist reaction and treason against Mexico?

This pernicious mission cannot be hidden, even with the joking, perverse, and foolish self-promotion (all three simultaneously) that *Excélsior* has adopted to disguise its fury. Because the *Excélsior* publishing house, that house of treason, does what it can to convince its readers that its larger newspaper was the first to print the materials that have culminated in the signing of the pact. What *Excélsior* really did was misrepresent things and try to sound the alarm that Lombardo Toledano was negotiating the suppression of the right to strike. The pact says the opposite: "without weakening those rights that current laws consecrate in our favor." The newspapers of this house of treason hoped to stop the pact, carrying out their mission as enemies of Mexico, its unity and progress.

AN ALLIANCE MADE TO LAST

The points of the alliance presented above are quite clear and not open to doubt. No one is tricking anyone else. No one is betraying their class. On the contrary, it is specific class interests, as well as the interests of the entire nation, which have made this pact possible. The working class and the capitalist class struggle to develop the country industrially and to raise the standard of living of the masses, each for their own reasons. This is why current conditions in Mexico and the world require an alliance of the workers and the capitalists for the same goals, without either renouncing their own interests or specific class purposes.

A joint Round Table Commission remains in operation to discuss problems and, as far as possible, elaborate common views. This commission must fulfill a great task, and the Mexican people hope that it will succeed in developing opinions on the majority of the problems faced by Mexico.

It is now possible and necessary to create the tripartite committees proposed in the following terms by the PCM on May 1, 1944: "There is a concrete measure which would contribute greatly to the solution of conflicts and the lightening the work load in the factories—the creation of tripartite committees in each workplace, where representatives of the workers, the company, and the government can discuss and resolve their differences and increase production by mitigating and improving labor methods." Many of these committees with their technical functions can now be created across the country.

Everything permits this alliance to be strengthened by the incorporation of non-participating workers' committees and capitalist organizations. Hopefully, the hostile campaign by *Últimas Noticias*, which has tried to take advantage of the declarations of some workers' groups, will be enough to convince the union federations that have not yet joined that their incorporation is the only patriotic path to follow.

The April 7 Pact expresses the understanding of the signers, with their great, representative power, that only this road leads to freedom and national progress.

This signifies that a wish of all Mexicans who love their country will be satisfied: this alliance will be consolidated and broadened even more, and will develop with great force in the peaceful, just, and victorious future.

THE PULACAYO THESES*

In November 1946, an extraordinary congress of the FSTMB (Bolivian Mineworkers' Federation) met in Pulacayo and approved a document that came to be known as the Pulacayo Theses. Militants of the POR (Revolutionary Workers Party, founded in 1934), particularly Guillermo Lora, drafted this text, which was clearly inspired by the Trotskyist theory of permanent revolution. It is therefore a notable exception to the general line of the Latin American workers' movement in this period, which was dominated by the extreme moderation of the "national unity" strategy put forward by the Communist parties.

The Pulacayo Theses became a central point of reference for the Bolivian workers' movement, and remain so even today.

1. FUNDAMENTAL PRINCIPLES

1. The proletariat, even in Bolivia, is the revolutionary social class *par excellence*. The mineworkers, the most advanced and combative sector of the national proletariat, determine the direction of struggle of the FSTMB.

---

*"Tesis central de la Federación de Trabajadores Mineros de Bolivia: Tesis de Pulacayo," in Guillermo Lora, ed., *Documentos políticos de Bolivia* (Cochabamba: Ed. Los Amigos del Libro, 1970).

2. Bolivia is an underdeveloped capitalist country. While its economy is a combination of the most diverse stages of economic evolution, capitalist exploitation is qualitatively predominant, and other socioeconomic formations constitute an inheritance from our past. This is the reason that the proletariat dominates national politics.

3. Bolivia, despite being an underdeveloped country, is only a link in the world capitalist chain. Its national peculiarities themselves represent a combination of the fundamental characteristics of the world economy.

4. The particularity of Bolivia is that no bourgeoisie capable of liquidating the *latifundio*, realizing the unification of the nation, and liberating it from the yoke of imperialism has appeared on the political scene. These unfulfilled bourgeois tasks are the bourgeois-democratic objectives that must be carried out without delay. The central question for the semicolonial countries is the agrarian revolution: that is, the liquidation of our feudal heritage and the establishment of national independence, which means shaking off the imperialist yoke; these tasks are intimately connected.

5. "The distinctive characteristics of the national economy, as great as they are, form an integral and increasingly larger part of a higher reality that is known as the world economy; working-class internationalism has its basis in this fact." Capitalist development is characterized by the growth of international relations, which is expressed in the volume of foreign trade.

6. As backward countries change under imperialist pressure, their development has a combined character; they unite the most primitive economic forms and the latest in capitalist technique and civilization. The proletariats of the underdeveloped countries are obliged to combine the struggle for bourgeois-democratic goals with the struggle for socialist demands. These stages, the democratic and the socialist, "are not separated in the struggle by historical eras, but grow immediately out of each other."

7. The feudal landowners have merged their interests with those of international imperialism and have thereby become its unconditional servants.

This is why the ruling class is a truly feudal bourgeoisie. Given its technical primitivism, their exploitation of the *latifundio* would be inconceivable if imperialism did not artificially maintain their existence by throwing them crumbs. Imperialist domination is unimaginable without such local rulers. Bolivian capitalism is highly concentrated: three companies control production in the mines, the economic axis of national life. The ruling class is pathetic, insofar as it is incapable of realizing its own historical objectives and finds itself tied as much to feudal interests as it is to imperialists. The feudal-bourgeois state finds its justification as an organ of the violence necessary to maintain the privileges of the *gamonal* and the capitalist. The state is a powerful instrument of the ruling class for crushing its adversaries. Only traitors or fools would maintain that the state can raise itself above classes and paternally decide between them.

The middle class or the petty bourgeoisie is numerically the largest class, but its weight in the national economy is insignificant. Small businessmen, small landowners, technicians, bureaucrats, artisans, and peasants have not yet been able to develop their own independent class politics and will be even less able to do so in the future. The countryside follows the city, and here the proletariat is the leader. The petty bourgeoisie follows the capitalists during periods of "social tranquillity" and when parliamentary activity is prospering. It follows the proletariat during those moments when the class struggle is extremely sharp (for example, during the revolution) and when it is certain that only the proletariat is pointing the way toward emancipation. Between these extremes, the independence of the middle class is a myth. Obviously, the revolutionary potential of broad layers of the middle class is enormous (just recall the objectives of the bourgeois-democratic revolution), but it is also true that they cannot realize these goals by themselves.

The proletariat has the power to achieve its own objectives and even those of other classes. Its enormous weight in politics is determined by the place it occupies in the productive process, and not by its numerical weakness. The economic axis of national life will also be the political axis of the future revolution. The Bolivian miners' movement is one of the most advanced in Latin America. Reformists argue that this country cannot have a social movement that is more advanced than those in more technologically evolved nations. History has proven innumerable times that this mechanistic conception of the relationship between the development of machinery and the political consciousness of the masses is incorrect. Because of its extreme youthfulness and incomparable energy, because it has remained almost virginal in a political sense, because it has no tradition of parliamentarism and class collaboration, and finally because of its presence in a country where the class struggle has acquired an extreme belligerence, we say that the Bolivian proletariat has become among the most radical. We say to the reformists and to those who have sold out to the *rosca* that a proletariat of such quality will put forward revolutionary demands and display an audacious bravery in the struggle.

II. THE TYPE OF REVOLUTION WE MUST CARRY OUT

1. We underground workers are not suggesting we should pass over the bourgeois-democratic stage: the struggle for basic democratic demands and for the agrarian, anti-imperialist revolution. Nor do we deny the existence of the petty bourgeoisie, above all the peasants and artisans. We point out

that the bourgeois-democratic revolution, if it is not to be strangled, must become only one phase of the proletarian revolution.

2. Those who claim we are proponents of an immediate socialist revolution in Bolivia are lying, since we know that the objective conditions do not exist. We have already clearly stated that the revolution will be bourgeois-democratic in regard to its objectives and will be but one episode in a revolution that must be proletarian, because this is the social class that will lead it. The proletarian revolution in Bolivia will not exclude other exploited social layers of the nation, but will be a revolutionary alliance of the proletariat with the peasants, artisans, and other sectors of the petty bourgeoisie.

3. The dictatorship of the proletariat is the expression of this alliance at the state level. The slogan of revolution and proletarian dictatorship puts in clear relief the fact that the working class will be the leading nucleus of this transformation and this state. To maintain the contrary, that the bourgeois-democratic revolution as such will be carried out by the "progressive" sectors of the bourgeoisie, and that the future state will be a government of national unity and concord, indicates a firm intention to strangle the revolutionary movement within the framework of bourgeois democracy. Once in power, the workers cannot indefinitely stay within bourgeois-democratic limits and will be obliged, to a greater and greater degree, to make ever deeper inroads into the regime of private property. In this way, the revolution will acquire a permanent character.

Before the exploited, we mineworkers denounce all of those who claim to substitute for the proletarian revolution with palace mutinies fomented by different sectors of the feudal bourgeoisie.

III. THE STRUGGLE AGAINST CLASS COLLABORATIONISM

1. The class struggle is, in its final determination, the struggle for the appropriation of surplus value. Workers who sell their labor power, struggling to do this under the best conditions, and the owners of the means of production (capitalists) who struggle to continue to usurp an unpaid portion of their labor, pursue contradictory and therefore irreconcilable objectives. We cannot close our eyes to the evidence that the struggle against the bosses is a struggle to the death, since the destiny of private property is determined thereby. Unlike our enemies, we recognize no truce in the class struggle. The present historical stage, a shameful stage for humanity, can only be overcome when social classes disappear, when neither exploiters nor exploited continue to exist. It is a stupid sophism of class collaborationists that we should not destroy the rich, but make the poor rich. Our objective is the expropriation of the expropriators.

2. Any attempt to collaborate with our executioners, any attempt at making concessions to our enemy in this struggle, is nothing less than a betrayal of the working class to the bourgeoisie. Class collaboration means the renunciation of our objectives. All the conquests of the workers, even the smallest, have been gained after bloody struggle against the capitalist system. We cannot even think of reaching an understanding with our subjugators, because we subordinate our program of transitional demands to the proletarian revolution. Even though we put forward the most advanced programmatic demands to the workers, we are not reformists; we are revolutionaries above all else, because we intend to transform the very structure of society.

3. We reject the petty bourgeois illusion that the problems of the worker can be solved by leaving them to the state or any other institution that hopes to solve them through organs that mediate between struggling social classes. The history of the national and international movement teaches that such a solution has always meant compromise with the interests of capitalism at the cost of hunger and oppression for the proletariat. Arbitration and legal control of the workers' methods of struggle are generally the origin of defeat. As far as possible, we work to smash compulsory arbitration. Let conflicts be resolved by the workers themselves, under their own leadership!

4. The achievement of our program of transitional demands, which should lead to the proletarian revolution, is always subordinate to the class struggle. We are proud of being the most intransigent opponents of compromises with the bosses. This is why it is a major task to struggle with and destroy the reformists who extol class collaboration, those who advise us to tighten our belts on the altar of so-called national salvation. Where hunger and oppression exist for the worker, there can be no national glory—only misery and national weakness. We will abolish capitalist exploitation.

War to the death against capitalism! War to the death against reformist class collaboration! For the road of class struggle until the destruction of capitalist society!

IV. The Struggle against Imperialism

1. For the mineworkers, class struggle means the struggle against the largest mine owners—that is, against a sector of Yankee imperialism that oppresses us. The liberation of the exploited is subordinate to the struggle against imperialism. Since we struggle against international capitalism, we represent the interests of our whole society, and we have objectives in common with the exploited of the world. The destruction of imperialism is preliminary to the introduction of more advanced agricultural techniques and the creation of light and heavy industry. We occupy the same position

as the international proletariat because we are engaged in the destruction of an international power: imperialism.

2. We denounce as declared enemies of the proletariat those "leftists" who have sold out to Yankee imperialism and tell us of the greatness of Northern "democracy" and its international superiority. One cannot speak of democracy when sixty families dominate the United States, and when these sixty families suck the blood of semi-colonial countries like ours. Yankee predominance corresponds to an enormous accumulation and sharpening of the antagonisms and contradictions of the capitalist system. The United States is a powder keg that needs only a single spark to explode. We declare our solidarity with the North American proletariat and our irreconcilable opposition to its bourgeoisie, which lives from the plunder and oppression of the world.

3. Imperialist politics, which determine Bolivian politics, are themselves determined by the monopoly stage of capitalism. This is why imperialist politics can only lead to oppression, plunder, and the incessant transformation of the state into a weak instrument controlled by the exploiters. Postures such as the "Good Neighbor" policy, "Pan-Americanism," etc., are only disguises used by Yankee imperialism and the native feudal bourgeoisie to deceive the peoples of Latin America. The system of reciprocal diplomatic consultation, the creation of international banking institutions with money from the oppressed nations, the concessions of strategic military bases to the Yankees, unfair contracts for raw materials, etc., are different forms of the shameless sellout of Latin American countries by their rulers. Struggling against this betrayal and denouncing imperialism whenever it displays its claws are elementary duties of the proletariat. The Yankees are not content to decide the composition of our ministries; they now go further and have taken upon themselves the task of guiding the activity of the police of the semi-colonial countries, announcing their intention to attack anti-imperialist revolutionaries.

Workers of Bolivia: Support your cadre and struggle against rapacious Yankee imperialism!

V. THE STRUGGLE AGAINST FASCISM

1. Our struggle against imperialism must be paralleled by our struggle against the sellout feudal bourgeoisie. Antifascism is, in practice, one aspect of this struggle: the acquisition and defense of democratic rights and the destruction of armed bands supported by the bourgeoisie.

2. Fascism is a product of international capitalism. Fascism is the final stage in the decomposition of imperialism, but nevertheless continues to be a phase of imperialism. When violence is organized by the state to defend

the privileges of the capitalists and destroy the workers' movement, we are in the presence of a fascist regime. Bourgeois democracy is an excessively dear luxury that can only be afforded by those countries that have accumulated their fat at the cost of world hunger. In poor countries like ours, workers are condemned at particular moments to face the barrels of rifles. It matters little which political party must resort to fascist measures to better serve imperialist interests. If it persists in supporting capitalist oppression, its destiny is already writ: the use of violence against the workers.

3. The struggle against fascist grouplets is subordinate to the struggle against imperialism and the feudal bourgeoisie. Those who claim to struggle against fascism by surrendering to "democratic" imperialism and the feudal bourgeoisie do nothing but prepare the way for the inevitable coming of a fascist regime.

To definitively destroy the fascist danger, we must destroy capitalism as a system.

To struggle against fascism, we must revive the class struggle, not artificially attenuate class contradictions.

Workers and the exploited: Destroy capitalism to definitively destroy the fascist danger and fascist grouplets! We can only defeat fascism with the methods of the proletarian revolution within the framework of class struggle!

VI. THE FSTMB AND THE CURRENT SITUATION

1. The revolutionary situation of July 21 was created by the irruption into the streets of the exploited masses, deprived of bread and freedom, and by the defensive and belligerent action of the miners, brought on by the need to defend their social conquests and achieve more advanced victories; it has allowed the representatives of the mine owners to take command of their state apparatus, thanks to the betrayal by the reformists who collaborated with the feudal bourgeoisie. The people's blood allowed these executioners to consolidate their position in power. The fact that the Government Council is a provisional institution in no way changes this situation.

The mine workers are right to eagerly organize themselves and confront the government to demand they force the enterprises to obey the country's laws. We cannot and should not solidarize with any government that is not our own—that is, not a workers' government. This is because we know the state represents the interests of the socially dominant class.

2. "Worker" ministers do not change the structure of bourgeois governments. While the state defends capitalist society, the "worker" ministers become vulgar pimps for the bourgeoisie. The worker who is weak enough to exchange his place in the revolutionary ranks for a portfolio as a bourgeois minister joins the ranks of traitors. The bourgeoisie creates

"worker" ministers to better fool the workers, to make the exploited abandon their own methods of struggle and surrender themselves body and soul to the tutelage of the "worker" minister. *The FSTMB will never be part of a bourgeois government, since this would signify the most naked betrayal of the exploited and mean denying our line, the revolutionary line of class struggle.*

3. The next election will result in a government in the service of the big mine owners, since these elections have nothing to do with democracy. The majority of the population, the indigenous peoples and an enormous percentage of the proletariat, are not allowed near the ballot boxes because of obstacles in the Electoral Law or because they are illiterate. Sections of the petty bourgeoisie corrupted by the ruling class determine the results of the election. We cannot have any illusion in the electoral struggle. The workers cannot gain power by the ballot; we will gain power through the work of the social revolution. This is why we maintain that our relations with the next government will be the same as with the current Government Council. If they carry out the laws, all well and good; this is why they were put in power. If they do not, they will face our energetic protests.

VII. Transitional Demands

Each union and each mining region has its particular problems, and unionists must adjust their daily struggle to these peculiarities. But there are problems that agitate and unify worker cadres throughout the nation; these are their growing misery and the employers' lockout that are daily more threatening. Against these dangers, the FSTMB proposes the following radical measures:

1. A Living Minimum Wage and a Sliding Scale of Wages. The termination of the system of inexpensive company stores and the excessive disproportion between the cost of living and real wages demand the establishment of a living minimum wage.

A scientific study of the needs of a worker's family should serve as the basis for setting a living minimum wage—that is, a salary that allows a family to lead a life that can be considered human. As we maintained at our Third Congress, this wage should be supplemented by a sliding scale. This will keep price increases from never fully being compensated by the periodic readjustment of wages. We must put an end to the regular gimmick of nullifying wage increase through depreciation of the monetary unit and the artificial increase in the prices of the means of subsistence. The unions ought to take charge of controlling the cost of living and demand automatic wage increases in accord with these costs. The minimum wage, rather than being static, should follow the rise in prices of the basic necessities.

2. The Forty-Hour Week and a Sliding Scale of Hours. Mechanization in the mines increases the worker's pace. The very nature of underground work makes an eight-hour day excessive, destroying the worker's vitality in an inhuman way. The struggle for a better world requires that man be liberated in some manner from slavery in the mines. This is why the FSTMB will struggle to attain the 40-hour week, which should be supplemented by a sliding scale of working hours.

The only way to struggle effectively against permanent danger of unemployment is to attain a sliding scale of hours, which would decrease the length of the work day in the same proportion that the number of unemployed increases. This decrease would not mean a cut in wages, since these wages are a vital necessity.

Only these measures will let us keep the worker cadres from being destroyed by misery and stop the employers' lockout from artificially creating an army of the unemployed.

NOTE: The First Extraordinary Congress complemented this point by demanding a thirty-six-hour week for women and children.

3. *Occupation of the Mines.* The capitalists hope to contain the rising workers' movement with threats about what they will have to do if they have financial losses. They hope to fetter the workers by raising the specter of unemployment. Moreover, experience has shown that the temporary shutdown of the mines has only served as an excuse to flout the full range of social laws and to force workers pressured by hunger to recontract under truly shameful conditions.

The companies keep two sets of books: one to show the workers and pay taxes, and the other to set their dividends. We cannot give up our aspirations because of some numbers on a balance sheet.

The workers who have sacrificed their lives on the altar of private property have the right to demand that they not be denied the right to work, even when the times are not prosperous for the capitalists.

The right to work is not a demand directed at this or that particular capitalist, but at the system as a whole, which is why we are not interested in the laments of a few small, bankrupt businessmen.

If the bosses are unable to offer their slaves an extra piece of bread; if capitalism, to survive, is forced to attack our wages and the gains we have achieved; if the capitalists respond to all our demands with the threat to shut down their operations, the workers have no recourse but to occupy the mines and take charge of production themselves.

The occupation of the mines passes beyond the limits of capitalism, since it raises the question of who really owns the mines. Occupation should not be confused with the socialization of the mines; it is merely a question of keeping the lockout from succeeding and the workers being condemned to die of hunger. Strikes that include the occupation of the mines are becoming one of the main objectives of the FSTMB.

For these reasons, it is obvious that the occupation of the mines is an illegal measure. It could not be otherwise. A step that from any point of view surpasses the limits of capitalism will not be covered in established legislation. We know that by occupying the mines, we are breaking bourgeois law, and that we thereby create a new situation; afterwards, legislators in the service of the exploiters will introduce the matter into the legal codes and attempt to control it through regulation.

The Supreme Decree of the Governing Council prohibiting the legal attachment of the mines by the workers will not effect our position. We know that in such cases, we cannot count on the collaboration of the government, and since we have evidence that we do not work under the protection of the law, we have no other recourse than to occupy the mines, with no right to compensation for the capitalists.

The occupation of the mines should be led by a Mines Committee that is formed with the assistance of all the workers, including non-union workers. The Mines Committee will have to decide the future of the mines and the workers who take part in production.

Mineworkers! To fight the lockout, *occupy the mines!*

4. *Collective Contracts.* Under our laws, a boss can freely choose between individual contracts and collective contracts. Because this is important to the companies, it has not been possible until now to win collective contracts in practice. We must struggle, because there is only one form of labor contract: the collective contract.

We cannot allow the tremendous power of the capitalist to trample on the individual worker, who cannot give his free consent; there is no free consent whenever misery obliges the acceptance of the most pathetic labor contract.

In opposition to the organized capitalists who work together to extort the worker through the individual contract, we propose a collective contract for workers organized together in unions.

1. A collective work contract, above all, should be able to be abrogated at any time by decision of the unions alone.
2. New workers will find the relevant conditions already established, since adherence to the contract will be mandatory even for non-unionists.
3. The collective contract should not eliminate the more favorable conditions found in individual contracts.
4. The execution of the contract itself should be controlled by the unions.

The collective contract is the point of departure for our platform of transitional demands.

5. Union Independence. The realization of our aspirations is only possible if we are able to free ourselves from the influence of all sections of the bourgeoisie and its "left" agents. Controlled unions are the syphilis of the workers' movement. When unions become appendages of the government, they lose their freedom of action and drag the masses down the road to defeat.

We denounce the CSTB as an agency of the government inside the workers' movement. We cannot trust organizations with their permanent secretariat in the Labor Ministry that send their members to spread government propaganda.

The FSTMB is absolutely independent of any sector of the bourgeoisie, the reformist left, or the government. It carries out the policies of revolutionary unionism and denounces any compromise with the bourgeoisie or the government as treason.

War to the death against controlled unionism!

6. Workers' Control in the Mines. The FSTMB supports all measures taken by the unions to achieve effective control by the workers over all aspects of the operation of the mines. We must end the bosses' secrets in production, accounting, technique, transport, etc., and establish workers' intervention into these matters. Since our objective is the occupation of the mines, we must become interested in bringing these secrets to light.

The workers should control the technical management of extraction and accounting, take part in selecting lead workers, and above all, publicize the profits of the big mine owners and the frauds they carry out when paying taxes and making Social Security payments.

In opposition to the reformists who speak of the sacred rights of the bosses, we propose the slogan of *workers' control of the mines.*

7. Arming the Workers. We have stated that as long as capitalism exists, violent repression against the workers' movement is a potential danger. If we hope to avoid future massacres like Catavi, we must arm the workers. To repel the fascist bands and the strikebreakers, we will create duly armed worker pickets. Where will we get arms? The main thing is to educate the rank-and-file workers that they must arm themselves to the teeth against the armed bourgeoisie; they will find the means to do it. Have we perhaps forgotten that we work with powerful explosives every day?

Any strike is potentially the beginning of a civil war, and we definitely must be armed when we start. Our objective is to win, and this is why we must not forget that the bourgeoisie can count on armies, police, and fascist bands. We must therefore organize the first cells of the proletarian army. All unions should form armed pickets among the youth and the most combative elements.

Union pickets should be militarily organized as quickly as possible.

8. Strike Benefits. The company stores and the miserable wages that give the worker no resources but his daily pay are means of control for the companies. The hunger that strikers suffer is the worst enemy of a strike. For a strike to end happily, the adverse pressure on the worker's family must be eliminated. Unions must designate a portion of their receipts to increasing their strike funds, so they can offer the necessary aid in the event of a strike.

Let us end the bosses' control of strikes through hunger by immediately organizing strike funds!

9. Regulate the Abolition of Company Stores. We have already stated that the system of company stores allows the bosses to enrich themselves at the expense of workers' wages. Simply abolishing the company stores does nothing more than aggravate the workers' situation and is against the workers' interests.

To properly abolish the company stores, this must be done in conjunction with a sliding scale of wages and the establishment of a living minimum wage.

10. End "Contracted" Work. To flout the maximum legal work day and exploit the worker even more, the companies have contrived different labor techniques that they call "contracts." We must stop this new capitalist maneuver that is being used for robbery. The daily wage should be established as the only wage system.

VIII. DIRECT MASS ACTION AND PARLIAMENTARY STRUGGLE

Direct mass action is regaining its leading role among the methods of proletarian struggle. We know abundantly well that we must liberate ourselves, and in achieving this goal, we cannot expect the collaboration of those alien to us. This is why direct mass action, particularly the strike and occupation of the mines, is the preferred method of struggle at this juncture in the rise of the movement. As far as possible, we avoid strikes over insignificant matters so that we will not weaken our forces. We are overcoming the stage of local struggles. Isolated strikes allow the bourgeoisie to concentrate their attention and their forces at a single point. Any strike must be begun with the intention of becoming a general strike. Moreover, a miners' strike ought to be extended to other proletarian sectors and to the middle class. Strikes that include mine occupations are on the order of the day. From the first, the strikers must control the key points of the mines and, above all, the stores of explosives.

We state that as direct mass action moves to the forefront, we do not need to import other methods of struggle.

Revolutionaries ought to be wherever social life places the classes in struggle.

The electoral struggle is important, but in a stage when the revolutionary movement is in ascent, it acquires a secondary character. For electoralism to play a transcendental role, it must be subordinated to direct mass action. When it is in retreat, when the masses are abandoning the struggle and the bourgeoisie is taking the positions they have surrendered, electoralism can play a key role. Generally, bourgeois parliaments do not resolve the fundamental question of our epoch: the destiny of private property. Its destiny will be determined by the workers in the street. If we do not deny the need for the electoral struggle, we do subject it to particular conditions. We should elect proven revolutionary elements who identify with our union activities. The parliament should become a revolutionary tribune. We know that our representatives will be a minority, but they will be charged with unmasking the maneuvers of the bourgeoisie from the parliament itself. Above all, the parliamentary struggle should be directly linked to the direct action of the masses. Worker and mineworker deputies should follow a single lead: the principles of these theses.

Our task in the next electoral struggle is to send the strongest possible workers' bloc to parliament. Despite being anti-parliamentarists, we repeat that we cannot leave this field open to our class enemies. Our voice will also be heard inside the parliament.

In opposition to the electoral maneuvers of left traitors, we propose the formation of a Miners' Parliamentary Bloc!

IX. In Opposition to the Bourgeois Slogan of National Unity, We Propose a Proletarian United Front

1. We are soldiers in the class struggle. We have said that the war against the exploiters is a war to the death. This is why we will destroy any attempt at collaboration from the side of the workers. The road to betrayal was opened by the famous "popular fronts": that is, a front that neglects the class struggle and unites the proletariat, the petty bourgeoisie, and even some sectors of the bourgeoisie. The popular front has cost the international proletariat numerous defeats. So-called national unity, the culmination of the degeneration of popular fronts, is the most cynical negation of the class struggle and the betrayal of the oppressed to their executioners. This bourgeois slogan has been put forward by the reformists. "National unity" means the unity of the bourgeoisie and its servants to handcuff the workers. "National unity" means defeat for the exploited and victory for the *rosca*. We cannot speak of national unity when the nation is divided into social classes bound together in a struggle to the death. While the regime of

private property exists, only traitors or agents in the pay of imperialism can dare speak of "national unity."

2. In opposition to the bourgeois slogan of "national unity," we propose the proletarian united front (FUP). The unification of the exploited and the revolutionary elements into a bloc that is as strong as granite is a powerful necessity for the destruction of capitalism, which is united in a single bloc.

We are forging a proletarian united front because we use the methods of proletarian revolution and because we never abandon the framework of the class struggle.

To avoid bourgeois influences, to turn our aspirations into realities, to mobilize the masses for the proletarian revolution, we need a proletarian united front. The revolutionary elements that identify with our fundamental statements and the proletarian organizations (railroads, textiles, graphics, drivers, etc.) will be well received in this united front. Recently, the CSTB has agitated for a left front. At this point, we don't know for what purposes this front is being formed. If it is merely a pre-electoral maneuver and an attempt to impose a petty-bourgeois leadership (and the CSTB is petty-bourgeois), we declare that we will have nothing to do with such a left front. But if proletarian ideas can become predominant and if its objectives are those of these theses, we and all our forces would join such a front, which in this latter case would be no more than a proletarian front with some slight variations and a different name.

Against the *rosca*, which is united in a single front, against the fronts that petty-bourgeois reformists dream up daily, *we are forging the proletarian united front!*

X. WORKERS' CONFEDERATION

The proletarian struggle needs a single authority. We must create a powerful Workers' Confederation. The shameful history of the CSTB demonstrates the way we should proceed to reach this goal. When the federations become docile instruments in the service of the petty-bourgeois political parties, when they make agreements with the bourgeoisie, they have stopped being representatives of the exploited. Our mission is to avoid the maneuvers of the union bureaucrats and the layers of craftsmen corrupted by the bourgeoisie. The confederation of Bolivians workers should be organized on a truly democratic basis. We are sick and tired of petty frauds committed to create majorities. We cannot allow an organization of a hundred craftsmen to weigh as heavily in the electoral balance as the FSTMB with 70,000 workers. The ideas of organizations that make up a majority should not be annulled by the vote of nearly non-existent organizations. The percentage of influence of the different federations should be determined by the size of their membership. *Proletarian thought, not petty-bourgeois ideology, should have primacy in the Workers' Confederation.* And it is our task to give it a truly revolutionary program that finds its inspiration in the ideas of this document.

XI. AGREEMENTS AND COMPROMISES

We can have no blocs or agreements with the bourgeoisie.

We can create blocs and sign agreements with the petty bourgeoisie as a class, but not with its political parties. The left front and the Workers' Confederation are examples of such blocs, but we definitely struggle for the proletariat to lead them. If it seems that we are following the petty bourgeoisie, we should reject and break such blocs.

Many pacts and agreements with different sectors might be unachievable, but are still powerful instruments in our hands. These commitments, if they are made with a revolutionary spirit, allow us to unmask the betrayals of the petty-bourgeoisie's caudillos and move their ranks to our positions. The July worker-university pact is an example of how an unfulfilled agreement can become a weapon for destroying our enemies. When some unauthorized university students abused our organizations in Oruro, the workers and revolutionary sectors in the university attacked the authors of this outrage and gave direction to the students. The declarations contained in the present document ought to be the starting point for any agreement.

The fulfillment of a pact depends on the miners' beginning an attack on the bourgeoisie, and we cannot wait for petty-bourgeois sectors to take such a step. The proletariat will be the leader of the revolution.

Revolutionary collaboration between the miners and the peasants is a central task of the FSTMB; such collaboration is the key to the future revolution. The workers should organize peasant unions and work together with their communities. To do this, the miners must support the peasant struggle against the *latifundio* and aid their revolutionary activities.

We must unite with the other proletarian sectors, and this unity should include the other exploited sectors of the craft workshops—the journeymen and apprentices.

NOTE: The First Extraordinary Congress ratified the worker-university pact signed in Oruro on July 29, 1946 (the program approved was based on that of the Third Miners' Congress of Catavi).

Pulacayo, November 8, 1946

10

The Cold War

FOR A DEMOCRATIC AND
ANTI-IMPERIALIST NATIONAL FRONT*
Mexican Communist Party

In 1946, the PCM called for support to the candidacy of Michael Alemán (of the
official government party, the PRM) for the presidency of the republic. It continued
supporting him until 1948, but with the beginning of the Cold War and the
government's anticommunist campaign, the PCM went into opposition. This 1951
document harshly criticizes the Alemán regime on behalf of a national-democratic
alternative; the radicalization of the party's policies during the Cold War did not
change its basic analysis of the character and tasks of the Mexican Revolution.

Mexicans:

Our people now face the decisive question of the presidential succession.
It is barely one year until the election of the next president of the republic
and the members of the Chamber of Deputies and the Senate, and the
unshakable decision of the Mexican people to resolve the presidential succession in accord with the national interests, their own sovereign will, and
the aspirations of the broadest popular masses is being displayed and is
growing—despite the proposals and maneuvers hatched in the highest
circles of the government and among anti-national forces serving the goals
of Yankee imperialism and reaction.

With the start of the struggle for the presidential succession, grave problems are weighing down upon the Mexican people, and Mexico is living
through one of the most serious and crucial situations in its history.

The resolution of this situation will determine whether Mexico will exist
as an independent and democratic nation, or if it will be completely dominated and colonized by Yankee imperialism and driven into backwardness,
misery, exploitation, and reactionary dictatorship to more easily impose the

---

*"Un Frente Nacional Democrático y Anti-imperialista," Political Commission of the Central
Committee of the PCM, July 1951.

will of the monopolistic circles of the United States and their policies of war and fascism.

THE POLITICS OF AN ANTI-POPULAR AND REACTIONARY REGIME

The threat of becoming cannon fodder, of going to die at distant battle-fronts in an unjust war of plunder, and the danger that Mexico will be dragged into a war of aggression being prepared by the North American imperialists to dominate the world and enslave all its peoples, hovers over our people and their youth.

Our country's dependence in relation to the United States and the intervention and colonial penetration of Yankee imperialism in Mexico have never been as shamefaced and obvious.

The unbridled cost of living is sinking its claws into the vast majority of the population; with the passive complicity of the current government, workers' wages are suffering blow after blow, and their families are being condemned to hunger. Meanwhile, with the dreadful rise in misery among the people, the ruling circles and the dominant classes make a show of a supposed but false era of "prosperity and national ascent," whose only manifestation is an insulting display of extravagance, waste, and ill-gotten wealth by an exploitative minority. The government claims to be fighting inflation, shortages, and high prices—the results of policies that condemn the masses to hunger and misery—by freezing and controlling workers' wages and repressing their struggles.

The working class is suffering under the attack of anti-worker and pro-boss government policies that are destroying the conquests of the workers, freezing their wages, flouting labor laws, destroying and obstructing trade union unity, intervening in the unions and imposing government control, making use of police repression to crush the revolutionary struggle of the proletariat, fomenting a considerable degree of corruption, and bribing insidious leaders of the workers' movement.

Along with the unrelenting destruction of the agrarian reform and the complete abandonment of the distribution of land to the peasants and harvest gleanings to the members of the *ejido*, a new caste of landowners is being formed that, along with the owners of the large *latifundios* that still exist and with the open connivance of official circles, condemns our country's vast peasant masses to a life of monstrous misery and unrestrained exploitation by landowners, speculators, functionaries of the Banco Ejidal, and private loan sharks.

These conditions are intensifying discontent among the popular masses and leading them to reject the policies of a government that has betrayed the Mexican Revolution and revealed its reactionary, anti-popular character and its submission to Yankee imperialism. The democratic liberties and political rights of the Mexican people are being violated and restricted, the Constitution is being attacked, and a shameless Penal Code is being adopted to repress the freedom of expression, the right of assembly, the right to strike, and the democratic struggles of the people and the working class of Mexico in defense of peace, national independence, and their own rights.

Along with the numerous Yankee loans which mortgage and give away our country, our national economy is tied and subordinate to the U.S. economy of war and crisis. The giant North American monopolies increasingly appropriate our national wealth and destroy the independent national economy of Mexico, with its own development and economic progress thereby obstructed.

Corruption and administrative immorality have invaded the state apparatus to an unprecedented degree, and millionaire public functionaries are being created overnight through the looting of the public treasury.

These facts, principally, describe the reactionary and anti-popular policies perpetuated by the government of President Alemán and indicate the grave situation and the serious problems that weigh upon our homeland and the Mexican people.

ANTI-IMPERIALISM IN BRAZIL*
Brazilian Communist Party

The Cold War period was characterized by the persecution of the Latin America Communist Parties and by their turn toward a policy of radical opposition to U.S. imperialism and their own governments. This orientation at times led to oversimplification, as in this 1952 Brazilian Communist Party (PCB) document that defines the populist regime of Vargas as pre-fascist and "a cynical agent of U.S. imperialism." Actually, Vargas zigzagged between accepting American impositions (a military assistance pact) and adopting timid nationalist initiatives; this provoked his downfall (and suicide) in 1954.

This document also shows the preoccupation of the Brazilian CP with the Korean War and the struggle against sending Brazilian troops to fight on the side of the North American interventionist forces. Its radical anti-imperialism corresponded to the Soviet foreign policy of the moment, but also to the sentiments of important sectors of the popular masses in Brazil, as shown by the success of the PCB's campaign against foreign oil companies, carried out under the slogan "The oil is ours!"

ONE MORE STEP TOWARD WAR

With the signing in Itamaratí on March 15 of last year of the so-called Military Assistance Accord between Brazil and the United States, the Vargas govern-

---

*"Resolução do PC do Brasil," in *Problemas*, n. 39, March–April 1952, pp. 3–6.

ment has taken a new and serious step toward dragging the country into an imperialist war and has committed a new crime against the security and sovereignty of the homeland and the lives of the Brazilian people.

The Executive Committee of the Communist Party of Brazil, confronting the seriousness of this event and convinced that it is expressing the hopes for peace of the vast majority of the nation, raises its most vehement protest against this new step along the path of war and national betrayal, and asks the people to stay alert to the growing danger that threatens us all.

This "Military Assistance Accord" is really a pact for war, drawn up secretly behind the backs of the people, and is contrary to the vital interests of the nation. It is above all an attempt to drag our nation behind the warmongering acts of the United States and send Brazilian troops to Korea, or any other part of the world, according to Truman's will. It is not by chance that this document repeats that it is the wish of the Vargas government "to provide armed forces to the United Nations," an organization that today is notorious for becoming the mere instrument of North American aggression in Korea.

Second, Mr. Vargas aims to legalize the concession of military bases to the United States with this new "Accord" and facilitate the occupation of our soil by North American troops. And since this so-called military assistance is directed against supposed external or even internal aggression, the terms of the "Accord" permit the automatic occupation of our territory by North American troops in case of any popular movement against our country's government, which could be easily termed aggression by "international Communism." It is obvious that Mr. Vargas, fearing the people, is already soliciting help from his Yankee bosses to make our homeland another Greece, with American soldiers coming to kill Brazilians to preserve the interests of traitors and enemies of the people. Beyond these fundamental objectives, the new "Accord" completely submits the Brazilian armed forces to the control of the American imperialists. They aim to transform it into a body of mercenaries under the command of Yankee generals and officers, so it can be launched not only against the Korean people and other free peoples, but equally against our own people, who are against imperialist war and are showing that they are not prepared to die slowly of hunger or allow themselves to be enslaved by fascists and agents of American imperialism.

Finally, in the terms of the new "Accord," the Vargas government freely surrenders all our nation's wealth to American imperialism, completely opens the country's ports to the invasion of Yankee agents and spies with their privileges and diplomatic immunity, and cynically violates the nation's laws, assuring rights of territoriality and even guarantees against legal suits to Truman's agents.

This is, in short, the content of this "Accord," a clear attack on the manifest will for peace of the whole people and a true crime of treason against our national sovereignty and the lives and liberty of the Brazilians.

The signing of this "Accord" thus shows the nation the real meaning of the policies of Mr. Vargas and once again confirms what the Communist Party of Brazil has repeatedly said in this regard: that this is a government of war and national betrayal, a government of the most cynical agents of American imperialism, which since its first days has been attempting to drag the country into direct participation in the aggressive acts of the American warmongers. This shameless participation by Mr. Vargas in the war plans of American imperialism is what leads him to suppress the Continental Peace Conference—the expression of the desire for peace among the peoples of the American continent—and to unleash terror against people struggling against hunger and for peace and democratic rights. This is how the Vargas government is preparing the conditions for implanting fascism in the country, under the well-known pretext of fighting the Communists. This is the reason for the police provocations, the supposed "armed coups" of which the Communists have been accused, which serve to justify the unleashing of police terror against the people, and the legalization of exceptional measures to crush the people's struggles, drag the country into war, and give away Brazil's petroleum to Standard Oil and satisfy the other demands of the American warmongers.

Only the power of the united and organized people can stop these criminal policies and keep Mr. Vargas from freely following the path to war. Only the people's power can save the country from the catastrophe that threatens it. With the seriousness of this situation and the growing danger that threatens the nation and the people's very existence, no patriot can stand with his arms crossed, passive and indifferent.

The Executive Committee of the Communist Party of Brazil therefore calls upon all people to unequivocally oppose the monstrous plans of the Vargas government and the North American imperialists. Today more than ever, it is indispensable that the voice of the people make itself heard, that energetic and resolute protests—the broadest possible—rise throughout the country against the crime signified by the signing of this new war covenant with the American imperialists. Using all forms of protest, the great popular masses must demonstrate their repudiation of this criminal pact against the homeland and promote the widest possible actions to keep the National Congress from ratifying it. Popular action can overcome these war accords and paralyze the government's war policies. If the great popular masses take the defense of peace and national sovereignty into their own hands, the warmongers' plans can be defeated.

The Executive Committee of the Communist Party of Brazil calls on all patriots, both men and women; mothers, wives, daughters, and girlfriends that feel the danger that threatens the lives of their loved ones; the youth, whether workers, peasants, or students, soldiers, sailors, or air corpsmen, who are threatened with death because of the sinister and criminal plans of Mr. Vargas. To all, we make a passionate call to intensify the struggle for peace and against the Vargas government of national treason, against sending Brazilian troops to Korea, and against the concession of Brazilian oil to American imperialism.

The Executive Committee of the Communist Party of Brazil especially calls on the workers and peasants to intensify their struggle for peace, against Mr. Vargas' politics of war, hunger, and reaction, for national liberation from the imperialist yoke, and for a democratic and popular government.

In this emergency, each party organization and each Communist has the duty to redouble their efforts with all other partisans of peace in the struggle for the defense of peace and national independence.

REVOLUTIONARY SOCIALISM IN ECUADOR*
Manuel Agustín Aguirre

During the Cold War, the Latin American Communist movement was not alone in raising the banner of radical anti-imperialism. Some revolutionary socialist currents developed that were more or less influenced by the ideas of Trotsky, especially in Chile and Ecuador; their orientation was both anti-imperialist and anti-capitalist (see, for example, the work of Oscar Waiss of the Chilean Socialist Party, *Nacionalismo y Socialismo en America Latina* [Santiago: Prensa Latinoamericana, 1954]).

Manuel Agustín Aguirre was one of the founders of the Socialist Party of Ecuador (1933) and its General Secretary for many years. Elected senator in 1944, he was imprisoned and exiled by the dictatorship of Velásco Ibarra (1946). He was also the first dean of the faculty of economic sciences and later the rector of the Central University of Ecuador. In 1960, Manuel Agustín Aguirre led the majority of the party rank-and-file in a left split that created the Revolutionary Socialist Party of Ecuador.

The selections we reprint here are from a speech he gave on May 1, 1952, and summarize some of the central themes of revolutionary socialism in Latin America (notably the strategic principle of the socialist character of the continental revolution).

---

*Manuel Agustín Aguirre, *América Latina y el Ecuador (apuntes para un estudio socioeconómico)*, 1952 (Quito: Associación de la Escuela de la Facultad de Ciencias Administrativas, 1972).

A BOURGEOIS REVOLUTION IN LATIN AMERICA AND ECUADOR?

Following on this summary analysis, I feel it would be absurd to await a messianic (and long frustrated) 1789 to liquidate what remains of our feudal structure and move us forward to an industrial, progressive capitalism. How can we expect the landowning bourgeoisie or the bourgeois landowners to destroy the very structure that serves as their base of support? How can we believe these feudal-bourgeois castes will solve the agrarian problem by giving land to the peasants if they basically live from the exploitation of this very peasantry? How can the laissez-faire economy of a liberal state (which for years has been displaying its incompetence) advance our delayed and paralyzed economic development? How can we expect those who live from the misery and exploitation of the people to be capable of liberating and redeeming them?

Metaphysical theoreticians who think that bourgeois classes and liberal ideas ought to have the same relevance in the middle of the twentieth century in Indian America as they did during the industrialization of Europe and the United States in the eighteenth and nineteenth centuries, so foreign and different a time, lead us to such unsustainable positions. It is these scandalous incongruities that have led us to consistently put forward the unavoidable necessity of dealing with our own Latin American and Ecuadorian problems. We must honestly put ourselves in the category of semicolonial and semi-capitalist countries, hitched to the wagon of world imperialism.

So, how can we imagine that the landowning national bourgeoisie will struggle against imperialism, an ally on which it is fully dependent? Don't we realize that the Latin American economies, especially Ecuador's, are still tied to the import and export trade, which establishes their essential character and rhythm? Then it isn't difficult to understand that the landowners who produce raw materials for imperialism, as well as the layer of major import and export merchants who live by foreign trade, will not struggle against imperialism, to which they are tied so intimately. If our incipient national industrial capital does at times oppose the imperialists as competitors, they nevertheless are not sufficiently capable of anti-imperialist struggle. Whenever they feel threatened, they rush to join the imperialist bourgeoisie, who extend a helping hand in continental solidarity to guarantee their salvation . . . .

As we have shown in this short essay, it is undeniable that there are major vestiges of feudalism, supported by the landowning bourgeoisie and imperialism, particularly in the countryside, that have limited and delayed our progress. But denying that capitalism is the fundamental form of productive relations and that there is a proletariat with sufficient capacity to constitute itself as the leading force of the Latin American and Ecuadorian revolution reflects the distance between comfortable opportunism and a truly revolutionary attitude. And while the proletariat, like any class for itself, perhaps, is not a numerical majority, it is a qualitative majority, as Lenin says, because of its strength and revolutionary capacity.

In addition, if we consider not only the industrial proletariat, but also the proletarians and semi-proletarians in the city and the countryside who sweat and die to feed and enrich the national landowning bourgeoisie and the international bourgeoisie, we see that they form the great majority of the nation. Or does the tiny bourgeois-landowning class constitute a majority?

And even supposing that some underdeveloped nations of Latin America, like Ecuador, were fundamentally feudal and therefore the proletariat was an insignificant minority, as some theoreticians claim—not even then could we conclude that the bourgeois revolution and not the proletarian revolution was the only possible revolution in our America. We have already proved *ad nauseam* how impossible and absurd it is to expect a revolution by a bourgeois-landowning class that is committed to maintaining the feudal-bourgeois-imperialist structure of our nations. History has shown us that numerical majorities are not necessary for a revolution. The proletariat, though a minority, is the only class capable of leading the socialist transformation in Ecuador, our continent, and the entire world that is needed to save humanity.

Also, we must once and for all negate the pseudo-Marxist thesis that maintains the impossibility of socialism in countries like ours that have not yet reached their full capitalist development. These theoreticians ignore the fact that after the worldwide growth of capitalism and the arrival of imperialism, nations cannot be considered isolated and independent units, but are simply weak or strong links in the chain of world capitalism. These gentlemen forget the great Russian Revolution and that capitalism, decadent world capitalism, exists as a whole and must be transcended, as quickly as possible, by the revolutionary advent of socialism . . . .

A LATIN AMERICAN WORKER-PEASANT FRONT AND THE UNITED SOCIALIST STATES OF LATIN AMERICA

This leads us to maintain the necessity of forming a single front of workers and poor peasants in Latin America, supported by the world proletariat, to push forward the socialist revolution that will rescue our countries from their backwardness, destroy exploitation and misery, and establish real freedom, peace, and justice.

Just as the landholding bourgeoisie knew to unite during the great War of Independence (during which, given its class nature, the people's blood was disgracefully spilled for bourgeois interests), the proletarian and peasant classes of Latin America now must join in a continental embrace of solidarity and create a real struggle, in the broadest sense, for the liberation and independence of Latin American humanity. The working classes, to liberate themselves from the yoke of exploitation, will liberate all humanity by building a classless socialist society.

Only a worker and peasant front will create true freedom in America, break the chains of slavery and servitude both internally and externally, and give full liberty to American humanity.

Only the Latin American socialist revolution, by planning our economies not only in a national but an international manner, adjusting and perfecting them as a whole, will make it possible to form the United Socialist States of Latin America, which ought to be our greatest continental aspiration. Bolivar's dream was the dream of the American bourgeois-landholding class. It could not be fulfilled because this class was built upon rivalry and competition, which separates nations into dominators and dominated, exploiters and exploited. This is why only socialism, which is the suppression of the exploitation of man by man and of nation by nation, will make possible a Latin American unity based on true equity and justice.

This is the greatest duty of the worker and peasant classes of Latin America. This is the greatest duty and responsibility of the truly revolutionary leftist youth of America, especially the university youth, who ought to be the most conscious of their historic mission. This is the greatest duty of all people who aspire to real peace and justice—the great duty to which we must pledge ourselves this May Day, 1952.

GUATEMALA: THE COMMUNIST SELF-CRITICISM*

Guatemalan Labor Party

The overthrow of the progressive regime of Jacobo Arbenz in Guatemala (1951–54), which followed an invasion by "volunteers" that had been directly inspired and organized by the U.S., was one of the most crucial episodes of the Cold War years on the continent. In this document, published a year after the invasion, the Guatemalan Labor Party (the country's Communist Party), which had played an important role in the Arbenz government, develops a self-critical balance sheet of its line during this period; it recognizes that it had committed a certain number of errors, particularly in its relations with the national bourgeoisie, whose influence on the party had been so profound that it was able to restrain many of its activities.

---

*Political Commission of the PGT, *La intervención norteamericana en Guatemala y el derrocamiento del régimen democrático* (1955), pp. 3–4, 30–36.

This critique shows that the Cold War had not changed the fundamental strategic orientation of the Latin American Communist movement: an alliance with the democratic bourgeoisie to reach the first historical stage of the revolution.

The democratic, freely elected government of Guatemala, which had been presided over by Colonel Jacobo Arbenz since March 15, 1951, was over-thrown on June 27, 1954. Since that time, the Guatemalan people have been preoccupied with establishing what factors led to the temporary defeat of the Guatemalan revolutionary movement. The peoples of the world in turn have also asked why there was not greater and more prolonged resistance to the North American aggression in Guatemala. Many diverse, even quite unserious versions of the events have been given. But there has been a lack of serious and profound analysis of the fundamental reason for this defeat that could draw out the principal lessons of these events for the people and conse-quently illuminate the road that the popular masses must follow to make of our country a democratic, prosperous, and independent Guatemala.

The Political Commission of the Central Committee of the Guatemalan Labor Party (PGT), with the aid of Marxism-Leninism, the proven, scien-tific theory of the working class, has attempted a serious effort to make a proper examination of that experience, which quite understandably could not be made public until this time. This undoubtedly will be of great use for the elaboration of the party's political line and at the same time help the Guatemalan working class and popular masses to better orient themselves in their struggle against the falsification of the facts, and to shake off the yoke of tyranny and imperialist domination from North America.

WHERE THE AGGRESSION CAME FROM

The United States government has tried in vain to disguise the facts and hide its responsibilities as the organizer of this intervention, attributing the overthrow of this democratic regime to the Guatemalan people, who had enjoyed the broadest freedom in its history under this very regime. The truth, known by our people and proven even more every day, is that the overthrow of Arbenz's legitimate government, the brutal crushing of all our liberties, and the destruction of all our revolutionary and democratic conquests were the work of the Yankee monopolies, particularly those that have investments in Guatemala or covet the natural wealth of our country, such as the United Fruit Company, among others. It was the work, there-fore, of the United States government, which for years has been under the control of the great North American monopolies, in whose name it prac-tices aggressive policies and the colonial subjugation of our countries. It was also the work of the reactionary bourgeois-landowning clique upon which

North American imperialism has always relied to oppress our people and plunder our country mercilessly.

The invaders who violated our fatherland's borders at two points and moved into our territory from Honduras, sowing desolation, terror, and death as they passed, were in their overwhelming majority Nicaraguan, Honduran, Salvadoran, Dominican, and Cuban mercenaries (with only a minimal number of Guatemalans). They ran the gamut from failed adventurers to *mafiosi* of the lowest type to professional criminals, recruited and paid by United Fruit and trained for months in Nicaragua and Honduras by U.S. Army officers. These bands of hoodlums were armed to the teeth by Yankee corporations, primarily United Fruit, with weapons supplied by the U.S. government, which was hiding behind the facade of puppet regimes in Honduras and Nicaragua.

The fact that a group of Guatemalan traitors, headed by the most traitorous Carlos Castillo Armas, seemed to lead the invasion in no way changes the foreign character of the invasion. The whole world knows that Castillo Armas and his tiny gang of adventurers couldn't raise a nickel to finance an invasion, and that the contributions of plantation owners, large merchants, and reactionary bosses could barely whet the appetite of this group of lowlifes. Everyone knows that the United Fruit plantations in Honduras, which extend right to the borders of Guatemala, had become the main center of the conspiracy against Guatemala's democratic regime over recent years. It was here that plans were developed to be approved later in Washington and Boston; it was here that the saboteurs and terrorists were recruited and later dispatched inside Guatemala; it was here that the propaganda, dirty lies, and slanders against the democratic forces and the Guatemalan revolutionary movement were cooked up; it was here that the so-called anticommunist civic marches were planned and arranged; it was to here that the conspirators came to coordinate their activity with Somoza, Pérez Jiménez, Trujillo, and Batista, all of whom had been ordered by the Yankee State Department to "cooperate" in carrying out these plans to crush democracy in Guatemala; and it was here, finally, that the mercenaries who made up the misnamed "liberation army" were recruited and paid.

The United States government supplied the planes that flew over cities and towns in Guatemala for ten consecutive days, bombing and burning not only military targets, but humble homes, churches, and schools. The planes that gunned down the peaceful population of Guatemala City, Chiquimula, Zacapa, and other towns with the purpose of sowing terror and desperation were piloted by North American fliers who later cynically boasted of their "exploits."

The coup d'état by the military traitors who overthrew President Arbenz's government when all the conditions were in place to defeat this foreign aggression, was planned, financed, and directed by the United States Embassy in Guatemala. The Yankee ambassador, John Peurifoy, a gangster and provocateur with a sorry record in Greece, where he had been commissioned to organize the slaughter of Greek patriots, was the man chosen by the United States government to execute the orders of the North American monopolies and drown Guatemala's democratic regime in blood.

To better understand why the Yankee imperialists organized their intervention and attacked our country to crush the revolutionary movement and overthrow the Arbenz government, we should recall some prominent characteristics of the situation and the struggles of our people.

THE EXPERIENCES OF THE PARTY

THE DEVELOPMENT OF THE PARTY OF GUATEMALAN COMMUNISTS

The Guatemalan Labor Party, founded on September 28, 1949, has accumulated a rich fund of experience in a short time. Our party has had to confront very complex situations and problems and deal with tasks that transcended its strength, experience, and theoretical level. It has quite often been successful in such situations, while in others its inexperience and theoretical weaknesses were obstacles to victory, or it did not have the necessary strength to move forward successfully.

Our party has had to work in a quite backward arena, where the enemies of the working class and the people had carried out poisonous anti-communist propaganda for decades before the birth of our party as an organization that could adequately answer the dirty lies of this anti-communist propaganda: an arena in which clericalism and alcoholism have been the main weapons of the dominant reactionary classes, aiming to sap the will and the combative, rebellious spirit of the working class and all the oppressed working masses.

Our party, thanks to the self-denying labors of our few cadres and militants, most of whom had only recently been won to the cause of socialism, succeeded in breaking the political blockade that the reactionaries had attempted to impose since its birth, and won the support and sympathy of a large part of the working class and important sectors of the peasant masses, intellectuals, and progressive professionals. Our party was the principal motor force, organizer, and leader of the struggle for working-class unity, the most important defender of this unity when it found its organic form in the CGTG, the organizer and leader of the major battles for the workers' demands, the guiding force of the working class in defense of the peasants' demands, most importantly the agrarian reform, and the driving force of the struggle for the rapid granting of land to the peasants.

It was our own party that was the most concerned about defending the rights and demands of youth and women. Our party was the biggest fighter for the unity of democratic and anti-imperialist forces. It supported and defended the democratic regime of Colonel Arbenz with the greatest firmness and patriotism, insofar as the regime adopted policies with an anti-feudal and anti-imperialist content.

As a consequence of its struggle in defense of the interests of democracy, national independence, and the interests of the working masses, the party has won the ferocious hatred of the reactionary classes, a hatred that is more than compensated for by the growing affection, respect, and sympathy of the working class, the peasant masses, and the honest elements among the democratic intellectuals.

With the affection and respect of working people that our party has won thanks to the importance and selflessness of its struggle, no fascist law, no slander campaign, no type of brutal terror, can keep the people from increasingly placing its trust in our party. Nothing can liquidate the party of the Guatemalan Communists, because our party did not develop accidentally, but grew in the process of the working-class struggle for national liberation and against class exploitation. It has tied its destiny, its life, and its lot to the historic development of the society at whose head the working class must inevitably march.

The development of the Guatemalan Labor Party is indissolubly linked to its struggle in defense of the interests of the people and the homeland; this will remain the source of its strength and its future expansion.

Along with its noted successes, our party has committed serious errors that we must frankly recognize to learn the lessons of these experiences, so we can keep them from again obstructing the successful struggle of the party.

The Political Commission of the Central Committee considers that the party's errors and weakness basically grew out of its political line. The party's political line was generally correct, but was nevertheless insufficient and incomplete in some aspects insofar as it did not lay down a concrete perspective to confront certain problems that later had to be addressed by the party leadership. This inadequacy in our political line was undoubtedly due to the low theoretical level of our party and to the fact that our congress (the Second Party Congress, in December 1952) did not deepen the discussion of the most important problems for the development of the revolution.

But, above all, the origin of the party's errors was in the insufficient assimilation and poor application of the party's political line. Certain questions that were highlighted at the congress, such as the character of the bourgeois-democratic revolution in a semi-colonial country like ours and the role of the proletariat as the leading force of such a revolution, were not taken into account later, or were in some cases underestimated and not developed in a consistent manner during the revolutionary struggle.

Let us examine the major errors of the party.

THE ALLIANCE WITH THE NATIONAL BOURGEOISIE

The Guatemalan Labor Party did not follow a sufficiently independent line in relation to the democratic national bourgeoisie. Its alliance with the democratic bourgeoisie had notable successes, but at the same time, the bourgeoisie exercised a certain influence in our party that in practice constituted a break upon many of its activities.

The PGT did not correctly estimate the weakness of the bourgeoisie's capacity for resistance and did not always take into account its conciliatory character in relation to imperialism and the reactionary classes. It thereby held some illusions in the patriotism, loyalty, and steadfastness of the national bourgeoisie in regard to the attacks of North American imperialism.

The PGT theoretically maintained the Leninist criterion that the national bourgeoisie is no longer a consistently revolutionary class in the imperialist epoch, and therefore it must be the working class that puts itself at the head of and exercises hegemony over the bourgeois-democratic revolution. But in practice, it limited itself to constantly repeating this Leninist concept without understanding its full depth. It did not struggle with the necessary tenacity for the working class to conquer the leadership of the revolutionary movement, nor did it put forward or resolve the concrete tasks necessary to assure the hegemony of the working class in the revolutionary movement.

Our party was aware that many leaders of the bourgeois parties and important elements of the government, of whose vacillations it was already conscious, would capitulate to imperialism. It understood that the vacillations of the revolutionary movement were due particularly to the fact that the bourgeoisie was still playing the leading role for most of the revolutionary movement and that it was necessary for the working class to become the hegemonic force among the totality of revolutionary forces. Yet our party, at bottom, nourished the false idea that it was still not possible for the Guatemalan working class to win the leadership of the revolutionary movement because it was numerically very weak and politically quite backward. Nevertheless, this way of putting things was leading to a dead end and could only leave the leadership of the revolutionary movement in the hands of the democratic bourgeoisie to the extent that the working class was not growing and developing politically.

It is clear that our party unconsciously fell into opportunist positions demolished more than fifty years ago by the great Lenin. A paper from the Marx-Engels-Lenin-Stalin Institute, "The Fiftieth Anniversary of the first Russian Revolution," says the following on this question:

The course of the revolution confirmed the correctness and vitality of the strategy and tactics of the Bolsheviks. The Leninist thesis that the proletariat can and must play the leading role in the revolutionary movement was fully confirmed . . . .

In a backward peasant country like Russia, the working class demonstrated that the real power and role of the proletariat do not depend on whether it constitutes a majority of the population of a country, but upon its revolutionary energy, its political consciousness, its capacity to lead the people's revolutionary struggle, and its ability to attract the peasant masses as allies of the revolution.

If our party had stopped to examine the question in the light of Marxism-Leninism, it would have understood that the numerical weakness of the Guatemalan working class was not an insuperable obstacle to its assuming the leadership of the revolutionary movement. In regard to the political backwardness of the working class, the question depended entirely on the party itself, on what it did to arm itself and the working class with Marxist-Leninist theory, on the will, energy, and audacity displayed by the party in the task of raising the political level of the working class, and particularly its consciousness of its own leading role in the anti-feudal and anti-imperialist revolution.

There are other important indications of the practical concessions made by the party to the democratic bourgeoisie.

The PGT, for example, committed the serious error of not denouncing and struggling publicly against those members of the army High Command that it knew, because of their class and ideology, were the enemies of the revolutionary movement and of the fundamental transformations that were taking place in Guatemala. The party put no trust in traitors like Monzón, Sánchez, Aldana Sandoval, Parinello, and others. But because of an incorrect manner of confronting the issue—to a certain degree accepting the false, bourgeois idea of an "apolitical army" (really a smokescreen behind which the generals have always pursued reactionary politics)—and fearing that the party could be accused of creating a provocation, it did not publicly unmask them, but limited itself to putting forward its views among narrow circles of the democratic camp and to President Arbenz. The PGT contributed to sowing illusions in the army and did not unmask the true positions and counterrevolutionary activities of the army High Command. It published in its newspaper, without the necessary criticism, speeches by Arbenz in which he discussed the "loyalty" of the generals and their hypocritical declarations, although it was useless to wait for them to confront Yankee imperialism even if our country were attacked.

Our party did not assume a consistent, critical attitude toward the democratic bourgeoisie and was complacent with them at times. It forgot that an alliance with the bourgeoisie should not tie the party's hands or keep it from criticizing or condemning their many vices and inconsistent actions toward the people and the revolutionary movement.

We will return to this question in examining our united front work.

THE PARTY'S WORK IN THE WORKING CLASS

The Guatemalan Labor Party conducted much fruitful work in the working class, carried out the correct united-front policies in the union movement, fought sectarianism and factionalism inside and outside the party, and led great, victorious workers' struggles in defense of wages and other major demands. But our party limited itself to economic activity in the class and did not know how to connect the struggle for economic demands and work in the union arena with the daily political activity of a revolutionary working-class party, and how to carry out political agitation and propaganda so that the class could correctly understand those social and political phenomena that were taking place, the positions of the various parties and classes in regard to these phenomena, and the positions and political line of our party.

The party lacked tenacity and intransigence in its organizing work in the class, which kept it from taking full advantage of the great influence and authority of the party in general, and of certain comrades in particular, in the workers' movement.

Long before the North American invasion and the army traitors' coup, the PGT definitely favored the workers' and peasants' arming themselves, considering this task as the key to the victory of the democratic forces in confronting imminent foreign intervention. Yet the party did not lay this task before the working class with the necessary energy and audacity; it only put it forward to some allies, and afterwards, confronting imminent foreign invasion, explained it too late and quite weakly to the working masses.

The principal actions in this regard were taken by the party from above, with some of its allies. The party was dominated by the fear that it might precipitate an army coup, or at least a political push from this quarter, if it openly put forward the question of arming the working class and the peasants, and could not find the method or opportunity to raise the question when it could have done so. Even when the North American invasion began, the issue was not posed well, since the party left the initiative to the popular organizations to demand military instruction at first, and later, the right to fight alongside the army in the defense of the fatherland.

This manner of posing the question fed illusions among the masses on the role the army would play, since it left them to suppose that the army was loyal in its totality and would fight with dignity against the invader and honorably maintain its oath to defend the inviolability of our national territory and sovereignty, our democratic institutions, and the legitimate government elected by the people.

It is true that the party organized numerous brigades of workers, peasants, and youth to fight against the intervention; it is certainly true that these brigades, armed only with machetes and sticks, confronted reactionary groups in different parts of the country. But the party basically waited for the army to distribute arms under order from President Arbenz. For its part, the army, which only received this order the day before the coup, repeatedly rejected the requests of the unions and the peasant and popular organizations for military training and weapons.

Our party did not fight with the masses against the army's refusal to arm the workers and peasants and did not publicly unmask the class basis of this refusal (which was hypocritically hidden behind feigned declarations of patriotism and self-sufficiency in fighting off an invasion). Our party did not carry out energetic activities to make the slogan of the arming of the people understood by each worker, peasant, and anti-imperialist fighter to the point where they would feel the need to arm themselves at all costs. Since this work was never carried out, the peasants innocently proceeded to turn over weapons, which had been dropped by parachute from invading planes, to the military and civil authorities. The party committed a serious error by praising this naive act of the peasants and giving instructions in some places to do the same, fearing a "premature" conflict with the army and maintaining the hope that they could reach an agreement to arm the people "from above." It is true that there were not many such weapons and that most of them were old or useless, but this fact does not in the least mitigate the party's errors.

Finally, the party committed the error of not concerning itself with organizing revolutionary work in the army. It did not take advantage of the tremendous opportunity given by the agrarian reform to approach the soldiers, who in their great majority are of peasant origin, on behalf of the working class, and carry out the serious work of agitation and propaganda for the goals of the revolutionary movement, against the venomous anti-Communist and counterrevolutionary work of the reactionary officers and general staff.

THE UNITED FRONT OF REVOLUTIONARY FORCES

The party followed the correct line of allying with all democratic and anti-imperialist forces against the feudal landowners, the reactionary bourgeoisie, and Yankee imperialism. Nevertheless, in applying the correct united front line, the party conceded more importance to the alliance with the bourgeois-democratic parties than to forging a firm alliance between the working class and the peasantry. The party did not sufficiently take into account that the united front of all democratic forces ought to have the alliance of workers and peasants as its fundamental basis, since the peasants are the most natural and closest allies of the working class and such an alliance is indispensable for the working class to exercise hegemony in the revolutionary movement and guarantee its consistent growth.

The party created the conditions for a close alliance between the workers and peasants by leading the working-class struggle for agrarian reform, making this a demand of the working class itself, by struggling consistently for the demands of the peasants, and by demanding the immediate delivery of land to the peasants, irrespective of their political or religious views or membership in a mass organization. But these favorable conditions were not fully taken advantage of, nor did the party discover the many concrete ways to use them to strengthen the worker-peasant alliance.

As to the alliance of the party with the bourgeois-democratic parties, we ought to point out that this was the result of a correct tactic that corresponded to the interests of the people and the objectives of the revolutionary and democratic movement. The party persevered in its efforts to maintain and perfect it. We should recognize that, along with the capitulators and encrusted reactionaries, there were elements and forces in the bourgeois-democratic parties who responded consistently to the line of unity among the revolutionary forces, thanks to which some important economic, social, and political conquests were made.

GUATEMALA: THE TROTSKYIST POSITION*
Ismael Frías

Shortly before the pro-American coup in Guatemala (June 1954), the Latin American Trotskyist Ismael Frias published an analysis of the situation, along with concrete proposals for the workers' movement: the creation of soldiers' committees to purge the army, the organization of workers' militias under the control of the unions, and so forth. This article from the journal *Fourth International* also contains an interpretation of the contradictory and unstable nature of the Arbenz regime and the reasons it did not enjoy the support of the bourgeoisie.

THE BOURGEOISIE AND THE GOVERNMENT

The Arbenz government is a bourgeois government. We should not be confused about this if we want to understand what is happening in Guatemala. José Manuel Fortuny, the General Secretary of the Communist Party

---

*Ismael Frías, "La Révolution guatémaltèque," *Quatrième Internationale*, v. 12, n. 3–5, March 1954.

(now called the Guatemalan Labor Party), in his report to the Second Party Congress on behalf of the Central Committee, himself recognizes that "the Arbenz government . . . is a government of the national bourgeoisie and the petty bourgeoisie, serving the nationalist interests of the bourgeoisie and leading its revolutionary activity against feudalism." What Fortuny passes over in silence, which as a Stalinist he must, is that the Guatemalan bourgeoisie is far from fully in support of its own government, especially in regard to the revolutionary measures it has had to sanction under the pressure of the masses and, most of all, its bold attempts to rely on the masses to resist imperialism. The Arbenz government is a Bonapartist bourgeois government that, while always defending the general political interests of the bourgeoisie, maintains an equilibrium between the bourgeoisie and the masses and between the masses and imperialism, thereby establishing its relative independence. In his article "Nationalized Industry and Workers' Management," Leon Trotsky, studying the Cárdenas government, wrote:

> The government oscillates between foreign and domestic capital, between the weak national bourgeoisie and the relatively powerful proletariat. This gives the government a distinctive character. It raises itself, so to speak, above classes. In reality, it can govern . . . by maneuvering with the proletariat, going so far as making concessions to it, thereby gaining the possibility of a certain independence in relation to foreign capitalists.[1]

The Arbenz government is of this type.

The difference between the current government and Arévalo's is that the Arbenz government has been subjected to much stronger popular pressure, forcing it to make much greater concessions to the workers. In the report cited above, Fortuny admits a great part of the truth when he says: "The new correlation of forces and the change of government have been characterized by more important popular organizations and mobilizations that have allowed the Arbenz government to show a much greater independence."

We should not nourish illusions in the anti-imperialist capacity of the Guatemalan bourgeoisie and, in consequence, its government. Again, as Fortuny tells us in his report: "The fact that a small part of the Guatemalan bourgeoisie is resisting imperialism and concerning itself with the defense of our national sovereignty does not mean that the Guatemalan bourgeoisie in general, being weak and immature, is disposed to defend the national interest, since it values its relations with imperialism above the interests of the nation."

---

[1] See Leon Trotsky, "Nationalized Industry and Workers' Management," *Writings, 1938–39* (New York: Pathfinder Press, 1974), pp. 326–329—Translator.

A government like that of Arbenz is extremely transitory, given that it represents an unstable factor in the social equilibrium. Either it will be overthrown by imperialism and the Idigorista feudal bourgeoisie or it will give way to a government of the Communist Party, the General Workers' Confederation, and the National Peasant Confederation that will actually emancipate the country from imperialism and complete the agrarian reform. Clearly Guatemala's revolutionary Marxists must struggle untiringly for the latter solution.

Between now and then, our duty is to defend the Arbenz government, arms in hand, against all attacks by the pro-Yankee counterrevolution. This naturally does not mean that we should give it the least political support, conceal its limitations and ephemeral character, or sow illusions about its ability to lead the anti-imperialist struggle. It is precisely this that differentiates revolutionary Marxists from opportunist bureaucrats like Fortuny; the former tell the truth to the workers and prepare them to defend the government against reaction and replace it with their own government, while the latter deceive the workers and disorient them, keeping them from preparing for both these tasks.

___11___

After the Twentieth Congress

FOR CAPITALIST ECONOMIC
DEVELOPMENT IN BRAZIL*
Brazilian Communist Party

A reorientation of the politics of Latin American Communism took place after the end of the Cold War, especially after the Twentieth Congress of the Communist Party of the Soviet Union. The 1949–54 line was criticized as sectarian and ultra-left, and a much more moderate orientation was put in place, with the theory of a "peaceful road" to socialism as its central axis. We can also observe a certain rapprochement with the "developmentalist" conceptions then predominant in political and academic milieus in Latin America. The following selections, from a March 1958 declaration of the Brazilian CP, clearly and systematically present the central ideas of this new period: capitalist development corresponds with the interests of all the people, and the main contradiction is between the developing nation and North American imperialism.

Let us note in passing that the text also insists upon the importance of "feudal remnants" as a break upon the capitalist development of the country.

The documents of the Twentieth Congress of the Communist Party of the Soviet Union led to an intense discussion in the ranks of our party, during which serious political errors of a dogmatic and sectarian character were submitted to criticism.

The examination of these errors and the necessity of overcoming them have led the Central Committee of the PCB to lay out the new political orientation put forward in the present declaration. In the process, the Central Committee has considered the past experience of the party and the basic changes that have occurred in the Brazilian and world situation.

The Central Committee hopes that the politics laid out here will be submitted to verification in the process of their practical application, and be enriched by the experience of the party and the Brazilian people . . . .

---

*Declaração sobre a política do Partido Comunista do Brasil, Rio de Janeiro, March 1958, pp. 3, 14–16, 24–26.

THE CONTRADICTION DEEPENS BETWEEN THE BRAZILIAN NATION AND NORTH AMERICAN IMPERIALISM

The changes in the country's economic and political situation, as well as the international situation, determine important changes in the arrangement of social forces and define the path for solving the problems of the Brazilian revolution. As a consequence of North American imperialist exploitation and the maintenance of a monopoly of land ownership, Brazilian society is subjected to two fundamental contradictions in the current historical stage. The first is the contradiction between the nation and North American imperialism and its local agents. The second is the contradiction between the developing productive forces and the semi-feudal relations of production. The economic and social development of Brazil necessarily revolves around the resolution of these two fundamental contradictions.

Brazilian society also encompasses the contradiction between the proletariat and the bourgeoisie, which expresses itself in various forms of class struggle between workers and capitalists. But this contradiction does not demand a radical solution at the current stage. In the country's present condition, capitalist development corresponds to the interests of the proletariat and the whole people.

The revolution in Brazil, therefore, is not socialist, but anti-imperialist and anti-feudal, national and democratic. The complete solution to the problems thus outlined must lead toward our full economic and political liberation from dependence upon North American imperialism, the radical transformation of the agrarian structure with the liquidation of the monopoly of land ownership and pre-capitalist labor relations, the independent and progressive development of the national economy, and the radical democratization of political life. These transformations will remove the deeper causes of our people's backwardness and, with the strength of the anti-imperialist and anti-feudal forces under the leadership of the proletariat, create the conditions for the transition to socialism, which is not the immediate but the final goal of the Brazilian working class.

In Brazil's current situation, capitalist economic development enters into conflict with North American imperialist exploitation, deepening the contradiction between the developing national and progressive forces and North American imperialism, which blocks their expansion. In these conditions, the contradiction between the developing nation and North American imperialism and its local agents becomes the principal contradiction of Brazilian society.

For this reason, the principal thrust of the national, progressive, and democratic forces is currently directed against North American imperialism and the compradors who support them. The political defeat of the North

American imperialists and their local agents will open the way to the solution of all the other problems of the national and democratic revolution in Brazil.

North American imperialism counts on the support of the bourgeois and landowning sectors to realize their political plans for exploiting our country and tying it to their warlike policies. Landowners whose interests are connected to imperialist exploitation, many intermediaries in foreign trade, partners in businesses controlled by North American monopoly capital, and certain bankers and businessmen serve North American imperialism.

These sectors—a truly abject minority—constitute the capitulationist forces inside and outside the state apparatus that support political dependence on North American imperialism.

Very broad forces, though, stand opposed to the principal enemy of the Brazilian nation. These forces include the proletariat, the most consistent fighter for the general interests of the nation; the peasants, interested in liquidating a backward structure that is based upon imperialist exploitation; the urban petty bourgeoisie, which cannot expand its activities because of the backwardness of the country; the bourgeoisie, interested in the independent and progressive development of the national economy; those sectors of the landowning class whose interests are in contradiction with North American imperialism in regard to export prices, competition in the international market, or acts of extortion by North American firms and their agents in the internal market; and bourgeois groups with links to the imperialist rivals of the U.S. monopolies whose interests are prejudiced by the latter.

These forces are extremely heterogeneous in their class character. They range from the proletariat, which is interested in the most profound social transformations, to some sections of the most conservative forces in Brazilian society. Their reliability in the struggle against North American imperialism obviously is not the same, but all these forces do have reasons to unite against the politics of submission to North American imperialism. The broader this unity, the greater are the possibilities of inflicting a total defeat upon these politics so as to guarantee an independent, progressive, and democratic path of development for Brazilian society . . . .

THE UNITED FRONT AND THE STRUGGLE FOR A NATIONALIST AND DEMOCRATIC GOVERNMENT

No social force in isolation can resolve the tasks imposed by the need for the independent and progressive development of the country. This is the reason for the objective necessity of an alliance between all forces interested in the struggle against the politics of submission to imperialism. The experience of Brazilian political life has demonstrated that anti-imperialist and democratic victories can only be won through the actions of a united front of these forces.

Since it is inevitably heterogeneous, the nationalist and democratic united front implies contradictions. On one hand, there are common interests, and therefore there is unity. This is the fundamental factor that explains the need for the existence of the united front and its ability to overcome the internal contradictions among its components. On the other hand, there are contradictory interests, and therefore the social forces that make up the united front are opposed on certain questions, each striving to make its interests and point of view prevail.

The proletariat and the bourgeoisie are allied around the common objective of struggling for independent and progressive development against North American imperialism. Although exploited by the bourgeoisie, it is in the interests of the proletariat to ally with it, since we suffer even more from the consequences of the country's backwardness and imperialist exploitation than from those of capitalist development. Yet, while marching together for a common objective, the bourgeoisie and the proletariat still have contradictory interests.

The bourgeoisie insists upon gathering for itself all the benefits of the country's development, intensifying its exploitation of the working masses, and imposing the burden of all its problems upon them. For this reason, the bourgeoisie is an inconsistent revolutionary force that vacillates at times, tends toward compromise with the capitulationist sectors, and fears independent action by the masses.

The proletariat has an interest in consistent anti-imperialist development and in democracy.

To assure these interests, the proletariat defends its specific interests and those of the vast working masses and struggles for the broadest democratic liberties to facilitate independent mass action. Meanwhile, it struggles for the common interests of all classes and social layers opposed to North American imperialist exploitation. The proletariat, for this reason, must safeguard its ideological, political, and organizational independence inside the united front.

Meanwhile, it must never forget that the struggle within the united front is different in principle from the struggle waged by the united front against North American imperialism and the capitulationists. In the latter case, the objective is to isolate the main enemy of the Brazilian nation and defeat it politically. The struggle of the proletariat inside the united front, though, does not aim to isolate the bourgeoisie or break the alliance with it, but to defend the specific interests of the proletariat and the broader masses, winning over the bourgeoisie itself and other forces to increase the cohesion of the united front. For the united front to succeed, this struggle must be led in a proper manner, through criticism and other forms, to avoid raising the internal contradictions within the united front to the level of the principal contradiction between the nation and North American imperialism and its agents. Thus we must always take into account that the conflicts of interests and the differences of opinion within the united front, while they should not be hidden and thereby cause problems, can be confronted and overcome without breaking this unity.

THESES OF THE ARGENTINE REVOLUTIONARY LEFT*
Silvio Frondizi

In certain Latin American countries, some revolutionary left currents grew while opposing the orientation of the official Communist movement (peaceful coexistence on the international level, support to bourgeois parties or governments they considered progressive, etc.). In Argentina, Silvio Frondizi (1907–74), a Marxist historian and sociologist who was politically close to Trotskyism, created a small organization that was the first to call itself the MIR (Revolutionary Left Movement). An original and compelling thinker, the author of important philosophical, economic, and political works (including *The International Integration of Capitalism,* 1947; *The Modern State,* 1954; *Argentine Reality,* 1955–56; *The Dialectical Materialist View of Our Epoch,* 1960) and a lawyer for guerrilla fighters jailed by the Argentine regime (1966–73), Silvio Frondizi was assassinated in 1974 by the Argentine Anti-Communist Alliance (AAA), a terrorist group of the extreme right.

The following passages are taken from his response to a 1958–59 survey of the Argentine left.

PERONISM

For us, Peronism has been the most important and only attempt to carry out the bourgeois-democratic revolution in Argentina; it failed because of the inability of the national bourgeoisie to fulfill this task.

As it developed, Peronism came to represent the Argentine bourgeoisie in general, rather than exclusively representing any one of its sectors—either the industrialists or the landlords. This representation was direct, but was exercised through a bureaucratic project that gave it a partial and momentary independence from this very bourgeoisie. This allowed it to channel mass pressure in a manner favoring the survival of the system—through certain concessions forced by this very popular pressure, the country's exceptional commercial and financial situation, and the regime's demagogic

---

*"Contesta el doctor Silvio Frondizi," in *Las izquierdas en el proceso político argentino* (Buenos Aires: Ed. Palestra, 1959), pp. 28–33, 40–46.

needs. It was precisely the country's flourishing economic situation at the end of World War II that constituted the objective basis for Peronism's activities. At the outset, it could count on copious reserves of gold and foreign currency. And it confidently hoped that the situation that had created these circumstances would constantly improve, because of the needs of the countries affected by the war and because of the new war that seemed imminent.

One more exceptional and temporary circumstance contributed to nourishing illusions about the future possibilities of the Peronist experiment. We are referring to the emergence of a sort of interregnum, during which English imperialism saw its control over Argentina diminish while North American imperialism had not yet established its definitive and substantial domination of the world and of our country. This allowed a certain international Bonapartism—a parallel to that occurring on the national level—and created illusions among almost all the country's political currents about the possibilities of economic independence and national revolution.

This broad material basis for maneuver allowed the Peronist government, in the first place, to plan and begin to carry out a series of projects of economic development and national renewal, with all the limitations inherent in any attempt at planning within the context of capitalism. The traditional structure of the Argentine economy underwent no essential change; the roots of dependency and deformation were not destroyed. The revolution did not come to the countryside—not even a tepid reform. Imperialist interests were respected and even called upon to collaborate in mixed enterprises. Nor were national and imperialist big capital made to pay for these economic development projects. The First Five Year Plan, to the degree it was carried out, was financed mainly from the profits of international trade. On the other hand, this fundamental source of revenue soon became insufficient for a series of reasons and had to be supplemented with budgetary manipulations and open inflation. Because of this inflation, the costs of Peronist economic planning soon fell on the urban petty bourgeoisie and the proletariat.

But during its early period of expansion and euphoria, Peronism had realized important accomplishments in different areas of the economy. In transportation, the railroads were nationalized and new stock was added; the Argentine merchant marine grew, as did its total tonnage transported. Around the same time, aviation received strong support, the nationalization of the ports was completed, etc. Another recuperative accomplishment of Peronism at its height was the repatriation of the foreign debt. It claimed to have solved the problem of energy in general and petroleum in particular, but without attacking the matter at its roots. It carried out a series of measures favorable to industry and supplemented the base of state-owned heavy industry that it had inherited from its predecessor, increasing the degree of state participation. The direct intervention of the state in industry had a dual purpose: to take charge of necessary economic tasks that the weak national bourgeoisie was unable to carry out itself, and to give the Bonapartist bureaucracy a new store of power and an additional source of profits. Generous grants of state credit were another way to favor native and foreign capitalism.

Maintaining an appreciable degree of social peace was one of the most important contributions of the Peronist state to the prosperity of the Argentine agro-industrial bourgeoisie during this early period of expansion. The general prosperity itself was a fundamental factor in the temporary attenuation of class struggles in Argentina, as was state policy; on the one hand, it promoted high salaries while subsidizing big businesses to keep them from raising prices too high, and on the other, it harnessed the workers to a flexible but forceful and efficient government-controlled union machine.

Understanding this balancing act (as we have done for many years) has kept us from falling into the two errors committed in regard to Peronism: the idealization of its progressive possibilities, magnifying its gains and concealing its failures; and negative and reactionary criticism, like the "democratic opposition" that, for example, accused Peronism of being fascist.

The result of this balancing act was the betrayal of national capitalism to imperialism by the former's governmental agent, Peronism. In fact, once the early years of prosperity had passed, the critical and fundamental factor in all semicolonial countries—imperialism—came into play with full force. Slowly but surely, it successfully strangled the national bourgeoisie and its government by a variety of means (dumping, changing terms of trade, etc.). The different treaties with imperialism, which were truly injurious to the country, were the culmination of this process of betrayal. In the end, the result of the bourgeois-nationalist experiment of Peronism was crisis: industrial stagnation and retrogression, a decline in industrial employment and real wages, a chronic energy deficit, the crisis of the agrarian economy and foreign trade, inflation, etc.

Moving on to its political aspects, the fundamental characteristic of Peronism was its desire to simultaneously develop and channel the growing pressure of the proletariat to the benefit, first, of the governing clique and, then, the exploiting classes. This is why we have classified Peronism as Bonapartism—that is, an intermediate form, particularly in the political realm, which is applicable at a moment when social tension has not yet required the use of violence. Bonapartism tends to conciliate antagonistic classes through its control of a state apparatus and government that is apparently equidistant from the classes, but always benefits one of them—in this case, the bourgeoisie.

Capitalism, confronting the eruption of the popular masses onto the political stage and with no immediate need to sweep away a parody of democracy that reinforces it, tries to channel these popular forces. To do this, at least at first, it needs to cultivate the working class with social measures such as raising wages and shortening the work day, etc. But since these measures are taken, by definition, in a period of social tension, big capital is not in the material or psychological position to bear the weight of its own policies. It must logically, then, lay the burden on the middle class, which rapidly loses strength and becomes pauperized. This adds a new factor to the process of polarization of social forces.

The policy of aiding the workers referred to above actually occurs on a very small scale, if at all, but all sorts of methods are used to make it seem enormous.

The consequences of such demagogy are easily predictable: even more disruption of the capitalist system, more anarchy, and therefore the acceleration of the crisis. Moreover, these demagogic policies relax labor discipline: this explains why, when capitalism needs to intensify the pace of work, it must employ methods of compulsion. This is a new cause for totalitarianism and a new demonstration that the liberal state is an inoperative value in the current period.

This demagogic process does produce some beneficial results, particularly in the social and political sphere. Since it bases itself on the people, it develops the political class consciousness of the worker. We believe that the major positive aspect of Peronism is its incorporation of the masses into active political life; in this way, it has psychologically liberated them. In this sense, Perón fulfilled the role that Yrigoyen played in relation to the middle class. He helped the worker participate in public life, even if at a distance, and let him hear the discussion of basic political problems, both national and international, from official sources.

It was these aspects of Peronism that were seen as dangerous by big capital. This is why, as we said in the first volume of *Argentine Reality*, written in 1953, the United States "needs a government of more formal personalities" than the Peronists—which allowed us to predict "that once this moment [of profound social convulsions] has come, General Perón, the instrument of the capitalist system during one stage of its evolution, will be displaced."

The loss of material room for maneuver on the part of Peronism ended any possibility of continuing these policies and finally led to its fall.

The accusation that the Peronist regime was fascist lacks as much foundation as the claim it was a national liberation movement. To demonstrate that it was Bonapartist and not fascist, suffice it to say it found support in the extreme classes, big capital and the proletariat, while the petty bourgeoisie and the middle class in general suffered the impact of the government's actions.

On the contrary, under fascism, the petty bourgeoisie constitutes the social shock force of big capital. This explains why the persecution of the proletariat is so serious in a fascist regime, since repression is under the control of a whole class. We must distinguish between a class dictatorship and a political dictatorship.

It was the Democratic Union, now but a sad memory, that made this stupid and reactionary accusation about fascism. The darkest forces in Argentine politics, united in the Democratic Union (which didn't lack its left hangers-on), were unable or did not want to understand the full importance of the new phenomenon represented by Peronism; their effort to gain power reaped the harvest of this failure and of their poor reputation. Thus, we were able to predict the victory of Colonel Perón in our work, "The Argentine Political Crisis."

The "democratic opposition" had such great hatred for the regime because the latter uncovered the rotten pot of bourgeois society, showing things as they are. Bourgeois legality and the nation's sacrosanct Constitution lost their political virginity; their servile role came into the open. The unity of the army was destroyed, and the regime collaborated in the decomposition of the political parties, etc. Actually, as we later saw, what differentiated Peronism from the "democratic opposition" was not its negative aspects: adventurism, political and administrative corruption, etc.—the "pornocracy"; the bureaucratization and state control of the workers' movement; and repressive legislation that is now stronger than ever. Likewise, these defects were not corrected with the fall of Perón; only the excessive demagogy ended, as it was already too dangerous in a period of economic contraction. The coup d'état of 1955 fulfilled this objective of native-foreign big capital . . . .

We believe that the conditions exist for a socialist revolution in Latin America, but some subjective conditions are still lacking. It is clear that analyzing this situation means resolving the serious problem—perhaps the most serious problem that confronts the socialist revolution internationally—of the relation between the masses, the party, and the leadership.

The Revolutionary Left Movement (MIR-Praxis) has confronted and sought solutions to these problems through the formation of intermediate cadres, both manual and intellectual workers, who can become great social leaders. This way, when the revolution begins to advance in our country—as it must—it will not fail, as in Bolivia, for example, where the objective conditions were ripe, but little or nothing occurred because of the lack of a numerous and conscious leadership.

The first requisite of a conscious leadership is a firm belief in the importance of the working masses and the need to respect the dictates of their magnificent creative capacity.

We will now dedicate our attention to those elements of the other classes that can join with the proletariat in the struggle for the liberation of humanity. Above all, this means the study of the pauperized petty bourgeoisie.

This group suffers the direct consequences of monopolistic economic concentration. The situation of this subclass should especially be taken into account, as its intermediate social position makes it capable of moving in any direction. It should be made to understand that its future is connected to the interests of proletariat, which can liberate it from the economic and social oppression it suffers.

Along with these social elements, we must also consider individuals or groups of intellectuals who have shed light on the social problem and passed into the revolutionary camp.

The taking of power by the proletariat with the collaboration of these other social elements produces a qualitative leap. While this matter is sufficiently clear, it is not always understood because of the social, intellectual, and moral deformation caused by all sorts of propaganda that begins in elementary school and follows individuals throughout their lives. This is why, when we think about the possibilities and consequences of social change, it is done within old mental modes and in accord with traditional possibilities. But things are not like this; the taking of power by the proletariat produces a qualitative leap that opens possibilities unimagined in the earlier formation.

The working class can carry out this transformation thanks to its greater independence from the deformations produced by capitalist society. And the proletariat, as it does not share certain of the advantages of bourgeois society, has the good fortune of not sharing in many of its deformations; this is the case with social conventions that, for example, stifle the lives of the petty bourgeoisie.

We should point out one more element: the tremendous and growing alienation endured by workers under capitalism creates a legitimate and often unconscious resistance to any productive or creative efforts, even if they offer immediate benefits.

The transition to a new, socialist society involves an important question, since it is obvious that not all aspects of the bourgeois-democratic revolution have been carried out. Since the bourgeoisie has burned out as a force capable of accomplishing them and it is the proletariat, as a superior power, which must be charged with this mission, we can resolve the issue by realizing it is not a question of carrying out the bourgeois revolution as a stage in itself, an end, but of accomplishing the bourgeois-democratic tasks in the forward march of the socialist revolution.

Among these immediate tasks figures the struggle against imperialism, which can only be accomplished by a revolutionary Marxist party based in the masses. Moreover, it is necessary to resolve the serious problems that hinder industrial and agricultural development in our country. First, the major sources of production ought to be concentrated in the hands of the collectivity, which will give a powerful impulse to economic accumulation. In regard to agriculture, the socialist forces must carry out not just a single step or leap forward, but a complete agrarian revolution whose first manifestation will be the nationalization of the *latifundios*. This nationalization should not be carried out by distributing small plots but through collectivization, which will allow, among other things, the massive use of agricultural machinery.

Of course, the realization of these tasks requires a qualitative change in the state apparatus. This cannot be left in the hands of a privileged sector of society, but in the hands of the social collectivity itself; in other words, this implies that the community must change the state.

Only a socialist organization can resolve the issue of the freedom of conscience, effectively separate church from state, and keep confessional interests from intruding in sociopolitical problems, as some hope to do, in an impossible attempt to return to the Middle Ages.

Finally, the socialist organization of society is the only form that can insure the people's freedom; the traditional parties have been unable to do this, either in the country or inside their own organizations. This is why a new power must insure political and spiritual freedom for humanity.

But the socialist revolution has one more meaning—an international one. This is important because different left tendencies seemingly propose the same thing, but with a different content and completely different results.

Actually, representatives of petty-bourgeois currents, whether of the bourgeois or Marxist camp, also support the idea of Latin American integration. The problem involves knowing if this task can be realized by the national bourgeoisies or, on the contrary, can only be fulfilled by the forces that are moving toward the socialist revolution. We maintain the latter since, from a general point of view, the national bourgeoisies are by definition national and were born, have lived, and will die as such. And this is even more true in our era, when the bourgeoisies must struggle, tooth and nail, among themselves in order to survive. Along with this dissociative activity comes the dissolvent behavior of imperialism, creating or encouraging conflict. To these we can add the historical aspect—that is, the fact that international unity has not been attained by the bourgeoisie, given its fundamentally competitive nature.

The only possibility of achieving Latin American unity is the taking of power by socialist forces. Only a class free of the national and international interests of the bourgeoisie can carry out this task. For the survival of an attempt at socialism in any Latin American country, we assign such importance to the internationalization of the revolution that we think this must be one of the central tasks of any revolution. A good portion of its energy and resources should be destined to this purpose. The resources that the national bourgeoisies and their states take from the community and senselessly waste should be set aside by the first socialist revolution to extend the revolutionary victory to the other Latin American countries.

It is impossible to predict in what country the struggle will begin, but clearly the struggle must begin soon. No matter what, our country will have an important and decisive task to fulfill: the Argentine revolution will mean the effective consolidation of the Latin American socialist revolution. This is because of our relatively high level of development and the consequent specific weight we have thereby acquired in all order of economic and ideological activities, etc. Along these lines, just imagine the vast prairies of Argentina and the mineral-rich mountains of Brazil, Chile, Bolivia, Peru, etc., to get an idea of the enormous possibilities for economic integration in this part of the world. And we speak of integration, because once competition is suppressed, the law of combined development will tend to stop functioning.

This economic integration will multiply the productive power of our nations a hundredfold. And any new country that joins the revolutionary process deals a mortal blow to imperialism from many points of view. This forces imperialism to divide the financial and military resources available for international repression. It shrinks its market for production and investment, sharpens its internal social and political contradictions, and reduces the material bases of the relative equilibrium that various imperialisms have enjoyed to varying degrees for decades.

In general outline, this is the strategic perspective that establishes the enormous tasks the MIR (Praxis) has set for itself and which it has begun to carry out through tireless practical and theoretical work. We think this is the time for the left to abandon old rivalries and false positions, and finally decide to form a giant front to unleash the definitive battle against capitalist oppression.

If the old leaderships that have marched apart from the Argentine proletariat for decades still insist upon choosing not among left movements, but from the different fractions of the bourgeoisie (whether called the Democratic Union, Peronism, or Frondizism), they will be deserted by their own ranks, who are tired of walking in circles and getting nowhere. The question of the moment is clear: revolutionary socialism or bourgeois dictatorship. Let every one choose their place in the struggle.

12

Marxist Economic History

THE COLONIAL ECONOMY*
Sergio Bagú

Sergio Bagú, the Argentine historian and economist (and author of various works on historical materialism), is one of the most important representatives of Marxist social science in Latin America. His writings on economic history show that it was possible to accomplish serious theoretical work, even during the period when the most shallow dogmatism was hegemonic in the Marxist movement. His book *The Economy of Colonial Society* (1949) was a pioneering work and probably the first to explicitly and systematically question the traditional schema of "Latin American feudalism" by emphasizing the capitalist dimension of the Iberian colonization of America.

THE NATURE OF THE COLONIAL ECONOMY

Determining the nature of the colonial economy is somewhat more than a strictly technical task. It affects one's very interpretation of its economic history and acquires an immediate practical importance if we consider that the present economies of the countries of Latin America still maintain many of the fundamental characteristics of their colonial structure.

The economic structure of Iberian colonial society began acquiring its definitive traits near the middle of the sixteenth century, and these traits were notably accentuated during later centuries. By the time of independence, the colonial regime had been functioning for three long centuries, and in one colony, Cuba, for almost four. And in Puerto Rico, the most unfortunate of all, it still continues in operation under a different form. This long life helps explain the profound colonial imprint inherited by the independent states of Latin America. Meanwhile, in the Anglo-Saxon colonies to the north, the imperial regime did not last even two centuries, and most of this time they were left to their own devices.

---

*Sergio Bagú, *Economía de la sociedad colonial* (Buenos Aires: Ed. El Ateneo, 1949), pp. 97–98, 103–104, 117–120, 142–143.

What type of economy did the Spanish and Portuguese establish here among the enormous native populations of America and Africa? Was it feudalism, then declining on the old continent? Was it capitalism, whose brilliance and power were documented at the time in the heights reached by the Italian Renaissance and the Iberian navigators? Was it something different from either that took some of its basic characteristics from both? . . .

But it is an indisputable fact that the Iberian colonies of America were not established to renew the feudal order, but to be integrated into a new capitalist order being inaugurated worldwide.

Their discovery and conquest was one more episode in the vast period of expansion of European commercial capital. The colonial economic regime was organized to strengthen the metropolitan economies and create a colonial market. Within a few years, the orientation of the mines and agricultural enterprises clearly showed they were responding to the predominant interests of the large commercial centers of the Old World.

Still, we must observe there was a combination of apparently contradictory factors at work in the socioeconomic configuration of our America. They should be studied in detail to draw a broad and clear idea of the nature of the colonial economy from this general overview.

PRODUCTION FOR THE MARKET

If we wish to find some well-defined and indisputable characteristic of the colonial economy, it is production for the market. From the beginning to the end of the colonial regime, this fact conditioned all productive activities.

The owners of the sugar plantations of Bahia, Rio, and São Vicente were producing for the market by the middle of the colony's first century, as were the owners of the mines of Minas Gerais and the Diamantina District (which were later monopolized by the Portuguese crown in the eighteenth century). Cotton was cultivated in Maranhão for the same reason in the eighteenth century, as was coffee on southern Brazilian plantations toward the end of the colonial era. The cattle ranchers of the Northeast produced for the internal market starting in the sixteenth century, as did their southern competitors later on. Grains were cultivated for the internal market in different regions . . . .

The Iberian colonies not only rapidly incorporated themselves into the commercial revolution that had begun in Europe, but as a whole soon constituted one of its most important elements.

Moreover, there are abundant signs of the high degree of commercial sensibility that presided over the economic development of these colonies. Tools, credit, and slaves became available to increase production when it was discovered that colonial products could be launched onto the international market on the grand scale. At times there were also armies of men available to conquer productive areas to take advantage of their riches.

The Dutch West India Company, which invaded the northeastern coast of Brazil in 1630, sought to dominate the production of sugar, a product for which there was such great interest in Holland that a company had already been created to market it by the sixteenth century. This company still owned a coastal fringe of the Portuguese colony, but its need for greater quantities of the product led it to offer capital, tools, slaves, and cane cuttings to English colonists in Barbados—everything they needed to begin cultivation. After their first attempts failed because their sugar was not of good quality, they brought English colonists to their own model plantations in Brazil so they could better learn the proper techniques. When the Portuguese and Brazilians expelled the Dutch from Brazil in 1654, Barbados had already begun to export sugar to Europe—to the great pleasure of the stockholders and directors of the Dutch company, without whose help Barbados would never have been transformed into what it later became: a giant sugar plantation.

In the eighteenth century, when the colonial techniques of international commerce had already been perfected, examples like this began to multiply. Slave traders, by making credit available to farmers, helped stimulate the production of sugar in Cuba. The *Companhia Geral do Comércio de Grão Pará e Maranhão* supplied credit to the colonists of Maranhão so they could acquire slaves and farm implements for the cultivation of cotton, which was being sought by insatiable European looms. The *Compañía Guipuzcoana* offered credits to small landowners in Venezuela to produce cacao and other fruits, which were then sold at a good price on the old continent.

These examples should be enough to confirm the fact that the Iberian colonies formed a fundamental part of the world capitalist system and developed as a complement to the European economy. This is why the products that were most desired in the Old World were those whose production boomed in the new. The colonial market itself was larger than most of our nineteenth century historians had supposed, but could not compare to the gravitational pull exerted by the European market in configuring the American economy . . . .

THE COLONIAL ECONOMY AS A CAPITALIST ECONOMY

We are now in the position to offer a response to the questions with which we opened this chapter. The economic system of the Iberian colonial period was not feudalism. It was colonial capitalism.

When historians and economists say that feudalism, in its death agony in Europe, was revived in America, they are referring to certain factors: the transfer of certain institutions already in their decadence in Europe, the flourishing of an aristocracy created by elements displaced from Europe, and certain characteristics of the large agricultural, mining, and ranching units we have analyzed that evoke the dependent relationship between servant and master as well as the seigniorial belligerence of the feudal era. But these factors do not sufficiently define a feudal economic system.

In every continent, moreover, colonial capitalism has repeatedly had certain external characteristics that seem feudal. It is a system with an ambiguous profile, but this does not change its unquestionably capitalist nature.

Far from reviving the feudal order, America entered into the orbit of commercial capitalism with surprising speed. And America contributed to giving this system a tremendous vigor, making possible the beginnings of industrial capitalism centuries later.

Slavery has nothing to do with feudalism, but everything to do with capitalism, as we have proved in the American case. Iberian America had to receive a formidable graft from Africa to become integrated into the commercial order. Indigenous and African labor were the pillars of colonial America. America and Africa, their blood distilled by the alchemists of international commerce, were indispensable to the dazzling growth of capitalist Europe.

THE ECONOMIC NATURE OF THE COLONIZATION OF THE TROPICS*
Caio Prado Jr.

Caio Prado Jr., the eminent Brazilian historian and Communist Party militant, was the author of several classic works on the economic history of Brazil. Along with Bagú, he was one of the first Latin American Marxists to question the traditional theories of the Communist parties on the "feudal" character of the colonial economy, especially in his *Economic History of Brazil* in 1951. However, as he later explained, his scientific discoveries never influenced the fixed ideas of his party on the necessity of an "anti-feudal" revolution in twentieth-century Brazil.

The passage below analyzes the characteristics of the colonization of the Latin American tropics in general and of Brazil in particular, underlining its specifically capitalist dimension.

Let us imagine ourselves in Europe before the sixteenth century: far from the tropics, which are only remotely and indirectly accessible; deprived of products which today seem of secondary importance because of their ordinariness, but which were then prized as the height of luxury. Take sugar,

---

*Caio Prado Jr., *Historia económica do Brasil* (São Paulo: Ed. Brasiliense, 1959), pp. 20–23.

for example, which was cultivated on a small scale in Sicily and was a rare and much sought-after article; it even figured as a precious and highly prized gift in the dowry of queens. For centuries, pepper imported from the Orient was the principal article of commerce for the Italian merchant republics; the long and arduous route to the Indies served no other purpose than to provide this product to Europe. Tobacco, which originated in America and was therefore unknown before the Discovery, became no less important. And didn't this later become true for indigo, rice, cotton, and so many other tropical products?

This gives us an idea of what sort of attraction the tropics represented to frigid, far off Europe. America placed at its disposition immense spaces, territories that only awaited the initiative and labor of humanity. This is what stimulates the occupation of the American tropics. But having this intense interest, the European colonist would not bring the disposition to invest the energy of his own physical labor in such a difficult and foreign environment. He comes to organize the production of goods with great commercial value; he is an entrepreneur in this profitable enterprise, but only to his distaste a worker. Others would work for him.

Here lies the major distinction between the colonists who left for the different parts of the New World—the temperate and the tropical zones. The European freely and spontaneously goes to the tropics only when he can be a master, when he disposes of the resources and aptitude for it, and when he can rely on other people to work for him. One other circumstance reinforces this tendency: the nature of agricultural exploitation in the tropics. This takes place on the large scale—that is, in large productive units: ranches, sugar mills, and plantations, each one bringing together a relatively large number of workers. In other words, for each owner (rancher, landlord, or planter), there are many subordinate and landless workers . . . .

As we can see, the tropical colonies take a completely different path from those in the temperate zones. The latter are created as true colonial settlements (*peuplements*, in the phrase from the classic work of Leroy-Beaulieu, *Colonization among Modern Peoples*), outlets for the demographic surplus of Europe. These New World settlements recreated an organization and a society similar to their original European model. In the tropics, on the other hand, an entirely original type of society is created. It is not the simple commercial trading post that we have already seen was impossible to create in America. But it nevertheless has a particularly commercial character. It is an undertaking of the white colonist, who unites the prodigious natural resources appropriate for the production of commodities of great commercial value with the labor of the subordinate races he dominates, the indigenous peoples and Africans. The traditional mercantile objectives that determined the origins of the overseas expansion of Europe adjust under the new conditions in which this venture takes place. These objectives, which are relegated to a secondary place in the temperate colonies, are maintained here, profoundly affecting the nature of colonies of our type and dictating their destiny. As a whole, seen from an international perspective, the colonization seems a vast commercial enterprise. The colony is more complex than the old trading post, but always has a somewhat similar character. Its purpose is to exploit the natural resources of a virgin territory in the interest of European commerce. This is the real nature of the colonization of the tropics, of which Brazil is one result. This explains the fundamental elements, both social and economic, of the formation and historical evolution of the American tropics. If we look at the essence of our social formation, we see that we were actually created to furnish sugar, tobacco, and a few other products—gold and diamonds next, then cotton, and finally coffee—for European commerce. This is all. Brazil's society and economy are organized for this purpose, a foreign purpose directed outward from the country, without regard for any consideration not in the interest of this commerce. Everything is arranged for this purpose: the social structure and all the other activities of the country. The white European comes to speculate, start a business, invest his wealth, and recruit the manual labor he needs, whether indigenous or African. The Brazilian colony is created with these characteristics, articulated in a purely productive and mercantile organizational form.

These origins, whose basic character has been maintained throughout the history of the Brazilian social formation, are deeply and fully engraved into the forms and the very life of the country, particularly its economic structure. And this remains true, as we are barely beginning to free ourselves from this long colonial past. To keep this in mind is to understand the essence of the economic evolution of Brazil.

THE DEVELOPMENT OF CAPITALISM IN CHILE*
Marcelo Segall

The Chilean historian Marcelo Segall was also one of the first Marxist writers to criticize the theory of Latin American feudalism. Born in Santiago in 1920, Segall was the founder and rector of the Independent (Popular) University of Santiago, as well as a professor and researcher at the University of Chile. Arrested in 1973 and

---

*Marcelo Segall, *El desarrollo del capitalismo en Chile, cinco ensayos dialécticos* (Santiago: n.p., 1953), pp. 90–91, 96–97, 98–99.

imprisoned for a year by Pinochet's military junta, he was freed after an international campaign; he later became the director of the Latin American section of the International Institute of Social History in Amsterdam. Segall was a Communist militant from the thirties; in 1957, he left the Communist Party under the influence of Trotskyism, while organizationally remaining an independent. In addition to his pioneering 1953 book on the development of capitalism in Chile, Segall authored several important works of economic and social history: *The Social Biography of Scrip* (Santiago: Mapocho, 1964), and *Scrip Wages around the World* (Boletin de la Universidad de Chile, 1967), to mention only two.

The following are selections from his book, *The Development of Capitalism in Chile: Five Dialectical Essays.* We should note that Segall later considered his ideas of this period to be partially obsolete. In a letter to us (dated April 23, 1976), he emphasized: "My former position was presented somewhat mechanically: it showed Chilean society as capitalist from the colonial period onward, after the historical leap that signified the passage of the land from common use to private commercial property and the passage from a natural economy to a money economy. . . . But this does not explain the totality of the process. . . . My current view is more dialectical and more universal. It starts from this historical leap, but sees it as one part of the uneven and combined development of this society. The Spanish conquest brought with it private property relations, but on top of the existing culture, that is, the Andean culture, which constituted an original type of evolution. Andean Latin America is the product of the combined development of societies at different and quite unequal cultural levels that, as a whole, can be considered capitalist since the Conquest."

Modern agriculture was born with the *encomienda* and the distribution of the land by the conquistadors. This entailed the violent, bloody, and inevitable expropriation of the land from its aboriginal inhabitants and their reduction to slavery. Such use of labor developed through a revolution in the relations of production—that is, from primitive communal gathering in a tribal system to the system of exploitation of one class by another.

The agricultural system in Chile, from the time of the *encomienda* until today, has been likened to the European feudal stage that succeeded the ancient slave system.

To avoid confusion and misunderstanding, both about this system and its terminological signifier, we will pause briefly to define and specify the meaning of capitalism and feudalism.

Feudalism, in its economic sense, is the dominant relation of production in a stage of society specifically characterized by small-scale agricultural and artisanal production for the direct consumption of the lord and his servants.

On the contrary, capitalism, in its commercial sense, is a mode of production destined to a greater or lesser degree for the market, whether national or foreign. This in turn signifies commercial exchange or the production of commodities (or exchange values), in this case agricultural products. It is a mode of production characterized by the sale of labor power by the worker.

The *encomienda* was begun, in part, for the private use of the conquistador, but its general purpose was to produce commodities for the consumption and provisioning of the cities and mines—to produce goods for exchange and pay duties to the Spanish crown. In short, this is capitalist development, but of a colonial type . . . .

The reason for the subjection of the *inquilinos* is not a hypothetical "feudal social system," but their permanent indebtedness, which forces them to spend all their time working for free for a "benevolent" creditor: their boss.

The key to the liberation of the Chilean peasantry lies in the effort made by the *inquilino* to fulfill his obligations and still maintain some surplus for his own use and nourishment, which forces him to work from sunup to sundown. And not only must he work; so must his family. "This condition is inherited by the family and by future generations, who in this way effectively belong to the creditor"(K. Marx).

As a debtor, it is obvious that if the climate permits or demands (because of the unpredictable nature of agriculture), he will work at a rhythm that he would otherwise never maintain (forcing his pace, working at night, using his family) if he worked under a simpler form of subordination—which might be difficult, but from which he could escape with a little cleverness.

It seems to me that we can put an end to the patriarchal (or semi-feudal) legend that familial relationships exist between landowners and *inquilinos*. This legend was restated by MacBride, a researcher, in the early pages of his book.[1] To the defenders of the current agrarian regime, the landowner is a generous patriarch. To its uninformed enemies, he is a feudalist. The historian and agriculturalist Francisco Encina calls them "patriarchs" of a basically benevolent feudalism. The socialist historian Julio César Jobet, from the other camp, refers to them as "feudal or semi-feudal."

My opinion is not in accord with the general wisdom. Everyone, from MacBride to the authors of impersonal political programs, agrees that Chilean agriculture still maintains a modified medieval or semi-feudal structure. This is a common position throughout America, with a few notable exceptions, such as the North American William Z. Foster, the Mexicans Jan Bazant and Silvio Zavala, and the Argentine Sergio Bagú, all of whom (except Zavala) use the economic method of Marx and define the matter in another way. Foster[2] classifies Latin American agriculture as an underdeveloped capitalist activity, and Bazant defines the *encomienda* as a capitalist organizational form that uses the methods and forms of a slave system . . . .

Another element that contributes to the false idea of Chilean feudalism is

---

[1] *Chile: Its Land and People.* Despite its defects, it is a most valuable contribution to the question. Its investigations of agriculture are quite often correct and precise.

[2] *An Outline of the Political History of the Americas* (New York: International Publishers, 1952).

the confusion of this term with *latifundismo*. The presence of large landholdings is not the fundamental characteristic of feudalism. These can be present
in feudal societies, as in slave societies and the Roman Empire. But they also
exist in capitalist England. What characterizes feudalism is the class relation
between lord and serf. Another factor used to define the national landowning class as feudal, quite prominent in the work of Julio César Jobet, is based
on their familial and external customs—in other words, upon acts of a
moral nature. This approach draws on the fact that the great majority of
landed proprietors are descended from the *mayorazgos* and *encomenderos*,
which allows for the continued existence of their privileged caste traditions
and lordly ostentation. But this does not affect the capitalist nature of
production, which is the essential factor.

THE COMBINED DEVELOPMENT OF THE COLONIAL ECONOMY*
Milcíades Peña

Milcíades Peña was a Trotskyist militant, theoretician, and author of several studies
of the economic and social history of Argentina (*Before May*, *The Landowners'
Paradise*, *Caudillos and Elites*); until his death in 1965, he was also the moving force
(under the pseudonym Alfredo Parrera Dennis) of *Fichas*, a journal of Marxist social
science. His analysis of the colonial economy, written during the years 1955–57, was
published for the first time in 1966 in this journal. Peña attempted to apply Trotsky's theory of uneven and combined development to the Latin American social
structure. The passage below is a polemic on this subject directed against the
Argentine Communist Party historian Rodolfo Puiggrós.

Undoubtedly, throughout its colonial history, there has existed a type of
Spanish American landowner whose habits, actions, and mentality have
been quite similar to that of a medieval lord. The *senhor do engenho* (sugar
mill owner) and the *fazhendeiro de ganado o café* (cattle rancher or coffee
grower) in Brazil; the *encomendero*, mine owner, *latifundista*, the cacao and
sugar grower, the bishop, the rancher, and the *estanciero* in the Spanish
colonies: all have a striking tendency to consider themselves absolute lords
of their domains, to act like military chiefs disdainful of the central authorities, and to exercise a feudal-style justice over their subordinates. One
could say the same of the plantation owners of the British Antilles and the
tobacco planters of Virginia and the Carolinas. But the "feudal lords" of
America differ notably from their European counterparts; the material

---

*Milcíades Peña, *Antes de mayo, formas sociales del transplante español al Nuevo Mundo* (Buenos
Aires: Ed. Fichas, 1973), pp. 51–54.

sources of their wealth are not enclosed fiefs, self-sufficient units, but rather mines producing for the external market, Indians subjected to the regime of the *encomienda*, or sugar mills, *estancias*, or ranches whose products are exported. As Bagú has said, America was a "caste ideal imposed upon a class reality."

Rodolfo Puiggrós, a historian of the Stalinist school, wrote a history of Argentina some years ago with the purpose of finding feudal elements (or inventing them if necessary) to which he could counterpose a correspondingly progressive bourgeoisie. Puiggrós made a discovery that, despite their differences, was at least as transcendent as the discovery of America itself: "The conquest and colonization transferred the methods of production . . . of a declining Iberian feudalism," and "America helped sustain the dying feudalism . . . of the Iberian peninsula." Following Puiggrós, Leonardo Paso also claimed that, in America, "the colonization was feudal," but with characteristics of slave societies grafted onto it. And an apostle of this nonsense, Jorge Abelardo Ramos, wrote a book entitled *Latin America: One Country*, saying that the Spanish colonies "developed their economies on a feudal basis."

Despite such statements on the feudal nature of the colonization, this same Puiggrós recognizes that "the discovery of America was an enterprise carried out by navigators and traders," with fully commercial aims. There is an obvious contradiction between this remark and his thesis on the nature of the colonization; Puiggrós dodges this with his "bridge" theory, according to which the commercial objectives of the Conquest served as a bridge for the Spanish, so they could establish feudalism in these new territories. Evidently, Puiggrós and Company understand feudalism to mean the large-scale production of commodities for the world market through the use of concentrations of semi-free labor, similar to the system used centuries later by international finance capital on African and Asian plantations. If this is feudalism, we might ask with a certain uneasiness, exactly what is capitalism? But this question doesn't bother Puiggrós, who explains the "eminently feudal character of the Spanish empire in America" from the fact that "the Crown considered the new continent to be its direct fief and its inhabitants as its vassals, rather than as colonies in the sense that it used the term for its commercial domains from the 17th century on." Appearances to the contrary, these are not the words of a specialist in comparative law, but of a historian who considers himself a Marxist. But nothing is more alien to Marxism than legal cretinism, and nothing more revealing of an unrepentant legal cretin than characterizing the Spanish colonization as feudal *not* because of the structure of its relations of production, but because of the juridical form assumed by the connection between the colonies and the Spanish crown. The form taken by the relation between the colonies and

Spain undoubtedly had a particularly feudal flavor in its juridical aspects. But, underneath this juridical form, the socioeconomic content of the colonies centered on production for the market and the creation of profits, which gave this content a decisively capitalist character, despite all the feudal nuances involved.

Once again, in Puiggrós' thesis, we run into the type of schematic and formal thinking that is at the origin of so many errors in the development of knowledge: Spain was feudal, so therefore its colonies were feudal. This is a perfectly formal and perfectly incorrect deduction. The Spanish, upon their arrival in America, encountered a new reality that did not exist in Spain. The result was that, however much they subjectively wished to reproduce the structure of Spanish society, they objectively built something quite different. Spain constructed a basically capitalist society in America: a colonial capitalism, certainly—just as inversely, in the imperialist epoch, finance capital creates capitalist structures in its colonies that are reminiscent of feudal and slave societies. This is precisely the combined nature of historical development. Formal thought is incapable of capturing this, which is why it is generally incapable of capturing anything essential.

THE FEUDAL ECONOMY IN LATIN AMERICA*
Rodney Arismendi

Despite the work of Marxist historians in the forties and fifties, the Latin American Communist parties continued to maintain the theory of the feudal or semi-feudal character of the continent's colonial economy and its modern-day vestiges.

The selection below is a short summary of this historical position, presenting a view of the total socioeconomic structure of the Latin American colonies. It is taken from a 1961 essay (published in the Moscow journal *Communist*) by Rodney Arismendi, a Marxist sociologist and philosopher, General Secretary of the Communist Party of Uruguay, and one of the leading theoreticians of traditional Latin American Communism.

Let us review the socioeconomic structure of the Iberian-American colonies. If the discovery of America and its Indian gold and silver, the transformation of slavery into a commercial enterprise based on the hunting and selling of African slaves, the development of navigation and technology, etc., historically belong to that bloody, rapacious, and astonishing period of the dawn of capitalism and the formation of the world market, the

---

*Rodney Arismendi, "Problèmes d'une révolution continentale," in *Recherches internationales à la lumière du marxisme*, n. 32, July 1962, pp. 31–34.

social institutions and the relations of production that Spain and Portugal transplanted to the lands of the New World were feudal or of a feudal cast, and not capitalist. These institutions had to be adapted to American conditions, to the presence or lack of precious metals, to the climate (a primary and natural condition of production), and to the possibilities of using native labor. But these newly created economies were basically stamped with a more-or-less classic feudal character.

This is not the place to re-discuss the positions of those Latin American historians and sociologists who deny the predominantly feudal character of the relations of production of the Spanish and Portuguese colonies and characterize them under a variety of names, including "colonial capitalism." We will limit ourselves here to discovering the roots of our current economic structure in its colonial past. Fundamentally, these are the *latifundista* regime of landed property and the subjection of the colonial economy to the metropolitan economy. Taken together, these two features clearly give the plantation, the Brazilian sugar *engenhio*, and the cattle ranch of the Platte their character as enclosed economic units, typical of the feudal economy. These units produce for the metropolis, but the relations of production that predominate in the majority of these countries are based on servile Indian labor (*encomiendas*, *yanaconas*, etc.) and African slave labor or semi-slave Indian labor (the *mita*). Surrounding these export-producing economies, which are based on feudal property, is a natural economy where pre-capitalist forms of rent predominate (labor, farm products, and much later, pre-capitalist money rent).

As the eighteenth century proceeds, one can find sporadic manifestations of wage labor, individual petty production, and a simple mercantile economy. Artisanal guilds of a medieval type are organized, using the labor of both African slaves and Indians. But the predominant and essential form is still the feudal or semi-feudal *latifundio*.

The Spaniards divide the land among the colonists in different ways: by royal grants or through the *composición*, which is a feudal land sale. The Portuguese lay the basis for the *latifundio* by dividing the legendary brazil-wood lands into "captaincies" and grants called *sesmarias*. Various economic units of a feudal type develop from the *latifundio*: the mines and *latifundios* of Mexico, Peru, etc., which are highly stratified; the Brazilian *engenhio*, where the *latifundio* and the sugar mill are based on African slave labor combined with peasant petty production dependent on the *engenhio*'s owner; the vast Jesuit enterprises (in Paraguay, northeastern Argentina, and the "Misiones" region now in Brazil), which despite their peculiarities were indeed of a feudal character. In the regions where there are neither Indians for the *encomienda*, nor precious metals, nor products with great commercial value, nor a tropical climate—and where colonization occurs later, such as Buenos

Aires and Uruguay—the cattle *latifundio* is established to produce leather, tallow, horns, meat, and later, jerked beef by exploiting forced labor, some African slaves, and sporadically, patriarchal wage labor. Near these cattle ranches, social relations are established which represent a special type of sharecropping. The plantation, organized as a colonial commercial investment with the utilization of abundant African slave labor, exists only in the Caribbean islands colonized by the French, English, and Dutch.

Along with the *latifundio* and the production of minerals and foodstuffs, the colonial period leaves as its heritage an overgrowth of intermediary commercial capital and various forms of usurers' capital. Marx and Lenin have already shown that the independent development of commercial capital is in inverse proportion to degree of capitalist development. This is a factor that has contributed to the formation of the large South American port cities, which developed as true commercial marketplaces.

In the eighteenth and early nineteenth centuries, the Latin American economies were openly incorporated into the world capitalist market because of changes in the colonial policies of the Spanish monarchy and, later, through the political independence of the various nations. European, especially English, merchandise entered the breach and led to the ruin of the domestic industries of many countries, while tying Latin American primary production to European, particularly English, industry.

This connection to the world market led to capitalist development. But the world capitalist economy, while wearing down and subordinating the former colonial economies and unleashing internal capitalist development, deformed these economies at the same time. This process was more or less rapid, depending on the strength of the feudal institutions in each country (for example, we could compare the Río de la Plata and Bolivia or Peru); but in no case was this a normal transition from feudalism and semi-feudal colonialism to capitalism. This was a slow, painful, complex process that occurred while the *latifundio* continued producing for the external market. The *latifundio*, adapting to the export of foreign capital, the extension of the railroads, improvements in navigation, etc., later became a conditional and determining factor in the transition to the imperialist stage of capitalism. During this process, capitalist forms combined with and adapted to precapitalist forms. Thus, the primitive accumulation of national capital, the formation of the internal market, and the creation of a proletariat and a modern bourgeoisie were delayed for several decades, with the most painful consequences for the masses.

PART IV
The New
Revolutionary Period

13

The Cuban Revolution

THE POPULAR SOCIALIST PARTY AND THE CUBAN REVOLUTION*

A. Díaz

The triumph of the Cuban Revolution took place in 1959, but its roots go back to the celebrated assault on the Moncada Barracks in 1953 that gave birth to the July 26 Movement. It is interesting to look at the position taken by the Popular Socialist Party (the Cuban Communist Party) in relation to this action and, generally, in regard to the methods of struggle against the Batista dictatorship, to better understand the difference between the ideas of the new Castroist Communism that crystalized in the sixties and those of traditional Stalinized Latin American Communism. The following selection (taken from an article in *Fundamentos*, the organ of the PSP, in 1954) also allows us to understand why the PSP did not stand at the head of the most important revolutionary movement in the history of the continent.

Comrades,

On July 26, 1953, the bourgeois-*latifundista* and pro-imperialist clique that imposed itself upon the country in the reactionary coup of March 10, 1952, in effect carried out a new coup d'etat, this time to reinforce the reactionary nature of its government and eliminate a whole series of obstacles to its plans.

Despite the good intentions of its authors, the sterile and wrong-headed Eastern rising, targeting the barracks of Santiago and Bayamo, was easily defeated by the military machine of the de facto regime. It served as an opportune pretext to sweep away what little remained of democratic legality and to sharply attack the mass democratic movement, which at that time was growing and seriously threatened to disturb all the government's plans.

The weeks preceding July 26 saw a rapid growth of popular protest, which little by little was translated into various actions, even strikes, that shook the de facto regime. The government had promised its godfathers

---

*A. Díaz, "Balance de la actividad de la Dirección Nacional del Partido desde el 26 de julio hasta la fecha," *Fundamentos* (Havana), May 1954, pp. 111–113, 133–137.

and protectors, the Yankee imperialists, to impose a "readjustment plan" in Cuba that would lower wages, create mass unemployment, and abolish social legislation won through great workers' struggles under our party's leadership. Being a faithful executor of the Yankees' expansionist and militarist policies that are opening the country to their monopolies' insatiable thirst for exploitation, and having committed itself to making Cuba an open colony, this government was confronting great difficulties in carrying out what was demanded of it. Moreover, with increasing mass mobilizations and growing resistance to its policies, the possibility of assuring their application was becoming increasingly precarious. The government ran the danger of an overwhelming oppositional vote in the electoral farce that it was planning to create the legal cover it had sought since March 10.

This is why the leaders of the March 10 coup welcomed the events in eastern Cuba with such savage excitement and indecent passion, as a useful pretext to undertake a quick, violent offensive against the remnants of democratic legality we have mentioned and unleash a wave of persecutions and outrages that have so disturbed the nation. As a result of this offensive, besides the innumerable street assassinations in the East, the hundreds imprisoned, the mass searches, the closing of our dear *Hoy* and other periodicals, Cuba has had to submit to the suspension of all constitutional guarantees (those few that remained after March 10!), and to a reign of violence unleashed by the regime's assassins, the hated SIM—that Gestapo without peer, even in Machado's political police.

July 26 brought on the total suppression of the rights of free speech and assembly, repression against our party, new restrictions on the workers' and popular movement, the tyrannical Law of Public "Order" that in practice has suppressed the freedom of the press, and other unpublicized measures suppressing and strangling democratic rights. The fascist Anti-Communist Law adopted two months later only gave "legal" cover to the outlawing of our party and has created a weapon to blackmail and persecute the whole anti-imperialist and workers' movement, including the bourgeois opposition to Batista.

The government later "reestablished" constitutional guarantees, but who is unaware that there are no guarantees in Cuba and that, in practice, this is still a regime of exception, arbitrariness, persecution, and the absence of democratic rights.

As everyone knows, the most violent attacks and most aggressive governmental measures are directed against our party. It is well established that our party took no part in the events in the East, and in fact opposes these bourgeois-putschist tactics as incorrect, isolated from the masses, and obstructive of the mass struggle—the only strategy that, by inevitably rising toward higher and more combative forms, can defeat reaction and imperialism, as we saw in 1933, and later, in another form, in 1938–39. If this is true, why the furious persecution of the party? The reason should be clear to all: our party is the strongest and most decisive obstacle to the plans of the North American imperialists and their agents inside and outside Batista's government. Our party alone cannot be intimidated, coerced, bought, or corrupted. Our party alone is anti-imperialist, refuses to bow down to Washington, and unhesitatingly and unreservedly raises the banner of full national independence from foreign oppression. Our party is the only party of the working class, of all the workers and peasants, of workers' unity and union democracy, of unemployment compensation, of real agrarian reform to freely distribute land to the peasants, of people's unity, and of a Democratic National Front to lead the country out of its crisis and toward higher levels of progress and national development. Our party, in short, is the party of peace and socialism.

Because of this, because it is the most consistent fighter against the "readjustment plan" and Batista's pro-imperialist and reactionary politics, because it is the party of democratic struggle for elections and a democratic solution to Cuba's crisis, the Popular Socialist Party is the target of the worst attacks and the most brutal persecution by the reactionary government that tarnishes Cuba.

The ferocity of this persecution of our Popular Socialist Party—incited by periodic anti-Communist declarations from abroad by Prío and his friends—is dictated to a great degree by the de facto regime's interest in remaining in Washington's favor by adding to the chorus of dirty and repulsive anticommunist and anti-Soviet hysteria, and maintaining the support of the Yankee imperialists by joining the fascist policy of rabid anticommunism.

These persecutions and legal measures taken against our party are therefore neither accidental nor temporary. They are the result of a plan that aims not only to outlaw the party but, as its authors hope, to conclusively destroy it. But for the results of this plan to be permanent from a historical perspective is another kettle of fish. With the people, we can defeat this and all other enemy plans to "sweep away" Communism, which at the moment is victorious in a third of the world and is the hope of all humanity . . . .

Our position is well known.

Since the days immediately following March 10, we have supported a line that has proven to be correct.

We do not imagine Cuban problems—as we have said—in terms of a simple "institutional crisis."

We get to the bottom of things and propose profound solutions for problems that come not only from the coup and the reactionary de facto regime, but most importantly from the economic crisis that is spreading across the country, and from the stifling of national development by imperialist interference.

This is why our line does not proceed from the circumstances of the electoral contest alone, but aims to provide profound solutions for this crisis.

This is why our line calls for immediate, free elections, not as an end in itself, but as a possible route toward a democratic solution to the crisis.

This is why our program calls for the formation of a National Democratic Front to organize a government able to apply a Cuban and patriotic program for the democratic resolution of the crisis.

We reject adventurism and "putschism" as well as electoral sellouts. We are opposed to all unprincipled conspiracies, coup attempts, terrorism, and other activities of groups isolated from the masses, whose futility and negativity have been proven by history. We are opposed to "quietism," abstentionism, and other formulas that condemn the people to passivity, simply waiting for the development of events. We are opposed to electoral sellouts, which seek merely petty concessions and immediate advantages and neglect real problems that demand solution.

In opposition to these bourgeois and petty-bourgeois methods, we resolutely propose proletarian methods of mass struggle, mass mobilization, mass propaganda, and mass unity.

Our tactic is clear: we propose a united front, a popular union, an agreement between the parties of the opposition to defend democratic rights, win freedom for political prisoners, fight the wage cuts, unemployment, dispossession of the peasants, racial discrimination, etc., to struggle for free elections and eventually participate in them with the program of the National Democratic Front, the democratic solution to the crisis.

Our goal is clear: a democratic solution to Cuba's crisis, the defeat of this de facto government and its submission to imperialism, and the creation of a patriotic government of the National Democratic Front.

What have we done to apply and develop these politics?

The events of July 26 have not led the party to deviate from its line. Despite the terror and other new conditions, the party has not abandoned the struggle for the United Front, but has reinforced it by all means at its disposal. It has not desperately withdrawn the slogan of immediate and democratic general elections, but has put it forward with even more force, demanding that the Supreme Electoral Tribunal and the government open a new period for party registration and make the necessary changes so the elections would be a real consultation of the people. With redoubled energy, the party has put forward the necessity of building the united front as an electoral vehicle.

The party accepted these tasks energetically, and united front committees quickly spread from one end of the country to the other. The Havana united front movement, which was older and stronger, since it dated from before July 26, led the way by initiating the creation of a National United Front Party (FUN) with the collaboration of men and women of all parties, including our own.

To a great degree, it was because of this struggle—the petition of the United Front of Havana to the government and the Supreme Electoral Tribunal, demanding new elections—that the government was obliged to maneuver, creating an Electoral Commission "to hear the opposition." Along with the clear, resolute voice of our party, an avalanche of demands and petitions in favor of democratic elections came to this government commission. And the government was obliged not only to postpone the elections—which fit with its plans—but also to open a new period for party registration and speak of "concessions to the opposition."

Given this opportunity, united-front committees around the country presented the signatures of over 8,000 voters to register as a party. Having done this, the movement's vigor frightened the reactionary government. It was on the verge of becoming a truly popular electoral instrument for the opposition. Its existence opened new possibilities for unity among the masses, for a united struggle for free elections, democratic demands, freedom for all political prisoners, etc., and for the defeat of the government. The Batista clique could find no other way to confront this situation than arbitrarily refusing the registration of the FUN. It thereby ran the risk of revealing, as it finally did, its plans to forbid any democratic opposition in the elections, or to call them to a halt if circumstances demanded. The refusal to register the FUN showed that the government's autocratic measures were not temporary, but rather formed a permanent part of its plans.

Later, when the registration took place and our party was arbitrarily forbidden to participate in the electoral process, it took advantage of the opportunity to again denounce the reorganization process as a masquerade and to call for the masses to refuse affiliation with any of the parties that were participating in this masquerade, whether with the government or the supposed opposition.

The masses repudiated the reorganization, as is well known. Batista and his comrades turned up two million signatures, but the people know that this number included hundreds of thousands of voters whose identification cards had been stolen or taken by force, or who had been dropped from the census lists.

Precisely because of the failure of this maneuver, the government had to resort to another shameful special decree.

Recently, continuing our line of struggle and mass unity and welcoming the initiative of the United Front, our party approached the Permanent Executive Committee of the Orthodox Party to support the demands they had presented to the nation, despite their insufficiency. We invited the *Orthodoxos* to help create a united movement for these demands, which could and ought to serve as a basis for uniting not only with the *Orthodoxos*, but with the whole opposition, in common activity for various democratic demands and for free elections. While this Permanent Executive Committee did not respond to our party, our declaration could only move things in our direction.

In fact, if we continue in this direction, if we seriously struggle to involve the *Orthodoxos* in common activity for *their* own program, if we tirelessly and patiently promote united struggle with the *Orthodoxos* and other oppositionists both from above and below, and if we do not disparage smaller united rank-and-file actions for economic and political demands in the factories and workshops, the countryside and the *barrios*, and among the youth and students, the idea of the united front will decisively gain support. It will take flesh and blood among the masses, who will force those leaders who fear unity to join the people and the mass struggle against the regime and its major supporter, Yankee imperialism, the biggest obstacle to democracy in Cuba.

Finally and concretely, the proper road for the people in the current circumstances is:

1. Unite the opposition and the masses to win free elections, defeat "putschism" and "possibilism," and stop any compromising behind the backs of and against the masses.
2. In any event, keep alive the mass struggle for economic demands and democratic slogans, for free elections and the program of the Democratic National Front, and prepare to use the government's very own electoral farce in the struggle for these demands.

The situation is not easy by any means. The government is resolutely opposed to free elections and democratic rights. It obstinately sticks to its farcical electoral plans. The government can still maneuver and resist the solution the country needs, because unity among the opposition is conspicuous by its absence and because "putschism" and abstentionism still hold back the masses.

This is why our party must increase its activity in favor of unity and mass mobilization, continue performing its duties, and not allow itself to be dragged down by certain electoralist currents that persist in certain party circles or by pseudo-leftist currents that would place us with the "abstentionists"; we must rather keep fighting with renewed energy for our correct line.

We insist the situation is not easy, but it is not impossible to win our demands. We should not forget that the mass struggle for economic and political demands tends to grow, and if we help move the masses, they can definitely impose their own solution.

Batista, with the collaboration of elements of the opposition, is resisting the advance of democracy. He relies upon force. He uses the machinery of power so that elections are at his whim and convenience, without any real popular participation.

Understanding this, we must act with even more tenacity to quickly change this situation and carry our struggle to the enemies' territory.

The people have one slogan: free elections and the defeat of the anti-Cuban de facto government, to open the way for a democratic solution and a National Democratic Front government.

To this end, we are ready to unite with any party, political group, or citizen.

We base ourselves on the interests of the people, and their interests only. This is how we behave and will continue to behave. Other parties should do the same if they really want to free Cuba from its dark and difficult circumstances!

In conclusion, we must:

* Step up the struggle for immediate, free elections.
* Step up the struggle to unite the masses, the opposition parties, etc., for demands such as:
  —amnesty for political and social prisoners;
  —repeal of the anti-Communist and public-order decree laws;
  —end the closure of *Hoy, La Calle*, and other periodicals and reestablish the freedom of the press;
  —reestablishment of democratic rights, including the right of workers to meet, organize, and demonstrate against wage and salary cuts;
  —repeal of the fascist trade union tax;
  —facilitation of the electoral registration of all democratic, labor, anti-imperialist, socialist, and progressive parties and groups in elections, reestablishing the principles of the 1940 Constitution;
  —free and direct voting.
* Step up the struggle for the united front; for the creation of increasingly active united-front committees in the workshops, workplaces, plantations, schools, offices, neighborhoods, and cities; unite all the united-front committees in a powerful and solid movement.
* More forcefully spread and defend the idea of the National Democratic Front as the Cuban solution to Cuban problems.
* Finally, if no better can be won, use the government's own electoral process to the maximum, despite its limited possibilities, to carry out the mass struggle, defend the line of the party and the program of the National Democratic Front, and unite the masses against the Batista government and in favor of the democratic solution to Cuba's crisis.

SOCIALIST AND DEMOCRATIC REVOLUTION IN CUBA*

Fidel Castro

The growing over of the Cuban Revolution into a socialist revolution took place in October 1960, but it was only in April 1961 that this "qualitative leap" in the revolutionary process was explicitly recognized and proclaimed.

In this historic speech, made on April 16, 1961, at the burial of the victims of a counterrevolutionary air attack launched from Guatemala, Castro for the first time announced the socialist and democratic character of the Cuban Revolution. The next day, April 17, several thousand counterrevolutionary Cubans (armed and trained by the C.I.A.) landed at the Bay of Pigs, but they were routed within 72 hours by workers' and peasants' militias that had been formed in 1960.

The imperialists cannot forgive us because we exist. The imperialists cannot forgive the dignity, the integrity, the bravery, the ideological firmness, the spirit of sacrifice, and the revolutionary spirit of the people of Cuba.

This is what they cannot forgive: that we are here under their noses. And that we have made a socialist revolution right under the nose of the United States!

We are defending the socialist revolution with these rifles. We are defending this socialist revolution with the bravery our anti-aircraft artillerymen displayed while shooting down the aggressor's planes.

And we are not defending this revolution with mercenaries. We defend it with men and women of the people.

And who bears these arms? Maybe a mercenary? Maybe a millionaire? Because mercenaries and millionaires are the same. Are little rich kids bearing these arms?

Are foremen carrying these weapons? Who has these weapons? Whose hands are raising these weapons? Are they the hands of little gentlemen? Are they the hands of the rich? Are they the hands of the exploiters? Whose hands are raising these weapons? Aren't they workers' hands? Aren't they peasants' hands? Aren't they hands hardened by work? Aren't they productive hands? Aren't they the humble hands of the people? And who are the majority of the people? Are they millionaires or workers? The exploiters or the exploited? The privileged or the humble? Do the privileged have weapons? Don't the humble have them? Aren't the privileged a minority? Aren't the humble a majority? When the humble have weapons—isn't this a democratic revolution!

Comrade workers and peasants, this is a socialist and democratic revolution of the humble, with the humble, and for the humble. And for this

*Fidel Castro, *La Revolución Cubana, 1953–62*, (Mexico City: Ed. Era, 1976), pp. 328–329.

revolution of the humble, by the humble, and for the humble, we are ready
to give our lives.

Workers and peasants, humble men and women of the homeland, do you
swear to defend this revolution of the humble, by the humble, and for the
humble with your last drop of blood?

Comrade workers and peasants, yesterday's attack was the prelude to
mercenary aggression. Yesterday's attack cost seven heroic lives. Its goal
was to destroy our airplanes on the ground, but they failed. They did not
destroy our planes, and most of the enemy planes were damaged or destroyed. Here, before the grave of our fallen comrades, along with the rest
of our heroic youth, children of the workers and children of the humble, we
reaffirm our decision that, just like those who braved bullets with their
chests bared, like those who gave their lives, when the mercenaries seek
vengeance, we, proud of our revolution, proud to defend this revolution of
the humble, by the humble, and for the humble—we will not waver in
defending it against any foe, to our last drop of blood.

Long live the working class! Long live the peasants! Long live the humble! Long live our homeland's martyrs! May the heroes of the nation live
forever! Long live the socialist revolution! Long live free Cuba!

Homeland or Death! We shall win!

FROM MARTÍ TO MARX*
Fidel Castro

This speech of December 2, 1961, is a key document of the Cuban Revolution: it is
the first time that Fidel explicitly declares himself a Marxist, and explains his
ideological itinerary from radical anti-imperialism (Martí) to Marx and Lenin. He
also sheds light on how and why the Cuban Revolution "grows over" to socialism.
We also find here some of the principal characteristics of the Castroist interpretation
of Marxism: a view of the political arena as an alternative between imperialism and
socialism, and an intense ethical emotionalism. Also note the homage to Mella,
Martínez Villena (a Communist poet and leader who died in 1935), and Guiteras.

Really, we thought that here was a truly heroic kind of worker. How did he
work? He worked fifteen days in the plains, got together fifteen or twenty
pesos, bought some salt and a little butter, and returned to the hills. And so
it went for years. While he harvested prime coffee beans, no one helped
him. But not only that. As soon as this peasant cleared a little piece of
mountainside, a couple of rural guards would come around—or if not the

---

*Fidel Castro, *La Revolución Cubana, 1953–62* (Mexico City: Ed. Era, 1976), pp. 394–399,
434–439.

rural guard, then someone sent by the chief of the nearest post—to collect a fee for the clearing.

So this unfortunate peasant came down to the plains, worked for a couple of weeks burdened by a thousand hardships—since they paid him a peso— so he could have a little piece of land to grow coffee, and a corporal of the rural guard or the sergeant of a nearby post sends out somebody to take his money whenever he clears land.

These same peasants had the problem that they were paid thirteen or fourteen pesos for their coffee; money was lent them and they were charged the highest interest. And the BANFAIC was already operating. Sure, the BANFAIC was operating, but to whom did the BANFAIC give money? The BANFAIC gave money to the peasants who already had a crop, the person who had money, who was almost a capitalist, or to someone who through hard work had been able to plant a half *caballería* and had already harvested a hundred quintals. They gave more to someone who had harvested a hundred quintals, but they didn't lend money to people who hadn't harvested anything—the overwhelming majority of the highland peasants—since they didn't have title to the land. The BANFAIC demanded title to the land and demanded they already have a harvest—that they had already harvested coffee beans; if not, they did not lend. This was the situation of the peasant.

Besides, when the rural guard came by, they were sure to take at least a fine rooster. At least! That is if they didn't take a little pig, too, and things like that. Merchandise that was sold to the peasants was sold quite dear. There weren't any schools there. There weren't any teachers. Of course, if the peasants had known what it was possible to do with just six rifles, they could have at least set themselves up independently in the mountains— because the conditions were optimal. It was a much better fate for any peasant to grab a rifle and rise up than to be driven off his land and endure hardship and misery.

These are the conditions we encountered in the Sierra Maestra: that is, the objective conditions. Everything else—the organization of a military apparatus, the organization of a political apparatus, everything!—was yet to be done. This is exactly what had happened in the plains. The corresponding organization had been done in the plains, but it was very embryonic, very new, and therefore didn't have the discipline of a revolutionary organization forged by many years of struggle.

Obviously, many young people struggled in the plains, sacrificed, risked their lives, and fought heroically. But it was basically a heroic struggle that could not reap the fruits we had already begun to harvest in the mountains.

The mountains were the field for the struggle. Our task of organizing the guerrilla movement began there, giving us experience, gaining experience, while at the same time winning, conquering the peasant masses for the revolution. It was perfectly logical that our revolutionary work would develop in the objective conditions that existed in the Sierra Maestra, to the point that we could count on the practically unanimous support of the peasants of the Sierra Maestra.

That is, we already could rely on a social force, despite having few arms and series of problems. The struggle kept developing; it developed in the second front in Las Villas, and later, in the second front in Oriente. The tactic that we promoted had triumphed. That is, the facts had shown that this road, under particular conditions, was correct. Tactics of a putschist type, organizing forces and attempting to conquer power in a frontal struggle against the armed forces, under great disadvantages, began to be abandoned. The tactics that we recommended were wearing down the forces of the tyranny.

Needless to say, this is why we have had a profound faith in the guerrilla struggle. We believe in the guerrilla struggle under the conditions that exist in our country, which are similar to the conditions in many countries of Latin America. And don't think because of this that we are promoting. . . . You didn't let me finish. We believe it quite seriously. We have the right to believe it, since we have gone through this experience.

Of course, we know that when this conviction comes to other peoples who are similarly oppressed by imperialism, by cliques in the service of imperialism and by military castes, and similarly exploited by *latifundistas*—another people where exactly the same thing is happening as happened in Cuba: hungry, exploited peasants, without land, without schools, without doctors, without credit, without any kind of aid—when they are convinced of what we were convinced (and we were convinced, above all, by the reality of events), I am sure that there will be no imperialist or reactionary power, or military caste, or NATO army that will be able to contain the revolutionary movement.

We sincerely believe that, under Cuban conditions, we have to guard against this one tactic. This is just what our enemies are trying to do, but with one single difference, a single difference: they are trying to make a revolution among a peasantry that has finished with the *latifundistas*; where rent has been abolished and there is a teacher in every neighborhood; with hospitals, doctors, credits, and aid; where the middleman and the speculator is done for and the harvest guaranteed—in other words, under conditions that are completely the opposite of the conditions under which we made ours.

So it is that we made a revolution under certain conditions, and the counterrevolutionaries come and want to create a war under conditions that are the opposite of those under which we struggled. In short, everything that happened to them, had to happen to them. There in the Sierra Maestra, in that zone, whenever they tried to form a counterrevolutionary group, they were put out of action within forty-eight hours.

That is, they copied one part, but not the other. In short, it couldn't be copied. But even our enemies, even the reactionaries, copied the idea of creating a guerrilla struggle. Even the Pentagon finally copied our ideas, but chose the other side of the coin. We don't have to copy anything: simply leave things alone and see how they develop. We know that all the military science of the Pentagon will clash against our reality. Our reality is the situation in which the people of Latin America live.

There is only one way of combating the revolutionary guerrilla: the dissolution of imperialist monopolies and imperialist exploitation. This is why no one is bothered when we hear that General Taylor, or any other general who was in Korea or where ever, is heading an anti-guerrilla school in Panama. This is a waste of time.

In short, they're afraid; they're showing that they're really afraid. But they wallow in the illusion that the revolutionary peoples' struggle can be averted. There is no remedy of any kind for the peoples' revolutionary struggle—only the disappearance of the causes that lead the people to revolt. That's why we can't help laughing at all the schools like Taylor's. We are certain that if any handful of men launch a struggle in those countries where objective conditions are like those that existed in Cuba—and I'm not referring to any country in particular—and if that revolutionary movement, that group, follows the rules that a guerrilla must, we are completely sure that this will be the spark that will light a fire.

We were just like a little match in a haystack—I won't say a cane field, because a match in a cane field is quite serious—a match in a haystack. That's what the revolutionary movement was, given the conditions that existed in our country. Little by little, the struggle became a struggle of a whole people. It was the people, the whole people, who were the only actors in this struggle. It was the masses who decided the contest.

When our tactic proved itself, the people immediately began to join, all the revolutionaries began to join, and it became the tactic and the struggle of the whole Cuban revolutionary movement, of all revolutionaries, and finally the struggle of the whole people.

Even though it's true at the final stage, at the end of December, the tyranny's regular army was quite broken, how can the revolutionary movement avoid what's happening now in Santo Domingo—avoid what reaction and imperialism always has tried to do throughout America? Only revolutionary consciousness that has developed among the people, the active participation of the masses, can do this.

What made the maneuvers of the American Embassy and the reactionaries melt away like candy in a school yard? Simply, the general strike. There was no need to take another shot. That was the right moment to raise the slogan of a general strike.

Certainly we raised it quite prematurely. What does that mean? Subjective criteria predominated; we didn't know the objective situation. Our own revolution has examples of everything. We wanted these conditions to be ready. We wanted to unleash a general strike with a simple slogan and have the tyranny collapse. This was what we wanted, what we hoped for. But it so happened that we made these wishes into reality, but only in our imagination.

And what does a revolutionary have to do? He must interpret reality. We were not interpreting this reality, and we committed an error. The result was that there was no such strike, because the conditions weren't fully ripe and because of the tactics employed. In short, the conditions basically weren't ripe. The revolution's military force amounted to less than two hundred men.

When the slogan was raised for a second time, we already had isolated entire provinces, destroyed complete enemy units, and the enemy was really broken—while at this other time, the enemy was always crossing the territory we wanted and dominating the situation in the country. When the slogan is raised at the right time, then it's easy to carry out the strategy: the revolutionary conquest of power by the masses. This was the difference between a really revolutionary movement and a coup d'état.

What factor mobilized the masses? The guerrilla struggle became a factor that mobilized the masses, that sharpened the struggle, the repression, sharpened the regime's contradictions. And simply, the people took power; power was taken by the masses. This was the first basic characteristic.

It is possible to liquidate the power, the military apparatus, the machinery that has supported the regime. That is, a series of revolutionary laws were being fulfilled; first, the conquest of power by the masses, and second, the destruction of the apparatus, the military machine that supported this whole regime of privilege.

What are the reactionaries and imperialism attempting? What are they trying to preserve in this crisis? The history of Latin America is full of examples; what they are trying to preserve at all costs is the military apparatus, the system's military machine. Neither imperialism nor the ruling classes ultimately care who is president, who is a representative, who is a senator.

Of course, imperialism and reaction would rather the president not be a total thief, if possible. They would rather he be honorable, if possible, and that he invest money properly to advance the interests of the ruling class. They would rather the public administration function honestly. And finally, they prefer a government of people who steal less to a government that steals more.

What does imperialism want? It wants, of course, a government that guarantees profits for its monopolies. It's all the same to them whether it's Pérez Jiménez or Rómulo Betancourt. There's an example, if you like . . . .

From the point of view of the march of world history, from the point of view of the great efforts of all the world's peoples to free themselves from hunger, misery, exploitation, colonialism, and discrimination—for example, the struggles of the peoples of Asia, Africa, and Latin America—we could never consciously be on the side of imperialism. Many people, stuffed with *Readers' Digest*, Yankee movies, *Life* magazine and UPI and AP cables that have told so many lies, might believe that the policies of the United States have been proper, noble, and humanitarian, as they would like you to believe.

What thinking person, what reasonable person who knows what's going on in the whole world today, could honestly be on the side of the politics of imperialism?

From the point of view of the universal interests of humanity, rather than those of national values and sentiments, it is logical that our country would never be on the side of these policies, but on the side of the policies that it supports today, defending the rights of all these peoples. It is possible that some people see this more clearly than their own economic problems. For those who don't understand, our country had to choose between two options: the policies of capitalism, the policies of imperialism; or anti-imperialist policies, the policies of socialism.

We must take into account that there is no middle way between capitalism and socialism. Those who persist in seeking third ways fall into a quite false and utopian position. This would be like fooling oneself; this would mean complicity with imperialism. It is perfectly understandable that anyone who remains indifferent to the struggle of the Algerians is an accomplice of French imperialism. Whoever is indifferent to Yankee intervention in the Dominican Republic is an accomplice of this Yankee intervention in the Dominican Republic. Whoever remains aloof from the persecution unleashed by the traitor Rómulo Betancourt against the workers and the students of Venezuela—the same workers and students who defend us—is an accomplice of that oppression. Whoever is indifferent to Franco in Spain, to German rearmament, to the fact that German warmongers, Nazi officers, are now armed and are even demanding thermonuclear weapons, whoever is indifferent to what is happening in South Vietnam, in the Congo, in Angola, whoever is indifferent and proposes to adopt a third position on these events isn't really adopting a third position, but is adopting in practice a position of complicity with imperialism.

There are some people—people who consider themselves quite smart—who claim what the Cuban Revolution ought to have done was grab money from the Americans and from the Russians.

There's no lack of people who preach such repugnant, such cowardly, such cheap and base policies. That is—sell yourself, sell your country as if you were selling any piece of merchandise to the imperialists. Take from the imperialists while frightening them with the friendship of the Soviet Union—that is, be blackmailers. And there were those who put forward this blackmail theory.

But how could we accomplish this blackmail? How could we carry out this blackmail theory? There wasn't really anything to blackmail. This would have meant maintaining the status quo in our country, respecting all of imperialism's interests, their thousands of acres, their sugar mills, their electric monopoly, their telephone company, their control of our foreign and domestic trade and our banks. And any country that decides to free itself from the North American trade monopoly, that decides to carry out a land reform, that decides to have its own industry, to have independent politics, has to confront imperialism.

That is, the revolution wouldn't be a revolution; it had to be betrayed. The revolution had to choose between these two: treason or revolution.

And we remember the people who have died for this revolution; we remember our comrades cut down in struggle, as all revolutionaries should remember those who have fallen since Guiteras, since Martínez Villena—although Martínez Villena wasn't actually assassinated but died as a result of that struggle's failure—and Mella. All these revolutionaries didn't think of today's revolutionaries, but of Martí, who also had a brilliant vision.

Because, those of us who admire Martí—what was Martí's merit? Was Martí a Marxist-Leninist? No, Martí wasn't a Marxist-Leninist. Martí said of Marx that he had all his sympathy, since he placed himself on the side of the poor.

This is because the Cuban Revolution was a national, liberating revolution against the Spanish colonial power. It was not a social struggle; it was a struggle that first sought national independence. And even then, in that period, Martí said of Marx: "Since he put himself on the side of the poor, he deserves my respect."

And what other vision did Martí have? He had another brilliant vision in the year 1895. He had a vision of North American imperialism, when North American imperialism had not yet become imperialist. That's called having long-range political vision!

Because North American imperialism began to develop actively after its intervention in Cuba, when it practically took possession of the country's wealth, took possession of Puerto Rico, took possession of the Philippines, and thereby began the imperialist stage of North American capitalism.

Martí foresaw the development of the United States as an imperialist power in 1895. And he wrote, alerted the public, and pronounced himself against this. You can see that Martí was indeed a brilliant revolutionary who warned against the rise of imperialism in 1895, when it had not yet begun to show itself as an international power.

So, we must think of all of those who fell, all of those who died, all of those who struggled. Why did they struggle? So the electric company could remain a Yankee company? So that 600,000 acres along the Atlantic Gulf could remain foreign-owned land? So that our peasants should remain landless, stay hungry, and remain in misery? So the banks could remain foreign property? So that they could drain hundreds of millions of dollars from our country every year? So there would still be a million illiterates in our country? So the peasants could remain without schools, without hospitals, without homes, living in shacks and slums? So our people would stay like this, fifty years after they supposedly had won their independence?

Of course, I'm not saying this for the revolutionaries. And it's possible I don't have to say this to revolutionaries. This must be said to the insensitive, to the indifferent, to the confused, to those who don't understand why this and why that.

And have all these people died so the *latifundistas* can remain the masters of thousands of *caballerías* of land? No. Anybody can understand this. Anybody can understand that the leaders of the revolution would have been traitors if they made a revolution, if they had led so many youths into combat and struggle, if they had sacrificed so many lives for this. Such little glory would not have been worth a single Cuban life! For such little glory, it wouldn't have been worth raising one weapon! To use a weapon, to fight, to struggle, to suffer what our country has suffered, had to have been for something much greater than this.

And some claimed men were dying precisely for this system of exploitation to continue: so a thousand families could keep living like princes in our capitals and our cities; so this regime of exploitation, of hunger, of misery, of discrimination, of abuses, could continue. Some claimed this. And it seems they believed that the revolution could be just like this. There were some who even bought bonds and did things like that at the last moment. How wrong they were! They thought that certain gains for our country, which had been laid out as far back as the war of 1895, were going to be cut short and things would go on as always!

It's clear that these honest politics, these revolutionary politics, these policies that march in step with history, are in accord with the sentiments and the interests of the underdeveloped and exploited peoples of the whole world, in accord with national interests and national honor. These are not easy politics. They are necessarily a politics of sacrifice, because if we wanted to redeem our people from a lack of culture, from unemployment, from hunger, from misery, to develop our economy, to have our own economy, an independent economy, and along with an independent economy, an independent policy that ends unemployment, the lack of culture, misery, backwardness, poverty, ignorance, sickness, and the unhappy situation in which the majority of our people live, we had to carry out consistently revolutionary policies. To do it meant confronting imperialism with all our strength. And this is what we have done.

Of course, we leaders of the revolution are revolutionaries. If we were not revolutionaries, we would simply not be making a revolution. What I mean is that the revolutionaries, and the people with the revolutionaries, that is, the vast exploited mass of the people, are ready to make whatever sacrifice and pay whatever price is necessary for all this.

The potbellies, the indifferent, the insensitive, the corrupted could say that the best thing was not to look for trouble, to simply respect all these interests. They could say this, and they did.

We had to choose between remaining under imperialist domination, exploitation, and insolence, putting up with Yankee ambassadors giving us orders while our country remained in its state of misery, or making an anti-imperialist revolution and making a socialist revolution.

There was no alternative. We chose the only honorable road, the only road for our country that we could loyally follow, in accord with the tradition of our *mambises*, in accord with the traditions of all those who have struggled for our country's well-being. This is the road we have followed: the road of anti-imperialist struggle, the road of socialist revolution. Because there was no place for any other position, anyway. Any other position would have been wrong, absurd. And we will never take such a position. We will never vacillate. Never!

Imperialism should know that we will never have anything to do with them, ever, and imperialism should know that no matter how great our difficulties, no matter how hard the struggle to build our country, to build a future for our country, to make a history worthy of our country, imperialism should never have the smallest hope for us.

Many who didn't understand this, understand it today. And they will understand it more and more. For us, all these things are more clear, more obvious, more indisputable.

This was the road the revolution had to follow: the road of anti-imperialist struggle and the road of socialism. That is, the nationalization of all the big industries, the big businesses, the nationalization and social ownership of the basic means of production and the planned development of our economy at the quickest pace our resources and the aid we are receiving from abroad will permit. This has been the other really favorable thing for our revolution—the fact that we can count on the aid and solidarity that allow us to move our revolution forward without the enormous sacrifices that other peoples have had to make.

We had to make an anti-imperialist and socialist revolution. Well, the anti-imperialist and socialist revolution could only be one revolution, because there is only one revolution. This is the great dialectical truth of humanity: imperialism, and socialism against imperialism. The result of this is the victory of socialism, the transcendence of the socialist epoch, the overcoming of the stage of capitalism and imperialism, the establishment of the socialist era, and then the era of communism.

Nobody should be frightened—in case there are still some anti-communists here—there won't be communism for thirty years, at least.

And here are a few words so even our enemies can learn what Marxism is. Simply, we cannot jump over a historical stage. Perhaps the building of capitalism is a historical stage that some underdeveloped countries can leap over today. This means they can begin the development of a country's economy through the road of planning, the road of socialism. What can't be skipped over is socialism. And even the Soviet Union, after forty years, is beginning the construction of communism and hopes to have advanced considerably along this road after twenty years. Therefore, we are in the stage of the construction of socialism.

And socialism, what kind of socialism must we apply here? Utopian socialism? Simply, we have to apply scientific socialism. This is why I began by saying with all honesty that we believe in Marxism, we believe that it is the most correct, most scientific, and only true theory—the only really revolutionary theory. I say here with complete satisfaction and complete confidence: I am a Marxist-Leninist, and I will be a Marxist-Leninist until the last day of my life.

14

Castroism and Guevarism

GUERRILLA WARFARE: A METHOD*
Ernesto Che Guevara

This article by Guevara, which dates from 1963, is one of the most interesting attempts to generalize certain lessons of the Cuban Revolution to the Latin American struggle. One of the central theses of the article, the socialist nature of the Latin American revolution, is directly connected to its analysis of the national bourgeoisies. Guevara also presents his conception of guerrilla warfare on a continental scale in a concise and rigorous way; we should point out that while his superficial critics misunderstand the point, Guevara saw guerrilla warfare as a political-military process with a mass-struggle character. Of course, his ideas on guerrilla warfare were directly inspired by the Cuban example: the priority of struggle in the countryside, the key role of the initial *foco*, and so forth.

Guerrilla warfare has been employed innumerable times in history, under different conditions and in pursuit of different ends. Lately, it has been employed in various popular wars of liberation, where the people's vanguard has chosen the road of irregular armed struggle against enemies of greater military potential. Asia, Africa, and America have been the scene of this activity during attempts to take power in the struggle against feudal, colonial, or neo-colonial exploitation. In Europe, it has been employed as a complement to one's own or allied regular armies.

Guerrilla warfare has been resorted to in America at various times. As the most immediate precedent, we could refer to the experience of Augusto César Sandino, struggling against the Yankee expeditionary force on the Coco River of Nicaragua, and more recently, the revolutionary war in Cuba. Since then, the problems of guerrilla warfare have been raised in the theoretical discussions of the progressive political parties of the continent, and the possibility and suitability of its use are the subject of contentious polemics.

---

*Ernesto Che Guevara, "Guerra de guerrillas, un método," in *Obra revolucionaria* (Mexico City: Ed. Era, 1973), pp. 551–52, 556–563.

These notes will attempt to express our ideas on guerrilla warfare and its correct utilization.

First, we must specify that this form of struggle is a method—a method to reach a goal. This goal, which is indispensable and unavoidable for all revolutionaries, is the conquest of political power. For this reason, in our analysis of the specific situations of the different countries of America, we should use the concept of guerrilla war as a simple category—a method of struggle to achieve this end.

Almost immediately, the question arises: Is the method of guerrilla warfare the only formula for the taking of power in the whole of the Americas? Or, in any case, will it be the predominant form? Or will it simply be one form among others used in the struggle? And lastly, it is asked if the example of Cuba is applicable to other situations on the continent. In the course of polemics, it is the custom to criticize those who wish to carry out guerrilla warfare, alleging that they neglect the mass struggle, almost as if these were counterposed methods. We reject the idea that underlies this position; guerrilla war is a people's war, a mass struggle. To attempt to carry out this type of warfare without the support of the population is the prelude to inevitable disaster. The guerrillas are the fighting vanguard of the people, situated in a particular location in a given territory, armed and ready to carry out a series of warlike actions with the sole possible strategic goal of taking power. They are supported by the worker and peasant masses of the region and the whole territory in which they act. Without these preconditions, guerrilla warfare is impossible.

"In the situation in our America, we think that the Cuban Revolution has made three fundamental contributions to the technique of revolutionary movements in America. They are: first, the popular forces can win a war against the army; second, one does not always have to wait for all the conditions for the revolution to be in place—the insurrectionary *foco* can create them; third, in underdeveloped America, the field of armed struggle must fundamentally be the countryside" (*Guerrilla Warfare*).

These are our contributions to the development of the revolutionary struggle in America, and they can be applied in whichever countries of our continent that a guerrilla war is to be carried out . . . .

During the development of the revolutionary struggle in America, there are two moments of extreme danger for the revolution's future. The first of these occurs during the preparatory stage, and the way it is resolved shows the measure of determination to struggle and the clarity of purpose of the popular forces. When the bourgeois state advances against the people's positions, a defense must obviously be organized against the enemy, who is attacking while he has superiority. If the minimum objective and subjective conditions have developed, this defense should be armed, but in such a way that the popular forces do not become mere objects of the enemy's blows; they should not let the scene of armed defense become the last refuge of the hunted. While at a particular moment the guerrillas are a defensive people's movement, they have and must constantly develop an ability to attack the enemy. This capacity, in time, is what determines its character as a catalyst of the popular forces. That is, the guerrilla struggle is not passive self-defense; it is defense and attack. And the moment that it is established as such, the conquest of power becomes the final prospect.

This moment is important. The difference between violence and non-violence in social processes cannot be measured by the number of shots exchanged; it corresponds to concrete and changing circumstances. And we must be able to recognize the instant at which the popular forces, conscious of their relative weakness but at the same time of their strategic power, should force the enemy to take the necessary steps to keep the situation from deteriorating. We must violate the equilibrium between the oligarchic dictatorship and popular pressure. The dictatorship constantly attempts to function without the ostentatious use of force; forcing it to present itself without a disguise, that is to say, in its true aspect as a violent dictatorship of the reactionary classes, will contribute to its unmasking, which will deepen the struggle to such extremes that no retreat will be possible. The solid beginning of a long-term armed action depends on how the people's forces fulfill their function when confronting this task of forcing the dictatorship to make a decision between retreating and unleashing the struggle.

Avoiding another dangerous moment depends on the growing power of the popular forces. Marx always recommended that once the revolutionary process has begun, the proletariat must strike, and strike relentlessly. A revolution that does not deepen constantly is a revolution that is moving backward. The fighters, being tired, begin to lose faith; at this point, some of the maneuvers to which the bourgeoisie has made us so accustomed can bear fruit. These might include elections, with the transfer of power to another gentleman with a more mellifluous voice and a more angelic face than the dictator of the moment, or a coup by reactionaries, generally led by the army, which finds direct or indirect support among progressive forces. There are other tactical strategems, but it is not our intention to analyze them.

Let us look principally at the tactic of a military coup that we mentioned above. What can the military contribute to true democracy? What loyalty can they demand if they are mere instruments of the domination of the reactionary classes and imperialist monopolies, and if, as a caste whose worth rests on the arms they possess, they only aspire to maintain their prerogatives?

When the situation is difficult for the oppressors, and the military conspires and overthrows a dictator (who actually has already been defeated), we should infer that this occurs because he can no longer maintain their class privileges without extreme violence, which is generally inconvenient at the moment for the oligarchies' interests.

This statement is in no way meant to exclude the use of military men as individual fighters, when separated from the social environment in which they functioned and actually rebelled against. And this should be done in the context of a revolutionary leadership to which they belong as fighters, not as representatives of a caste.

Long ago, in the preface to the third edition of *The Civil War in France*, Engels said that the workers, after each revolution, were armed: "Therefore the disarming of the workers was the commandment for the bourgeois, who were at the helm of the state. Hence, after every revolution won by the workers, a new struggle, ending with the defeat of the workers" (cited by Lenin in *The State and Revolution*).

This game of continual struggles, in which some kind of formal change is won and then strategically withdrawn, has been repeated for decades in the capitalist world. Even worse, the regular deception of the proletariat in this regard has been practiced periodically for more than a century.

There is also the danger that the leaders of the progressive parties, because of their desire to maintain, as long as possible, the most favorable conditions for revolutionary activity by using certain aspects of bourgeois legality, could neglect their goals (which is very common during such activity), and forget the definite, strategic objective: the taking of power.

The two difficult moments for the revolution that we have summarized can be avoided if the Marxist-Leninist party leaders are able to see the implications of the moment clearly, and mobilize the masses to the maximum, leading them along the correct path to resolving the fundamental contradictions.

In developing this theme, we have supposed that the idea of armed struggle and the formula of guerrilla warfare as a method of struggle will eventually be accepted. Why do we think that guerrilla warfare is the correct road in the current conditions in America? There are fundamental arguments that in our view determine the necessity of guerrilla activity in America as the central axis of the struggle.

First, accepting as true that the enemy will struggle to remain in power, we must consider the destruction of the oppressor army; to destroy it, we must directly confront it with a popular army. Such an army is not created spontaneously, but must be armed with the arsenal that its enemy offers, which means a hard and very long struggle in which the popular forces and their leaders will always be exposed to attack by superior forces, without adequate conditions for defense or maneuver.

On the other hand, the guerrilla nucleus, established on terrain favorable to the struggle, guarantees the security and continuity of the revolutionary command. The urban forces, under the direction of the general staff of the people's army, can carry out actions of incalculable importance. The eventual destruction of these groups will not destroy the revolution's soul—its leadership—since it will continue catalyzing the masses' revolutionary spirit and organizing new forces for other battles from its rural fortress.

Moreover, the structuring of the future state apparatus that will be charged with effectively leading the class dictatorship during the whole transitional period starts in this zone. The longer the struggle, the greater and more complex will be the administrative problems, and their solution will train the cadres for the difficult task of consolidating power and developing the economy in a future stage.

Second, there is the general situation of the Latin American peasantry and the increasingly explosive character of its struggle against feudal structures, in the context of the existence of a social alliance between the local and foreign exploiters.

Returning to the Second Declaration of Havana:

> The peoples of America liberated themselves from Spanish colonialism at the beginning of the last century, but they did not liberate themselves from exploitation. The feudal landlords assumed the authority of the Spanish rulers, the Indians remained in punishing servitude, the Latin American people remained slaves in one form or another, and their smallest hopes were crushed under the oligarchy's power and the yoke of foreign capital. This has been America's reality, with one or another nuance or variation. Today, Latin America suffers under a much more ferocious, much more powerful and more merciless imperialism than Spanish colonial imperialism.
>
> And what is the attitude of Yankee imperialism to the objective and historically inexorable reality of the Latin American revolution? It is prepared to unleash a colonial war against the peoples of Latin America and create the coercive apparatus, the political pretexts, and the pseudo-legal mechanisms consented to by the reactionary oligarchies to repress the struggles of the Latin America people with blood and fire.

This objective situation shows us the dormant power of our peasants and the need to use it for America's liberation.

Third is the continental character of the struggle.

Can this new stage in the emancipation of America be seen as a confrontation between two local forces struggling for power in a particular territory? Only with difficulty. It will be a fight to the death between all the popular forces and all the forces of repression. The paragraph quoted above also predicts this.

The Yankees will intervene because of their common interests and because the American struggle is decisive. In fact, they are already intervening in the preparation of repressive forces and the organization of a fighting continental apparatus. But from now on, they will do this with all their energies: they will punish the popular forces with all the weapons of destruction at their disposal, and they will not allow a revolutionary power to be consolidated; if it is, they will continue attacking. They will not recognize it and will try to divide the revolutionary forces, introduce saboteurs of all kinds, create border conflicts, launch other reactionary states against it, and attempt to economically isolate the new state—in a word, try to annihilate it.

Given this American panorama, it is difficult for victory to be won and consolidated in one isolated country. The unity of repressive forces must be met by the unity of the popular forces. The banner of rebellion must be raised in all the countries where oppression is reaching unsustainable levels, and this banner, by historical necessity, will have a continental character. As Fidel has said, the Andes cordillera will be the Sierra Maestra of America, and all the immense territories that make up this continent will be scenes of the struggle to the death against imperialist power.

We cannot say when the struggle will take on this continental character, nor how long it will last; but we can predict its coming and its victory, because it is the result of inevitable historical, economic, and political circumstances whose course cannot be deflected. The task of the revolutionary forces in each country is to start when the conditions are ripe, independent of the situation in other countries. The development of the struggle will condition our general strategy; our prediction of its continental character is the result of an analysis of each contender's forces, but does not at all exclude independent outbursts. Just as the initiation of the struggle at one location in a country will cause it to develop in a whole area, the launching of a revolutionary war contributes to creating new conditions in neighboring countries.

The development of revolutions has normally occurred in inversely proportional flows and counterflows. A revolutionary tide corresponds to a counterrevolutionary retreat; and vice versa, when the revolution is retreating there is a rise in the counterrevolution. At these times, the situation of the revolutionary forces grows difficult, and they must resort to better defensive measures to suffer the least possible damage. The enemy is extremely strong and continent-wide. This is why one cannot analyze the relative weaknesses of the local bourgeoisies to make decisions about limited areas. Still less can we consider an eventual alliance between these oligarchies and the people in arms. The Cuban Revolution sounded the alarm. The polarization of forces will be total: the exploiters on one side and the exploited on the other. The mass of the petty bourgeoisie will lean toward one camp or the other, according to their interests and the political skill with which they are treated; neutrality will be an exception. This is how the revolutionary war will be.

Let us consider how we might start a guerrilla *foco*.

Relatively small nuclei select sites for guerrilla warfare that are favorable for unleashing a counterattack or weathering a storm, and begin to act there. We must clearly establish the following: at first, the relative weakness of the guerrillas is such that they should aim to merely fix themselves in the terrain, learn about their environment, establish connections with the population, and reinforce the locations that will eventually become their support bases.

There are three conditions for the survival of a guerrilla movement that begins to develop under the conditions described here: constant mobility, constant vigilance, and constant distrust. Without adequately using these three elements of military tactics, the guerrilla force will find it hard to survive. It must be remembered that, for the guerrilla, heroism at these times is found in the breadth of their goals and the enormous series of sacrifices that they must endure to fulfill them.

These sacrifices do not include daily, face-to-face combat with the enemy; they have more subtle forms, and are more difficult for the body and mind of the individual guerrilla to bear.

Perhaps they will be severely punished by the enemy armies, divided into groups at times. Those who fall prisoner may be martyred. They could be chased like hunted animals in the areas they have chosen to fight, with the constant fear of having enemies on their trail. They constantly mistrust everyone, since the territory's peasants in some cases will betray them to the repressive troops to save themselves. There are no alternatives other than death or victory, with death a constant presence and victory a myth of which a revolutionary can only dream.

This is the heroism of the guerrilla. This is why it is said that marching is a form of combat, and that sometimes fleeing from combat is only another way of fighting. Facing the enemy's general superiority, the policy is to find the tactical way to achieve a relative superiority at a particular point, whether by concentrating more forces than the enemy or by assuring an advantage in the use of the terrain that changes the balance of forces. In these conditions, one insures a tactical victory; if this relative superiority is not certain, it is preferable not to act. As long as one can choose the "how" and "when," one should not give fight unless it will lead to a victory.

The guerrilla movement continues growing and consolidating in the context of the great politico-military activity of which it is a part. They continue creating their support bases, a fundamental element if the guerrilla army is to prosper. These support bases are points where the enemy army can only penetrate at the cost of heavy losses; they are bastions of the revolution, refuge and springboard for increasingly daring and distant raids.

This moment arrives if they have simultaneously overcome difficulties of both a tactical and political order. Guerrillas can never forget their function, the role they incarnate as the vanguard of the people, and therefore must create the political conditions necessary to establish a revolutionary power based on the full support of the masses. The major demands of the peasantry must be satisfied to the degree and in the form that circumstances allow, making the whole population a close and committed group.

If the military situation is difficult at first, the political situation is no less delicate; if a single military error can finish off the guerrillas, a political error can hold back their development for long periods.

The struggle is a political-military one, and it must develop and be understood as such.

The guerrilla movement, as it grows, comes to a point where its ability to act covers a particular region in which there are too many fighters, and the zone becomes excessively concentrated. The "beehive" effect begins here, when one of the leaders, a distinguished guerrilla, leaps to another region and starts repeating the chain of development of the guerrilla war—subject, of course, to the central command.

We must now point out that we cannot aspire to victory without forming a popular army. The guerrilla forces can grow to a certain size, the popular forces in the cities and other penetrable enemy zones can wreak havoc, but the military potential of reaction could remain intact. We should always remember that the final result must be the annihilation of the enemy. For this reason, all the new zones that are created, the areas behind enemy lines that have been penetrated, and the forces that operate in the major cities must have a dependent relation to the central command. We cannot claim to have the closed, hierarchical ranks of an army, but yes, a strategic chain of command. While having freedom of action under determined conditions, the guerrillas must carry out all the strategic orders of the central command, which is located in the strongest, most secure zone, preparing the conditions for the unity of all forces at a particular moment. Are there any less cruel alternatives?

The guerrilla liberation war will generally have three phases. The first is the phase of the strategic defensive, where a small force nibbles at the enemy and flees. They do not seek refuge to establish a passive defense in a little circle; rather their defense consists of the limited attacks they can carry out. After this, a point of equilibrium is reached, when the potential for action of the enemy and the guerrillas are balanced. And then there is the final moment of overwhelming the repressive army, which leads to the taking of the large cities, the great decisive encounters, and the total annihilation of the enemy.

After the point of equilibrium has been reached, when both forces respect each other, and the guerrilla war continues to develop, it acquires new characteristics. The concept of maneuver is introduced: large columns attacking strong points, a war of movement with the transfer of relatively powerful forces and equipment. But, because of the capacity for resistance and counterattack that the enemy still maintains, this war of maneuver does not definitively substitute for the guerrillas. It is merely another form of doing the same thing—a greater number of guerrilla forces—until a popular army with full army corps is finally created. Even then, however, the guerrillas remain in their "pure state," destroying communications and sabotaging the enemy's whole defensive apparatus.

We have predicted that the war will be continent-wide. This also means that it will be prolonged. There will be many fronts, and it will cost much blood and innumerable lives for quite a long time. But the phenomenon of the polarization of forces that is occurring in America—the clear division between exploiters and exploited that will exist in future revolutionary wars—means that when the people's armed vanguard takes power, the country or countries that do this will have simultaneously destroyed both of their oppressors, the imperialists and the local exploiters. The first stage of the social revolution will have crystallized; the peoples will be ready to bind their wounds and initiate the construction of socialism.

Are there other, less bloody possibilities?

It was some time ago that the last division of the world took place, with the United States taking the lion's share of our continent. Today, the imperialists of the Old World are again developing, and the vigor of the European Common Market is frightening these same North Americans. This might lead us to think it is possible for us to remain spectators to this inter-imperialist struggle, and then make our advance, perhaps in alliance with the strongest national bourgeoisies. Without even considering that passive politics never bring positive results in the class struggle and that alliances with the bourgeoisie, as revolutionary as they might appear at a particular moment, only have a transitory character, there is the question of timing that leads us to take action now. The sharpening of fundamental contradictions in America seems so rapid that it is affecting the "normal" development of contradictions within the imperialist camp in the struggle for markets.

The national bourgeoisies have, in their great majority, fused with North American imperialism, and will face the same fate as imperialism in each country. However, in those cases where agreements and coincidences of interest develop between the national bourgeoisie and other imperialisms, this occurs in the context of a fundamental struggle that necessarily will unite, in the course of its development, *all the exploited and all the exploiters.* The polarization of the antagonistic forces of the class enemies is, up to this point, more rapid than the development of contradictions between the exploiters over the division of the spoils. There are two camps; the alternative is becoming clearer for each individual and for each social layer of the population.

The Alliance for Progress is an attempt to stop the unstoppable.

But if the advance of the European Common Market or any other imperialist grouping upon American markets were more rapid than the development of this fundamental contradiction, our only choice would be to move the popular forces into the breech as a wedge, leading their whole struggle and taking advantage of the new intruders, while clearly understanding their ultimate intentions.

We must not surrender one position, one weapon, or one secret to the class enemy, under penalty of losing everything.

In fact, the eruption of the American struggle has already occurred. Will its center be in Venezuela, Guatemala, Colombia, Peru, or Ecuador? Are today's skirmishes only manifestations of a restlessness that has not yet borne fruit? The results of today's struggles do not matter. Whether one or another movement is temporarily defeated will not bear on the final result. What is definitive is the decision to struggle—which is maturing daily—the consciousness of the need for revolutionary change, and the certainty that it is possible.

This is a prediction. We make it with the conviction that history will prove us right. An analysis of the objective and subjective factors in America and the imperialist world indicates to us the certainty of these assertions based on the Second Declaration of Havana.

MESSAGE TO THE TRICONTINENTAL CONGRESS*
Ernesto Che Guevara

This document, written in the Bolivian bush toward the beginning of 1967, develops Guevara's ideas on the world revolution and proletarian internationalism in the form of a letter to the Executive Secretariat of the Organization of Solidarity with the Peoples of Asia, Africa, and Latin America (OSPAAL), which had been formed by the Tricontinental Congress of 1966.

The passage on Latin America that we reprint here insists on both the socialist

*Ernesto Che Guevara, "Mensaje a la Tricontinental," in *Obra Revolucionaria* (Mexico City: Ed. Era, 1973), pp. 643–645, 646–648.

character of the revolution and the inevitability of armed struggle. It has been used as a programmatic document by Latin American Castroists and Trotskyists.

The fundamental field for imperialist exploitation comprises the three underdeveloped continents: America, Asia, and Africa. Each country has its own characteristics, but so does each continent as a whole.

America constitutes a more or less homogeneous unit, and North American monopoly capital maintains an absolute supremacy through almost all its territory. Its puppet governments or, in the best of cases, its weak and cowardly governments, cannot defy the orders of their Yankee master. The North Americans have almost reached the apex of their political and economic domination, and have little room for improvement. Any change in the situation might lead to a weakening of their supremacy. Their policy is to maintain what they have conquered. Their line of action at the moment has been reduced to the brutal use of force to stop liberation movements of any type.

Under the slogan "No more Cubas" lurks the possibility of cowardly aggression, like that perpetrated against the Dominican Republic or the massacre in Panama before that, and the clear threat that Yankee troops are prepared to intervene anywhere in America where the established order is being changed and its interests endangered.

This policy can count on nearly total impunity. The O.A.S. is a useful masquerade, despite its poor reputation. Whether absurd or tragic, the U.N. is similarly ineffectual. The armies of all the countries of America are prepared to intervene to crush their own people. In fact, an International of crime and treason has been organized.

On the other hand, the national bourgeoisies have totally lost their ability to resist imperialism—if they ever had any—and now form its rear guard. There are no other alternatives: either a socialist revolution or a caricature of revolution.

In Latin America, the struggle is being carried out with arms in hand in Guatemala, Colombia, Venezuela, and Bolivia, and its first shoots are blossoming in Brazil. There are other centers of resistance that appear and are extinguished. But almost all the countries of the continent are ripe for a type of struggle that, to be victorious, can settle for nothing less than establishing a government of a socialist character.

For all practical purposes, only one language is spoken on this continent, with the exception of Brazil, whose people can understand Spanish given the similarity between the two languages. There is such a great identity between the classes of these countries that a "transnational American" type can be identified to a much greater degree than in other continents. Language, custom, religion, and a common master unite them. The degree and forms of exploitation are similar in their effects on both the exploiters and the exploited in most countries of our America. And rebellion is maturing rapidly here.

We might ask ourselves: How will this rebellion come to fruition? What kind will it be? We have maintained for some time that, given these similar characteristics, the struggle in America will, in its time, acquire continental dimensions. America will be the scene of many great battles fought by humanity for its liberation.

In the context of this continent-wide struggle, those struggles currently being fought are merely episodes, yet they have already furnished martyrs that will figure in American history as having given their necessary quota of blood in this final stage of the struggle for humanity's complete liberation. Here will figure the names of Commandante Turcios Lima, of the priest Camilo Torres, of Commandante Fabricio Ojeda, of Commandantes Lobatón and Luis de la Puente Uceda, key figures in the revolutionary movements of Guatemala, Colombia, Venezuela, and Peru.

But the active mobilization of the people creates its new leaders: César Montes and Yon Sosa raising the banner in Guatemala; Fabio Vázquez and Marulanda doing the same in Colombia; Douglas Bravo in the West and Américo Martín in El Bachiller, leading their respective fronts in Venezuela.

New outbreaks of war will develop in these and other countries, as has already occurred in Bolivia, and they will continue to grow with all the vicissitudes that are involved in the dangerous profession of the modern revolutionary. Many will die, victims of their own mistakes; others will fall in the hard combat that lies ahead. New fighters and new leaders will arise in the heat of the revolutionary struggle. The people will produce their fighters and leaders in the selective process of this very war, and the agents of Yankee repression will grow in number. Today, there are advisers in all the countries where armed struggle is being waged, and the Peruvian army, it seems, advised and trained by the Yankees, has carried out a successful campaign against this country's revolutionaries. But if these guerrilla *focos* are led with sufficient political and military skill, they will be practically invincible and require the dispatch of more Yankee troops. In Peru itself, new leaders, still unknown, are reorganizing the guerrilla struggle with tenacity and firmness. Little by little, obsolete weapons that are sufficient for the suppression of small armed groups will become modern armaments and North American advisers will become combatants, until the time when they will be forced to send growing numbers of regular troops to assure the relative stability of a government whose puppet army is disintegrating in the face of guerrilla attacks. This is the Vietnamese road. This is the road our peoples must follow. This is the road that America will follow, with the special feature that its armed groups might create something like Coordinating Councils to make the repressive tasks of Yankee imperialism more difficult and to facilitate their own cause.

America, a continent left behind by recent political liberation struggles, a continent beginning to make itself felt through the Tricontinental in the voice of its peoples' vanguard—the Cuban Revolution—will have a task of much greater import: the creation of the world's second or third Vietnam, or the second *and* third Vietnam.

We must definitely take into account that imperialism is a world system, the final stage of capitalism, and that it must be defeated in a great worldwide confrontation. The strategic goal of this struggle must be the destruction of imperialism. The role that falls to us, the exploited and underdeveloped of the world, is to eliminate the foundations of imperialism: our oppressed nations—from which they extract capital, raw materials, and cheap technical and manual labor, and to which they export new capital (instruments of domination), arms, and all types of goods, submerging us in absolute dependence.

The fundamental element of this strategic goal will therefore be the real liberation of our peoples, a liberation that will be carried out through armed struggle in the majority of cases, and which will have the almost inevitable tendency to turn into a socialist revolution.

In focusing on the destruction of imperialism, we must identify its head, which is none other than the United States of America.

We must carry out a general task whose tactical goal is to draw the enemy from his own environment, forcing him to fight in places where his living habits clash with the existing reality. We must not underestimate our adversary. The North American soldier has technical ability and is backed by means of such magnitude as to make him frightening. What he lacks is the ideological motivation that his most bitter enemy, the Vietnamese soldier, has to the highest degree. We can only triumph over this army to the degree that we undermine its morale. And this is done by inflicting defeats and causing repeated suffering.

But this simple schema for victory entails immense sacrifices by our peoples, sacrifices that we must openly demand from today on, but that will perhaps be less painful than those they would have to bear if we constantly fled from the struggle, letting others pull our chestnuts out of the fire.

It is true that the last country to liberate itself will probably do so without an armed struggle, and the people of this country will be spared the suffering of the long and cruel war that imperialists can inflict. But perhaps it will be impossible to avoid this struggle or its effects in a conflict of world proportions, and it will suffer equally, or even more. We cannot predict the future, but we must never give in to the spineless temptation to be the flag-bearers of a people who yearn for freedom but renounce the struggle that it entails, and wait for it as for a fallen crumb of bread.

It is absolutely correct to avoid any useless sacrifice. For this reason, it is important to be clear about any realistic possibilities that dependent America has to liberate itself by peaceful means. For us, the answer to this question is clear: this might or might not be the right moment to begin the struggle, but we cannot have any illusion, nor do we have the right to gain our freedom without fighting for it. And the battles will not be mere street fights of stones against tear gas, nor peaceful general strikes, nor will they be the struggle of an enraged people that destroys the repressive apparatus of the governing oligarchies in two or three days. It will be a long, bloody struggle whose fronts will be in the guerrilla sanctuaries, in the cities, in fighters' homes, where the repressive forces will go seeking easy victims among their families, in massacred peasant villages, in towns and cities destroyed by enemy bombardment.

They are forcing us into this struggle; we have no recourse other than to prepare for it and decide to undertake it.

THE VENEZUELAN GUERRILLA MOVEMENT*
Douglas Bravo

Douglas Bravo, a leader of the Venezuelan Communist Party (PCV) and its representative in the leadership of the National Liberation Front (FLN)—a guerrilla alliance of the PCV, the MIR, and other independent sectors during the early sixties—quickly became one of the legendary figures of the armed new left that developed in Latin America under the influence of the Cuban Revolution. He broke from the PCV in 1965, when the party began to distance itself from the armed struggle. Bravo created his own organization, the PRV (Party of the Venezuelan Revolution) some years later, while remaining in the *sierra* with a small guerrilla nucleus during the seventies. He received an amnesty in 1979, ending a period of almost thirty years underground to carry out legal political activity.

The following are selections from a document written by Douglas Bravo and Elías Manuit of the Mountain Regional Committee of the FLN in 1964, in which they explain their ideas on the peculiarities of the Venezuelan revolution.

---

*Douglas Bravo, "Informe del Comité Regional de la Montaña, aprobado por el FLN y por la Comandancia General del Frente Guerrillero José Leonardo Chirinos," October 18, 1964.

THE VENEZUELAN ROAD

Starting with the particular characteristics of our liberation war that we have already noted, we move on to formulate the fundamental laws that govern and will continue to govern our revolutionary process. Similarly, starting from an understanding of these fundamental laws, both general and particular, we come to a formulation that serves as a basis for the tactical line we will follow. An examination of our economic, social, and political reality allowed our Central Committee to explain the prolonged character of our liberation war. But in applying this concept, it committed a serious error. On the one hand, as we have already said, we exaggerated our peculiarities and developed tactics that were too short-term, reflecting illusions both in electoralism and in the possibilities of a coup. On the other hand, we abandoned these approaches and hoped to apply a scheme that was foreign to our reality—a classic, three-stage, prolonged war.

International experience has shown us two roads of armed struggle that have been travelled in our fellow countries: the classic short-term insurrection and the classic long-term liberation war. Our country, with the characteristics and laws we have pointed out, needs a new kind of formula that will definitely be the same for other Latin American countries. We are very far from the classic, St. Petersburg-style insurrection, where a conjunctural moment of crisis was taken advantage of within forty-eight hours to lead an assault on state power and change the old order. In that case, the cities were the fundamental factor and the countryside a secondary factor. In the case of China and other Asian countries, the three-stage, prolonged war was the path of development. These countries had to develop a war where an incipient army moved to a second stage of equilibrium, then to a level of superiority (the so-called stage of the strategic military offensive), and then to the preparation for the taking of power. In this case, the superiority of the revolutionary movement was in direct relation to the existence of a regular army with its own liberated territories and full reign for conventional warfare. To be more graphic, we could say that starting from *zero* degrees, they could only reach *one hundred*, the boiling point, through great military strength, which was their key premise—an army strategically and tactically on the offensive.

In our case, things are different—neither a classic urban insurrection nor a classic three-stage, prolonged war. We can properly speak of a Venezuelan road, which we can call a *Combined Insurrection*. The nature of the prolonged war will not change, but the very factors of our reality allow us to skip stages and reach the boiling point. But this will not be the result of the existence of a regular army, a conventional war, and a full strategic and tactical military offensive. In our case, rather, superiority will be won through a conjunction of political and military factors precisely arranged in rural, suburban, and urban areas, making use of multiple forms of struggle—armed and unarmed, legal and illegal, mass economic and political struggle—incorporated into an insurrectionary explosion. The *Combined Insurrection*, as a strategic line to be followed, is a permanent process that takes advantage of all the benefits of multiple forms of struggle and strategically subordinates them to the development of the armed struggle—particularly to the rural guerrilla movement, the fundamental form of the struggle for power. That is, it harmonizes the fundamental factors of insurrection that exist in our situation with the fundamental factors of prolonged war that also exist, producing a dialectical interrelationship among the fundamental and secondary factors, the political and military factors, the social and economic factors, etc., that exist in our country. These factors are reflected in the potential mass upsurge we have been unable to take advantage of, or to channel, before an insurrectionary explosion because we have lacked adequate political and military tactics. This is why we say that the laws of our revolution can be summarized in the tactical line of *Combined Insurrection* . . . .

Starting from this situation, the *Combined Insurrection* bases its political-military strategy on forcing the enemy to keep the majority of its troops protecting the urban and suburban areas by using the proper combination of military activities by Tactical Combat Units, suburban guerrillas, and various forms of unarmed activity by the masses in populated areas. *Permanent* political-military activity in the cities and suburban zones will reduce the number of troops able to fight the peasant guerrilla, making it easier for them to destroy the repressive apparatus. This strategy for the revolutionary movement, applied through a *permanent combined insurrection*, creates an insuperable contradiction for the enemy, since he will never have sufficient repressive troops and will have to remove some from those fronts under attack, thereby facilitating our destructive blows. In addition, this strategy allows the revolutionary movement to transcend the current vanguard character of our liberation war and convert it into a *true peoples' war*, with the participation of the masses in strikes, demonstrations, protests, etc., until the moment they *take up arms* and begin the *taking of power*.

> Douglas Bravo
> Elías Manuit
> For the Regional Committee of the
> Falcón Sierra-in-Arms
> Iracara, October 18, 1964

A MESSAGE TO CHRISTIANS*
Camilo Torres

Camilo Torres was born in Bogota in 1929 and ordained as a priest in 1954. That same year, he travelled to Europe to study sociology at the University of Louvain, where he remained until the end of 1958. Returning to Colombia in 1959, he became a professor of sociology at the National University. During the sixties, he committed himself more and more directly to the popular struggle in his country.

This first appeal, published in August 1965 in *Frente Unido*, the organ of the People's United Front, is a very important document; it shows the ideological mediations through which a radicalized Christian commits himself to the revolutionary movement. In a deeply sincere way, it combines the religious problematic of love for one's fellow humans with the Marxist theory of class struggle, and the duty of charity with the duty of making the revolution.

A year later, Camilo Torres, finding himself increasingly restricted leading the propaganda work of the People's United Front, made contact with the National Liberation Army (led by Fabio Vázquez) and decided to join the guerrilla movement. Like Che Guevara, Camilo Torres believed in the need for leaders to give a personal example of engagement in the struggle. In February 1966, he fell in an encounter with the Colombian armed forces. The second document explains the reasons for this commitment.

A MESSAGE TO CHRISTIANS

The convulsions caused by recent political, religious, and social events may have confused the Christians of Colombia. At this decisive moment in our history, it is necessary that we Christians be steadfast in the essential bases of our religion.

The essence of Catholicism is love for our neighbor. "He who loves his fellow man has fulfilled the law" (St. Paul, Romans 13:8). To be real, this love must aim to be effective. If kindness, alms, a few free schools, a few housing projects—what is known as "charity"—are not able to feed the majority of the hungry, or clothe the majority of the naked, or teach the majority of the ignorant, we must seek effective means for the well-being of these majorities.

The privileged minorities who hold power will not seek these means because, generally, such effective means would oblige these minorities to sacrifice their privileges. For example, for there to be more jobs in Colombia, it would be better for them to invest in sources of employment in this country, rather than sending their capital abroad in the form of dollars. But since the Colombian peso is devalued daily, those with money and

---

*Camilo Torres, "Mensaje a los cristianos," 1965, and "Al pueblo colombiano desde las montañas," 1966, in *Cristianismo y revolución* (Mexico City: Ed. Era, 1972), pp. 525–528, 571–572.

power will never prohibit the export of capital, because by exporting it they free themselves from the effects of devaluation.

It is therefore necessary to take power from the privileged minorities and give it to the poor majorities. This, if it is done rapidly, is the essence of a revolution. The revolution can be peaceful if the minorities do not put up violent resistance. The revolution, therefore, is the method of obtaining a government that will feed the hungry, dress the naked, teach the ignorant— that will carry out works of charity, of love of one's neighbor, not only occasionally and briefly, not only for a few, but for the majority of our fellows. This is why the revolution is not only permissible but obligatory for Christians who see in it the only effective and far-reaching way of realizing their love for all. It is true that "there is no law but God's law" (St. Paul, Romans 13:1). But St. Thomas says that the concrete attribution of authority is made by the people.

When authority stands against the people, this authority is illegitimate and is called tyranny. Christians can and must struggle against tyranny. The current government is tyrannical because it is only supported by 20 percent of the electorate and because its decisions emanate from the privileged minorities.

The temporal defects of the Church should not scandalize us. The Church is human. What is important is to believe that it is also divine, and that if we Christians fulfill our duty to love our fellow man, we will be strengthening the Church.

I have given up the duties and privileges of the clergy, but I have not ceased being a priest. I believe that I have joined the revolution out of love for my fellow man. I have given up saying mass to realize this brotherly love on the temporal, economic, and social plane. When my fellow man holds nothing against me, when the revolution has occurred, I will return to saying mass, if God permits. I believe that I am thereby following Christ's injunction: "If you bring your offering to the altar and there you remember that your brother has something against you, leave your offering there and go; first make peace with your brother, and then come and present your offering" (Matthew, 5:23–24).

After the revolution, we Christians will have the knowledge that we are establishing a system that is oriented toward the love of our fellow man.

The struggle is long; let us begin now.

To the Colombian People, from the Mountains

Colombians:

For many years, our country's poor have awaited the battle cry to throw themselves into the final struggle against the oligarchy.

At those times when the people's desperation has reached its limit, the ruling class has always found a way to fool the people, distract them, and appease them with new schemes that always have the same result: suffering for the people and happiness for the privileged caste.

When the people sought a leader and found one in Jorge Eliécer Gaitán, the oligarchy killed him. When the people asked for peace, the oligarchy sowed the country with violence. When the people could no longer hold back from violence and organized guerrillas to take power, the oligarchy staged a military coup so the guerrillas could be fooled into surrendering. When the people called for democracy, they were again tricked into a plebiscite and a National Front that imposed the oligarchy's dictatorship.

Now, the people will never believe them again. The people do not believe in elections. The people know that the legal means have been exhausted. The people know that nothing remains but the armed road. The people are desperate and resolved to risk their lives so the next generation of Colombians will not be slaves; so that the children of those who are willing to give their lives can have an education, a roof over their heads, food, clothing, and above all, Dignity; so that future Colombians can have their own homeland, independent of North American domination.

All sincere revolutionaries must recognize that the armed struggle is the only remaining path. Yet the people are waiting for their leaders to give the battle cry with their presence and by their example.

I wish to tell the Colombian people that now is the time; that I have not betrayed you; that I have crossed the plazas of towns and cities campaigning for the unity and organization of the popular class for the taking of power; and I have asked that we devote ourselves to these objectives to the end.

All is ready. The oligarchy wants to organize another electoral farce, with candidates who decline and then accept nomination, with bipartisan committees, with movements for renewal based on ideas and individuals that are not only old but have betrayed the people. What more are we waiting for, Colombians?

I have joined the armed struggle.

I plan to continue the struggle from the Colombian mountains, with arm in hand, until we conquer power for the people. I have joined the National Liberation Army (ELN) because I have found here the very ideals of the United Front. I have found the desire for and fulfillment of unity at the base, the peasant base, without regard to religion or party tradition, with no intention of fighting the revolutionary elements of any sector, movement, or party, and without *caudillos*: a movement that aims to liberate the people from exploitation by the oligarchies and imperialism; that will not lay down its arms until power is fully in the hands of the people; that accepts the platform of the United Front as its goal.

All Colombian patriots should go on a war footing. Little by little, experienced guerrilla leaders will develop in all corners of the country. Meanwhile, we must be prepared.

We must collect arms and munitions, seek guerrilla training, talk with our closest friends, gather clothing, drugs, and provisions, and prepare ourselves for a prolonged struggle.

Let us make small attacks on the enemy when victory is certain. Let us test those who call themselves revolutionaries. Let us get rid of traitors. We should not hesitate to act, but we should not be impatient. In a prolonged war, everyone will have to act at some point. What matters is that we are ready and prepared for the revolution at the right moment. We do not all need to do everything. We must divide our work. The militants of the United Front should be in the vanguard of initiative and action. Let us be patient while we wait, and confident of the final victory.

The people's struggle must become a national struggle. We have already begun because the journey is long.

Colombians, let us not fail to respond to the call of the people and the revolution.

Militants of the United Front, let us make a reality of our slogans:

> For the unity of the popular class unto death!
> For the organization of the popular class unto death!
> For the taking of power by the working class unto death!

Unto death, because we have decided to go to the end; unto victory, because a people that is devoted unto death always gains victory. Until the final victory, with the slogans of the National Liberation Army!

Not one step backward!

Liberation or death!

THE DECLARATION OF THE OLAS*
Organization of Latin American Solidarity

In August 1967, the first (and only) congress of the Organization of Latin American Solidarity (OLAS) took place in Havana, joining representatives of all the Latin American political parties that had oriented toward the Cuban Revolution. The Castroist current was clearly dominant, but some representatives of the traditional Communist parties (particularly Rodney Arismendi of the Uruguayan CP) also

---

*"Declaración General de la Primera Conferencia Latinoamericana de Solidaridad," in *Primera Conferencia de la OLAS (Documentos)* (Havana: Ed. El orientador revolucionario, Instituto del Libro, 1967), pp. 68–78. For the complete text, along with Castro's speech to the OLAS conference, see *International Socialist Review*, v. 28, n. 6, November 1967.

played an important role. On the other hand, the Brazilian, Venezuelan, and Argentine parties boycotted the congress.

The OLAS documents had a quite profound impact throughout Latin America, especially in Brazil, where they accelerated a political crisis in the Communist Party. But the OLAS was never able to organize itself on the continental level.

The general declaration that we excerpt here summarizes the central themes of the congress and recaptures the "Bolivarian" perspective of continental revolution in a Marxist context.

The First Conference of the Organization of Latin American Solidarity met in Havana, the capital of the Republic of Cuba, from July 31 until August 10, 1967.

The conference constituted a shining guidepost for the revolutionary struggle being waged by our continent's peoples in the mountains and the cities for definitive and total national and social liberation. For the first time in the history of Latin America, the genuine representatives of the exploited, hungry, and oppressed masses met to discuss, organize, and promote revolutionary solidarity, exchange experiences, coordinate their actions on a solid ideological basis, and confront the global counterrevolutionary strategy of imperialism and the national oligarchies in the light of the lessons of the revolutionary past and of present conditions.

The main objective of the conference has been, in brief, to strengthen the ties of militant solidarity among the fighting anti-imperialists of Latin America and to lay down the fundamental lines for the development of the continental revolution. This great assembly has opened the possibility for a broad and profound discussion of old problems of revolutionary strategy and tactics, as well as for an interchange of opinions in relation to the role of different classes and social layers in the continent's current historical process. The exchange of opinion, the elaboration of a common line, and the creation of a permanent organization of solidarity constitute an important step toward the encouragement and promotion of revolutionary struggle in Latin America. The revolutionary armed struggle that has been victorious in Cuba and has already begun in Venezuela, Colombia, Guatemala, and Bolivia will not be finished until it destroys the bureaucratic and military apparatus of the bourgeoisie and the landlords and establishes the revolutionary power of the working people, confronting both internal counterrevolution and Yankee intervention and implacably tearing out imperialist domination at the roots.

The battle that has begun will only end with the victory of the legitimate descendants of those who supported the heroic and self-denying armies of the liberators. We are living under the banner of the second war of independence . . . .

We, the representatives of the peoples of our America, conscious of the conditions that exist in the continent and aware of a common counterrevolutionary strategy led by Yankee imperialism,

PROCLAIM:

1. That making the Revolution is a right and a duty of the peoples of Latin America.

2. That the Latin American revolution has its deepest historical roots in the nineteenth-century liberation movement against European colonialism and this century's struggle against imperialism. The epic struggle of the American peoples and the great class battles against imperialism that our peoples have undertaken in previous decades constitute the sources of historical inspiration for the Latin American revolutionary movement.

3. That the essential content of the Latin American revolution is found in its confrontation with imperialism and the bourgeois and landowning oligarchies. Consequently, the character of the revolution is one of struggle for national independence, emancipation from the oligarchies, and the socialist road to full economic and social development.

4. That the principles of Marxism-Leninism guide the revolutionary movement of Latin America.

5. That armed revolutionary struggle constitutes the fundamental line of the Latin American revolution.

6. That all other forms of struggle should serve and not hold back the development of the fundamental line, which is the armed struggle.

7. That for the majority of the countries of the continent, the problem of organizing, initiating, developing, and completing the armed struggle is today the immediate and fundamental task of the revolutionary movement.

8. That in those countries where this task is not immediately posed, all forms should be considered with the perspective of the inevitability of the development of revolutionary struggle in the country.

9. That the peoples and revolutionary vanguards of each country have the historic responsibility of moving the Revolution forward in their own country.

10. That the guerrilla movement—as the embryo of the liberation army—is the most effective method for initiating and developing the revolutionary struggle in the majority of our countries.

11. That to guarantee its success, the leadership of the Revolution requires the existence of a united political and military command as an organizing principle.

12. That the most effective solidarity that revolutionary movements can offer each other is the development and completion of the struggle in their own country.

13. That solidarity with Cuba and collaboration and cooperation with armed revolutionary movements constitute an inevitable internationalist duty for all the anti-imperialist organizations of the continent.

14. That the Cuban Revolution, as a symbol of the triumph of the armed revolutionary movement, is the vanguard of the Latin American anti-imperialist movement. Peoples who carry out their armed struggle will also stand in the vanguard to the degree they advance along this road.

15. That the peoples directly colonized by the European metropolises or subject to the direct colonial domination of the United States, in their road to liberation, have as an immediate and fundamental objective the struggle for independence and the maintenance of their links to the general continental struggle, which is the only way to avoid being absorbed by North American neo-colonialism.

16. That the Second Declaration of Havana, summarizing the beautiful and glorious revolutionary traditions of the last 150 years of American history, constitutes a programmatic document for the Latin American revolution that has been confirmed, deepened, enriched, and radicalized by the peoples of our continent over the last five years.

17. That the peoples of Latin America hold no antagonism toward any other people in the world, and extend a fraternal hand to the people of the United States, whom they urge to struggle against the repressive politics of the imperialist monopolies.

18. That the Latin American struggle is strengthening its ties of solidarity with the peoples of Asia and Africa, the socialist countries, and the workers of the capitalist countries, especially with the Black population of the United States, who at once suffer class exploitation, misery, unemployment, racial discrimination, and the denial of their most elementary human rights and constitute an important force to consider in the context of the revolutionary struggle.

19. That the heroic struggle of the people of Vietnam represents an inestimable source of support for all revolutionary peoples fighting imperialism and constitutes an inspiring example for the peoples of Latin America.

20. That we have approved the Statutes of the Organization of Latin American Solidarity, the real representative of the peoples of Latin America, and have created a Permanent Committee with its seat in Havana.

We, the revolutionaries of our America, the America south of the Río Bravo, the successors of the men who won our first independence, armed with an unshakable will to struggle and a revolutionary and scientific orientation, and with nothing to lose but the chains which oppress us,

AFFIRM:

that our struggle stands as a decisive contribution to the historic struggle of humanity to free itself from slavery and exploitation.

The duty of every revolutionary is to make the Revolution.

THE TUPAMARO URBAN GUERRILLAS*

The Tupamaros National Liberation Movement was founded by Raúl Sendic (b. 1925), a lawyer, member of the Uruguayan Socialist Party, and organizer of farm workers in the country's north. At first, the Tupamaros were a sort of "armed wing" of the Socialist Party, but shortly after their first armed actions in 1963, they became an independent organization, while still open to socialist, Communist, and anarchist militants. During the years 1965–72, the Tupamaros (whose name refers to Tupac Amaru, the leader of an eighteenth-century indigenous revolt against the Spanish) grew tremendously, winning the sympathy and support of a significant part of the population (especially young people) through a series of spectacular armed urban actions that included expropriations, kidnapping of diplomats, and the execution of torturers. But, decimated by repression and weakened by splits, the movement experienced a profound crisis after 1972.

The following is a selection from the document "Thirty Questions to a Tupamaro," published on June 2, 1968, in *Punto Final* (a Chilean magazine influenced by the MIR), which served as a political and strategic platform for the movement.

THIRTY QUESTIONS FOR A TUPAMARO

Upon what fundamental principle has your organization based its activity up to now?

Our fundamental principle is that revolutionary action itself, the very act of arming, preparing, and provisioning oneself and carrying out actions that violate bourgeois legality, will create consciousness, organization, and revolutionary conditions.

What is the fundamental difference between your organization and other organizations of the left?

The majority of the latter appear to trust more in manifestos and theoretical declarations on the revolution to prepare militants and create revolutionary conditions, without understanding that fundamentally it is revolutionary action that precipitates revolutionary situations.

---

*"Treinta preguntas a un Tupamaro," 1968, in Omar Costa, *Los Tupamaros* (Mexico City: Ed. Era, 1975), pp. 68–73.

Can you give me a historical example that illustrates this principle, that revolutionary action generates consciousness, organization, and revolutionary circumstances?

Cuba is an example. Instead of a long process of forming a mass party, the Cubans created a guerrilla *foco* with a dozen men, and this action generated the consciousness, organization, and revolutionary circumstances that culminated in a real socialist revolution. Faced with this revolutionary deed, all true revolutionaries were obliged to fall in line behind it.

Do you mean that once a revolutionary action has been launched, the much-vaunted unity of the left will be created in the struggle?

Yes, if the forces that call themselves revolutionaries must choose between supporting the action or perishing. In Cuba, the Popular Socialist Party chose to support a struggle that it neither initiated nor led, and they continued to exist. But Prío Socarrás, who claimed he was the main opposition to Batista, did not support it and perished.

This is in respect to the left. What about the people generally?

For the people who really disagree with the regime, the choice is really much simpler. They want a change and must choose between the improbable and far off changes that some groups offer them through proclamations, manifestos, or parliamentary activity and the direct route represented by the armed groups and their revolutionary actions.

Do you mean that the armed struggle, while it is destroying bourgeois power, will also be creating the mass movement that an insurrectionary organization needs to make the revolution?

Yes. Leaving aside the effort lost in attempting to create a party or mass movement before launching an armed struggle, we should recognize that the armed struggle hastens and stimulates the mass movement. And it was not only in Cuba, but also in China, that the mass party was created in the course of the armed struggle. That is, the rigid formula of certain theoreticians, "first create the party, then launch the revolution," is historically more the exception than the rule. At this advanced historical stage, no one can deny that an armed group, as small as it may be, has a greater possibility of becoming a mass popular army than a group that limits itself to putting forward "revolutionary positions."

Nevertheless, a revolutionary movement needs platforms, documents, etc.

Of course, but we should not be confused about this. The revolution is not made by merely perfecting platforms and programs. The basic principles of the socialist revolution have been laid down and experienced in countries like Cuba, and there is nothing more to discuss. It is enough to adhere to these principles and let our deeds point the way forward on the road of insurrection—that is, apply these principles.

Do you think that a revolutionary movement ought to prepare the armed struggle at any stage, even when the conditions for armed struggle do not yet exist?

Yes, for at least two reasons. Because an armed leftist movement can be struck by repression at any point in its development and should be prepared to defend its existence (remember Argentina and Brazil).

Also, if every militant is not inculcated with a combatant's mentality from the very beginning, we will be building something else—a mere support movement for a revolution made by others, for example, but not the revolutionary movement itself.

Can this be interpreted as underemphasizing all activities other than preparing for combat?

No. Mass work that moves people to revolutionary positions is also important. What militants, even those leading the masses, must know is that on the day the armed struggle is launched, they cannot stay home and await the results. They must therefore prepare themselves, even if their current activity is on another front. This, moreover, will lend authority, authenticity, sincerity, and seriousness to their ongoing revolutionary evangelism.

What are the concrete tasks of a militant in your organization who works in the mass movement?

A militant in a trade union or mass movement should try to create an arena, either a group inside the union or the whole union, where he can organize support for the activity of the armed organization and prepare for joining it. The main concrete tasks in this arena are theoretical and practical training, recruitment, propaganda on behalf of the armed struggle, and, as far as possible, involving the union in more radical struggles and a more advanced level of class struggle.

What are the fundamental objectives of the movement at this stage?

To create an armed group, as well prepared and equipped as possible, that is tested in action. To have good relations with all the popular movements that support this type of struggle. To create propaganda organs to radicalize the struggles and raise consciousness. To create an efficient apparatus for the recruitment of militants capable of theoretical development and form groups inside the mass movement to fulfill the aforementioned functions.

Does the importance you place on the preparation of the armed struggle imply that the combatants cannot improvise?

The armed struggle is a technical activity that therefore requires technical knowledge, training, practice, materiel, and a fighting psychology. Improvisation on this front is paid for harshly in lives and catastrophes. Spontaneity, supported by those who vaguely speak of a "revolution that will be made by the people" or "the masses," either means merely procrastinating, or leaving the final stage of the struggle to improvisation. All vanguard movements, to maintain their vanguard character at the culminating moment of the struggle, must intervene and know how to technically organize popular violence against oppression so that the objective can be achieved with the least possible sacrifice.

Do you feel that the left parties can carry out this preparation for the armed struggle by maintaining a small "shock troop" or self-defense group?

No party fulfills its revolutionary principles if it does not face this question seriously at every level of the party. There is no other way to reach the highest possible level of effectiveness in confronting reaction at every stage of the struggle. This might otherwise result in fatal negligence (as in Brazil and Argentina) or in missing a revolutionary opportunity.

Lacking specific aims, a small, armed party group can be transformed into the miserable instrument of political maneuvers. A sad example of this occurred during last year's May Day rally: armed groups reduced to protecting the distribution of a manifesto attacking other left groups, with other armed groups attempting to stop its distribution.

What do you think that the militants of the armed party organizations should demand of their respective leaderships?

That their activities only be directed against the class enemy, the bourgeois apparatus, and their agents. No armed group can fulfill its specific objective if its leadership does not fulfill the following minimum requirements:

1. That they be consistent, show their unwavering adherence to the principle of armed struggle, and give it the importance and the material means necessary for its organization.
2. That they offer the necessary security and discretion to those militants engaged in illegal activities.
3. That, because of the movement's breadth and its correct line, they have an immediate possibility of leading the proletarian masses.

Don't you think that an armed organization should be linked to a political party?

I feel that any armed organization should be part of a mass political organization at a particular stage of the revolutionary process, and that if such an organization does not exist, it should contribute to its creation. I do not mean that it is obliged, considering the current panorama on the left, to link itself to one of the existing political groups or create a new one. This would mean perpetuating the current state of the movement or accepting this situation. We must combat the petty idea that identifies a party as a headquarters, meetings, a newspaper, positions on all the issues, and the conformist expectation that the other left parties will wither away before its verbal attacks and that their base and the people generally will one day follow its lead. This has been going on in Uruguay for sixty years, and you can see the results. We should recognize there are authentic revolutionaries in all the parties of the left, and many more that are not organized. Taking these elements and groups, wherever they may be, and uniting them is a task for the left in general when it forsakes sectarianism. This is something that does not depend upon us. But until then, the revolution cannot stop and wait. Every revolutionary, every revolutionary group, has but one duty: to prepare themselves to make the revolution. As Fidel said in one of his recent speeches, "with a party or without a party." The revolution cannot wait.

Can you detail the strategy for taking state power in Uruguay?

No, I cannot give you a detailed strategy. On the other hand, I can explain a general strategic orientation, and even this is subject to modification as circumstances change—that is, a general strategic orientation for the day, month, and year that it is enunciated.

Why can't you give me a detailed and definitive strategy?

Because a strategy is developed on the basis of the real situation, and reality changes independently of our will. Understand that a strategy based on the existence of a strong, organized labor movement is different from one where this movement has been destroyed, for example.

What is the current situation upon which your organization bases its general strategic orientation?

To cite the most important circumstances:

Our conviction that the crisis, far from being overcome, keeps deepening daily. The country is floundering, and a capitalist plan for development based on increasing exports, if applied, will produce quite meager results, and that only after some years. This means that for some years ahead, the people will have to keep tightening their belts. And with a foreign debt of $500 million, one cannot expect the large quantities of credit to come from abroad that could reestablish the standard of living among those sectors where it has declined. This is a concrete reality: there will be economic shortages and popular discontent in the coming years.

A second basic factor for our strategy is the high degree of unionization among Uruguayan workers. While all of these unions do not have a high level of combativity, either because of their composition or because of their leadership, the mere fact that practically all the basic government services, banking, industry, and commerce, are organized is a tremendously positive factor that has no precedent in America. The possibility of paralyzing government services has created and can create quite interesting circumstances for an insurrection, since, for example, it is not the same thing to attack a fully potent government as to attack a government that has been semi-paralyzed by strikes.

Another strategic factor that must be taken into account, a negative one, is geographic. There are no unassailable sites on our territory where one can locate a long-term guerrilla *foco*, although there are places in the countryside that are difficult to reach. On the other hand, we have a large city, with more than 300 square kilometers of built-up area—which allows for the development of an urban struggle. This means that we cannot copy the strategy of those countries where a guerrilla *foco* can be built and stabilized in the mountains or jungles. On the contrary, we must develop an autonomous strategy suited to a reality that is different from the majority of the countries of America.

EL SALVADOR, THE ISTHMUS, AND REVOLUTION*
Roque Dalton

Roque Dalton, a poet, writer, and Salvadoran Communist militant, lived for many years in Cuban exile. In 1971, he published eyewitness accounts and documents of the 1932 revolt in El Salvador in the journal *Pensamiento Critico*; this is how the historic importance of this great experience of popular insurrection first came to light. It was as a (dissident) member of the Communist Party of El Salvador that he wrote this article in 1969. A few years later, he secretly returned to El Salvador, broke with the Communist Party, and joined a guerrilla organization. In 1974, Roque Dalton was assassinated by members of one of the factions of this group—an absurd and inexplicable act.

This process had made El Salvador a quite unusual Central American country. The process of national integration had been completed from an ethnic point of view by the beginning of the century. While not seeming to be a large imperialist plantation, *à la* Honduras and the United Fruit Company, its dense population and small size has exacerbated the explosiveness of the social question because of the intimacy of relations between the people and the coffee oligarchy. The popular struggle quickly led to popular organization, which obliged the ruling class to concentrate its repressive

*Roque Dalton, "El Salvador, el istmo y la revolución," *Tricontinental*, (Havana), n. 11, March–April 1969, pp. 9–10, 20–22.

response both in time and space. Basically, the character of the local oligarchy, the character of imperialist exploitation in the country, and the development of the local commercial sector led to a tendency for capitalist development to have a faster rhythm here than in the other countries of the isthmus. El Salvador, as the nucleus of the Pacific coast of Central America, began to appear as both the city and suburb of Central America (speaking the language of modern revolutionary writings from Mao Tse-tung to Regis Debray), which imposes specific characteristics and demands on its revolutionary struggle.

Popular class organization appears in El Salvador after 1914, with trade organizations of urban, suburban, and rural artisans. In the twenties, this organizing work reached an important stage of development on the national level among wide layers of urban and rural workers. Groups were founded on somewhat ambiguous political and trade lines (anarchist, anarchosyndicalist, reformist, and Marxist), with a vanguard slowly organizing the incipient Marxists among the still incipient working class and agricultural proletariat.

The Communist Party of El Salvador arose in 1930 from this surge of organization and began to carry out extraordinary work in association with the Communist International—so extraordinary that after barely two years, in the midst of the *revolutionary situation* that developed in El Salvador in 1931–32 as a national result of the world economic crisis, our party called the people to armed insurrection to take political power in the country. The details and an analysis of this historic action are beyond our purposes here; suffice it to say the Salvadoran insurrection of 1932, still quite unknown in our country, is one of the key events of the history of contemporary Latin America and remains an unstudied lesson for our continent's revolutionaries. Basically because of military and organizational errors, the insurrection was defeated by the first Salvadoran government that could properly be called oligarchic-imperialist: the dictatorship of Maximiliano Martínez. The people were massacred; the revolutionary organizations destroyed. The number of worker and peasant victims approached 30,000 after less than a month. *For decades, this profound defeat, which was never properly analyzed by El Salvador's revolutionary organizations, determined the organizational ideas and the relations with the masses of the Communist Party* (the country's major revolutionary organization, despite its weakness and its sometimes incorrect strategies and tactics). *It served as a negative point of reference for the undertaking of revolutionary armed struggle in El Salvador, and in fact led to a serious rupture between our people's revolutionary traditions and the perspective of taking power.* These were the subjective results. Objectively, *the defeat of 1932 was the material basis for the construction of an extremely effective oligarchicimperialist apparatus, because it had faced the problem of defending the system against a revolutionary armed struggle for Socialist Revolution on an operative level (both locally and nationally) as early as 1932.*

The long military dictatorship (which, with changes in personnel, continues until today) began at that point. Following the Martínez government (which was overthrown in 1944 by a student-led national general strike, the culmination of an insurrectionary process that had begun with a failed military rising) came the government of the bloody Colonel Osmín Aguirre (who survived a series of armed attacks and an invasion from Guatemala by students, professionals, and young military men who reached Ahuachapán, where they were defeated by the national guard and the army), and the governments of General Salvador Castaneda Castro, Colonel Oscar Osorio, and Colonel José María Lemus (1956–60). Popular struggles against the Lemus government opened a new stage in the situation and the country's political possibilities just when the victory of the Cuban insurrection was doing the same in Latin America as a whole . . . .

A downturn in mass revolutionary activity began after 1962. The party suffered serious blows (betrayals, desertions, paralysis of whole fields of work, etc.), but was able to recover to a sufficient degree to be in the leadership of the workers' movement during the great strikes of 1966, 1967, and 1968. Nevertheless, new conceptions of armed struggle have been seriously questioned by Salvadoran Communists (in two ways: by those affected by the downturn, and by the de facto counterposition of the legal-strike movement and the insurrectionary movement, a counterposition which for many embodied the difference between the political lines—and the practical results—of the Guatemalan Labor Party and the Communist Party of El Salvador) to the extent that one could claim that at the moment, this questioning has become the most important activity of the conservative current that predominates in the leadership and among wide sectors of the party's base. All of this is reflected in different aspects of the party's practical activity: tendencies in its policy of alliances; electoralist politics; its descent into economistic and legalistic deviations in the workers' movement, especially its failure to provide a revolutionary perspective to the union masses after the legal struggle had been raised to a certain level; an unprecedented number of splits and schisms in the party ranks, with unprecedented results in recent years; a variety of deficiencies on the military front, etc.

And what was our enemy doing during this period? After 1961, imperialism began to emphasize political-military solutions to the revolutionary problems of Central America to an even greater degree. The perspectives brought on by the beginning of the guerrilla war in Guatemala accelerated this counterrevolutionary activity even more. In regard to El Salvador, the army now became the main instrument of the government, which concentrated a large part of its administrative activity in the hands of the officer corps. With the growth of Central American economic integration and the creation of a common market in the area came the integration of the Central American armies under a joint general staff, with a common executive and planning organ, the Central American Defense Council. This whole regional military apparatus has acted jointly, at the necessary level, against the guerrilla movements that have appeared in our countries. To sum up the recent actions of imperialism in this arena, we would say that the United States Government *has created and put into operation the institutions and organs of special warfare in Central America.* This means that, in broad terms, imperialism *has already begun institutionalized warfare against the people of Central America* in complicity with the local oligarchies and armed forces. The finishing touches are being put on this strategy with, for example, the interpenetration between the army and the integrated mixed enterprises, turning officers into stockholders, administrators, or high functionaries of the large industrial and commercial firms or the state institutions that are carrying out this economic integration.

In El Salvador, the traditional cunning of the native oligarchy and their experiences in the struggle against the people and the guerrillas of Guatemala have led the army to try to carry out imperialist plans to organize violence against the popular masses. Colonel José Alberto Medrano, the coordinator of the nation's intelligence services and a high-level C.I.A. operative, has proclaimed the creation of a rural paramilitary organization known as ORDEN (Democratic Nationalist Organization), which by the end of last year had organized 4,000 cells of 15 people each, some 60,000 peasants throughout the country, for "anti-communist and anti-guerrilla" activities. This organization, along with the members of the army (infantry, military police, tank corpsmen, aviators, paratroopers, artillerymen, marines, etc.), the national guard, rural police, national police, local police, etc., form a large, coordinated anti-democratic network whose actual role is impossible to ignore on the path to the revolution.

Facts such as these, along with others like them that are traditionally cited (our small, overpopulated territory, crossed by good roads in all directions, without mountains or other inaccessible locations; the presence of a relatively large army with a knowledge of the local terrain; the lack of revolutionary bases in the countryside and the concentration of revolutionary forces in the two or three main cities), have helped in various ways to spread a tendency toward non-revolutionary quietism. *The fact that revolutionary armed struggle presents special difficulties and particular technical and practical problems in our country leads many to the conclusion that revolutionary struggle is impossible here.* This is not always said straightforwardly in the documents, but it can be clearly inferred from their content with the slightest analysis.

This dangerous tendency toward quietism, which is in the final instance counterrevolutionary, can only be avoided by the concrete elaboration of a strategy for armed struggle in El Salvador that is in accord with the concrete conditions of the country, and through the practical undertaking of the tasks imposed by this strategic perspective. This strategic perspective must be developed from an analysis of our country, not in isolation, but as a nation that is part of the Central American region at a time when imperialism is imposing a new, unified development upon us that is contrary to the interests of our peoples. The strategy of the Salvadoran revolution must be a Central American political-military strategy . . . .

The Central American character of the peoples' struggles in Guatemala, Honduras, El Salvador, Nicaragua, and Costa Rica is establishing a real unity that the imperialist enemy has again posed for the region in the form we have already outlined. The basic economic unit is no longer El Salvador, Guatemala, etc., but the totality of Central American countries that make up our Common Market. To defend this new economic framework (whose structural crisis is beginning to become evident), imperialism has built and continues to build a Central American apparatus of domination and repression. The revolutionaries' response must also be at the Central American level. The men fighting under the leadership of César Montes and Carlos Fonseca Amador in Guatemala and Nicaragua have already begun to give this response. The Salvadoran revolutionary organizations cannot be indifferent to these extraordinary and self-sacrificing efforts, since they foreshadow their own future. Overemphasizing the internal character of the class struggle in our countries, as the Political Committee of our party does in its epilogue to the *Diary of Che Guevara*, is counterposed to the necessity of regionalizing the struggle. This absurdity is based on an obsolete analysis . . . .

Those who can definitively abandon the pacifist illusions that our enemy always attempts to arouse, those Communists who have decided to take the hard road of peoples' war, have the duty to carry Che's lessons to their ultimate conclusions. Little by little, the leaderships of the Latin American Communist parties have developed a pessimistic view of their parties' participation in revolutionary armed struggle. Haven't the concrete activities of Venezuelan, Peruvian, Honduran, Nicaraguan, and Brazilian parties and the theoretical positions of the Communist parties of Argentina, Costa Rica, Ecuador, and now El Salvador been more or less similar to those of the PCB in this matter? Is there a pacifist line in the Latin American Communist movement that until now has hidden behind successive declarations in favor of armed struggle? This is why any discussion with these parties would be impossible, since a revolutionary discussion of the problems of armed struggle can only take place among revolutionaries who have taken the road of armed struggle.

In our party's case, we feel the moment is serious and full of disquieting alternatives. Undoubtedly, it is one of the most mature, strong, and influential revolutionary organizations of Central America, whose political positions and organic structure are superior to the parties of Honduras, Nicaragua, and Costa Rica, to mention some concrete examples. Nevertheless, its conservative habits still determine and limit its potential activities. These bad habits could become a definitive brake on the ability of the party to occupy the vanguard of the struggle of the Salvadoran people and force it from its destined place in the struggle of the Central American masses against their common enemy. There are various examples of such regression in our region. Only an in-depth discussion of Central American reality, carried out in a constructive and independent spirit, and the initiation of those actions demanded by these conclusions, can avert this danger. Otherwise, our party, a prisoner of the dogmatism that has already been reflected, if only partially, in the epilogue to the *Diary of Che Guevara*, will find it impossible to follow the path we have laid out: taking political power for the people, making and leading the revolution. There are other examples of this process in Latin America, at different levels of development. One only has to open one's eyes to see them.

THE DECLARATION OF PRINCIPLES OF THE MIR*
Revolutionary Left Movement of Chile

The Chilean Revolutionary Left Movement (MIR), founded in 1965 in a fusion of sectors of the Socialist, Communist, and Trotskyist youth movements, became one of the largest and most influential Castroist groups in Latin America within several years.

The *Declaration of Principles* adopted at its founding conference demonstrates the preponderant Trotskyist influence inside the MIR during its early period. This influence could also be seen in the party program adopted in 1965, which proclaimed, for example: "The MIR declares itself in favor of the defense of the socialist countries in the case of aggression. In those socialist countries dominated by reformism or revisionism, we support the revolutionary people, not the bureaucratic leaderships who have deformed the process of socialist construction and betrayed revolutionary Marxism."

In 1967, the Trotskyist militants were expelled and a group of student leaders from Concepción (Bautista von Schowen, Luciano Cruz, and Miguel Enríquez) took over the leadership of the organization. A new line was adopted in the *Programmatic Document* of 1967, reaffirming the Trotskyist theory of a democratic

---

*Revolutionary Left Movement, *Declaración de Principios*, Santiago, September 1965.

and socialist proletarian revolution while, on the other hand, supporting the ideas of Debray on the centrality of the rural guerrilla movement.

1. The MIR is organized to be the Marxist-Leninist vanguard of the working class and the oppressed layers of Chile who seek national and social emancipation. The MIR considers itself the authentic heir of the Chilean revolutionary tradition and the continuator of the socialist path of Luis Emilio Recabarren, the leader of the Chilean proletariat. The goal of the MIR is the overthrow of the capitalist system and its replacement by a workers' and peasants' government headed by organs of proletarian power, whose task will be to construct socialism and gradually suppress the state until the arrival of a classless society. The destruction of capitalism implies a revolutionary confrontation between antagonistic classes.

2. The MIR bases its revolutionary activity in the historic reality of the class struggle: the exploiters on one side, based in the private ownership of the means of production and exchange; the exploited, the overwhelming majority of the population who own only their labor power and from whom the bourgeois class extracts surplus value, on the other. The MIR recognizes the proletariat as the revolutionary vanguard class that must win the peasants, intellectuals, technicians, and the impoverished middle class to its cause. The MIR intransigently fights the exploiters, bases itself on the principle of class against class, and categorically rejects any strategy that tends to mitigate this struggle.

3. The twentieth century is the century of the death agony of the capitalist system. The development of technology has not served to avert periodic crises and the idleness and impoverishment of millions, because in the capitalist system, production is social but appropriation is individual. The capitalist system in its highest stage, imperialism, can offer humanity no other perspective than dictatorship and war as a final attempt to overcome its chronic structural crisis. Although it seems to be hidden in certain periods, the regime of bourgeois dictatorship, which is exercised through an oppressive state, speaks in the abstract of freedom but inevitably tends toward fascism because of these contradictions.

4. The most prominent feature of our century is the international character acquired by the revolutionary process. Every continent has been shaken by history, and the relation of forces between the classes has changed to the disfavor of imperialism. A third of humanity, more than a billion people, has escaped the orbit of capitalism and is building socialism. The triumph of the revolution in many backward countries has shown that all countries have sufficient objective conditions to realize the socialist revolution; there are no "mature" or "immature" proletariats. The struggles for national liberation and agrarian reform have been transformed, through a process of

permanent and uninterrupted revolution, into social revolutions, demonstrating that without the overthrow of the bourgeoisie, there is no real possibility of national liberation and full agrarian reform—democratic tasks that are combined with socialist measures.

The revolution in the colonial and semi-colonial countries has not yet resolved the basic problems of socialism. As long as the revolution has not triumphed in the highly industrialized countries, the danger of nuclear war will exist and a classless society will not be achieved. Imperialism will not be defeated by mere economic competition between opposed social regimes in a world of formal peaceful coexistence, but by socialist revolution in the very bastions of imperialism.

5. The objective conditions are more than mature for the overthrow of the capitalist system. Despite this, reformism and revisionism continue betraying the interests of the proletariat. This is why the crisis of humanity is concretized in the worldwide crisis of leadership of the proletariat. Nevertheless, the revolutionary process has produced a crisis in the traditional parties of the left in recent decades, and new revolutionary movements have begun to grow, opening the historical perspective of overcoming the crisis of leadership of the proletariat.

6. Chile has become a semi-colonial country, with backward, uneven, and combined capitalist development. Despite its backwardness, Chile is not an agricultural country, but an industrial and mining nation. In their 150 years of misgovernment, the ruling castes have underdeveloped agriculture, mining, and industry, have turned over our major sources of production to imperialism, mortgaged our national independence with international agreements and concessions, and made Chile a country with one of the lowest standards of living and highest infant mortality rates, high levels of illiteracy, and shortages of food and housing. The trajectory of the ruling classes, from last century's declaration of independence until the present, has demonstrated the incapacity of the native bourgeoisie and its parties to resolve bourgeois-democratic tasks, fundamentally those of national liberation, agrarian reform, and the liquidation of semi-feudal remnants. Therefore, we reject any "stagist theory" that falsely claims we must first await a bourgeois-democratic stage led by the industrial bourgeoisie before the proletariat takes power.

We will fight any theory that encourages illusions in the "progressive bourgeoisie" and practices class collaboration. We emphatically maintain that the proletariat, at the head of the peasantry and the impoverished middle class, is the only class capable of carrying out "democratic" tasks along with socialist ones.

7. The bureaucratic leaderships of the traditional parties of the Chilean left defraud the hopes of the workers. Rather than struggling for the

overthrow of the bourgeoisie, they limit themselves to planning reforms of the capitalist regime on a class-collaborationist basis, and fool the workers with their permanent electoral waltz, neglecting mass action and the revolutionary traditions of the Chilean proletariat. In addition, they maintain that they can reach socialism by the "peaceful and parliamentary road," as if any ruling class in history has ever voluntarily given up power.

The MIR rejects the theory of the "peaceful road" because it politically disarms the proletariat and is inapplicable. The bourgeoisie itself would not follow this road, but would resist with totalitarian dictatorship and civil war rather than peacefully give up power. We reaffirm the Marxist-Leninist principle that popular armed insurrection is the only road to the overthrow of the capitalist regime.

8. Facing this reality, we have assumed the responsibility of founding the MIR to unify those militant revolutionary groups who are prepared, above and beyond any sectarianism, to quickly but seriously undertake the preparation and organization of the Chilean Socialist Revolution.

The MIR defines itself as a Marxist-Leninist organization led by the principles of democratic centralism.

THE CAUSES OF THE DEFEAT*
Miguel Enríquez

Miguel Enríquez (1944–74), the General Secretary and chief theoretician of the MIR, was one of the most notable representatives of the new generation of revolutionary Marxists in Latin America. As a student at the University of Concepcion, he was a member (along with Bautista von Schowen and Luciano Cruz) of the group that took over the leadership of the MIR in December 1967. He died in October 1974 in a confrontation with the Chilean military police.

This selection, an interview with the French Trotskyist weekly *Rouge* on the balance-sheet of the tragic experience of the Popular Unity (UP) government and the perspectives for the resistance to the military regime installed by the September 1973 coup, was one of his last.

During the last three years, we alerted the workers and the left to the catastrophe into which they were being led by reformist politics and did all that we could as a party and among the masses to avoid it.

The masses were not "ultra-leftists" when they expanded their mobilizations in defense of their own interests. After having brought the UP to power, they accelerated their pace on the sole road that history offered

---

*"Quelle stratégie pour la résistance? Quelle unité? La réponse de Miguel Enríquez," *Rouge*, 22 March 1974.

them. It was not the masses that kept the Christian Democrats from allying with the UP, but the laws of the class struggle in an underdeveloped and dependent country like Chile.

The working class and the people can constitute themselves as a social force (as they did when putting the UP into power) only to the degree that they fulfill their own interests as a class. And objectively, in Chile, a capitalist country, they could and will only be able to do this by incessantly attacking the interests of the ruling class—one of whose sectors, represented by the Christian Democratic Party, also understood this. From the start, the ruling class took on the defense of the capitalist system, the struggle against the advance of the workers, and the destruction of what this class had created—the Popular Unity government.

The masses were not mistaken in moving forward, just as history cannot be "mistaken." Nor was the Christian Democratic Party, a bourgeois party, driven away by the "ultra-lefts." What led Chile to the catastrophe we face today were reformist policies that systematically attacked, frustrated, and finally destroyed the social force that had created the government and was its principal source of strength—the working class and the people.

We were not "impatient" or "ultra-left." We gave leadership, as far as we could, to the historic march of the workers against the ruling class and the capitalist system in the factories, farms, camps, schools, and universities, and in the armed forces. But we were not able to take leadership of the movement from the reformists. This was our weaknesses and our failing—nothing else.

We are staying in Chile to reorganize the mass movement, seeking unity with the whole of the left and all sectors ready to fight against the dictatorship, in preparation for a long revolutionary war that will overturn the dictatorship, conquer power for the workers, and install a workers' and peasants' government.

But this is not the most important debate today in Chile. We are trying to attain unity among the whole of the left. However, what has occurred is a lesson for all the peoples of the world. There are few times when the disaster provoked by reformist politics has been so obvious. At the same time, we must respond to the attacks of certain European parties and individuals, so the truth may win out over the misrepresentation of the facts.

THE COUNCIL OF REVOLUTIONARY COORDINATION*

In 1972, during a meeting of the leaders of the MIR, the Tupamaros, and the Argentinian PRT, Miguel Enríquez proposed the creation of an international organization—a "little Zimmerwald," in his words—of the three revolutionary groups. His proposal was accepted, and the groups were soon joined by the ELN of Bolivia. After consolidating their links, the four organizations announced the formation of the Council of Revolutionary Coordination (JCR) in early 1974. Unlike the OLAS, the JCR, which remained active until 1977, was not an initiative of the Cuban leadership, despite their fraternal ties; its creation signified a certain autonomization of Latin American Guevarism in relation to Cuba.

> This is the Vietnamese road. This is the road our peoples must follow. This is the road that America will follow, with the special feature that its armed groups might create something like Coordinating Councils to make the repressive tasks of Yankee imperialism more difficult and to facilitate their own cause.
>
> Che Guevara, *Message to the Tricontinental*

The National Liberation Movement (Tupamaros) of Uruguay, the Revolutionary Left Movement (MIR) of Chile, the National Liberation Army of Bolivia, and the People's Revolutionary Army (ERP) of Argentina sign the present declaration to inform the workers, the poor peasants, the urban poor, the students and intellectuals, the indigenous peoples, and the millions of exploited laborers in our long-suffering Latin American homeland of our decision to unite in a Council of Revolutionary Coordination.

This important step is the result of a felt necessity: the need to join our peoples on the organizational terrain, to unify the revolutionary forces confronting the imperialist enemy, and to engage more effectively in the political and ideological struggle against bourgeois nationalism and reformism.

This important step concretizes one of the main strategic ideas of Commandante Che Guevara, the hero, symbol, and precursor of the continental socialist revolution. It is also a significant step toward reestablishing the fraternal traditions of our peoples, who acted as brothers and fought as one against our oppressors, the Spanish colonialists, in the past century . . . .

OUR PROGRAM

We are united by the understanding that there is no viable strategy in Latin America other than the strategy of guerrilla warfare. This guerrilla warfare is a complex process of mass struggle, armed and unarmed, peaceful and

---

*"A los pueblos de América Latina, declaración constitutiva de la JCR," *Che Guevara* (organ of the JCR), n. 1, November 1974.

violent, in which all forms of struggle develop in harmony, while centered on the axis of armed struggle. The victorious development of this whole process of guerrilla warfare requires the mobilization of the whole people under the leadership of the revolutionary proletariat. The proletarian leadership of the war is exercised by a Marxist-Leninist combat party with a proletarian character, able to centralize and lead all aspects of the popular struggle and guarantee a coordinated strategic leadership with a single powerful visage. Under the leadership of the proletarian party, we must structure a powerful popular army, the iron nucleus of the revolutionary forces; growing from smaller to larger, intimately connected to and sustained by the masses, it will become an impenetrable wall against which the military attempts of the reactionaries will be smashed, assuring the total annihilation of the counterrevolutionary armies. It is likewise necessary to build a broad workers' and peoples' front that mobilizes all progressive and revolutionary people, the different popular parties, the unions, and other similar organizations—in a word, the broadest masses—whose struggle runs parallel to and at each strategic moment converges with the military action of the peoples' army and the underground political action of the proletarian party.

Our response must be clear—nothing other than armed struggle, the main factor for polarizing, agitating, and finally defeating the enemy, and our only possibility for victory. This does not mean we will not utilize all possible forms of organization and struggle: legal and clandestine, peaceful and violent, economic and political, all converging with the greatest efficacy into the *armed struggle*, in accord with the peculiarities of every region and nation.

The continental character of the struggle is fundamentally determined by the presence of a common enemy. North American imperialism is developing an international strategy to stop the Socialist Revolution in Latin America. The imposition of fascist regimes in those countries where a rising mass movement threatens the stability of the oligarchy's power is not accidental. The revolutionaries' continental strategy corresponds to the international strategy of imperialism.

The path we must travel in this struggle is not short. The international bourgeoisie is prepared to stop the Revolution in every country by any means necessary. It has all kinds of resources at its disposal to use against the people. This is why ours is a war of attrition in its early stages, until we can form a peoples' army more powerful than that of our enemy. This process is slow, but paradoxically, it is the shortest and least costly path to reaching the strategic objectives of the neglected classes.

THE SANDINISTA FRONT IN NICARAGUA*

Carlos Fonseca Amador

Carlos Fonseca Amador (1936–76) was one of the most important members of the young Marxist generation born under the banner of the Cuban Revolution. Having joined the pro-Soviet Nicaraguan Socialist Party as a student, he soon left to find a more radical path. In 1959, shortly after the victory of the revolution in Cuba, he became a guerrilla and was seriously wounded in combat against Somoza's National Guard. In 1962, he was one of the founders of the Sandinista National Liberation Front (FSLN), which attempted to take up the torch of Sandino's peasant guerrilla war against North American imperialism and its local agents. The central leader and theorist of the FSLN, he was killed by Somoza's troops in 1976.

The selections below are from a 1969 text and contain two important elements that were not always present in the Castroist current: an explicit critique of the past and present politics of the traditional Communist parties and a clear statement of the democratic and socialist character of the Nicaraguan revolution.

From 1926 to 1936, the people of Nicaragua lived through one of the most intense periods in their history. The armed struggle, through which the people sought change, led to more than 20,000 deaths. It began as a struggle against a conservative government imposed by the North Americans, was continued by the Sandinista resistance, and ended with Anastasio Somoza's military coup against Juan B. Sacasa.

The struggle developed without the existence of an industrial proletariat. The incipient bourgeoisie betrayed the Nicaraguan people and sold them out to the Yankee intervention. The bourgeoisie could not be immediately replaced in the vanguard of the popular struggle by a revolutionary proletariat. The Sandinista resistance, which became the heroic vanguard of the people, was composed almost exclusively of peasants, and precisely in this fact lies the glory and tragedy of that revolutionary movement. It was a glory for the Nicaraguan people that this most humble class defended the stained honor of the homeland, and, at the same time, a tragedy that this peasantry lacked any political understanding. There were even leaders of important guerrilla columns that could not read a single letter. Because of this, the movement was unable to maintain its continuity once Sandino was assassinated.

The prolonged armed struggle, which ended in betrayal and frustration, exhausted the people's strength. The sector headed by Anastasio Somoza gained hegemony over the traditional Liberal party. The opposition to Somoza came to be dominated by the traditional Conservative Party, a reactionary

*Carlos Fonseca Amador, "Nicaragua hora H," *Tricontinental* (Havana), n. 14, September–October 1969, pp. 32–33, 40–41. For the complete text, see *Sandinistas Speak* (New York: Pathfinder Press, 1982), pp. 23–42.

political force profoundly weakened because the people's memory of their sellout to the Yankee interventionists was still fresh during the thirties.

An important factor that also seriously contributed to the interruption of the anti-imperialist struggle was the situation at the outbreak of World War II, which concentrated the focus of world reaction in Europe and Asia. Yankee imperialism, the traditional enemy of the Nicaraguan people, became an ally of the international antifascist front. The lack of a revolutionary leadership in Nicaragua kept this reality from being correctly interpreted, and Somoza took advantage of the situation to consolidate the rule of his clique.

THE RISE OF THE OLD MARXIST SECTOR

For many years, the influence of the Marxist sector within the opposition to the Somoza regime was extremely weak. The anti-Somoza opposition was under the nearly complete hegemony of the conservative sector, a political force representing the interests of a section of the capitalist class. One of the factors that contributed to the weakness of the Marxist sector originated in the conditions under which the Nicaraguan Socialist Party (the traditional Communist organization in Nicaragua) was formed. This organization was created in June 1944, when World War II had not yet ended. This was a period when the theories of Earl Browder, the General Secretary of the Communist Party of the United States who proposed conciliation with the capitalist class and North American imperialism in Latin America, were in full force.

During those years, the Nicaraguan workers' movement was made up mainly of artisans, and this provided the basis for anti-worker deviations. Also, the leadership of the Socialist Party was itself of artisanal and not proletarian origin, as the Nicaraguan Socialist Party demagogically claims. It was a leadership that suffered from an extremely low ideological level.

For many years, the revolutionary intellectual was a rare exception in Nicaragua. The radical intellectuals and free thinkers of the years of the U.S. armed intervention, who as a class represented a bourgeoisie that finally capitulated, could not be replaced by intellectuals identified with the working class, for reasons that we have explained. As a result, the intellectual movement in Nicaragua became the monopoly of a Catholic element that even openly identified with fascism for a period. In this manner, the door of thought remained closed to the revolutionary movement.

The Nicaraguan Socialist Party was formed at a meeting whose purpose was to proclaim support for the Somoza government. This took place on July 3, 1944, in the Managua Gymnasium. To be rigorously objective, we should explain this very serious error was not simply the result of bad faith on part of their leaders; we must take into account the factors that led to this. The Marxist leadership did not maintain the proper composure in confronting the hegemony of the conservative sector over the anti-Somoza movement; they did not know how to distinguish between the decency of the anti-Somoza opposition and the maneuvers of the conservative sector.

Once Somoza had used the pseudo-Marxist sector to his benefit, he unleashed repression against a workers' movement that, because of the comfortable circumstances in which it had been born, did not know how to defend itself with the proper revolutionary firmness . . . .

The Sandinista National Liberation Front considers that, at the present time and for a certain period, Nicaragua will be passing through a stage in which a radical political force will continue acquiring its own character. Consequently, at the present moment we must put great emphasis on the fact that our main objective is the socialist revolution, a revolution that aims to defeat Yankee imperialism, its local agents, fake oppositionists, and fake revolutionaries. This propaganda, with the consistent support of armed action, will permit the front to win the support of the section of the popular masses who are conscious of the profound nature of the struggle that we are carrying out.

To outline a strategy for the revolutionary movement, we must take into account the power represented by the capitalist parties, because of the influence they still exercise in the opposition. We must be alert to the danger that a revolutionary insurrection might serve as a steppingstone for the reactionary forces in opposition to the Somoza regime. The goal of our movement is a dual one: on the one hand, to overthrow the criminal and traitorous clique that has usurped power for many years and, on the other, to prevent the capitalist forces in the opposition, who are known to be under the control of Yankee imperialism, from taking advantage of the situation unleashed by the guerrilla struggle to seize control of state power. A revolutionary political and military force rooted in broad sectors of the population must play a decisive role in barring the way to the capitalist traitors. Sinking these roots depends on its ability to eradicate the influence of the Liberals and Conservatives in these sectors.

We will determine the policies to follow in regard to these parties in accord with the attitude taken by the people as a whole toward the old parties with capitalist leadership.

As to the situation of the Nicaraguan Socialist Party, we can state that the changes which have taken place in the leadership of this political organization are purely formal. The old leadership creates illusions in the Conservative sector and clamors for the construction of a political front with these contemptuous agents of imperialism. The so-called new leadership currently justifies its participation in the electoral farce of 1967, supporting the candidacy of the pseudo-oppositionist, Conservative Fernando Agüero. Just like the old leadership, the so-called "new leadership" ceaselessly speaks of the armed struggle, but in practice concentrates its energy on petty legalistic work.

These previous statements do not contradict the possibility of developing a certain general unity in the anti-Somoza sector. But this must be a unity at the base, with the most honest sectors of the different anti-Somoza tendencies. This is all the more possible because of the growing prestige of the Sandinista National Liberation Front and the increasing loss in standing of the capitalist parties and their like, along with the splintering of their leadership.

The Sandinista National Liberation Front understands the difficulties of the guerrilla road. But it is not prepared to retreat. We know that we are confronting a bloody, reactionary armed force in the National Guard, the ferocious GN, which still maintains the cruel practices inculcated by its creator, the United States Marines. The bombarding of villages, the butchering of children, the raping of women, the burning of huts with peasants still inside, mutilation as a form of torture: these were the subjects that the North American professors of civilization taught the GN during the epoch of the guerrilla resistance (1927–32) led by Augusto César Sandino.

The frustration that followed the period of Sandinista resistance does not have to be repeated today. The times are different. The current period is not like the time when Sandino and his fellow guerrillas fought alone against the Yankee empire. Today, revolutionaries of all subjugated countries are launching or preparing to unleash the battle against the empire of the dollar. At the apex of this battle is indomitable Vietnam, which with exemplary heroism is repelling the aggression of the blonde beast . . . .

We shall faithfully carry out our oath:

"Before the images of Augusto César Sandino and Ernesto Che Guevara, before the memory of the heroes and martyrs of Nicaragua, Latin America, and the whole of humanity, and before History, I place my hand on the red and black flag that signifies 'Free Homeland or Death,' and swear to defend the national honor with arms in hand and fight for the redemption of the oppressed and exploited of Nicaragua and the world. If I carry out this oath, the liberation of Nicaragua and all the peoples will be the reward; if I betray this oath, a shameful death and ignominy will be my punishment."

THE SANDINISTA PROGRAM FOR THE NICARAGUAN PEASANTRY*

Jaime Wheelock

A few weeks after the triumph of the Sandinista Revolution in Nicaragua, Jaime Wheelock, the new Minister of Agrarian Reform, gave the following interview to the Trotskyist journal *Perspectiva Mundial*, in which he developed a brief analysis of the agrarian structure of the country and presented the program of the new regime. Wheelock had been one of the main leaders of the Proletarian tendency of the FSLN, which had put forward a strategy of anti-imperialist and socialist revolution in Nicaragua.

To begin, perhaps you could describe a little bit of the structure of agricultural production during the last years of the dictatorship.

From the point of view of the technology and the destination of production, there were two basic types: the production of basic grains and seasonal cattle-raising for the internal market, and production for export. Most of this production was carried out under productive relations that left workers unemployed most of the time—that is, seasonal cultivation. At the same time, this production was intended to fulfill the needs of a very small number of landowners, the *latifundistas*.

There are 300,000 manzanas of cotton, some 150,000 manzanas of coffee, and 200,000 beef and milk cattle. Some 120,000 manzanas of sugar, along with tobacco and rice, were fundamentally controlled by the Somoza and Pelas families. While there was production for internal consumption, there was also a capitalist plantation sector and a sector of poor and middle peasants.

Practically 40 percent to 60 percent of the arable land was controlled by the Somoza family. If we add the *Somocistas*, this number might rise to 70 percent. Perhaps 60,000 peasants with a bit of land and some 100,000 peasants working both as wage laborers and on their own land worked the rest.

Clearly, many workers, including middle peasants with family farms, have to or had to join the planting or harvesting on the large farms. There were more than 250,000 agricultural workers involved in the cotton harvest alone. Coffee also required 150,000 people in the high season, and sugar some 15,000. This is a large proletariat, but a floating, seasonal proletariat.

What was happening? Extensive capitalist exploitation, as well as the harmful practices of the old oligarchy, were displacing the small producers, the small peasants. For example, in Chinandega, capitalist production has covered the land with sugar, cotton, and banana plantations, and the

---

*"La reforma agraria en marcha: El programa sandinista para los campesinos de Nicaragua," *Perspectiva Mundial* (New York), v. 3, n. 16, September 3, 1979.

peasant masses have been driven off their land. They lead miserable, marginal lives in the midst of the countryside, just like in the marginal barrios of the city. This is happening right in the countryside. This is incredible: leading marginal lives in the countryside, as if someone had moved them there from the city. But no, this is a different phenomenon, a retrogression—a drowning on land.

The opposite phenomenon has taken place in the cities. Some peasants driven off the land have moved to the periphery of the cities, creating marginal barrios. Other peasants from Chinandega are almost being thrown into the sea and must live by fishing.

What measures are you taking to resolve this terrible problem?

Here in Nicaragua, we have different types of agricultural situations. There are poor peasants in the northern departments, where there are no roads, no infrastructure, and the land, while it is available, is not productive. Here we would like to create a program to enlarge the peasants' landholdings, along with technical assistance and the development of the infrastructure.

On the other hand, in the Managua Valley, Masaya, and Carazo, where we have an older indigenous and peasant community that has been driven down by the expansion of the *latifundios*, there is a quite strong single-crop economy in the center of the country. We wish to resolve the land problem here by giving land to the peasants. Both in the north and here, we are going to give land to the peasants.

But in other regions—for example León, Chinandega, and Rivas—we do not wish to distribute land. We are going to create large-scale state enterprises that will be both an impulse to economic and social development in the region and a base for deepening this process. That is, in some cases, we want to resolve the problem of the poor, landless peasant with land; in other cases, we are going to solve the problem of the agricultural worker by incorporating him into production and giving him stable work the year round, as well as many social and economic benefits. And in the case of indigenous communities, we will give land to the indigenous people, but to the collectivity, not individual producers—enough to increase production and their standard of living.

What kind of administration is planned for this type of state enterprise?

I explained earlier about the question of social and economic development. We are going to create large-scale state enterprises where the workers will participate in management and fundamental decision-making. But a significant part of the product of each enterprise will go toward the social development, education, health, etc., of these workers and of the whole region.

For example, in Rivas, there is a large sugar mill called Dolores. This mill has a high level of production. With this production, we can probably solve the problem of the lack of hospitals in the whole department. And the workers ought to know this. This is the consciousness we want to instill in the workers, so they will know that it was with their production that the health problems of the whole department of Rivas have been solved. We will also provide homes and educational and literacy programs to these workers and, at the same time, socially incorporate them into productive activity and decision-making in the enterprise and in society as a whole.

There was an article in **Barricada** *a few days ago which reported that some peasants, I believe in León, demanded arms to defend their new situation. Are you encouraging the development of peasant militias?*

Yes. In fact, there already are peasant militias created during the war. There is a large peasant presence in our army.

What was the role of the peasants in the struggle against Somoza and the insurrection?

The peasantry has participated directly in the struggle for democracy, freedom, and progress in Nicaragua for many years.

This has been going on since the time of General Sandino. The peasants were numerically the most important force in this national liberation struggle. But also, in this new stage, the first nuclei of the Sandinista Front developed in the mountains with the support of the peasantry, and the peasantry has been the social sector hit hardest by repression.

As an example (and there are many more), recall the brutal repression, the repressive assault launched by Somoza in 1975–76 and 1977 against the peasants in the North. There were towns like Barial, Sofana, and Boca de Lulu that were totally demolished. Barial ceased to exist. Thousands of peasants were sacrificed by the *Somocista* gangs. Yet the peasantry remained active, combative, and patriotic.

Therefore, we have a great obligation to the peasantry. Besides, the peasantry is a motor force of this revolution and the first beneficiary of it. And, of course, it will have to work to consolidate its revolution.

THE REVOLUTION AND THE INDIGENOUS PEOPLES*
The EGP of Guatemala

The 1960s ended with the failure of a long period of guerrilla struggles in Guatemala, the destruction of the main columns of the FAR (Revolutionary Armed Forces)

---

*EGP of Guatemala, *Manifiesto Internacional*, October 1979, pp. 27–29, 35–36.

and the MR-13 (June 13 Revolutionary Movement), and the death of their central leaders (Turcios Lima and Yon Sosa). In 1973, some survivors of these groups united to form the EGP, the Guerrilla Army of the Poor, which within a few years became the country's principal revolutionary organization. Other political-military groups followed, including the reconstituted FAR and the ORPA (Revolutionary Organization of the Armed People). These three armed organizations later formed the *Coordinación Unitaria* (United Coordinator) along with the left wing of the PGT (Guatemalan Labor Party, the traditional Communist Party). Parallel to this, a process of popular mobilization developed under the leadership of the CENUS (National Council of Trade Union Unity) and the Democratic Front Against Repression (which included the major unions and organizations of peasants, teachers, students, and others) in solidarity with the objectives for which the political-military organizations were and are struggling.

The following are passages from the October 1979 EGP *Manifesto* that refer to the indigenous question in Guatemala. A leader of the FAR, Ricardo Ramírez, had already emphasized the importance of the indigenous peoples in the revolutionary process during the sixties, in his important book *Letters from the Guatemalan Front*. The EGP takes up this theme again and points out the necessity of a revolutionary socialist solution to the problem.

The Ethnic-National Problem and the Revolution

With all that it has in common structurally and geopolitically with the other Central American countries, Guatemala has a peculiarity that distinguishes it from the rest. One factor that introduces a distinctive element, without changing the essential dynamics of the social process and the class and revolutionary struggles, is also an additional need for revolutionary transformation in our country.

This is the national-ethnic question. The majority (60 percent) of the population of Guatemala belong to 22 indigenous ethnic minorities who in their totality constitute the majority of Guatemalans, the majority of the masters of our homeland.

These 60 percent of Guatemalans have been marginalized, discriminated against, and oppressed from colonial times until today. The most oppression and the most exploitation are concentrated here, since these people contribute the most cheap labor and form the largest section of the semi-proletariat.

In some regions, they have been relegated to the most isolated, inhospitable, and poor areas, so they receive neither the advantages nor disadvantages of the services, state power, and institutions of the ruling classes. The problems of communication, contact, and economic, social, and cultural interchange are also great.

Under these conditions, it is impossible to speak of the existence of one integrated nationality in Guatemala. The oppressors of the indigenous peoples of Guatemala, both yesterday's and today's, erroneously believed that servitude, exploitation, and marginalization would destroy the spirit of resistance of the Maya-Quiché peoples and that their social and cultural character would in time disappear, to be finally absorbed and destroyed by the system. This was a profound and fatal error. These conditions have accumulated and strengthened the very identity of the indigenous peoples; their mute rebelliousness has grown to the point that not only can its magnitude not be ignored as a political factor, but it has become a decisive element for our country's future.

The Guatemalan ethnic minorities cannot freely lead and organize their own cultural development or enjoy their legitimate right to participate in leading the nation and configuring its social and political character in a country where the system of production and development is determined by the laws of class exploitation and the oppression of races and cultures.

This is why no partial change in Guatemalan society or in its regime will eliminate these differences that make a subjugated mass of the majority of the Guatemalan population. History has proven that capitalism cannot resolve these problems, because the very dynamic of class rule leads it to incorporate national oppression into its operation. True and full liberation of oppressed nationalities is impossible in the context of a society divided into exploiting and exploited classes.

Only under socialism, which eliminates the confines of exploitation and the division of classes, will the indigenous peoples of Guatemala form part of the national and cultural community without losing their identity, since the factor to unite the component parts of the Guatemalan nation will be common interest, not the domination of one group over others. The community of Guatemalans will not be determined by the submission of all to an unequal fate, but by the sharing of the same united destiny under a mechanism of reciprocal communication, interaction, and influence. Only under these conditions will we be able to speak of a Guatemalan nation. And, along with the class struggle, this social imperative constitutes the essential impulse of the Guatemalan revolution . . . .

- There will be no revolutionary victory in Guatemala if there are no tranformations of its structures and institutions to reflect the basic needs and concrete historical interests of the working class and the other popular sectors of Guatemala.
- There will be no revolutionary victory in Guatemala if it does not bring with it the end of ethnic-cultural oppression, the incorporation of the indigenous peoples into the full range of economic, political, and social rights, and the creation of national harmony, without inequality, along and together with the *mestizo* population.
- In the context of the present international situation, the historical and socioeconomic development of our country, with its combination of

both archaic and modern features, creates an indivisible interconnection between our revolutionary, democratic, and socialist tasks that cannot be unraveled. The Guatemalan revolution will take part in this global problematic. This is where it derives its content.

• The geopolitical location of Guatemala and the current degree of development of the socialist camp explain and determine the fact that the revolutionary victory in Guatemala opens a necessary transitional phase from capitalism to socialism, which will last as long as socialism, as a global system, does not achieve a decisive correlation of forces in its favor.

• The liquidation of our dependency in relation to imperialism and the creation of a popular revolutionary power are the initial bases for this transitional period.

PROGRAM OF THE REVOLUTIONARY DEMOCRATIC GOVERNMENT*
Revolutionary Coordinator of the Masses of El Salvador

During 1979–80, an intensification and sharpening of class confrontations occurred in El Salvador; the replacement of General Romero's military regime by a civilian-military junta after the coup d'état of October 15, 1979, did not end the prerevolutionary crisis. In early 1980, the main popular organizations—three guerrilla groups, the Farabundo Martí Popular Liberation Army (EPL), the National Resistance, the Revolutionary Army of the People (ERP), along with the Communist Party—grew closer together. An agreement among the mass fronts connected to these organizations (BPR, FAPU, LP-28, UDN), which included the major unions, workers', peasants', and students' associations, was reached in February of the same year. The Revolutionary Coordinator of the Masses was created in this accord, and the following are the most significant sections of its program, which implicitly puts forward a dynamic of breaking with the bourgeois state and its military apparatus and liquidating capitalism.

The economic and social structures of our country, which have guaranteed the disproportionate enrichment of an oligarchic minority and the exploitation of our people by Yankee imperialism, are facing a profound and insoluble crisis.

The military dictatorship also finds itself in crisis, as is the whole legal order and the ideology that has defended oligarchic and North American imperialist interests, oppressing and subjugating the Salvadoran people for half a century. The ranks of these ruling classes have split, and both fascist and reformist attempts to overcome the crisis have failed, victims of their

---

Plataforma programática del Gobierno Democrático Revolucionario, El Salvador, February 1980, in *Combate* (Sweden), n. 55–56, March–April 1980, pp. 5–7.

own contradictions and beset by the decisive and heroic action of the popular movement. This failure has not even been reversed by the increasingly shameless North American intervention on behalf of these anti-popular projects.

The faithful attachment of the revolutionary organizations to the interests and aspirations of the Salvadoran people has allowed them to tremendously strengthen and deepen their roots among the vast laboring majority and the middle classes. The revolutionary movement is now indestructible because of its popular roots, and constitutes the only alternative for the Salvadoran people, who cannot be stopped or detoured in their struggle for a free homeland in which they can realize their vital aspirations.

The economic and political crisis of the ruling crisis, on one hand, and the strength of the popular movement that has become the decisive political force in our country, on the other, have initiated a revolutionary process and established the conditions for the people to take power.

The revolutionary transformation of our society, subject until now to injustice, betrayal, and pillage, is today a possible and near-at-hand reality. Only in this way will our people conquer and secure the freedoms and democratic rights they have been denied. Only the revolution will solve the agrarian problem, creating material and spiritual conditions favorable to the immense majority of our population on behalf of the peasant masses and the agricultural workers, who today are sunk in misery, cultural backwardness, and marginality. This revolution will win real political independence for our country, giving the Salvadoran people the right to freely determine their destiny and gain real economic independence.

This is why our revolution is popular, democratic, and anti-oligarchic and seeks to win effective, real national independence. Only a revolutionary victory will stop the criminal repression and make it possible for the people to win the peace they do not enjoy today—a solid peace based on freedom, social justice, and national independence.

This revolution under march is not, nor can it be, the work of a group of conspirators. On the contrary, it is the fruit of the struggle of the whole people—that is, the workers, peasants, the middle classes in general, and all the honestly democratic and patriotic sectors and individuals.

The most conscious and organized ranks of the Salvadoran people are increasingly numerous and increasingly united. With its fighting spirit, its level of consciousness, temperament, and organization, and its commitment to sacrifice for a popular victory, the alliance of workers and peasants has proven to be the strongest basis on which to guarantee the seriousness and solidity of the liberation movement, which unites the revolutionary and democratic forces, those two great currents created by the long struggle of the Salvadoran people, as an expression of the unity of the whole people.

The decisive task of the revolution, on which the fulfillment of all its tasks and objectives depends, is the conquest of power and the installation of a Revolutionary Democratic Government that will undertake the construction of a new society at the head of the people.

THE TASKS AND OBJECTIVES OF THE REVOLUTION

The tasks and objectives of the revolution in El Salvador are the following:

1. Defeat the reactionary military dictatorship of the oligarchy and Yankee imperialism, imposed and maintained against the will of the Salvadoran people for fifty years. Destroy its criminal political-military machine and establish a Revolutionary Democratic Government based on the unity of the revolutionary and democratic forces, the Popular Army, and the Salvadoran people.
2. End the power and the political, economic, and general social rule of the great lords of capital and the land.
3. Definitively liquidate the political, economic, and military dependence of our country in relation to Yankee imperialism.
4. Assure the rights and democratic freedoms of the whole people, particularly the working masses, who have least enjoyed them.
5. Transfer to the people, through the creation of collective and cooperative enterprises and the nationalization of the basic means of production and distribution now monopolized by the oligarchy and the U.S. monopolies: the land under the control of the big landowners, the companies that produce and distribute electricity, the oil refineries, monopoly enterprises in industry, commerce, and services, foreign trade, the banks, and the big transportation companies. All this should be done without affecting the small and medium private enterprises in the different branches of the national economy, which should be stimulated and fully supported.
6. Raise the material and cultural level of the population.
7. Create our country's new army, whose basic foundation will be the Popular Army built in the course of the revolutionary process—to which the healthy, patriotic, and worthy elements of the current army can incorporate themselves.
8. Give impulse to all forms of popular organization at all levels and in all sectors to guarantee the active, creative, and democratic incorporation of the people into the revolutionary process and create the closest connection between them and their government.
9. Orient our country's foreign policy and international relations according to the principles of independence and self-determination, solidarity, peaceful coexistence, and equal rights and mutual respect among states.
10. Assure peace, freedom, the well-being of our people, and continuing social progress through the above.

It is the unanimous opinion of the popular and democratic forces that only the realization of the measures in this platform can resolve our country's profound structural and political crisis to the benefit of the Salvadoran people.

Only the oligarchy, North American imperialism, and those who serve its anti-patriotic interests oppose and conspire against these changes. Since October 15, 1979, different parties and sectors in the government have vainly attempted to carry out a great number of the measures that we propose, without first destroying the old reactionary and repressive power and installing a truly revolutionary and popular power. This experience has clearly confirmed that this labor of transformation can only be realized by the united revolutionary movement, in alliance with all democratic forces.

The hour of this historic, liberating victory, for which the Salvadoran people have struggled and heroically spilled so much of its blood, is arriving. Nothing or no one can stop it.

For the unity of the revolutionary and democratic forces!

Toward the victory of the revolutionary democratic government!

> Revolutionary Coordinator of the Masses
>
> For the Executive Directory of the Popular Revolutionary Bloc (BPR),
> Juan Chacón, General Secretary;
> Julio Flores, Organization Secretary
>
> For the National Coordinating Committee of the FAPU,
> Héctor Recinos,
> José Napoleón Rodríguez Ruiz
>
> For the National Political Committee of the February 28 Popular Leagues,
> Leoncio Pichinte
>
> For the National Coordinating Committee of the National Democratic Union (UDN),
> Manuel Franco
>
> San Salvador, El Salvador, Central America
> February 23, 1980

15

Socialisms

SOCIALISM FOR VENEZUELA*
Teodoro Petkoff

The 1968 invasion of Czechoslovakia by the U.S.S.R. led the European Communist parties (Italy, Spain, Great Britain, France) to distance themselves from the Soviet leadership. In Latin America, the Venezuelan party was one of the few to enter this type of crisis, which led a large number of leaders and militants to break from the U.S.S.R. and create an independent party, the MAS (Movement toward Socialism), in 1971.

A book by Teodoro Petkoff, one of the best known leaders of the PCV, was published in July 1970, just before this split. The selections reprinted here are a powerful self-criticism of the party's traditional politics and an attempt at a Marxist analysis of the controversial and crucial question of the so-called national bourgeoisie.

The discussion of the character of the revolution is becoming quite complicated because it comes up against one of the sacrosanct myths of our theoretical formulations: the existence of the national bourgeoisie.

For many decades, the Communist parties of Latin America have put forward the idea that we can count on the participation of a section of the Latin American bourgeoisies, baptized with the ambiguous name of the *national bourgeoisie*, in the national liberation struggle. This schema presumes that a certain section of the Venezuelan bourgeoisie, in our case, has developed with no direct connection to imperialism and, under the immense pressure of competition from imported goods and devastated by the strength of the imperialist economies and the native big bourgeoisie, possesses an anti-imperialist potential allowing it to collaborate in a grand, multi-class front for national liberation. Consequently, for all its mature life (that is, since the forties), our party's politics have been oriented toward building this alliance with the national bourgeoisie. To this end, our party's program makes important concessions to this "national" bourgeoisie,

---

*Teodoro Petkoff, *Socialismo para Venezuela* (Caracas: Ed. Fuentes, 1972), pp. 89–90, 96–99.

223

including a fundamental one: limiting the objectives of a revolutionary transformation of the country to a bourgeois-democratic phase, offering the perspective of the *development* of "national" capitalism once imperialist domination is broken and the internal market is enlarged by an agrarian reform. The theory of an agrarian and anti-imperialist revolution is only the distillation of this political approach toward the "national" bourgeoisie.

Precisely this is one of the fundamental "theoretical" bases of the rightist politics carried out by the party leadership during certain periods, among them the crucial years after the overthrow of Pérez Jiménez in 1958. While always proclaiming "the hegemony of the proletariat" in this supposed alliance, in practice—because of our ideological weakness more than that of the masses—political developments always find us tailing the bourgeoisie, especially its non-national sector, which naturally dominates the "national" bourgeoisie. We will return to this later when we examine the question of stages in the revolution . . . .

This "national" bourgeoisie understands perfectly well that its survival as an exploiting class, that is, as a sector of society that acquires its wealth by exploiting wage labor, is indissolubly linked to the continuance of our neo-colonial status and the maintenance of the political and economic power of the imperialist-capitalist-oligarchic complex.

Whatever the degree of conflict that periodically opposes the "national" bourgeoisie to this complex of dependency, the solutions proposed to resolve them never suggest subverting the neo-colonial pact or changing the status quo. Maintaining the latter is the unchangeable premise that allows some spokesmen for the bourgeoisie to occasionally express their nationalist "audacity."

Similarly, the "national" bourgeoisie understands perfectly well that its survival as a socially dominant sector—a minor partner, but a partner nonetheless—is inseparably linked to the existence of the current Venezuelan state. It may struggle to better its position, but never proposes breaking the neo-colonial structure.

Even more serious is that the tendency of development of the "national" bourgeoisie's consciousness is precisely away from nationalism and ever more rapidly toward a "denationalization." This social class, like the whole of the bourgeoisie, is very sensitive to the communications media, which constantly sing the praises of imperialism and capitalism. The American presence; its tremendous capacity to impress the minds of those whose social situation makes them amenable to pro-capitalist arguments; the threat of world revolution; Cuba's example, which tangibly shows that a break with dependency is tied up with the liquidation of capitalism; and finally, the action of imperialism on consciousness (this subjective factor is far from being a mere reflex of the objective factors and can, with fearsome ease, become a *false consciousness*): all these work in favor of "denationalizing" the "national" bourgeoisie.

Clearly, this so-called national bourgeoisie does not have the revolutionary potential (the thesis of the Third Congress) or is not as easily neutralized (an alternative version of the same theory) as we have indefatigably claimed. It is a contradictory social sector that, in certain periods, when the popular movement does not threaten the established order, can allow itself a certain "impudence," but when confronted by the dilemma of choosing between change and the maintenance of the status quo will line up as it always has, against the revolutionary movement.

Conflicts between this social layer and imperialism are being, and ought to be, fomented and supported. Revolutionaries cannot excuse themselves from this task in regard to any manifestation of nationalism, wherever it may occur, as it helps to strengthen the nationalist consciousness of the Venezuelan people. These are conflicts that should not be tactically undervalued. But strategically—that is, from the point of view of the party's general program for the whole historic period, from the angle of the historic alliances for making a revolution, not just any political change—it should not continue to grant these conflicts a subversive potential expressly rejected by the "national" bourgeoisie itself, or continue seeing its qualities and virtues either as revolutionaries, as an "ally, no matter how small or weak," or as a "sector that it is possible to neutralize."

The attempt to win over or neutralize this sector supposes a particular content for our program and general political line, so as to carry out the concessions necessary to reach this goal. This can lessen the revolutionary content of the program, conceal the socialist character of the revolutionary change we promote, maintain bourgeois-democratic illusions, and stimulate rightist tendencies on the possibility of an independent development of our country by the capitalist road—if imperialist domination is broken—without associating this rupture with a whole revolutionary realignment of the country's socioeconomic pattern that would block the growth of capitalism and open the way to socialist development. Even more seriously, this conception affects the politics of the party and contributes to distancing it from the masses.

Lowering the revolutionary content of our program and activity means limiting our possibility of firmly winning the support of those social sectors that are the main class forces upon which the revolutionary process must be based. Our adamant search for this "grand alliance" with the national bourgeoisie (which we have never been able to concretize in any class front or particular activity) might be one of the reasons for our limited ability to attract the working class and other sectors of the poor. Trying not to "frighten" the "national" bourgeoisie, to "open the perspective [of an alliance]," to "neutralize" them, we so hide the revolutionary character of our movement and diminish its socialist content that we leave those sectors we hope to win to our cause completely open to the influence of neocolonial ideology. So far, "Operation National Bourgeoisie" has not allowed us to win over either this bourgeoisie—or the working class.

THE CHILEAN ROAD TO SOCIALISM*
Salvador Allende

The Socialist Party of Chile has often taken more radical positions than the Communist Party, and its members have been more greatly influenced by the Cuban Revolution. This speech by Salvador Allende, the long-time leader of the Chilean SP and President of Chile during the Popular Unity government, who was assassinated by the military during the September 1973 coup, is more representative of the party's moderate sectors. It puts forward quite radical plans for the socialist transformation of society and, at the same time, nourishes illusions about the possibility of a peaceful and constitutional road to socialism in Chile. It is testimony to both the generosity and the limitations of a man who was committed to his people and who died with a weapon in his hand, fighting for his ideals.

THE OVERTHROW OF CAPITALISM IN CHILE

The situations in Russia in 1917 and in Chile today are very different. Nevertheless, the historic challenge is similar.

Decisions were made in Russia in 1917 that had the greatest effect on contemporary history. It was decided there that backward Europe could jump ahead of advanced Europe, that the first socialist revolution would not necessarily take place in the heartland of the industrial powers. They accepted the challenge and established one of the forms for constructing a socialist society, namely, the dictatorship of the proletariat.

Today, no one doubts that nations with large populations can escape from their backwardness in this way and rise to the heights of contemporary civilization. The examples of the U.S.S.R. and the People's Republic of China are eloquent in this regard.

Like Russia then, Chile finds itself facing the necessity of initiating a new way to build a socialist society—our own revolutionary path, the pluralist road, anticipated by the Marxist classics but never before concretized. These social thinkers had supposed that the first on this road would be the more developed nations, probably Italy or France, with their powerful Marxist workers' parties.

---

*Salvador Allende, "La vía chilena hacia el socialismo," Message to Congress, May 21, 1971, in La vía chilena hacia el socialismo (Madrid: Ed. Fundamentos, 1971), pp. 28–32. For the full text, see Allende, Chile's Road to Socialism (Middlesex: Penguin Books, 1973).

However, history once again allows us to break with the past and create a new model of society, not where it was theoretically easier to foresee, but where conditions more favorable to its success have developed. Today, Chile is the first nation on earth called upon to create this second model of the transition to a socialist society.

This challenge is arousing lively interest beyond our country's borders. Everyone knows or feels that, here and now, history is beginning to take a new turn to the extent that we Chileans are conscious of our task. Some among us, perhaps only a few, see merely the enormous difficulties involved. Others of us, the majority, are looking for ways to confront them successfully. For my part, I am certain we will have the energy and capability to carry forward this effort, creating the first socialist society built on a democratic, pluralist, and libertarian model.

Skeptics and catastrophe-mongers will say this is impossible. They will say that a parliament that has served the ruling classes so well is not capable of transforming itself into a parliament of the Chilean people.

It has been said even more emphatically that the Armed Forces and the National Police, until now a base of support for the institutional order that we are overthrowing, will not support the popular will in its decision to build socialism in our country. These people overlook the patriotic consciousness of the Armed Forces and National Police, their professional tradition, and their submission to civilian rule. In the words of General Schneider himself, the Armed Forces, as "an integral and representative part of the Nation and a foundation of the State, serve both permanent and temporal interests, and counterbalance those periodic changes that govern political life under the rule of law."

For my part, Gentlemen Members of the National Congress, I declare that since this institution is based on the popular vote, there is nothing in its nature to keep it from renovating itself and becoming a true People's Parliament. And I assure you that the Chilean Armed Forces and National Police, faithful to their duty and tradition of not interfering in the political process, will be the backbone of a social order that corresponds to the popular will as expressed in terms established by the constitution—a more just, more humane, and more generous order for all, but especially for the workers, who until now have given so much and received almost nothing.

The difficulties we confront are not in this arena. They really are to be found in the extraordinary complexity of the tasks that await us: to institutionalize the political road to socialism—and do this starting from our present reality, a society oppressed by the backwardness and poverty of dependence and underdevelopment—to break with the factors that cause this backwardness and, meanwhile, build a new socioeconomic structure able to provide for collective prosperity.

The causes of our backwardness were and still are to be found in our traditional ruling classes' intimate connection to both external subordination and internal exploitation. They grew rich through their association with foreign interests and their appropriation of the surplus produced by the workers, leaving the latter only the absolute minimum necessary to restore their ability to labor.

Our first task is to undo this stifling structure that only generates a deformed type of growth. But we must build a new economy in a way that simultaneously follows on the old one without a loss of continuity; that, as far as possible, maintains the productive and technical capacity we have managed to develop despite the vicissitudes of underdevelopment; and that avoids a crisis artificially created by those who are seeing their archaic privileges abolished.

Beyond these basic problems, there is another challenge that seems the essential question of our times: How can we restore a sense of mission to humanity, especially the youth, that infuses us with a new joy of living and confers a dignity to our existence? There is no other way than being inspired by the noble effort to carry out great impersonal tasks like overcoming the human condition itself, until now debased by the division between the privileged and the dispossessed.

No one today can imagine solutions to the problems of the far-off future, when all peoples will have reached a level of abundance to satisfy their material necessities, and inherited the cultural patrimony of humanity. But here and now, in Chile and in Latin America, we have the possibility and the duty to unleash our creative energies, especially those of our youth, for missions that will move us far more than any past undertaking.

Such is our hope: to build a world that overcomes the division between rich and poor—and in our case, to build a society that outlaws the war of all against all in the economic realm, in which the struggle for professional advantage has no meaning, where there is not the indifference toward the fate of others that turns the powerful into exploiters of the weak.

There have been few times in which people have so needed faith in themselves and their ability to remake the world and renew life as we do now.

This is an unparalleled time, when the material means exist to realize the past's most exalted utopias. Only the weight of a heritage of greed, fear, and obsolete institutional traditions keeps us from reaching this goal. Overcoming this heritage is all that stands between our age and the era of a liberated humanity on the world scale. This is the only way to summon humanity to reconstruct themselves, not as the products of a past of slavery and exploitation, but as the conscious realization of their most noble potentialities. This is the socialist ideal.

16

The Communist Parties

A CONTINENTAL REVOLUTION*
Rodney Arismendi

Rodney Arismendi, General Secretary of the Uruguayan Communist Party, former congressman, and author of several political and philosophical works (including *Soviet Justice Defends the World: The Moscow Trials*, 1938; *Haya de la Torre and the Philosophy of Marxism*, 1946; *The Communist Party and the Intellectuals*, 1948), is certainly one of the most intelligent and cultured representatives of the pro-Soviet Marxist current.

Unlike other Communist leaders (for example the Argentines and Brazilians), Arismendi has collaborated with the Cuban leadership, playing an important role as conciliator between the Castroists and the Communist parties at the OLAS conference.

The following pages, taken from a 1961 article in the Soviet journal *Kommunist*, attempt to incorporate the Cuban experience and its results into the context of the traditional theories of the Latin American Communist parties.

REVOLUTIONARY THEORY VERIFIES ITS ABILITY TO RESOLVE THE BURNING PROBLEMS OF LATIN AMERICA

A second element to take into account in any understanding of the importance of the Cuban Revolution in Latin America is that, for the first time, it radically carried out the mature, fundamental tasks that our social development has placed before the continental revolution in general and before each people in particular. Until then, the struggles of the Latin American peoples had not been able to break the imperialist yoke and the power of the large landowners and big capitalists.[1]

The bourgeois-democratic revolutions that did begin in some countries— the Mexican Revolution during the imperialist epoch and the Bolivian

---

*Rodney Arismendi, *Problemas de una revolución continental* (Montevideo: Ed. Pueblos Unidos, n.d.), pp. 20–22, 50–54.
[1]The War of Independence (1810–30), which liberated the Iberian-American colonies from Spanish and Portuguese rule, won political independence but generally left unsolved the fundamental problems of the bourgeois-democratic revolution.

Revolution after World War II—only went halfway: this is one more proof of the contradictory and dual character of the national bourgeoisie and its organic inability to lead the democratic struggle for national liberation in Latin America in a profound manner.

The Cuban Revolution, on the contrary, quickly carried out the general anti-imperialist and democratic tasks of the revolution and laid the material bases for the transition to more advanced social forms.[2]

For these reasons, Cuba today incarnates, as the Declaration of the Communist and Workers Parties of Latin America, meeting in Havana in August 1960, correctly stated, *"the patriotic and democratic aspirations of all our peoples, whose riches are harvested by Yankee imperialism and its accomplices, the latifundistas and the anti-national big capitalists, and whose sovereignty is mediated by the dictates of North American foreign policy."*[3]

In this sense, it is the perfect example of an anti-imperialist and agrarian revolution. But, as the Cubans themselves point out, this revolution is an "advanced popular revolution" in regard to the class forces that sustain it and the radical methods it uses. The social classes that are objectively interested in the realization of these historic tasks are the workers, the peasants, the urban middle classes, and the national bourgeoisie. But the motor forces of the revolution, those that move it forward, are mainly the workers, the poor peasants, and the radical sectors of the urban petty bourgeoisie."[4]

This situation is undoubtedly a peculiarity of the Cuban Revolution; nevertheless, neither the specificity of its direction nor its advanced character lessens its consequences for all Latin American revolutions, whose rhythms of development are indeed different, but whose essential problems and general tasks are the same. While making this statement, we caution

---

[2]The revolution expropriated and nationalized North American imperialist corporations valued at a billion dollars; expropriated and nationalized the property of the supporters of the dictatorship and the enemies of the revolution; carried out a radical agrarian reform, destroyed the *latifundio*, divided the land among the peasants and agricultural workers and nationalized those lands whose division would not be economically feasible, and began a broad plan of industrial development and agricultural diversification with the generous aid of the socialist camp; adopted important measures to the material and cultural benefit of the workers; destroyed the old military apparatus and state bureaucracy and began the building of a new revolutionary power based on the armed people, organized in the rebel army and workers' and peasants' militias. In international relations, the new revolutionary Cuban government put into practice an independent and peaceful foreign policy, became the implacable opponent of North American imperialism, and opened friendly relations with the socialist camp and all peace-loving and anti-colonialist peoples.
[3]Reprinted in *Estudios* (theoretical and political journal edited by the Executive Committee of the Communist Party of Uruguay), n. 17, 1960.
[4]Blas Roca, "Report to the Eighth National Assembly of the Popular Socialist Party," *Estudios*, n. 17, 1960.

that we are referring to the revolution's content and most general experiences. There is no room here for a petty-bourgeois extremism that abstracts from objective conditions and takes this or that particular form of struggle employed by the Cuban revolutionaries as a unique recipe.

It would be a mistake to think that bells chime the same hour throughout the continent; this could lead us to an improper schematism or the infantile sin of skipping stages. But we feel that the Cuban Revolution, by its mere existence, has forced the pace of history's twists and turns, opened new wounds, and moved all struggles onto a higher plane. It would therefore be incredibly shortsighted to overlook the *qualitative change the Cuban Revolution has introduced in the continent's general situation, the experience of the masses, the direction of different classes and social layers and their mutual struggles, and the explosiveness of all these contradictions.*

The wave of mass action brought on by the Cuban Revolution confirms all this. The battle of ideas being fought in our countries over the last year and a half revolves around Cuba or is directly or indirectly connected to the debate stirred up by the revolution's actions. Imperialism, the *latifundistas*, and the big capitalists are filling the press and the airwaves with systematic slander against the Cuban Revolution. Workers, students, peasants, intellectuals, and the advanced sections of the national bourgeoisie are inundating the streets, factories, and classrooms with a passionate gust of solidarity through the most diverse and active forms of struggle.

Why We Speak of a Continental Revolution

When we speak of a qualitative change in the general continental situation, we are thinking precisely of the essential unity of the Latin American revolution in our epoch, and of the Cuban Revolution as an expression of this and as a factor that, acting back upon this unity, itself becomes a conditioning element within it.

One merit of the Cuban revolutionaries is their conception of the revolution in continental terms. This should not be understood in the provocative sense that Yankee imperialism and the traitorous ruling classes attribute to it; they accuse its revolutionary government of "exporting the revolution," while they organize an invasion of Cuba! Revolutions are not exported or imported!

Almost all the liberators of last century had a clear consciousness of the continental character of the revolution. "We are a nation of republics," said Simon Bolívar. Many things have changed since then, and our wishes cannot undo what history has done. There are more than twenty republics geographically located on our continent, if we include the islands and the French, Dutch, and British colonies. Yet this diversity, and at times fragmentation (as Lenin warned in his notes on imperialism), constitutes an obstacle to understanding the united and international character of the Latin American revolution.

At times, the need to struggle against petty-bourgeois utopians who babble about Latin American unity or confederation in the context of its current structures leads us to overlook the active, and not merely speculative, idea of the essential unity of the Latin American revolutionary process. The ruling classes and even the most shameless agents of Yankee imperialism use nationalism to pit one country against another and negate the idea of a common front. In the nineteenth century, English diplomacy proceeded similarly with the independence leaders, and Yankee imperialism aims to act this way in Central and South America.

Only the internationalist logic of the proletariat can practically resolve those problems that have been created by the unity and diversity of the Latin American revolution. This is why we believe that we can and must speak of a Latin American revolution, which does not invalidate the existence of the particular paths, rhythms, and timing of the Cuban, Brazilian, Argentine, and Chilean revolutions, etc. . . .

SOCIAL PHILOSOPHY AND THE PROGRAM OF THE CONCILIATIONIST BIG BOURGEOISIE

The principal political goal of the North American government is, first, to tie the interests of the old ruling classes, the *latifundistas*, and the antinational big bourgeoisie to its own. Yet at the same time, it must reluctantly face the new situation that has increased the role of the conciliationist big bourgeoisie in many Latin American countries. These elements occupy important positions in major political parties in Argentina, Uruguay, Chile, Brazil, and Colombia. Betancourt, the president of Venezuela, and some Central American politicians follow the sociopolitical philosophy of this layer of the Latin American big bourgeoisie. These economically powerful layers of the bourgeoisie are not directly connected to the imperialist monopolies, but do have certain links with them; they prefer, despite recurring friction, to negotiate with the Yankee imperialists to the detriment of the people and the nation. Their objective position is determined by their connections with the sectors of *latifundistas* that have evolved in a capitalist direction, by their privileged position in the socioeconomic structure, and by the history and severity of their class struggle with the proletariat.

In regard to its orientation toward foreign policy, the position of the conciliationist big bourgeoisie is expressed in its failed attempt to resolve frequent differences and consistently sharp quarrels with the U.S., while maintaining the fiction of Pan-Americanism and without breaking with the

O.A.S.—that is, within the context of Yankee international strategy. Internally, its economic program and propaganda include the ideas of "developing" capitalism and pursuing industrialization without breaking *latifundista* relations of production—developing capitalism in the most painful way, to the detriment of the working masses. Thus it falls into the apparent paradox of opposing the imperialist monopolies in the internal market, while asking the "aid" of foreign capital to accelerate this industrialization; it hopes to expand the internal market while avoiding any radical solution of the agrarian problem; it promotes commerce with the socialist countries at times, and then, despite its advantages, trembles if Yankee imperialism and the sellout bourgeoisie accuse it of playing the game of the Communists. In Uruguay, we say this layer of the big bourgeoisie "has its heart in Washington, but its wallet in Montevideo."

The material basis of these contradictory attitudes of the conciliationist big bourgeoisie must be sought in the relatively important but deformed process of capitalist development that is characteristic of our countries.

The sociopolitical thought of this important sector of the bourgeoisie is to be found in the so-called "development" theory that currently influences layers of both the national bourgeoisie and petty bourgeoisie. This theory, which was the subject of a sociology seminar organized by the Center for the Investigation of Social Science in Rio de Janeiro, substitutes the confused expression "undeveloped countries" for a scientific definition of the structure of the dependent countries. Underdevelopment, as we all know, is the result of the uneven development of capitalism, the frustration of the bourgeois-democratic revolution on whole continents because of the formation of the imperialist colonial system, and the maintenance of pre-capitalist relations in a good part of the world. "Development" theory avoids defining the structure of these countries as the consequence of the presence of imperialism and the *latifundio*, and promotes the goal of raising the per capita national product, seeing this as a simple quantitative development of the productive forces without breaking the old relations of production. From this, it infers the half-truth that a greater availability of "investment capital" is an urgent necessity; this could come from abroad, or from "greater productivity" achieved by the pillage of the peasantry and the intensified exploitation of the workers, or by avoiding "superfluous spending" on social legislation, culture, and public health.

"Development" theory reflects, on the one hand, the tendency toward capitalist development and, on the other, the lack of will to resolutely fight for national independence against imperialism and for profound democratic transformations against the *latifundistas*. The best-known example of this thinking and posture on the cardinal topics of the Latin American revolution was given by President Kubitschek of Brazil when he put forward his

Operation Pan-America in response to the anti-Nixon demonstrations. But sectors of the Battlistas in Uruguay, the Argentine and Chilean Radicals, Colombian Liberals, Betancourt in Venezuela, and many "superrevolutionaries" in the Mexican official party and other Central and South American politicians think basically along the same lines.

Their essential strategy is to get Washington to aid Latin America and ward off the "Communist threat" by demonstrating the continent's importance for the international strategy of the U.S.[5] They overlook the fact that a half-century of relations with the U.S. has shown what Perogrullo already knew—that you can't get a pear from an elm tree, or oil from a brick.

As a result of Operation Pan-America, but also because of the development of a nationalist trend, the U.S. had to organize the Committee of 21, which has already met three times amidst disasters, complaints, and flirtations directed at Yankee imperialism. The third meeting of the Committee of 21 took place in Bogota, after one in Costa Rica, where the leaders of Latin America, among them the representatives of the conciliationist big bourgeoisie, agreed to sign a declaration against Cuba based on a promise by Herter of a collective loan from the U.S.

During this last meeting of the 21, the U.S. again mocked the hopes of the southern governments by offering them . . . $500 million to divide among themselves, depending on the approval of the Congress in Washington!

The Cuban delegate, R. Botti, judged the results of the conference in this way:

> At bottom, what the U.S. is now proposing is a mechanism invented to quiet the militant hopes awakened among the working peoples by the Cuban revolution. . . . And, "on the other hand," it hopes to "shift attention from the fundamental problem: independent, self-sustaining economic development."

THE PRINCIPAL LINES OF DEVELOPMENT FOR LATIN AMERICA'S FUTURE ARE IN DISPUTE TODAY

The landowners and the sellout big bourgeoisie consent to aggression against Cuba; the conciliationist big bourgeoisie, for its part, uses the

---

[5]"This situation [the Latin American economy] is a fertile field for action by the Communists. There is no democratic government that can resist a prolonged economic crisis. If the U.S. wishes to maintain democratic governments, it must first contribute to supporting their economies" (from a speech by the Brazilian Schmidt at the Buenos Aires meeting of the Committee of 21). The Colombian Turbay Ayala, at the Third Conference of the 21 in Bogota, echoed this idea: "When we have asked the U.S. to assume a new attitude to her Latin American brothers, we are simply inviting them to complement our efforts to avoid uncontrollable situations that could certainly compromise the structure of our institutions, to the disadvantage of us all." We could gather a whole anthology of such speeches, with slight differences of nationality or style.

specter of revolution to horse trade with Yankee imperialism, in the absurd hope that this will make them stop plundering Latin America and instead aid its development.

On October 29, a new "high level committee to coordinate inter-American plans and studies on development" was created in Washington by the O.A.S. The committee members are J. Mora, O.A.S. President; Filipe Herrera, President of the Inter-American Development Bank; and R. Prebisch of CEPAL. In his speech, the Colombian Ambassador, Sans de Santamaría, said: *"Latin America is in a race between evolution and revolution in its struggle to achieve economic development."*[6]

Actually, this statement does reveal the basis of the dispute over the future of Latin America. Leaving aside the phraseology and its more-or-less plausible political cover, the class content and the essential programs of this dispute are here on display. Besides the *latifundistas* and the sellout big bourgeoisie, whose historical interests are intrinsically tied to imperialism and the worst characteristics of this crisis-ridden, decrepit socioeconomic structure, the struggle for the future of Latin America is being fought between the *"development" strategy of the conciliationist big bourgeoisie and the program of democratic revolution and national liberation.*

This struggle involves the whole of social and political life, is embodied in the sharp and complex class struggle, and is openly or covertly incorporated into the terrain of ideological confrontation. The dispute is joined as much on the plane of anti-imperialist struggle as in programmatic postulates on the agrarian question. In this field, the struggle goes beyond the two classic paths of bourgeois development that Lenin analyzed in his day. Today, the slow transformation of the *latifundios* in a bourgeois manner is confronted by the revolutionary line of a radical agrarian reform. Only the proletariat will be able to steadfastly maintain this second path, uniting the national and agrarian objectives of the revolution, the foundation of a solid worker-peasant alliance, and thereby guarantee the victory of the democratic revolution of national liberation.

The Declaration of the Communist and Workers Parties expresses this quite well:

> The alliance of the working class and the peasants is the most important force for conquering and defending national independence, carrying out profound democratic transformations and assuring social progress. This alliance must be the foundation of a broad national front. The degree of participation of the national bourgeoisie in the liberation struggle depends to no small degree on its strength and solidity.

---

[6]*El Pais*, Montevideo, November 1, 1960.

SOME WAYS TO BUILD THE DEMOCRATIC NATIONAL FRONT

The Latin American peoples are building the national democratic front, the social force capable of carrying out the verdict of history. Its vanguard is the proletariat and its foundation the worker-peasant alliance, around which are gathering the great masses of the middle layers and the advanced sections of the national bourgeoisie. To reach their strategic objectives, these social forces must win over or neutralize the larger part of the national bourgeoisie and find support in the whole gamut of contradictions with Yankee imperialism and the sellout ruling classes.

This front is being built in all of Latin America, according to the particularities of national politics, whose structure and development are uneven.

THE MASSES ABOVE ALL

The leading role of the masses, their collective experience, and their impassioned entrance into the sociopolitical arena constitute one of the obvious characteristics of the current correlation of forces. Even negative episodes have proven this: for example, the major electoral changes that have occurred in various countries, brought on by demagogic illusions. But more recent events also verify this fact.

The fall of the dictatorships imposed by Yankee imperialism during the Cold War were not the consequence of palace coups or back-room deals. A third presence appeared in the contest: the popular masses and the proletariat. This was true even in those cases where the ruling classes controlled the situation, as in Colombia. The masses who overthrew the most ferocious dictatorships did not confront these tyrants only but also the hidden power behind the throne—Yankee imperialism and the anti-national ruling classes.

Those who gave battle and changed the political face of Latin America were the proletariat, the peasantry, the students, the urban middle classes, and the advanced wing of the national bourgeoisie.

THE POPULAR UNITY GOVERNMENT*
Luis Corvalán

Shortly after the electoral victory of Salvador Allende and the creation of the Popular Unity government in November 1970, Luis Corvalán published an article

---

*Luis Corvalán, "Chile, el pueblo al poder," *Revista Internacional*, n. 12, December 1970, in L. Corvalán, *Camino de Victoria* (Santiago: Ed. de Homenaje al cincuentenario del PCCh, September 1971), pp. 424–426. The full text of the article is in "Chile: The People Take Over," *World Marxist Review*, v. 13, n. 12, December 1970, pp. 5–12.

in the *World Marxist Review* (the international journal of the pro-Soviet Communists), developing the essential strategic axes that oriented the Chilean CP for the three years of the Allende government. This strategy was based on two fundamental precepts: the possibility of governing with the cooperation of the Christian Democracy and the armed forces' loyalty to the constitutional regime.

Luis Corvalán was arrested after the September 1973 coup and interned for four years in a military concentration camp.

Three months after the election and a month after the inauguration of the Popular Unity Government, the correlation of forces has changed in favor of the new regime. While the Christian Democracy is in opposition, it is not at war against the government; the majority find themselves ready to support some of its projects and measures. And as important, or even more so, the popular masses who voted for their candidate are closing ranks with the left parties. Even a section of those who voted for Alessandri seems to have a positive attitude.

These facts open the possibility of consolidating and broadening the unity of all anti-imperialist and anti-oligarchic forces.

Because of the very nature of the Chilean Revolution, the interests of the popular classes and sectors, and the need to isolate the reactionaries and defeat their seditious maneuvers, prevent foreign intervention, confront imperialist pressures, and find nationwide support for the government, the unity of the people can and must be developed still further and become a truly invincible force. This is the main question that must be resolved in the days ahead!

As the President of Chile, Salvador Allende, has said, his election was not the victory of a man but the triumph of a people.

It was the victory of a vast union of social and political forces organized around a program of profound, revolutionary transformations. The program foresees the nationalization of the country's basic natural resources, now under the control of foreign monopoly capital and the financial oligarchy; the nationalization of private banks, insurance companies, foreign trade, and retail monopolies, strategic industrial monopolies, and those activities that condition the country's economic and social development. It also includes advancing the land reform begun by the Christian Democratic government in a deeper and more coherent manner.

Under the Popular Unity Government, there will be three sectors of the economy: the sector of social property, formed by those enterprises now owned by the state, along with those to be expropriated; the private sector, made up of artisans and small and mid-sized merchants, farmers, and businessmen; and the mixed sector, made up of those businesses with both state and private capital . . . .

In regard to the armed forces, the Popular Unity bloc is for guaranteeing their national character and professional orientation through "technical training informed by the contributions of military science," which will allow them "to contribute to the economic development of the country" without prejudice to their essential work, defending national sovereignty and matters related to this function. The program states that, on this basis, it "is necessary to assure the armed forces the necessary material and technical means, a just and democratic system of remuneration, promotions, and pensions that guarantee economic security for officers, non-commissioned officers, and troops during their enlistment and after retirement, and the realistic opportunity for all of promotion based on personal qualifications."

As President Allende has repeatedly stated, the Popular Unity parties did not come to power in a struggle against the armed forces or any of its sectors. Meanwhile, the armed forces remained on the sidelines in the electoral struggle. And once the popular victory had been achieved, and shortly after its ratification by the Congress, they officially recognized this fact.

It is true we should not overlook the conditions under which the armed forces have been formed, especially the education and training they have received in recent decades under the influence of the Pentagon. But this does not qualify them as obsequious servants of imperialism and the ruling classes. Their professional spirit and respect for a government established in accordance with the constitution is dominant. In addition, the army and navy were created during the struggle for independence. The soldiers and non-commissioned officers in the three branches come from modest social backgrounds, and almost all the officers come from the middle classes. It is a long time since the oligarchy and the richest of the bourgeoisie interested their children in a military career. We must especially take into account that no institution can remain impermeable to social convulsions, closed to the winds that move the rest of the world, and foreign or indifferent to the drama of the millions and millions of human beings who live in the most atrocious misery.

The behavior of a good part of the Dominican army during the Yankee invasion of their territory and the progressive character of the military government in Peru show that the armed forces need not be viewed with dogmatic criteria.

It is true that the military institutions also need changes, but they cannot be imposed. They must grow from inside, from the convictions of their own members.

As for the rest, time will tell.

In conclusion, the question of the character of the state and its institutions and the question of the role of the working class require practical solutions above all. This is what we seek, on the basis of constantly securing, not weakening, the unity of the people and the cohesion and functioning of the new government. Certainly, this cannot happen overnight. But the nature of the forces that are taking leadership in the country allows us to state that there has been a basic change in the class composition and orientation of the government and that this change can spread through all the institutions. The new constitutional state must be a popular state.

17

Revolutionary Historiography

LATIN AMERICA: FEUDAL OR CAPITALIST?*
Luis Vitale

The historian Luis Vitale (b.1927), an Argentine-born Chilean national and author of the remarkable *Marxist Interpretation of the History of Chile*, wrote the following article in 1966 and thereby stimulated an important polemic on the nature of Latin American social formations. Vitale's theoretical starting point is that Latin America is not a copy of nineteenth-century Europe, as it has not followed the same historical stages as European society. This debate has important political implications, as is recognized by Vitale in his conclusion.

A former leader of the MIR and a Trotskyist militant, Vitale was arrested after the 1973 coup and interned in a concentration camp for three years.

III

The reformist's third thesis maintains that a feudal aristocracy, born in the colonies, led the independence struggle against Spain. We say that Spain conquered America to incorporate it into a new system of capitalist production, not to reproduce the European feudal cycle. This "imprint" not only has repercussions in the development of social classes, but generates the causes of the American revolution of the early nineteenth century. The Spanish colonization created a native bourgeoisie that, upon developing and entering into contradiction with imperial interests, led the emancipation of Latin America.

From its birth, the development of Latin America was subordinated to its position as a colony. Its economy was born deformed, to serve the interests of the metropolis. This characteristic of Latin America, as a continent that produces raw materials, dates from the colonial era. The evolution of autonomous industry—a basic condition, along with an agrarian reform, for creating an internal market—was restricted by Spain. The colony ful-

---

*Luis Vitale, "América Latina, ¿feudal o capitalista?," *Estrategia* (Santiago), 1966.

filled its dual function as an exporter of raw materials and importer of finished products.

Spain exercised a monopoly of colonial exports and imports, making it impossible for native producers to obtain better prices in other markets and buy cheaper manufactures. To pacify protests against this monopoly, the Bourbon kings began a new, reformist policy, allowing the opening of thirty-three new ports for American trade in 1778. A relative apogee in commerce raised the expectations of the native bourgeoisie. The Bourbon concessions, instead of lessening discontent in the colonies, served as a spur to the aspirations of the native landowners, mine owners, and merchants. The reforms urged by Charles III's liberal ministers show that the colonies were already lost to Spain much before 1810.

The colonial economy generated a bourgeoisie that produced raw materials. The capitalist nature of the colonization determined that in Latin America, the bourgeoisie would be born directly from the colony rather than passing through the European cycle. But, given its condition as a dependent supplier of raw materials, this bourgeoisie did not attain a modern aspect. It was not an industrial bourgeoisie, but a bourgeoisie that produced and exported raw materials. Its interest was not in the development of an internal market, but in the positioning of its products in the European market.

The fact that well-to-do colonials acquired titles of nobility and established entailed estates and other vestiges of feudalism has led liberals and reformists to commit the sociological error of characterizing this social layer as a feudal aristocracy. The truth is that these feudal institutions were only the formal, exterior aspect of a social class based upon the inexorable laws of an international capitalist market in formation. Even their noble titles were acquired with money that the colonials had obtained from their essentially bourgeois activity, not by bathing themselves in the blue blood of the feudal nobility.

The very existence of other social classes demonstrates that the colonies did not develop in a feudal manner. The petty bourgeoisie, whose role has been underestimated by historians, was composed of public employees, retail merchants, small farmers, estate foremen, small industrialists, grocers, butchers, army officers, lawyers, etc. Such a structure among the middle classes is not characteristic of feudalism. The presence of artisans, who tended to overwhelm the medieval regime of corporations, and the development of *mestizo* wage labor in the mines, fields, plantations, construction sites, and the cattle industries show the capitalist road, however incipient and embryonic, followed by the colonies.

IV

The reformists' fourth thesis claims that the feudal aristocracy governed the Latin American countries during the nineteenth and twentieth centuries, retarding capitalist evolution and the rise of a national bourgeoisie. Their conclusion is that these countries have not yet completed the stage of capitalist development, a task that the "progressive bourgeoisie" must accomplish.

We believe, to the contrary, that our countries have been led, not by feudal lords, but by a bourgeoisie that has essentially been a producer of raw materials. This bourgeoisie had no interest in developing the internal market and national industry during the nineteenth century because its basic source of revenue was the export trade. After aborting the early plans for the development of industry outlined by the most advanced wing of the first revolutionary generation of 1810, the landowners and merchants—who had committed themselves with England and France to allow the introduction of foreign merchandise in return for good treatment of their raw materials—were the gravediggers of the incipient native artisanal industries. Free trade signified an advantage to the native bourgeois exporters who held power, but meant the destruction of the small regional workshops that had reached an apex during the Wars of Independence, supplying necessities to the patriot armies. The outward appearance of this social class, with no interest in the development of industry, has led it to be characterized as feudal. Although the exploitation of workers employed by the *gamonales* did maintain some vestiges of feudalism (*pongaje* in Bolivia, for example), the system of production was not feudal but capitalist, since its products were destined for the external market.

A few decades after independence, the process of primitive accumulation of land accelerated with the violent conquest of properties still held by indigenous communities. The system of large-scale *latifundios*, which some confuse with feudalism because of their size and backwardness, was thereby strengthened. During the second half of the nineteenth century, the basis was laid for the modern hacienda, the fruit of the process of development of agrarian capitalism conditioned by the highly industrialized nations' ever-growing demand for raw materials. Capitalist agriculture did not grow in Latin America because of the development of industrial production and the internal market, as in the Europe of the Industrial Revolution, but in direct connection to demand in the world market.

For certain economists, capitalist development and the social importance of the bourgeoisie are only connected to factory mechanization or advanced industry: that is, where there is no industry, there cannot be capitalism or a bourgeoisie. This criterion serves to measure whether one country is more advanced than another, but only sows confusion if it is applied to colonial or semi-colonial countries. These countries do not have advanced industry, but they do have a system of capitalist production in agriculture, cattle-raising, etc., and a social class—the national landowning and mining bourgeoisie—that is ruled by the laws of value, surplus value, and the rate of profit. Around the middle of the last century, this class introduced the most modern means of communication, the railroad, into Latin America, and started a banking system that began to finance farming, ranching, sugar mills, and foundries. Chilean copper and saltpeter mines reached a high level of productivity. Argentine landowners increased their export of cattle with the introduction of new techniques, and agrarian capitalism began to reach new heights. The Cuban landowning bourgeoisie became the world's largest producer of sugar, as did the Bolivians with tin. Our continent's exporting class was already riding a capitalist and not a feudal pony over a century ago. Latin America's backwardness was not produced by a feudal system that never existed, but by its role as a producer of raw materials dependent on the world market. It is true that there were (and are) indigenous communities and semifeudal vestiges in the relations between classes. But these factors of underdevelopment coexist with the most modern and advanced technology. Alongside small, family production and pitiful artisanal workshops arose great capitalist enterprises. These are the distinctive signs of the unequal and combined development that characterizes the backward nations, according to the astute judgment of Leon Trotsky, who complemented Marx and Lenin's theory of unequal development with the designation "combined."

The inauguration of a new stage of capitalism at the end of the nineteenth century—imperialism—sealed the fate of Latin America. Investments by foreign finance capital transformed our dependent countries into semi-colonial ones. Raw materials that had been in the hands of the national bourgeoisie passed to a great degree into the hands of, first, European and, later, Yankee imperialism. The history of the surrender of Chilean copper, Bolivian tin, Central American plantations, etc., is well known, which is why we will not discuss this phenomenon of semi-colonization. We do wish to look at industry, since the revisionists grant such importance to the progressivity and the national and anti-imperialist character of the industrial bourgeoisie.

The Latin American industrial bourgeoisie was born with direct links to the landowners and imperialism, unlike in Europe, where they were generated in the struggle against the landowning nobility in a historical epoch characterized by free trade and competitive capitalism. At the end of the last century, imperialism not only inundated our markets with its manufactures, but from the start also controlled the majority of the shares of the principal industries created in our countries. There was a relative growth of industry during the two world wars because of the difficulties in importing manufactured goods. This process, which happened during the stage of monopoly capitalism, occurred in the light industrial sector (textile, shoes, etc.).

Reformists believe there is a great contradiction between imperialism and the development of this industrial production. The truth is that the evolution of industry has occurred under the control of imperialism and has meant even greater dependence, since light industry must purchase machinery from foreign monopolies. The importation of machinery is precisely one of the conditions that characterize the semi-colonial countries. The development of light industry in the backward countries is in the interest of imperialism, especially North American imperialism, because it creates a new market for its heavy industry. One of the objectives of the Alliance for Progress, when it praises "agrarian reform," is the development of light industry in Latin America (as a result of an increase in the purchasing power of the peasantry), which would signify a greater demand for machinery and increase the sale of North American capital goods. This objective of the alliance has been shamelessly promoted by the spokesmen of Wall Street. By claiming that imperialism and industrial development are incompatible in backward nations, the revisionists seem to ignore that what is most important to the modern great monopolies is not the export of consumer goods (clothing, shoes, food, washing machines, etc.), but the sale of the products of its heavy industry (durable goods). According to Lenin, imperialism—the export of capital in the form of means of production—has succeeded the old capitalism, which was interested in the export of merchandise. Finally, the Latin American industrial bourgeoisie, which developed with intimate links to foreign monopoly capital at the height of the imperialist epoch, now more than ever depends on the importation of machinery produced by the metropolis.

The native industrial bourgeoisie was born in combination with the other ruling classes. The squalid capital of national industry comes from the investments of landowners or mine owners. The industrialists themselves acquire lands they then convert into *latifundios*. In Latin America, intimate links exist between foreign finance capital, the landowners, and the industrial bourgeoisie—sectors that are becoming increasingly monopolized.

In summary, it is untrue that a feudal aristocracy has ruled the Latin American countries. In fact, power has been exercised by a bourgeoisie that exports raw materials—which has conditioned the backwardness of our continent. The imperialist stage meant the transfer of these raw materials into the hands of foreign finance capital. Our teething industrial bourgeoisie has remained dependent on imperialism because of its historic inability to develop heavy industry, a basic condition for the progressive evolution of a country at the current stage of civilization. The backwardness of Latin America is not the product of feudalism, but of a bourgeoisie that has exhausted all the possibilities of development for a semi-colonial continent in the midst of the imperialist epoch. Therefore it is wrong to claim, as revisionists do, that we need a stage of practical capitalist development to be carried out by the "progressive bourgeoisie."

V

We now come to the reformists' final thesis, the goal of all this pseudo-historical labor by the revisionists: "The popular parties should support the progressive bourgeoisie against the feudal oligarchy, to carry out bourgeois-democratic tasks through a National Liberation Front."

The political strategy of the revisionists is based on the theory of revolution by stages. Since, in their view, Latin America has been ruled by a feudal oligarchy, we must first make an anti-feudal revolution, at whose head should be the progressive bourgeoisie, to carry out a stage of capitalist development that has not yet occurred. This historical schema, fabricated to justify a false political strategy, has nothing to do with reality. Latin America has not been a mechanical copy of eighteenth-century Europe, where the new, rising bourgeoisie had to overthrow feudalism to initiate the cycle of bourgeois-democratic revolutions. Our continent has not travelled through the classic Old World stages, but passed directly from primitive indigenous communities to an incipient capitalism introduced by the Spanish colonization. After its independence from Spain, Latin America was not governed by an imaginary feudal oligarchy, but by a bourgeoisie that produced raw materials, conditioning our continent's backwardness through its dependence on the world capitalist market.

History has shown this bourgeoisie is incapable of carrying out these democratic tasks. The combined character of the ruling classes determines that the national bourgeoisie, including its industrial wing, cannot and does not want to carry out an agrarian reform, because all these classes are involved in land ownership. Thus it is illusory, not to say criminal, to maintain that the industrial bourgeoisie, which has had a large share of power in the postwar Latin America, is leading the struggle for land reform. The industrial bourgeoisie is also unable to break with imperialism because of its level of dependence on finance capital. It may have certain conflicts with some foreign businesses that introduce products to compete with local light industry, but this contest never goes beyond imposing weak tariff barriers. A class whose very existence depends on imperialism cannot be asked to commit hara-kiri for the simple reason that a class never goes against its own interests. Therefore, land reform and the expulsion of imperialism have and will only be carried out against the industrial bourgeoisie. As Huberman and Sweezy have correctly pointed out: "While there are conflicting interests and ephemeral alliances, the supposed fundamental contradictions between the 'national bourgeoisie,' the 'feudal lords,' the 'comprador bourgeoisie,' and the 'imperialists,' . . . despite all the hubbub, are to a great degree a myth." To understand the relationship between the national bourgeoisie and imperialism, we only have to apply the geometric principle of identity, rather than that of equality. Imperialism is not exactly the same as the national bourgeoisie. The friction between the two occurs in the context of the unity of foreign finance capital, the landowners, and the industrial bourgeoisie. Therefore, their antagonisms are secondary, and these classes close ranks in the struggle against the common enemy: the proletariat and the peasantry. The policies of Bonapartist governments like those of Perón, Vargas, Goulart, Paz Estenssoro, etc., never intended to break with imperialism, merely to blackmail it to obtain a more advantageous agreement on the division of national income.

Reformist illusions in the capacity of the "progressive" bourgeoisie to lead a democratic stage of land reform, national independence, and industrial development have been swept away by historical experience. The course of the Russian, Chinese, Cuban, and other revolutions has demonstrated the Revolution is a single, permanent, and uninterrupted process. Just as Trotsky anticipated in 1905, there is not first a democratic stage, led by the bourgeoisie or in alliance with it, and then a socialist stage. If Fidel Castro and Che Guevara had stopped at the anti-imperialist and agrarian struggle, leaving the national bourgeoisie intact, church bells would be tolling for the dead in Cuba, as in Arbenz's Guatemala. Either the revolution advances, expropriating the expropriators, or the bourgeoisie prepares a counterrevolutionary bloodbath for the people, as happened in Indonesia, with its 100,000 Communists murdered for the "progressive" bourgeois government of Sukarno. The modern history of the semi-colonial countries has shown that only the proletariat, along with the peasantry and the other groups of the poor, can guarantee land reform and the destruction of imperialism through the social revolution. The revolutionary government, based on organs of the armed power of the workers and peasants, fulfills the democratic tasks that the bourgeoisie was unable to carry out, which also include tasks of a socialist variety, as the Russian, Chinese, and Cuban experiences have demonstrated. The fact that the Revolution in the backward countries cannot immediately carry out 100 percent of its socialist objectives does not mean that the bourgeoisie still has a progressive role to play.

The tactic of the peaceful road is determined by the theory of revolution by stages. The revisionists guarantee the respectable bourgeois midwife that the delivery of the antifeudal revolution will be painless. Otherwise, how could this lady possibly join a common front with those bug-eyed partisans of violence—guerrillas who, with no respect for good manners or gentleman's agreements, might jump over the agreed stages and expropriate not only imperialism and the "feudal oligarchy," but also their own local patrons, the "progressive" industrialists?

The new Latin American generation, arising from the furnace of the Cuban Revolution, already refuses to be mystified by the old schemas of revolution by stages, whether called democratic, antifeudal, agrarian, national, or anti-imperialist. It knows there is only one road to defeat our centuries-old enemies and our continent's backwardness: *the armed popular insurrection to establish socialism.*

For those theoreticians in unparalleled and cowardly retreat who claim that the working class and peasantry of our countries are not yet mature, history has been charged with writing their definitive epitaph: the first social revolution took place in one of the most backward countries in the world, as did the second, third, fourth, and fifth.

MEXICO: THE INTERRUPTED REVOLUTION*

Adolfo Gilly

Adolfo Gilly, an Argentinian Trotskyist, author of several works on the Cuban economy, and a collaborator of the North American journal *Monthly Review*, has lived in Mexico for many years. Arrested in April 1966 for participating in a "subversive conspiracy," he was imprisoned for six years. While in the Lecumberri prison in Mexico, he wrote *The Interrupted Revolution*, which was published in 1971; it was a great success and stimulated much discussion in the Mexican left. The book is a study of the Mexican revolution of 1910–20, in light of Trotsky's theory of permanent revolution.

The two selections below relate to the revolutionary role of the peasantry: the occupation of Mexico City in December 1914 by Pancho Villa's Division of the North and Emiliano Zapata's Liberating Army of the South, and the Zapatista peasant commune in Morelos State in Southern Mexico.

MEXICO CITY, DECEMBER 1914

The capital, occupied by the peasant armies, is the synthesis of what is happening in the country as a whole. The peasant war has reached its highest point. The old oligarchy has forever lost its power and most of its

---

*Adolfo Gilly, *La revolución interrumpida, Mexico, 1910–1920: una guerra campesina por la tierra y el poder* (Mexico City: Ed. El Caballito, 1977), pp. 139–141, 151–152, 236–237.

property; this is something that had never happened in any Latin American country, nor would it happen again for many years. But the representatives of the new bourgeoisie have not yet been able to take this power into their own hands. Not only have they been unable to do this; they have had to give way under the blows of peasant arms and abandon the political center of the country, the capital, and the material symbol of power, the National Palace, which is occupied by Zapata's troops.

In reality, no one holds power. For it is not enough for the oligarchy to lose it and the bourgeoisie not have the strength to maintain it; someone must take it. And the peasant leadership does not take it. They do no more than keep it "in custody" (as they do the National Palace), and then hand it over to the petty-bourgeois leaders of the Convention. To exercise power, one needs a program. Applying a program demands a political strategy. Carrying out a strategy requires a party. The peasants had none of these, nor could they have had.

The proletariat was absent as an independent political force. There were proletarians in Villa's army, especially miners and railroad workers, but as individuals, not as a class force or tendency. There were large numbers of agricultural workers in both peasant armies. But no tendency or individual leader represented or assumed a proletarian class position. The anarchists (the Magonistas) were not an independent organization, but a diffuse petty-bourgeois tendency in the leadership of the incipient trade unions. And in their role both as union leaders and as a political current, the inclination of the anarcho-syndicalist leaders was the same in Mexico in those days as it has always been, everywhere: to collaborate and become entangled with bourgeois state power, rather than run the risk of tying their lot to the uncertain destiny of the armed peasants. Moreover, they had no program to offer the peasants, because the Magonista line, besides being filtered through the bureaucratic prism of the anarcho-syndicalist union leaders, was never a class program, nor did it have any connection to the reality of the class struggle, either as it really existed or as anarchist speculation imagined it to be.

The workers and artisans of the capital looked on the peasant armies with sympathy. They expressed their class solidarity, fraternity, and friendship in a thousand spontaneous ways when they entered Mexico City. But these sentiments never succeeded in establishing a worker and peasant alliance, lacking a program and policies to express this alliance and the organs to carry them out. The incipient unions and their leaders had none of these; the peasant leaders did not and could not understand the need for this alliance, tossed as they were between the radical and revolutionary impulses of their armed rank-and-file and their naive and petty-bourgeois illusions about "good laws" and "good and wise men" that neither they nor the peasant masses themselves had forsaken, despite their natural class distrust toward these pretentious gentlemen. In fact, prior experience could not eliminate these illusions; only the appearance of an independent proletarian axis could do this, since they were fed by the contradictory and intermediary situation of the peasantry in bourgeois society and by the absence of such a national and international axis.

No proletarian leadership or center existed on a national level, nor was there a single workers' state in the world that could serve as a guide, center of attraction, or point of support for the Mexican Revolution. The world revolution was at its lowest point in many years.

The international isolation of the Mexican revolution at this culminating moment not only determines this factor. It also serves to measure the historical feat of the Mexican peasants who, without knowing it, were at the apex of the world revolution during this month of December 1914, when they made themselves masters of Mexico City and took on the task of representing the masses of the whole country. And, naively but resolutely, they attempted to move forward with the task that history and their own bravery had placed on their shoulders.

The occupation of Mexico City by the peasant armies is one of the most beautiful and moving episodes of the whole Mexican Revolution, a precocious, violent, and systematic expression of the power of the masses that has left its mark on the country until today; it is one of the historical foundations of the pride and dignity of the Mexican peasantry, which has been unshaken by defeat, betrayal, or opposition. In the historical consciousness of the masses, it is a bridge to the workers' uprising, the taking of power, and the socialist revolution . . . .

What this powerful revolutionary thrust shows is that the peasants attempted to make themselves politically independent of the bourgeois government by installing a government themselves in the occupied capital, and did not simply maintain the war in the countryside. But peasant power mediated through the petty bourgeoisie (the drawing-room types, and Pancho Villa would say), since it never became a proletarian power, could only be a bourgeois power, suspended in air, in contradiction with the real bourgeois government of Carranza. But fundamentally, it was much more in contradiction with the very insurgent peasant base that supported it against Carranza. This is why, in the end, it acted as an agent of the latter against the peasant leadership.

Years later, with all his lucidity and cynicism, Martín Luis Guzman, the chronicler of constitutionalist indecision, put the matter this way in his book, *The Eagle and the Serpent*:

Eulalio, who wasn't born yesterday, took precise note of the situation in which we found ourselves. Three or four weeks in power (or whatever it was) were enough to strengthen his original idea that nothing could be done quickly, except gain time and find a way to escape Villa without falling into the hands of Carranza. But waiting meant defending himself—defending himself from the closer danger, which was Villa and Zapata—which is why we had to carry out one of the most incongruous policies that might be imagined: help our declared enemies, the Carrancistas, to defeat our official supporters, the Villistas and Zapatistas, to free us a bit from the tremendous pressure to which the nearer power was subjecting us.

The government of the Convention, which had been installed in the capital and supported by the armies that ruled the largest and most important part of the country, essentially signified that the revolution's dynamic demanded an organ that would express the power of the peasant masses in political terms; while they were unable to create one, their revolutionary push surpassed and rejected the limits of bourgeois power. So the Convention could not become an organ of power—which Guzman himself recognizes when he speaks of his stay "in power (or whatever it was)"—but only an unstable and conflicted alliance with a sector of the radicalized petty bourgeoisie. It was a sort of pre-Constituent Assembly and, like any constituent assembly or the like, it advanced two questions, but could not answer them: Where was the country going and who would lead the march? It could not answer the first, much less the second (whose answer is, definitely, whoever decides the first), because it lacked not words but material power: a program, organization, and weapons. This couldn't last for long, and didn't.

The government itself fully reflected this contradiction. It was a heterogeneous combination, without its own class base and without confidence in the masses; it was hostile to them, instead, since they held it prisoner. Actually, its most conscious elements had the perspective of negotiating with Obregón, and through him with Carranza, taking advantage of the power of the peasantry. To be accepted as interlocutors in such negotiations, they would have had to show that they controlled this power; but they could only show that they were secretly sabotaging it and that they controlled absolutely nothing. The perspective of its other members was completely unstable and nebulous; they were adventurers or innocents caught up in the revolutionary upsurge. As a group, they were a collection of petty-bourgeois opportunists, fools, adventurers, vacillators, and parasites, or, in the best of cases, lost souls. Unlike the leaders of history's other "peasant parties," their armed peasant base dominated the country—they were not a simple electoral mass—and had their own leaderships, in particular the Zapatistas, who were politically decisive and displayed a profound and armed distrust for the petty-bourgeois leaders; these weapons stood in the way of their maneuvers. This contradiction had to explode in the short term.

These petty bourgeois, unwilling even to dictate an agrarian reform law because it would give the peasant rank-and-file an anti-bourgeois basis from which to oppose or pressure them, were an obstacle by their mere presence. They hated, despised, and feared Villa and Zapata. Their presence, their methods, their actions, and their inaction built a petty-bourgeois barrier between the Villista and Zapatista peasants and the proletariat—which was completed on the other side by the anarcho-syndicalist union leaders who saw careers with Obregón, not with Villa or Zapata. They paralyzed and betrayed everyone. The most corrupt lived in luxurious surroundings abandoned by the bourgeoisie; the most foolish lived in the clouds. No one represented anything, except the absence of the proletariat as an independent political force and the inability of the peasants to play this role.

In other words, they represented two absences, two negatives that did not make a positive.

But if the government of the Constitutionalists was all of this, the fact of its creation expressed something more profound and longer-lasting than the individuals who made it up. It also meant that the peasant masses, through the military organization and centralization represented by Villa and the political intransigence represented by Zapata, could make a supreme effort to break with the bourgeoisie, a capability previously unknown in the history of peasant wars; under these conditions, they constitute themselves an independent national force and drag one section of the petty bourgeoisie along with them, even if only conditionally and temporarily, and powerfully influence the other section—the radical and Jacobin tendency of constitutionalism, in which the peasantry's weight will be most permanently expressed in a political manner during the revolution.

This supreme effort, though doomed to failure, was nevertheless the harbinger of the imminence of the era of victorious proletarian revolutions that opened three years later with the Russian Revolution, and a sign that the peasantry would finally be drawn as a mass from a bourgeois perspective and won to the socialist revolution.

The peasant war and the Mexican Revolution come at the boundary between two world-historic eras. Its protagonist, the Mexican peasantry, in attempting to establish its own national power with the useless petty-bourgeois instruments at hand, was a historical precursor of the worker and peasant government—in the same way, but in a different context, that the utopian socialists, on the theoretical level, were precursors of Marxism as a scientific theory of socialism and proletarian revolution.

THE MORELOS COMMUNE

After the retreat from Mexico City in January 1915, the peasant revolution, which had been fragilely united in Xochimilco and in the occupation of the capital in December 1914, was again split into two sectors, North and South—this time definitively. Unlike the earlier period, during which both sectors were carried forward toward unification and toward the conquest of the country and its power centers by an ascendant wave of mass struggle, the retreat now takes the form of a mutual withdrawal toward their regions of origin, with no future other than, first, a defensive struggle and, later, guerrilla warfare.

Nevertheless, as in any peasant war, which is by definition scattered and has no single center, the rhythm and forms of the retreat had different characteristics. The Carrancistas, as we have seen, concentrated all their military effort in 1915 against Villa's army. That is, they concentrated on defeating the peasant revolution's decisive military force, which at the same time potentially represented a bourgeois alternative—in Felipe Ángeles— that was supported by a sector of the peasantry, while the Carrancista bourgeois government was supported by sectors of the urban petty bourgeoisie, the proletariat, and even the peasantry. The military struggle against the Zapatistas was basically a holding action during this period; it didn't hope to defeat them yet, but merely keep them from expanding.

This was a realizable objective, since it coincided with the very character of the Morelos movement, which was tied to its land and its region, even in the way its army was organized.

The Carrancistas and their military chief, Obregón, avoided fighting on two fronts, and not just because of their military weakness. They were also quite weak socially; the tumult of the peasant revolution was continuing and the tide was only just beginning to turn. There were indications of this, but no assurance. No one, not even Obregón, with his Bonapartist political instinct, could be certain of victory in the immediate future. The Army of Operations was still a transhumant force, no weaker but no stronger than the two peasant armies taken separately. On the other hand, Obregón understood that he had to carry out an essentially military war against Villa, army versus army, while it was much more a social war in military form against Zapata, who was entrenched in his own region. And Obregón was not the man to win such a war with weapons, but the type to gather its fruits afterward by political action.

For all of these reasons, while the army of petty-bourgeois democracy led by Obregón entered the fray to fight Villa's peasant army, the masses of the South had a relative respite from military activity, felt themselves to be the masters of the state of Morelos, and consequently developed their own peasant democracy.

This is one of the most historically significant and beautiful episodes of the Mexican Revolution, though also one of the least known.[1] The peasants of Morelos applied their own meaning to the Ayala Plan. Doing this, they gave it its true content: the revolutionary liquidation of the *latifundios*. But since the *latifundios* and their economic centers, the sugar mills, were the form of capitalism's presence in Morelos, they thereby liquidated the fundamental centers of capitalism in the region. They applied older, precapitalist and communal peasant ideas; but translating these into laws in the second decade of the twentieth century, they took an anti-capitalist form. The result was the expropriation and nationalization of the mills without compensation, putting them under the control of the peasants through their military leaders. Here, where the peasants and workers finally established their own direct government for a time, the Mexican Revolution acquired an empirical anti-capitalist character. This is why we find a conspiracy of silence about this crucial episode of the revolution among bourgeois writers and the theoreticians of revolution by stages. But there is no conspiracy of silence or distortion of history that can erase what remains in the collective consciousness of the masses through their own revolutionary experience. This is what reappears at each new stage of revolutionary ascent, because the conquests of experience and consciousness may remain hidden and live underground for a whole period, but they are never lost.

The armed struggle, the division of the land after 1911, the military victory over the federal army, the defeat of the bourgeois state of Díaz, Madero, and Huerta, and the occupation of the country's capital—this four-year-long rise in the struggle—gave the peasants of Morelos a great historical security: the security and confidence that they could decide for themselves. This is what they applied in their own territory.

At that point, the end of the revolutionary tide and the beginning of a retreat on the national level after December 1914 coincided with a continuation of the revolution's ascent on the local level. The national impulse was broken, but it continued in sectors—although this could not last for long. But the peasants and farm workers who began to reconstruct Morelos

---

[1]This period is described in detail by the North America historian John Womack in his study *Zapata and the Mexican Revolution* (New York: Vintage, 1968), on the basis of an exacting study of the archives, especially those of the Zapatistas. This book is the principal source for the facts in this chapter, but my interpretation differs from Womack's.

society according to their own conceptions could not have known or even suspected this.

This unevenness is a phenomenon typical of a peasant revolution. Its empiricism and the limited nature or absence of a national conception of the struggle alter the timing of the revolution, which decomposes by regions. In Morelos, the peasant leaders, supported by the strength and the aspirations of the peasants organized in the Zapatista army and in the region's towns, carried out what they had wanted to do, as a national power, through a national government they could not hold. They did it on the local level, where they knew the terrain and the people and felt themselves secure socially, organizationally, politically, and militarily. Their power came from a peasant revolution much deeper than even they knew, because its roots lay in the ancient collective communal traditions and a traditional social structure that had always been an instrument of struggle and resistance among the peasantry.

18

Trotskyism

MILITIA OR GUERRILLA MOVEMENT?*
Hugo Blanco

Hugo Blanco, an agronomist and founder of the FIR (Revolutionary Left Front, a Peruvian Trotskyist organization), was born in Cuzco in 1934. Blanco led one of the most important peasant movements of the 1960s; at the head of the Peasant Federation of the Convención and Lares Valleys, he helped organize strikes, land occupations, and union militias during the years 1961–63. He was arrested in 1963 and imprisoned for eight years. The following letter, written from his cell in 1964, draws a balance sheet of his experiences and analyzes the relation between party and union and between militias and guerrilla movements in the revolutionary peasant struggle.

After a 1970 amnesty, Blanco committed himself to other struggles in Peru and was deported from the country at various times. In 1978, he was a candidate of the FOCEP (Peruvian Workers', Peasants', and Students' Front) to the Constituent Assembly and was elected with the third highest number of votes of any candidate in the country. He is currently a member and leader of the PUM (United Mariateguista Party).

In their first stage, the Cuban, Chinese, and other experiences were characterized by the absence of fighting mass organizations, which until then had been considered a necessary preliminary condition [for armed struggle]. It was perfectly normal that the armed organization would not at first enjoy the confidence of the masses; this is what gave it a nomadic character. But when the armed organization succeeds in earning the confidence and support of the masses, it loses its nomadic character and establishes itself in a fixed location. Under these conditions, the guerrilla group constitutes the center of the people's struggle, its polarizing and organizing nucleus, its vanguard. It is therefore a group prepared and organized at the margin of a nearly non-existent mass movement, which the guerrilla organization, itself having risen from these masses, is called upon to organize.

---

*Hugo Blanco, "A propos des guérillas et des milices," *Quatrième Internationale*, n. 24, March 1965, p. 45–47.

In Peru, there are already organizations that organize broad sections of the masses. In the regions where they exist, few remain outside them.

The fundamental question is as follows: Do you think that a situation of dual power already exists in the countryside? If you do not think so, then you must pronounce yourself for the guerrillas. But if you are convinced that this situation does exist, then you must opt for the militias.

After April 1962, when I found myself separated from my comrades, and putschist shadows were still passing through my mind, I edited, under the pressure of that situation, a report entitled *The Liberated Zone Before the Insurrection*. This report certainly contained some errors in appraising the situation, but its very title reveals how dual power had been developing. You are also acquainted with what I wrote about the peasant unions. It seems unnecessary to point out these things to a member of the FIR, "the conscious factor in the awakening of the peasantry," as you put it. If I do, it is because it seems to me your ideas on the launching of the armed struggle are the result of your lack of knowledge and your isolation from the work of the ranks of the FIR.

If the launching of the armed struggle can begin from such different situations as those in China and Cuba, it is obvious that each struggle must differ from the others at the beginning. This is the "dialectical process."

The guerrilla organization, as you say, must "earn the sympathy of the peasantry."

A militia is the product of the rising of the peasantry. The masses, having understood the necessity of armed struggle, create the militias. They are generated by the peasantry itself and therefore enjoy its confidence and support, even before they develop. Don't forget, the peasants have already decided to create defense committees; they are conscious of the need for these committees and know that they themselves must create them.

To your sentence, "Here the mass movement unites itself in the embryonic forms of the armed struggle for power," I would have preferred, "Here the mass movement reaches the phase of armed struggle for power" (even if at first it does not consciously recognize this objective).

You ask, "What organization is destined to prepare and organize the armed struggle: the peasant union or the party?" To help us answer this question, I would ask in turn: Who will lead the land occupations in Cuzco? The unions? The party? And who took power in Russia? The soviets or the party? The answer in all three cases is: it was the party, through the mass organizations; in our case, the peasant unions. They have already shown that they agree with this. Nothing remains but to act.

"This form of struggle is practiced by organizations trained and disciplined in the art and science of revolutionary war. Thus, the union can neither organize nor lead the armed struggle." These organizations are precisely the defense committees of the revolutionary unions, led by the party.

I do not deny the great importance of the party. On the contrary, I recognize that the great deficiency in 1962 was the absence of a party, and that all our weaknesses derived from this.

It is the duty of the party to build cells in the peasant unions; this is necessary if we wish to lead the armed struggle in the best possible manner. We ought to learn from our experience. If a well-organized party had existed, at least in Convención and Lares, we would have obtained better results. It was an experience of the negative variety.

But we also should learn from positive experiences. Why were we (my comrades and I) able to maintain ourselves longer than any other group, despite the absence of a party, political clarity, technical knowledge, etc.? Because our group had grown out of the peasant union and was nourished and supported by the union.

There are lessons in our experience that a guerrilla would call "second stage." One gets to know the people in the area and the three or four scabs that live there (or at least those who had been chased from the area, as happened in Quochapampa, Mesada, etc.). Almost the whole town is organized. They will not only support the armed groups economically, protect, inform, and feed them, but will do even more: when the time is right, they will carry out acts of sabotage and even launch the mass armed struggle. This struggle would certainly be episodic if it were carried out before an insurrection, but there should be no lack of opportunities for this to happen. This is not to say that we must promote such activity in all circumstances, although at times we will have to. What I want to show you is how things stand and how they will be in the future; I have to point out that we already have a great deal of experience to start with, and we should not waste any of our strength. During the difficult period in Chaupimayo, all the unions took turns at guard duty. The richness of the information at the disposal of the unions was unexploited because of the lack of a party.

All of these conditions, similar to the "second guerrilla stage," offer an armed group the possibility of rooting itself in a favorable zone. If a tenacious manhunt for a particular member of the militia causes a problem, he would have to be transferred to a union in another region.

One of the fundamental conditions for a militia struggle is a broad territory in which it is to develop. Many militias are needed in the designated territory— one per union. Otherwise, the militia will actually take on the characteristics of a guerrilla movement, and the enemy will concentrate their attacks against it and its union. This is what happened to us; but we were not a classic "first stage" guerrilla movement. We will not behave as we did in Chaupimayo, where we attracted the enemy's concentrated power.

As to guerrilla tactics, I agree that we must teach them to the self-defense committees. They should not resort to empiricism, since the vanguard party does have its reason for being. We should exploit all our knowledge in the field of guerrilla warfare that can be adapted to our strategy.

And now, a question of supreme importance: Perhaps it would be easier to recruit guerrillas than recruit militiamen?

A large section of the peasantry is prepared to give their lives but not to leave their land and way of life. They therefore support the slogan "Land or death." This is why a guerrilla fighter leaves his home only to return at the end of the struggle. On the other hand, the militiaman stays at home, dedicating himself to his work, and when he has to fight, he fights. Of one hundred peasants prepared to struggle, 99 would prefer to be militiamen, and only one a guerrilla. I don't want to go into details here, but you can believe me—I've already had this experience. Manco II, who had surrounded Cuzco preparing an assault, was abandoned by his troops because the planting or harvesting season had arrived; I'm not sure which.

Nevertheless, there is nothing wrong with organizing guerrilla movements. They can be created by those willing to join and aid the militias. But the fundamental organization of the armed struggle in Peru is the union militia, led by the party.

We will take advantage of all the particularities of Peruvian reality. And we will not start all over again after having advanced so far.

You say, "The FIR ought to launch the armed struggle to take state power." Very well, this took place in Cuba, riding the back of the peasant movement. But the Cubans first took up arms and then mounted the horse, while we are mounting the horse but lack arms. Why don't we put our feet on the ground?

I am convinced that if my response doesn't succeed in convincing you, your connection to the rank-and-file militants will do so. And the sooner, the better.

Land or death! We will win!

Central Prison of Arequipa
April 7, 1964

THESES ON THE MEXICAN REVOLUTION*

Revolutionary Workers Party

The first nucleus of the Mexican GCI (Internationalist Communist Group) developed during the 1968 movement, inside the National Strike Committee. Through a process of fusions (and splits), this group later became the PRT (Revolutionary Workers Party), the Mexican section of the Fourth International. In 1981, the PRT was conditionally registered as a political party; currently, it is the most important Fourth Internationalist organization in Latin America.

During its founding conference (1976), the PRT approved a document that is both a historical analysis of the development of the class struggle in Mexico from the revolution in 1910 until the 1968 movement and a program for the coming socialist revolution in Mexico.

THE REVOLUTIONARY REGIME: MEXICAN BONAPARTISM

The failure of Constitutionalist democracy, bloodily incarnated in the execution of Venustiano Carranza—a consequence of a rapid succession of events: the generals' revolt of 1919 in Agua Prieta; the arrival in power of the Sonora team with the inauguration of Adolfo de la Huerta as provisional president; Obregón's populist campaign, crossing the entire republic in search of votes in the 1920 elections, and his rise to power that same year—marked the birth of the "regime of the Mexican Revolution," which has now remained solidly in power for nearly sixty years.

The internal bases of this post-revolutionary regime were the army, the police, and control of the worker and peasant masses through the unions and agrarian leagues. Externally, it painstakingly sought and fortunately acquired the recognition of the United States. The longevity of this regime is based on the fact that these fundamental axes are partially and mutually counterbalanced. This regime, established by the counterrevolution that placed the Sonora team in power, has all the characteristics of a *Bonapartist regime in a semi-colonial country.*

Bonapartism (a form of government comparable to Caesarism in antiquity) exists in embryo in all bourgeois governments. As Friedrich Engels said: "All governments today are becoming Bonapartist, *noles volens* [like it or not]." In the epoch of capitalist decline, this form of governing is more justified than ever to the extent that the essential conflict of capitalist society, that between the bourgeoisie and the proletariat, is not definitively resolved in the favor of one (fascism) or the other (socialism). Class conciliation, which can occur through parliamentary democracy in the era of

---

* Tesis del PRT sobre la Revolución Mexicana (pasada y futuro), Folletos Bandera Socialista n. 36, September 1976, pp. 16–18, 31–35.

capitalism's ascent, is more difficult than ever when the exacerbation of class tensions puts all of society in danger. The bourgeoisie must resort to another form of rule to guarantee its dominance. This is Bonapartism, which is based on the strength of a bureaucratic-military apparatus that raises itself as the apparent arbiter between the fighting classes and establishes itself as the savior of the homeland, incarnated in the national *caudillo*.

Bonapartism assumes this role as arbiter from the start; it is then reinforced by its unique position as mediator between imperialism and the revolutionary masses. This factor determines both the "anti-imperialist" role it has inherited from the revolution and its supposedly popular character—which is actually populist, manipulative, and domineering.

In Mexico, Bonapartism is also the product of a post-revolutionary situation in a semi-colonial country, which gives it much more stability than a regime that is simply transitional between democracy and fascism or socialism. While some argue it is difficult for a transitional regime like Bonapartism to be as stable and long-lasting as in Mexico, they forget that political definitions do not measure the duration of the processes they define. Bonapartist forms of government are actually determined by class relations that ultimately are expressed at the governmental level; they can last for longer or shorter periods, and be transitional or not.

The impotency of bourgeois democracy in Mexico, the absence of a proletarian, revolutionary socialist alternative, and the presence of an extremely aggressive peasant movement that is heir to revolutionary struggles have served as the heavy anchors of Bonapartist stability. These massive struggles and their resulting anti-imperialist sentiments constitute the other major foundations for the Mexican regime's policies.

Mexican Bonapartism is bourgeois and ultimately quite reactionary. This does not mean that Obregón, in 1920, turned the clock back to the prerevolutionary period before 1910. Nor does it mean the bourgeoisie fully identifies with the revolution or with all its measures, some of which are totally repudiated by the national capitalist class (land reform affecting the *latifundistas*) or by imperialism (the oil expropriations that affected the North American and, mainly, the English capitalists).

1968: THE BEGINNING OF THE END

The year 1968 historically represents a fundamental turning point in the long-term trajectory of the Bonapartist system: clearly, the beginning of its decline. If the system had begun to visibly harden and erode since the time of Alemán, it had nevertheless been able, without much difficulty, to pass all the tests to which it was subjected. This was not true in 1968.

The imprint stamped upon Bonapartism by that year's popular movement still remains. To millions of Mexicans, Tlatelolco is the symbol of the bankruptcy and infamy of a repressive and anti-democratic regime.

The mobilization of 1968 combined the characteristic elements that undoubtedly will be identified with the coming revolutionary mobilizations that will shake our country. They are:

- Its independence from the government. That is, for the first time since the twenties, the leadership of a large mass movement did not respond to the needs of the government or accept the orientation of its different factions (either liberals, moderates, progressives, or reactionaries). The National Strike Committee (CNH) is the most important example of a revolutionary organ of mass self-organization and leadership that has yet arisen in the history of our popular struggles.
- Its democratic character. The masses found their own channels of expression, broadening their ideas and reorienting their vision, which had traditionally been subordinated to the state, toward new political and social forms and contents presaging life in the socialist future.
- Its mass, rather than corporate, character. Unlike *Vallejismo* and so many other peasant movements, popular protest in 1968 connected with the country's broadest and most deeply felt popular interests. From this point of view, it was a *revolutionary political* movement that overflowed the bounds of narrow corporate interests, despite its origins among students and the fact that the left political parties were not in the lead.

The ferment of 1968 did not end at Tlatelolco. Since then, its effects have been seen around the country. Its importance is most evident today in its repercussions inside the workers' movement. The union insurgency that has developed, with ups and downs, since 1971 is one of the main processes that has resulted. The peasant movement has experienced a rebirth since then and is taking an independent course for the first time since the era of the Mexican revolution.

In 1968, Mexico fully participated in a modern, international revolutionary upsurge. Along with the May movement in France, the anti-bureaucratic protests in Czechoslovakia, and the heroic Vietnamese struggle, the student and popular process of 1968 joined in the new rise of the world revolution that is broadening and deepening its course across the length and breadth of the planet.

The stage of the preparation and intensification of the processes that will culminate in the rapidly approaching second Mexican (socialist and democratic) revolution opened wide in 1968.

PERSPECTIVES ON THE SOCIALIST AND DEMOCRATIC SECOND
MEXICAN REVOLUTION

THE PERMANENT REVOLUTION IN MEXICO

The main objective of the second revolution that is now gestating in Mexico is the completion of those tasks left unfulfilled by the first Mexican revolution of the twentieth century.

Mexico is a semi-colonial country, only partially industrialized, subject to the disequilibrium of uneven and combined development in the context of a predominantly agrarian structure, and increasingly dominated by imperialist capital. For the second time this century, the country will witness the outbreak of a process of permanent revolution—the struggle of its working and exploited masses to acquire their democratic rights, which they will only attain through a fight to the death against the "national" and foreign capitalists and their Bonapartist government. This combination of the dynamic of the democratic revolution and the objectives and methods of an anti-capitalist revolution is the essential aspect of the second Mexican revolution. This will be a socialist and democratic revolution because its stimulus and initial strength will grow in response to the repression and anti-democratic despotism of the regime, but will not stop at a mere liberal bourgeois reform: it will have to strike at the capitalist origins, causes, and structures that obstruct democracy in Mexico. It will be a democratic revolution, because the Mexican people will exercise the rights they have been denied over the centuries; a socialist revolution, because it is impossible for working people to aspire to free and democratic self-determination within the capitalist system; and finally, a proletarian revolution, because a revolutionary mass mobilization can only defeat and crush its principal enemies, the capitalist class and its imperialist allies, under the leadership and hegemony of the working class.

Transcending the counterrevolutionary period signified by Bonapartist rule since 1920, the second revolution will reconnect with the unrealized objectives of the first Mexican revolution, led by Zapata and Villa, which was unable to reach on the subjective, political, and conscious level what it had objectively achieved in practice, in the class struggle: liquidating the capitalist landowners and confronting their rebirth. It will also be more exacting in carrying out the task of building a truly revolutionary government—based on democratic organs of the workers and peasants—on the ruins of the old regime, eliminating any possibility that a tyrannical clique will steal the revolutionary victories won by the masses through the most violent class struggles.

The subjective conditions lacking in 1910–17, a revolutionary Marxist party and a working class conscious of its socialist interests, are the factors being forged today. They will guarantee the revolutionary triumph of the second wave of massive transformations and struggles of the Mexican people. These factors will definitely lead to the expropriation and nationalization of the means of production, commerce, and exchange, which will lay the basis to start the construction of a socialist economy and inaugurate the democratic planning of those priorities deemed fundamental by the Mexican masses. The Mexican working class will play a key role in this, as the most conscious and self-sacrificing force for socialism.

In the countryside, the socialist revolution will offer private property to all those peasants who want it, and loyally and disinterestedly aid them with the credits and machinery the Bonapartist government has always promised but never delivered. At the same time, the revolution will not hide its objectives: to inaugurate a new system of collective enterprises, founded on the use of advanced techniques and the most varied resources to allow the growth of productivity to levels unimagined in bourgeois land reforms. But collectivization will not be forced. The Stalinist failures in this area will not be repeated, but rather, in the tradition of Marx and Engels, a procedure to consciously and voluntarily convince the small private farmer will be put into practice, to show him in deeds the greater advantages of collectivized agriculture at all levels.

The Mexican socialist revolution will be internationalist. It will identify with the struggles of the peoples of Latin America and reach out to them with all sorts of aid and solidarity. Through the international revolutionary Marxist organization, it will likewise identify with proletarian and revolutionary struggles on other continents: the colonial revolution of the peoples of Asia and Africa in their struggle against imperialism in a dynamic of permanent revolution, the political revolution of the workers and working masses of the bureaucratized workers' states, and the proletarian struggle of the working classes of the United States, Western Europe, Japan, and other imperialist countries.

The second Mexican socialist and democratic revolution will recover and put into practice the communist principles originated by Marx and Engels, and continued and enriched by Lenin, Trotsky, Rosa Luxemburg, and Ernesto Che Guevara—the highest expression in our century of the revolutionary communist struggle for the social liberation of mankind, against exploitative imperialism and the Stalinist bureaucratic usurpers, and for the inauguration of solidarity and socialist fraternity among all humanity.

19

New Tendencies

OUR SOCIALISM*
Brazilian Workers Party

The following document was approved by the Seventh National Conference of the Brazilian *Partido dos Trabalhadores* (PT), which took place in May 1990. The result of a public debate between the various tendencies of the PT, it was approved by a wide consensus at the conference. It reaffirms the party's commitment to socialist aims at the moment of the historic collapse of so-called really existing socialism. Although inspired by a Marxist anti-capitalist tradition, it expresses a pluralist political culture, looking forward to a democratic and libertarian socialism. It is one of the most significant and rich documents of the "new thinking" developing in the Latin American left at the end of the twentieth century.

This resolution proposes to reaffirm our judgment of the capitalist system, consolidate our party's accumulated views on the socialist alternative, identify the fundamental historical and ideological challenges to the socialist cause, and propose a broad debate in the PT and in Brazilian society on the concrete transcendence of these challenges.

    1. The PT was created with radically democratic goals. We arose fighting the military dictatorship and bourgeois oppression, demanding respect for political freedom and social rights in the streets and the workplaces. We grew denouncing the conservative transition and building the foundation for popular sovereignty. In its ten years of existence, the PT always has been in the vanguard of the struggles for the democratization of Brazilian society: against censorship, for the right to strike, for freedom of expression and the right to protest, for amnesty, for multi-party democracy, for an autonomous Constituent Assembly, and for free and direct elections. We became a great mass party denouncing the expropriation of the rights of citizens by state power, the shackling of the unions to the state apparatus, and the trade union tax. Various comrades have given their lives in the workers' struggle for democracy: Santo Dias, Wilson Pinheiro,

---

O socialismo petista, Seventh National Conference of the PT, May 1990.

264

Margarida Alves, Father Josimo, Chico Mendes, and many others. At the root of our party's project is precisely the goal of making Brazil a democracy worthy of the name, because democracy has a strategic value for the PT. For us, it is simultaneously a means and an end, an instrument of transformation and a goal to be realized. We have learned with our own flesh that the bourgeoisie has no real historic commitment to democracy. The relation of the dominant elites to democracy is purely tactical: they take the democratic road when it pragmatically suits them. Actually, democracy is above all in the interests of the workers and the popular masses. Today, it is indispensable to deepen its material and political gains. This will be fundamental in overthrowing the unjust and oppressive society in which we live. It will also be decisive in the future for instituting a qualitatively superior democracy, to assure that the social majorities in fact rule the socialist society for which we are struggling.

2. The democratic calling of the PT nevertheless goes beyond the political slogans it has defended and still defends. Its internal organization also expresses our libertarian commitment. It reflects the constantly renewed commitment of the leadership and rank-and-file militants to make the PT itself a free and participative society: a precedent for another, larger one we propose to inaugurate in the country. In opposition to the monolithism and verticality of the traditional parties, even many left organizations, the PT seeks to practice internal democracy as an indispensable requisite for democratic conduct in social life and in the exercise of political power. The same is true for the relation of the party to its social bases and to civil society as a whole. Although it was born through the strength of the union and popular movements and maintains powerful ties of inspiration, interest, and dialogue with them, seeking to offer political leadership, the PT refuses in principle to constrict their autonomy and treat them as clients or transmission belts.

3. Another innately democratic dimension of the PT is its ideological-cultural pluralism. We are in fact a synthesis of libertarian cultures, united in our diversity. Different currents of democratic and revolutionary thought—Social Christianity, various Marxisms, non-Marxist socialisms, democratic radicalism, secular theories of revolutionary action, etc.—joined together to create the PT as an expression of their concrete, more-or-less institutionalized social subjectivities. The ideology of the party does not unilaterally express any of these sources. The PT does not have an "official" philosophy. The different theoretical formations live in dialectical tension, with no lack of dynamic syntheses on the level of concrete political work. What unites these various libertarian political cultures, not all of which are textually codified, is the common project of a new society to encourage the end of all exploitation and oppression.

4. This basic commitment to democracy also makes us anti-capitalist, in the same way our choice of anti-capitalism unequivocally determines our struggle for democracy. One of the most powerful stimuli to our organization as a political party with an alternative project of government and power was our discovery (practically, rather than theoretically, for the majority of PT members) of the structural perversity of capitalism. This was and still is an indignant response to the unnecessary suffering of millions as a logical consequence of capitalist barbarism. Concrete historical experience—in other words, the negative lesson of the "Brazilian miracle" and so many other tragic examples in national and international life—taught us that capitalism, whatever its material strength, is unjust and exclusive by vocation, naturally averse to the fraternal division of social wealth that is the premise of any authentic democracy.

It is this capitalist oppression that results in absolute misery for more than a third of humanity. It is imposing new forms of slavery upon Latin America that have reduced per capita income by 6.5 percent in recent years, forcing various countries back to levels of twenty years earlier. It is the capitalist system, based ultimately on the exploitation of man by man and the brutal commercialization of human life, that is responsible for odious crimes against democracy and human rights, from Hitler's crematoria to the recent genocide in Southern Africa, leaving aside our sadly famous torture chambers. And Brazilian capitalism, with its predatory dynamic, is responsible for the hunger of millions, illiteracy, marginality, and the violence that pervades all levels of national life. It is capitalism that maintains and deepens the objective foundation of social inequality in Brazil.

For this very reason, the founding documents of the PT—its Manifesto and Fundamental Program—already advocated the overthrow of capitalism as indispensable for the full democratization of Brazilian life. While our major documents did not deepen the internal outline of this socialist alternative, the PT's historical goal was already clearly socialist at its birth. And the following ten years of difficult and impassioned social struggle have only confirmed the PT's anti-capitalist option and strengthened our commitment to this transformation.

5. This anti-capitalist conviction, the fruit of Brazil's bitter social experience, also made us critical of social-democratic proposals. Today's social-democratic currents present no real perspective for the historical transcendence of capitalism. They have falsely thought it possible to arrive at socialism through government and state institutions, especially the parliament, without mobilizing the masses at the base. They have trusted in the neutrality of the machinery of state and the compatibility of capitalist efficiency with a peaceful transition to another economic and social logic. In time, they even have stopped believing in the possibility of a parliamentary

transition to socialism and have abandoned, not the parliamentary road, but socialism itself. A critical dialogue with such mass currents is certainly useful for the workers' struggle on the world scale. But its ideological project does not correspond to the anti-capitalist convictions or the emancipatory objectives of the PT.

6. At the same time, our strategic commitment to democracy—the democratic identity of the PT—led us to disavow the supposed models of so-called "really existing socialism." We never ignored the fallacy of the term. The conservative media use it to facilitate their ideological struggle against any historical project that rises against capitalist rule. According to its detractors, socialism, whenever it materializes, must be fatally averse to the ideals of progress and liberty. This is a reactionary idea that we vehemently repudiate. Having said this, the expression "really existing socialism," in its abstract generality, does not consider national peculiarities, different revolutionary processes, various economic and political contexts, etc. It equates different experiences of social transformation that are heterogeneous in their character and their results, discrediting historical conquests that surely are not irrelevant for those people who obtained them. Some of these self-proclaimed socialist experiences originated in popular revolutions, whereas others occurred through the defeat of Nazi Germany and the occupation of these countries by the Soviet Army, which redrew the political map of Europe and gave birth to the so-called socialist bloc controlled by the U.S.S.R. In some national processes, the masses gained a not dishonorable influence over the course of national life. And the Sandinista experience certainly deserves a separate evaluation and a positive appraisal to the extent that it assured an unprecedented political and civil equality to the Nicaraguan people.

The PT supports the struggle of the workers and the peoples for their liberation and assumes the defense of authentic revolutionary processes, but with total political independence, fully exercising its right of criticism. This is why the PT, since its foundation, identified the majority of experiences of "really existing socialism" with a theory and practice that is incompatible with our project of libertarian socialism—because of their profound lack of democracy, whether political, economic, or social; the monopoly of power by a single party, even where there was formally a multi-party system; the symbiosis of party and state; the rule of the bureaucracy, whether a privileged layer or caste; the lack of democracy at the base and of authentic representative institutions; open or veiled repression of ideological and cultural pluralism; and the administration of production through a vertical, authoritarian, and inefficient method of planning. All of this negates the very essence of Petista (PT) socialism.

Our criticism of such historical processes, made in the light of revolutionary struggle and diverse socialist experiences on the international level, has been consistent but limited. The PT was the first Brazilian political party to support the democratic struggle of Polish Solidarity, even though we lack any other ideological affinities. We have fought all attacks on union rights and political, religious, and other freedoms in the countries of "really existing socialism," for the same reason that we struggle for public freedoms in Brazil. We denounce the premeditated assassination of hundreds of rural workers in Brazil and the crimes against humanity committed in Bucharest or in Tiananmen Square with the same indignation. Socialism, for the PT, will either be radically democratic or it will not be socialism.

The movements that have led the reforms in Eastern Europe justly turned against totalitarianism and economic stagnation, intending to institutionalize democratic regimes and subvert the bureaucratic and ultracentralized administration of the economy. The result of this process remains open, and the political and social debate itself will determine its contours. But the PT is convinced that the changes that have occurred and are still in course in the countries of "really existing socialism" have a historically positive meaning, although the process, at the moment, is under the hegemony of reactionary currents in favor of capitalist retrogression. Such movements should be valued not because they themselves represent a project for the renewal of socialism, but because they break with political paralysis, openly restore the various actors to the political and social stage, give impulse to democratic victories, and open the perspective of new possibilities for socialism. The political energy liberated by such social mobilizations will not be easily domesticated by IMF prescriptions or the abstract paradise of capitalist propaganda.

7. Our original ideological equipment, enriched in the course of the political struggle itself and consolidated in the various national party conferences, oriented the work of the PT through the eighties and guaranteed the conquest of important historical objectives. With the general meaning of our politics—democratic and anti-capitalist—fully established, we chose to progressively build our concrete utopia: that is, the socialist society for which we are struggling. We wanted to avoid both ideological abstraction, the elitist offense of the traditional Brazilian left, and the frazzled pragmatism characteristic of so many other parties. A purely ideological profundity at the summit would serve no purpose unless it corresponded to the real political culture of our party and social rank-and-file. Besides, the leadership also lacked experience that only the patient, continuous, democratic mass struggle could provide. What legitimates the strategically defined contours of any socialist project are the radically democratic and revolutionary convictions of broad popular sectors. Without being triumphalist, we could say

that this political education, based on the self-education of the masses through their civic participation, was found to be generally appropriate.

8. We recognize the existence on the international level of forces and movements of a democratic, popular, socialist, and libertarian character that identify with the Petista project and with whom we maintain privileged relations. We are now facing unprecedented challenges that we will only overcome through greater political and ideological creativity. We are moving into a new historical period both on the national and international levels, which demands of the PT and all socialist forces an even more audacious and rigorous theoretical discourse.

With the projected restructuring of the Brazilian economy and the current recomposition of interbourgeois hegemony, political debate increasingly occurs over general projects, with notorious ideological implications. But whether it is a matter of the mere "stabilization" of the economy or its "adjustment," what is in play is the very character of Brazil's strategic insertion in the international context, whether as an economic or an ideological project.

On the other hand, to the extent that the PT galvanizes growing sectors of Brazilian society and is given credence as a political alternative for the country, our historic alternative must be more explicit. Many apparently conjunctural challenges—reform of the state, for example, or the struggle for the democratization of landed property—can only in fact be met and overcome in the light of better strategic definitions.

In the same way, the failure of so many experiences of "really existing socialism" and the conjunctural reinforcement of capitalist ideology—even in a country like ours, a victim of the sharpest and most destructive contradictions of capitalism—call for renewed critical and theoretical efforts that can ethically and historically re-launch the perspective of socialist democracy.

9. But what socialism? What society, what state are we struggling with so much effort to build? How should its productive structure be organized, and upon what political structures will it depend? How will the cunning ghosts of authoritarianism be exorcised on the practical political level? It is as useless to emphasize the magnitude of this historic task as it is to theoretically and practically respond to such questions. This task does not depend solely on the PT, but must engage all the libertarian energy available in our society, as well as make use of analogous efforts realized in other spheres.

To some of these questions, we could put forward answers that originate in our own experiences of activity and reflection. Dialectically, they have grown from the forms of domination that we are struggling against or result from the strategic concepts we have acquired during our struggles. The Fifth National Conference already indicated this road: to suppress capitalism and begin the construction of a socialist society, a radical political change will be necessary. The workers must transform themselves into a hegemonic class in civil society and in the state. Other aspects of our socialist project are open challenges, to which it would be presumptuous and incorrect to claim we can give immediate answers. Overcoming them will probably demand unexpected political imagination and practical creativity, legitimated not only by our ideological options, but by the concrete aspirations of the oppressed masses for a life of dignity.

10. The PT does not conceive of socialism as an inevitable future that will necessarily be produced through the economic laws of capitalism. For us, socialism is a human project whose realization is unthinkable without the conscious struggle of the exploited and the oppressed—a project that therefore will be truly emancipatory only to the degree we conceive it as such, or rather, to the degree it is a necessity and ideal for the oppressed masses, capable of developing an effectively libertarian consciousness and movement. For this reason, the recuperation of the ethical dimension of politics is an essential condition for reestablishing the unity between socialism and humanism.

11. The new society that we are struggling to build finds its concrete inspiration in Brazil's rich historical tradition of popular struggles. It should base itself on the principle of human solidarity and in the sum of individual aptitudes for the solution of common problems. It will seek to constitute itself as a collective democratic subject, without thereby negating a rich and desirable individuality. While assuring basic equality between citizens, it will be no less zealous in defense of the right to differ, whether politically, religiously, culturally, behaviorally, etc. It will struggle for the liberation of women and against racism and all forms of oppression on behalf of an integrated and universalist democracy. Pluralism and self-organization, more than simply allowed, should be rewarded at all levels of social life as an antidote to the bureaucratization of power, minds, and wills. While affirming national identity and independence, it will reject any imperial pretensions and contribute to inaugurating cooperative relations among all the world's peoples. Just as we today defend Cuba, Grenada, and so many other countries from North American imperialist aggression, the new society will actively support the peoples' self-determination and value internationalist action in the struggle against all forms of exploitation and oppression. Democratic and socialist internationalism will be its constant inspiration.

The socialism we desire, by its very nature, can only exist with an effective economic democracy. It should therefore be organized with the means of production as social property. This social property should not be confused with state property and should be administered through forms (individual, cooperative, state-run, etc.) that the society itself democratically chooses. This economic democracy will transcend both the perverse logic of the capitalist market and the intolerable, autocratic state planning of so many of the so-called socialist economies. Its priorities and productive goals will correspond to the social will and not to the supposed "strategic interests" of the state. It will take on the challenge of all challenges—to both increase productivity and satisfy material necessities—with a new organization of work capable of transcending its current alienation. This democracy will operate as much in the administration of each productive unit (factory councils are a necessary reference) as in the system as a whole, through strategic planning under social control.

12. On the political plane, we are struggling for a socialism that will not only maintain those democratic rights won through hard struggle in capitalist society, but will broaden and radicalize them. These freedoms are valid for all citizens, and their only limit is democratic institutionality itself: freedom of opinion, freedom to demonstrate, and freedom of civil and political organization. Instruments of direct democracy, guaranteeing the participation of the masses at the various levels of leadership of the political process and of economic administration, should be joined with instruments of representative democracy and active mechanisms for popular consultation, freed of the coercion of capital and enjoying a real ability to express collective interests.

13. The PT, struggling for such a socialism, does not underestimate the theoretical and practical challenges that must be overcome to obtain it. It knows that it confronts a gigantic labor of theoretical construction and social struggle and declares itself more than ever prepared to perform it, along with all the democratic and revolutionary forces in Brazilian life.

CHRISTIANITY AND MARXISM*
Frei Betto

Frei Betto is a Brazilian Dominican priest, known worldwide since he published a series of discussions on religion with Fidel Castro; they have been translated into fourteen languages and printed throughout Latin America. Imprisoned by the military dictatorship from 1969 to 1973 for aiding the revolutionary movement led by Carlos Marighella, Frei Betto in recent years has become one of the main advisors of the Base Communities in Brazil and a leading liberation theologian. He also maintains fraternal links with the new Brazilian trade union movement and the Workers Party.

Frei Betto is among a group of liberation theologians who have used the Marxist method extensively in their work. This does not imply an uncritical attitude, but an

---

*Frei Betto, *Cristianismo e Marxismo* (Petropolis: Ed. Vozes, 1986), pp. 35–43.

active interest in Marxism both as science and as utopia, as theory and as practice. This enables him to locate the convergence between Christians and Marxists on the most decisive field of all—that of revolutionary commitment.

Marxism is, above all, a theory of revolutionary practice. This doesn't keep certain Marxists from wanting to transform it into a kind of religion, with its own dogmas based on a fundamentalist reading that turns the works of Marx, Engels, and Lenin into a new Bible. After all, Marxism, like any other theoretical work, cannot have simply one reading. Epistemological method teaches us that a text is always read from the point of view of the reader. These "reality lenses" determine the interpretation of the theory. Thus, Marx's work could be read through the optic of the positivist materialism of Kautsky, the neo-Kantianism of M. Adler, the voluntarist Hegelianism of Gramsci, or the objectivist Hegelianism of Lukács, the existentialism of Sartre, the structuralism of Althusser—or in the light of Mao Tse-tung's peasant struggle, the Cuban guerrilla movement, the Peruvian reality of José Carlos Mariátegui, or the Sandinista popular insurrection.[1] What is important is using Marxist theory as a tool for the liberation of the oppressed peoples, not as a totem or a talisman. Marxism, the fruit of the proletarian struggle, should always be checked against this struggle itself, since only in this way will it not lose its revolutionary vigor and be transformed into an academic abstraction.[2]

In this sense, Marxism and Marxists cannot ignore the new role of Christianity as a leaven in the liberation of the oppressed masses of Latin America. However, to understand Christianity's revolutionary potential, Marxism must break out of the straightjacket of its objectivist optic and recognize the role of human subjectivity in history. This implies admitting to the relative autonomy of superstructures, overcoming economistic tendencies and a certain "state metaphysics" within the socialist regimes. Revolutionary practice extrapolates from theories that are not exhausted by strictly scientific analyses, since they necessarily include ethical, symbolic, and utopian dimensions. The advances achieved by the socialist countries and by the ideology embodied in the party are insufficient to resolve all aspects of interpersonal relations and their social and political consequences.

Besides, what contradiction could there be between the determining role of human subjectivity and historical materialism? As the determinant "in the last instance," the economic sphere results from a complex formed by the productive forces and the relations of production. It is these relations of

---

[1] Rubem Cesar Fernandes, "Qual a medida da 'ferramenta marxista'?" *Comunicações do Iser*, n. 6, October 1983, pp. 2–9.

[2] Pedro A. Ribeiro de Oliveira, "O marxismo como ferramenta de cristãos," *Comunicações do Iser*, n. 7, December 1983, pp. 2–6.

production that determine the character of the productive forces. To speak of relations of production is to admit that, "in the first instance," it is class relations, the revolutionary militancy of the dominated classes, whose consciousness and practice are determinants in the economic sphere. On the contrary, to deny the importance of human subjectivity and intentionality and pretend to reduce Marxism to a purely scientific theory is to fall into a kind of neo-Hegelianism that returns the march of history to the control of an absolute and universal reason. The richness and originality of Marxist theory are found precisely in its connection to revolutionary practice, which dynamically verifies and responds to the theories that inspire and orient it. Without this dialectical relation between theory and practice, Marxism hardens into an academic orthodoxy that is dangerously manipulable by whoever controls the levers of power.

This primacy of practice has led Marxists to recognize that their conceptions of religion are, at times, religious—meaning they are dogmatic and disconnected from historical practice. So that this will not happen in Latin America today, the Second Congress of the Cuban Communist Party, in December 1980, approved a resolution that proclaimed:

> The important process of the massive and active incorporation of Christian groups and organizations, including elements of the Catholic clergy and other denominations, in the struggles for national liberation and social justice of the peoples of Latin America, as in Nicaragua, El Salvador, and elsewhere, and the growth of ecumenical institutions and centers that organize decidedly progressive activities and support the political commitment and fighting union of revolutionary Christians and Marxists on behalf of profound social change on the Continent, demonstrate the desirability of continuing to contribute to the successive consolidation of a common front for indispensable structural transformations in our hemisphere and around the world.[3]

The largest advance in relations between Christianity and a popular regime is taking place today in Nicaragua, where, for the first time in history, Christians participated actively in the process of liberation. This fact by itself destroys the axiomatic character of the statement that "religion is the opium of the people." Also, for the first time in history, a revolutionary party in power—the Sandinista National Liberation Front—released an official communique on religion in October 1980 that said:

> Some writers claim that religion is a mechanism for the alienation of humanity that serves to justify the exploitation of one class by another. This claim undoubtedly has a historical value insofar as religion served as

---

[3] "O PC Cubano e a religião," *Revista Vozes*, n. 5, June 1982, p. 55.

a theoretical support for political domination in different historical epochs. It is enough to remember the role played by missionaries in the process of the domination and colonization of the indigenous peoples of our country. Nevertheless, we Sandinistas state that our experience shows that when Christians, basing themselves on their faith, are able to respond to the necessities of the people and of history, their very beliefs lead them toward revolutionary militancy. Our experience shows that one can be a believer and a consequential revolutionary at the same time and that there is no insoluble contradiction between the two.[4]

Moreover, false certainties are being contradicted by historical practice. In the last twenty years, Christianity has come to display its libertarian character in the countries of the Third World, especially in Latin America, as an expression of the resistance and struggle of the oppressed. Moreover, contrary to academic prognostications, religion had not disappeared in the socialist regimes. In fact, the churches today constitute an important force in the struggle for peace, and the number of the faithful is growing.[5] Yes, they endure difficulties inside and outside the Church. Inside the churches, bishops and priests are not sufficiently clear about how they fit into the socialist regimes. Externally, especially in the orbit of the party in power, certain anti-religious preconceptions foster discrimination, which reinforces the ties between Christians and counterrevolutionary sectors.

It is true that there are also taboos among Christians concerning socialism. Capitalist propaganda is strong enough to create terrible specters that provoke insecurity and fear. Many times, the sectarianism of certain Marxist militants reinforces the impression that they are new crusaders fighting in the name of a new faith, with totalitarian consequences. While it is more difficult today than in the time of Pius XII to encounter vehement anti-Communist proclamations in the official documents of the Catholic Church, sympathy for socialism certainly does not abound, either. But there are doctrinal and political openings: the primarily social character of property, the socialization of goods, the primacy of the right of use over the right of possession, and politically, the realistic diplomacy of the Vatican in strengthening relations with almost all the socialist countries. One of the rare examples of a clearly socialist choice on the part of the bishops is found in a regional document proclaimed during the darkest period of the Brazilian military dictatorship, when the Church itself was fiercely attacked.

It is necessary to defeat capitalism. It is the greater evil, the original sin, the root of corruption, the tree that bears the well-known fruits of

---

[4]"Sobre Religião," official communique of the FSLN Directorate, in Frei Betto, *Nicarágua Livre, o Primeiro Passo* (Rio de Janeiro: Civilizaçao Brasileira, 1980), pp. 122–128.

[5]Cf. "Document of the Cuban Episcopal Conference on Peace," in *Revista Vozes*, ibid., p. 56.

poverty, hunger, disease, and death for the vast majority. This is why the private ownership of the means of production (factories, land, commerce, banks, and sources of credit) must be overcome. . . . This is why we want a world in which there is only one people, with no division between rich and poor.[6]

The language of another document is better articulated, although in a less popular form:

The historical process of class society and capitalist domination leads inevitably to class confrontations. Although this fact is more obvious every day, this confrontation is denied by the oppressors; but it is also confirmed by this very negation. The oppressed masses of workers, peasants, and the numerous underemployed know this and are progressively taking on a new libertarian consciousness. The dominated class has no way to liberate itself but through the long and difficult road to the socialization of the means of production, which is already in progress. This is the fundamental principle of the gigantic historical project of globally transforming today's society into a new society, in which it will be possible to create the objective conditions for the oppressed to regain their despoiled humanity, cast down the shackles of their suffering, overcome class antagonisms, and finally win their freedom.[7]

Marxists and Christians have more common archetypes than our philosophies might suppose. One of these is a utopia of human happiness in the historical future—a hope that becomes symbolic in the practice of innumerable militants who are not afraid to sacrifice their own lives. Marx calls this abundance the realm of freedom; Christians, the reign of God. In the third volume of *Capital*, Marx writes: "The realm of freedom begins where work conditioned by necessity and external pressure ends; the realm of freedom naturally lies, then, beyond the sphere of material production." Nothing in politics or history guarantees the realization of this goal, just as the salvation sought by Christians has no historical explanation, but is the gift of God. But, in the deepest parts of our being, there is the common desire of innumerable Christians and Marxists that humanity eliminate all barriers and contradictions that divide or separate people, and the unrestrained hope that the future will be like a table around which we will all, united as brothers, share the abundance of bread and the joy of wine. The road that can lead us to this goal, upsetting preconceived notions and calling forth unity, will certainly not be one of theoretical discussion, but of effective commitment to the liberation struggle of the oppressed.

---

[6]*Marginalização de um povo*, Document of the Bishops of the Center-West, May 6, 1973, n. 6.3 (SEDOC, v. 6, n. 69, March 1974, col. 1019s).

[7]"Eu ouvi os clamores de meu povo," Document of the Bishops and Religious Superiors of the Northeast, May 6, 1973, p. 29 (SEDOC, v. 6, n. 66, November 1973, col. 628).

THE SÃO PAULO MANIFESTO OF THE LATIN AMERICAN LEFT*

Representatives of most Latin American leftist movements and organizations (including the Communist parties) met in São Paulo in July 1990 at the invitation of the Brazilian Workers Party. The manifesto that resulted from this meeting gives evidence that the majority of the left has been able to reach agreement on some ideas that will be of decisive importance for the future of the labor and popular movements of the continent: the need for unity, the desire for an anti-imperialist and socialist transformation of Latin America, and the importance of democracy and human rights. It shows the influence not only of the crisis in Eastern Europe, but particularly of the Sandinista experience (although the FSLN was unable to attend) and of the PT's socialist perspective, on the whole Latin American left.

Called together by the Workers Party (PT), we representatives of forty-eight left organizations, parties, and fronts of Latin America and the Caribbean have met in São Paulo, Brazil.

The meeting, unprecedented in the breadth of participation by the most diverse ideological currents of the left, reaffirmed in practice the desire of the forces of the socialist and anti-imperialist left of the subcontinent to share an analysis and a balance sheet of their experiences and of the world situation. We are hereby creating new openings to respond to the great challenges faced by our people and by our left, socialist, democratic, popular, and anti-imperialist ideals.

In the course of an intense, truly honest, pluralist, and democratic debate, we have dealt with some of the great problems we face. We analyzed the situation of the world capitalist system and the imperialist offensive, concealed behind a neo-liberal discourse that is directed against our countries and our peoples. We evaluated the crisis of Eastern Europe and the model of the transition to socialism imposed there. We reviewed the revolutionary strategies of the left in this part of the world and the challenges that the international context places before us. We will continue with these and other united efforts.

This meeting is a first step in identifying and approaching these problems. We will meet again in Mexico, where we will continue to join our minds and wills in the permanent analysis we have begun. We will deepen the debate and seek to put forward proposals of mutually acceptable united actions in the anti-imperialist and popular struggle. We will also promote specialized dialogues on the economic, political, social, and cultural problems that confront the continental left.

We have established that as organizations of the left, we all think that a

---

*Declaración de São Paulo, in Inprecor (Paris), n. 6, July 1990, pp. 5–6.

just, free, and sovereign society and socialism can only grow and sustain themselves through the people's will, which is bound up with their historical roots. We therefore declare our common will to renovate leftist thought and socialism, reaffirm its emancipatory character, correct erroneous ideas, and overcome all expressions of bureaucratism and the absence of true social and mass democracy. For us, the free, sovereign, and just society and the socialism to which we aspire can only be the most authentic democracy with the most profound justice for the peoples. Therefore we reject any attempt to take advantage of the crisis of Eastern Europe to encourage capitalist restoration, revoke gains in social rights, or nourish illusions in the non-existent virtues of liberalism and capitalism.

Through our historical experience of subjugation to capitalist regimes and imperialism, we know that the overwhelming deprivation and the most serious problems of our peoples have their roots in that system; they will not find any solutions there, or in the systems of restricted, controlled, and even militarized democracies that exist in many of our countries. The solution our peoples desire must include profound transformations driven by the masses.

We, the political organizations meeting in São Paulo, have been inspired to reaffirm our socialist, anti-imperialist, and popular ideas and goals by the rise and development of vast social, democratic, and popular forces on the continent that face the alternatives of imperialism and neo-liberal capitalism and their resulting suffering, backwardness, and anti-democratic repression. This reality confirms that the left and socialism are the necessary and emerging alternatives.

Our analysis of the pro-imperialist, neo-liberal policies applied by the majority of Latin American governments, their tragic results, and a review of President Bush's recent proposal for "American integration" to guide the relations of domination between the United States and Latin America and the Caribbean, reinforce our conviction that nothing positive can come in this way.

The recent proposal of the North American president is a well-known recipe that has been sweetened to make it more palatable. It implies liquidating our national patrimony through the privatization of strategic and profitable public enterprises in exchange for a laughable amount, a hundred million dollars, to be contributed by the United States. He seeks the permanent application of the fatal "economic adjustment policies" that have led to the deterioration of the quality of life of Latin Americans to unprecedented levels, in exchange for a minuscule and conditioned reduction in our official foreign debt to the imperial government. The offer to reduce the official Latin American debt with the government of the United States by barely $7 billion represents nothing to a Latin America whose foreign debt has risen to more than $430 billion, if we include debts to commercial banks and multilateral organizations. Moreover, the $100 million in "subsidies" promised to those countries that apply neo-liberal reforms is barely 0.5 percent of the $25 billion that Latin America sent abroad in 1989 in interest, principal, and the repatriation of profits by foreign capital. The Bush plan aims to completely open our national economies to manipulative and unequal competition with the imperialist economic apparatus, subjecting us fully to its hegemony and destroying our productive economic structures by integrating them into a commercial free trade zone dominated and organized by North American interests—while they maintain profoundly restrictive laws on foreign trade.

These proposals are therefore alien to the genuine interests of the economic and social development of our region, and compound restrictions on our sovereignty and the limitation of and tutelage over our democratic rights. Actually, they aim to impede an autonomous integration of our Latin America directed toward satisfying its most vital necessities.

We know the real face of the empire. This is what we see in the relentless blockade and renewed aggression against Cuba and the Sandinista Revolution in Nicaragua, in its open intervention and support for the military in El Salvador, in the North American invasion and military occupation of Panama, in the projects and the steps already taken to militarize the Andean region of South America, with the excuse of fighting against "narco-terrorism."

Therefore, we reaffirm our solidarity with the socialist revolution in Cuba that is steadfastly defending its sovereignty and its gains, with the Sandinista popular revolution that is resisting the attempts to dismantle its conquests and is regrouping its forces, with the democratic, popular, and revolutionary forces of El Salvador who are urging demilitarization and a political solution to the war, with the Panamanian people, invaded and occupied by North American imperialism, whose immediate withdrawal we demand, and with the Andean peoples who face the military presence of imperialism.

In opposition to the proposal of integration under imperialist domination, we are also laying the basis of a new concept of continental unity and integration. This requires the reaffirmation of the sovereignty and self-determination of Latin America and its nations, the full recuperation of our cultural and historical identity, and the urge toward internationalist solidarity among our peoples. It demands defending our Latin American patrimony, ending the flight and export of the subcontinent's capital, confronting the whip of the unpayable foreign debt together and united, and adopting economic policies in the interest of the majority that can combat the misery in which millions of Latin Americans live. Finally, it requires an active commitment to the significance of human rights and to democracy and popular sovereignty as strategic values, calling on the forces of the left, socialists, and progressives to face the challenge of constantly renewing their thinking and action.

In this context, we are today renewing our left and socialist projects, our commitment to the conquest of bread, beauty, and happiness, our work to gain economic and political sovereignty for our peoples, and the primacy of social values based in solidarity. We declare our full confidence in our peoples, who, mobilized, organized, and conscious, will create, win, and defend a power that will realize justice, democracy, and true freedom.

We have learned from errors that have been made, as well as from victories that have been achieved. We maintain a non-negotiable commitment to truth and to the cause of our peoples, and with this commitment we move forward, certain that, along with the other groupings of the Latin American and Caribbean left, we will fill the space we are now opening with new efforts at interchange and unity of action as the foundation of a free, just, and sovereign Latin America.

Those delegations present and signing:

Argentina: Movement toward Socialism (MAS), Communist Party, Popular Democracy Party (PDP), Intransigent Party (PI), Popular Intransigent Party (PIP), Peronist Base Party (PPB), Popular Socialist Party (PSP), Movement "From Below," Broad Liberation Front-United Left (FAL-IU), Workers Party (PT). Individuals: Nestor Vicente

Bolivia: Axis of Patriotic Convergence (ECP), Free Bolivia Movement (MBL)

Brazil: Workers Party (PT), Communist Party of Brazil, Brazilian Communist Party, Brazilian Socialist Party, Democratic Labor Party (PDL). Individuals: Frei Betto, Jacob Gorender, João Hermann, Luciano Coutinho, Mayor of São Paulo Luiza Erundina

Chile: United Popular Action Movement (MAPU), Revolutionary Left Movement (MIR), Communist Party. Individuals: Marta Harnecker

Colombia: Communist Party, Marxist-Leninist Communist Party (PCML), M-19

Cuba: Communist Party

Ecuador: Ecuadorian Socialist Party

El Salvador: Farabundo Marti National Liberation Front (FMLN)

Mexico: Party of the Democratic Revolution (PRD), Revolutionary Workers Party (PRT), Popular Socialist Party (PPS)

Peru: United Left (IU), Movement toward Socialism (MAS), United Mariateguista Party (PUM), Workers Party (PT), Popular Democratic Union (UDP)

Paraguay: Popular Democratic Party (PDP), Workers Party (PT)

Dominican Republic: Communist Party

Uruguay: Broad Front (FA), Communist Party, Vertiente Artiguista, Artiguism and Unity, Party for the People's Victory (PVP), Socialist Party, Independent Democratic Left (IDI), Tupamaros National Liberation Movement, Socialist Workers Party (PST), Popular Current (CP), March 26 Movement, Revolutionary Workers Party (POR)

Venezuela: Movement toward Socialism (MAS), Radical Cause (Causa R)

Glossary of Spanish, Portuguese, and Native American Terms

ayllu	Incan term referring to a group of people linked by ties of consaguinity; an indigenous community
caballería	a measure of land (in Cuba, equal to 33 acres)
caudillo	authoritarian ruler
ejido	common lands (Mexico)
encomendero	the Spanish recipient of an *encomienda*
encomienda	the assignment of a group of indigenous people to a particular Spaniard as slaves or serfs
enganche	literally, a hook; a method of forcibly recruiting labor gangs
engenhio	sugar plantation or mill (Portuguese)
foco	literally, focus; a center of guerrilla activity
gamonal	rural boss; large landowner
hacienda	large estate or ranch
hacendado	the owner of a hacienda
ingenio	sugar plantation and/or mill (Spanish)
inquilino	agricultural laborer paid mainly in land and in kind (Chile)
kelkere	notary, clerk (Quechua)
Kaswa	Incan dance
latifundio	large estate
latifundista	owner of a large estate
mambises	nickname for nineteenth-century Cuban independence fighters
mayorazgo	an entailed estate (inherited by primogeniture)

281

mestizo	of mixed nationality, usually Native American and European
mita (also *minka* or *minga*)	Quechua term for collective labor; group labor required by the Spanish of Incan communities and peasants
parcelero	owner of a small plot of land; smallholding peasant
peón	day laborer, agricultural worker
pongaje	domestic service to a landlord required of Native American peasants (Peru)
quintal	100 Kilograms
rosca	popular term referring to the Bolivian ruling elite
sesmaria	a royal land grant (Portuguese)
sierra	mountains, hills
yanacona	originally, a person who lost their link to the community; later, a Native American who belonged to an *encomienda*; now, a sharecropper

Index

283